F

M. J. ABADIE &
CLAUDIA BADER

DRAWINGS BY
MARK HASSELRIIS

A
FIRESIDE
BOOK

PUBLISHED BY
SIMON & SCHUSTER
NEW YORK   LONDON   TORONTO
SYDNEY   TOKYO
SINGAPORE

LOVE
planets

FIRESIDE

Rockefeller Center
1230 Avenue of the Americas
New York, New York 10020

FIRESIDE and colophon are registered trademarks
of Simon & Schuster Inc.

Designed by Bonni Leon

Manufactured in the United States of America

7   9   10   8

Library of Congress Cataloging in Publication Data

Abadie, M.J.
Love planets / M.J. Abadie & Claudia Bader ; drawings
by Mark Hasselriis.
p.   cm.
"A Fireside book."
1. Astrology.   2. Love—Miscellanea.   3. Mate selection—
Miscellanea.   4. Interpersonal relations—Miscellanea.   I. Bader,
Claudia.   II. Title.
BF1729.L6A24   1990
133.5'81582—dc20   90-31244
                                              CIP
ISBN 0-671-68958-4

ACKNOWLEDGMENTS

In keeping with our theatrical theme, we take a bow to each other. A collaborative effort is never easy—like a marriage, you don't know what you're getting into until it's too late to back out! In spite of the difficulties that are the natural result of two different personalities attempting to blend themselves into one, we feel we have produced a useful book, written in a clear and entertaining way, and we hope our readers will agree that the end product reflects our dedication.

Our highest appreciation goes to Mark Hasselriis, the wonderful artist and inspired metaphysician who created especially for this book the drawings and the verses in the Astroscripts section—a truly significant and special contribution!

We owe the late Joseph Campbell a debt of gratitude, not only as our common inspiration in things mythological, but for the fact that we met through the medium of his wonderful lectures.

Maura Cleary, Claudia Bader's first astrology teacher, was a profound influence, as was Jeff Jawer's seminal work on Astrodrama.

Bobby Stevenson gets special kudos for his support both emotional and practical, for unfailing understanding, and for inexhaustible good nature. The Zippin-Apon family—Gean, Tina, Nicole, George, and Courtney—gave of their love and patience, and even sent flowers!

Sallye Leventhal, the first editor who saw this book in nascent form, continued to believe in it and us, and helped keep us from discouragement until a sale was made.

Mary Orser generously gave permission to reproduce her most thorough data on time changes from her book *Instant Astrology*.

Fellow astrologers Alan Epstein, Vivien Goldstein, Gillien Goll, Michelle McKee, Linda Myers, and Christine Theoharis provided insights, time, love, and patience with much generosity.

Suzanne Bien and Gail Citron helped test our scoring system on themselves and their significant others, and Michael Hudson provided illuminating discussions on the gods and goddesses.

Andrew Ciccarelli was a bulwark of support in more ways than can be recounted here, and is deeply thanked for his friendship.

For providing a month's respite in the Vermont countryside during the heat of composition and the N.Y.C. summer, thanks to Ian Anderson.

Arizona compatriots Christopher Santini, Irma Call, Carla Ohlig, and Leonard Rynsburger provided much-needed moral support, transportation, and a variety of special services.

Indispensible feline friends—Mushkin, Pim, and Merlin—gave unstintingly of love and patience, warmth and understanding while often providing much-needed comic relief!

Our agents, Peter Miller and Harrilyn Mills, of The Peter Miller Agency, deserve our heartfelt thanks, as does our wonderful editor Barbara Gess, whose interest, support, and competence have made the work a pleasure.

In a work of this sort it is always proper to acknowledge the gods and goddesses, whom we call the planets. Without them, there would be no book, no astrology, no mind-and-soul enriching study of the nature of the cosmos as it operates in human beings. As the work progressed, we learned more and more of an admittedly vast subject, and saw even more clearly how the energies of the planets really *do* operate in each of us.

And we especially thank our readers, the true inspiration for this work, for being open to that magical storehouse of knowledge, astrology. We can only hope astrology will enrich your lives as much as it has ours.

TABLE OF CONTENTS

ALL THE WORLD'S A STAGE . . .

Why another book on astrology and relationships? How is this one different from all the others? What are *Love Planets?* How can knowing about them promote more successful relationships? *Why* have we written this book?

Our motivation, to answer the last question first, is to help *you*—the person who has been trying to develop, maintain, or improve intimate relationships in this confusing world that is the end of the twentieth century.

Even those of us who think we have grown accustomed to a highly accelerated way of life in which we must process and accept change constantly are sometimes dizzy from it all. We need tools with which to cope. As therapists and consulting astrologers in regular contact with clients whose major problem is either a relationship that isn't working or the lack of a suitable relationship, we are acutely aware of this need. What to do?

This book is our answer. We chose the title *Love Planets* to indicate that the astrological influences on relationships are more varied than just Sun-sign comparisons, about which most astrological books on relationships have been written. The great majority of these books, even when they have provocative and promising titles using the words *love* or *sex*, give only Sun-sign information. Valuable as this may be, it is only part of the picture. (Your Sun sign is what you answer when someone asks, "What's your sign?")

Probably you have sensed that you are a much more complex and varied person than you have seen indicated just by looking up your Sun-sign description in other popular astrology books. You may even have wondered what was missing when you read both your own and your partner's Sun-sign descriptions. Reading, say, "Cancer Man" and "Libra Woman," you might have felt you couldn't really relate your relationship (or identify yourself) with what you were reading. You felt a gap.

Our book is meant to fill that gap. By focusing on the *personal planets and points*, instead of the Sun sign alone, this book brings you important additional information not usually available unless you consult a professional astrologer. These planets and points are the Moon, Venus, Mars, and the Ascendant/Descendant. The Ascendant, or rising sign, is the most important personal point in your chart. It is determined by the exact time and place you alone were born. It is what makes your chart unique. This approach is what makes our book different from the usual Sun-sign book that purports to reveal the mysteries of relationships.

Inside each of us are many and varied planetary energies, symbolized by the mythological characters from whom the names of the planets are taken. These energies are the actors in our personal life drama, they are our cosmic connection, they make us the richly variegated beings that we all are. The "Astropoints" we will be describing in detail have the most influence on your love and relationship life.

Although our book is a bit more complex than what you are used to from the usual Sun-sign-only books, we believe our method will be easy, fun, and rewarding to use. In addition, it will provide you with a more complete picture both of yourself and of your lover, mate, friend, relative, or any other person. It will, properly followed, give you a solid basis for achieving successful relationships, particularly intimate ones.

Each successive chapter will take you further into an understanding of yourself, which we believe is the first step in achieving satisfying relationships. After all, if you don't know about yourself—your needs, wants, desires—and what makes you most comfortable or drives you nuts, how can you relate successfully to another person, who also has needs, wants, desires, and so on, which may be very different from yours?

As you practice our system for self-understanding, you will at the same time learn to evaluate and understand your partner or potential partner. We have devised a unique system that is simple, clear, and easy to use. Correctly evaluating Astropoints that affect relationships is the key to creating successful relationships.

You already know that certain things about your partner make you mad. But getting to *why* you're mad, or why you mutually irritate each other, and resolving it is another issue entirely! An important step in any romance is to understand just who your Mr. or Ms. Right *is*. You yourself carry the image of that person inside you, recorded in the Astropoints we are discussing. This is your co-star in your life drama.

For example, have you ever met someone and immediately *liked* him or her, felt irresistibly drawn to that person? Astrology can give you the clues as to why this is. Astrologers call it chart comparison, the basis of this book's system for evaluating relationships.

If you *say* you want true love and commitment but wind up with only long-distance or intermittent lovers, there's a reason. And the reason is *you*. You may have internal conflicts. Perhaps your Venus wants to be free and uncommited while your Moon needs domesticity and commitment. And the two energies fight each other, keeping you from getting what you want.

This is a sampling of what we will reveal to you. Your *needs* are symbolized by the Moon in your chart; your *wants*, by Venus; your *desires*, by Mars; and the *image* you project to others, by your Ascendant, while the Descendant describes *whom* you attract.

We have chosen a theatrical theme for our book because, as astrologers who study the vast human drama, we see life as a cosmic play in which each of us has our part to act. Each of our lives is a play and each of us has many players within. We will be describing the planets as the players, the signs as the roles (or parts played), and the houses (determined by the Ascendant) as the stage settings against which the drama unfolds.

We view the planets, signs, and other factors in the chart as symbols. Life is lived on many different levels. Astrology *describes*, it does not determine. Your chart is a map of your own personal potential. How you use this is up to you. What your chart shows is who you are naturally, what's automatic in you, how you act and react, and, most important of all, the *quality* of the energies that are *you*.

We believe that understanding these ideas and applying them to your daily life will give you the power to use your inherent energies to the fullest, to change what you can, work around what you can't, and to perceive the difference between the two—to paraphrase the popular "Serenity Prayer."

If your goal is to find true love and fulfillment in a satisfying relationship, the help you need is here. It's all a question of knowing where and how to look—and what you're looking for!

Different people have different needs and wants. One of the biggest mistakes that most everyone makes is to assume that another's wants and needs are identical to one's own. Knowing both your own and your partner's predispositions will put you on the path to finding the relationship you want, keeping the one you have, or improving one that's in trouble.

Our book utilizes a unique approach, "Astroplay." Once you've experimented with this technique, you'll find that it's immediate, entertaining, and gratifying.

Astroplay means *acting the roles inside you and others*, and we give you the Astroscripts. These are to be read both silently and *aloud*. Instantly, you can see what scripts you are playing out (perhaps unknowingly) in what parts of your love life or other relationships. By reading silently and speaking the parts aloud you create a "double effective." Each enhances the other. First read, then speak the script. You'll be surprised how much you will become aware of which may have been hidden or kept unconscious.

Our unique numerical scoring system lets you evaluate the compatability potential between the two of you. This system will enable you to decipher the inner dynamics of your relationship, spot trouble-prone areas, emphasize congenial aspects, and create balance and harmony.

If you are not currently in a relationship but desire one, it will help you to understand your own propensities and what is best for you in another person. If you have one or more failed relationships in the past, it will clue you in to what went wrong and how to avoid a repetition of an old, possibly neurotic, pattern. It can also help you figure out relationships between yourself and nonromantic others—parents, children, relatives, friends, bosses, employees.

There's nothing more exciting than finding true love—and keeping it running smoothly. Our book is a significant guide that will enable you to be more in control of your relationship life. We've tested it in our practices and developed it just for you.

We've enjoyed our twenty years of being professional astrological counselors and therapists. We hope you enjoy using our method.

CASTING CALL: HOW TO USE THIS BOOK

Part One, "The Players," is designed to acquaint you with the five Astropoints with which this book deals. These are the SUN, MOON, ASCENDANT, VENUS, and MARS. We call these Astropoints (instead of planets) for two reasons: (1) technically, the Sun and the Moon are not planets, but "lights" and the Ascendant is a point in space and time. These points in your chart and that of your partners are the most important "relationship points" in your charts.

This book is meant to be used as a *working tool,* not only to help you understand yourself and your relationship, but to assist you in deriving the deeper meanings from the planetary placements in your charts. For this reason, we have written (in Part One) fully about the Astropoints. Although you can use the book without bothering to read Part One, you won't have as thorough an understanding of your Astropoints if you skip over it.

However, we realize that there are those who will want to know your placements *right away.* For you, we have devised a "quick fix."

If you can't wait, or refuse to wade through the beginning of the book, turn at once to the ephemerides (tables of planetary placements) in Part Two, "Places Everyone." If you don't know your Sun sign, or aren't sure, look at the chart on page 21.

Then, using the Basic Astropoint form on page 79, fill in your Astropoint placements. (Either photocopy the form or copy it onto a separate sheet of paper.) After you have looked up your Astropoints (and anyone else's), turn at once to the key words in Part Three, and then to the Astroscripts, in Part Four. You can figure out your Element and Mode Themes from the Table of Signs, Elements, and Modes on page 159 and look up your themes in Chapter 12.

However, by taking the quick fix you will get only an overview, not an in-depth understanding. This book is meant to be read through and worked with like a textbook. Each chapter leads successively to the next, and none should be skipped or skimmed. Everything is important to the end result of your understanding yourself and your relationship. By using this book as it was meant to be used—seriously and step by step—you will get more than your money's worth, and you will have a valuable working tool in your library for years to come, one to which you can continually refer for deeper insights, as well as when a new relationship comes into your life.

Of course, if you do take the quick fix, you can always go back and learn the basics later on . . . but that's doing it in reverse. It's as if you first wanted to study interior decorating and then had to learn to build a house in order to decorate it.

Part Three is your basic tool for understanding your own and your partner's astrological components. In it, we introduce a "sample couple" whose charts we analyze as we go along, to give you a guiding hand with self-interpretation. Our "sample couple" will help guide you through our process, and, at the end of the book, we reveal the two famous people you already know about and can relate to—but don't peek to see who they are! This part has been carefully crafted to give you the fullest possible understanding of how the Astropoints are operating in *you*. In it, you will also learn how to determine your Astropoint Theme and your Element and Mode Themes. These are vital to the overall astrological picture of who you/your partner are.

Part Four provides you with the Astroscripts discussed on page 11. Part Five outlines the scoring system for evaluating your relationship both numerically and thematically.

That's it. We hope you find *Love Planets* useful and truly *enjoy* using it. We've put a lot of thought and effort into bringing this book to you because we truly believe our method can help you either to better the relationship you are in or find the right one in the future. We're just extending our one-on-one astrological counseling and therapy practices, because there's no way we can see each of you on an individual basis, even though we'd like to! If you have any questions or comments, please feel free to write to us at the address listed in Appendix II, under LOVESTAR. We'd love to hear from you and we'll answer if we can.

Enjoy your Astroplaying (remember, it's really *play*), and we hope your relationship gets a rave review!

part one

THE PLAYERS

BEYOND SUN SIGNS

Your Sun sign is the sign of the zodiac that the Sun was passing through on the day you were born, no matter what year. Popular books and newspaper or magazine columns, based on the Sun sign alone, have created an oversimplification of astrology in most people's minds, with the result that they think comparing Sun signs will be the definitive clue to whether a relationship will work or not.

However, as this book will demonstrate, Sun signs alone are not the most relevant factor in whether two persons will fall in love, stay in love, have a smooth or rocky romance, stay together awhile and then split up, remain wedded for life, become friends or enemies.

Therefore, when astrologers are asked—as they often are, especially at social gatherings—whether Leo gets along with Scorpio or if a Cancer woman and a Libra man will make it together, there simply is no pat answer. The Sun is only one of ten planets in your charts, and, of these ten, four are particularly relevant to relationships—so if you don't know about these four, you have only part of the picture.

Let's take an example.

He's a Taurus and she's a Sagittarius. On the basis of Sun signs alone, we'd have to say that's a very difficult combination, and we wouldn't give it much of a chance for success.

BUT if we look further, we find that *she* has her Moon in Taurus, the same sign as his Sun, and the woman's Moon in the same sign as the man's Sun is an indicator of lots of harmony between them, for they share the same vibration, from her feelings (Moon) to his basic nature (Sun). Therefore, they will respond similarly to many things and feel comfortable together on one important level.

Next, we find that *he* has a Sagittarius Ascendant, another favorable combination, for Ascendant with the Sun is very compatible. Further investigation shows a winning Venus-Mars combination. Now the original gloomy picture of the success potential of their relationship has changed considerably.

The above example shows why it's important when considering relationships to realize that your two Sun signs don't tell the whole story. Moon, Venus, Mars, and your Ascendants play a big part as well.

And, having said that, let's talk about what the Sun *does* represent in your chart, how it can affect relationships when in basically incompatible signs.

In interpreting the *individual* horoscope, the Sun sign is a vital component, for it represents the core of the personality. The Sun, as generator of life, indicates how a person expresses the basic life energy potential given at birth. It is the motive power behind action, the essential Self. It is the creative drive toward growth and development as an individual. It tells about your approach to *learning* what life's all about. As the next chapter explains, your Moon sign is most evident when you are a child, whereas you slowly *grow into your Sun sign potential as you mature*.

One of the reasons for studying your own Sun sign is to understand how your personal energies work. This is a prime factor in self-understanding, the basis of finding and building a good relationship.

Esoteric theory, to which most astrologers ascribe, says that the Sun sign indicates the stage of growth represented by the person's present incarnation, the lessons to be mastered. Thus, the Sun in your chart represents or symbolizes *your conscious purpose in life*— what you feel you are here on earth to do and accomplish.

Since your Sun sign is how you view life from the standpoint of your "I-consciousness," it symbolizes your world view. Naturally, this can affect relationships. If you and your partner have similar life purposes, you will have a more harmonious relationship. If you are at cross-purposes about something so basic as what life is all about, you will have difficulties. Incompatible Sun signs have very different world views—that is to say, their separate energies flowing into the field of life clash.

Let's take an example.

Mr. and Mrs. X receive the totally unexpected news of a large windfall of money. He's a Sagittarius, she's a Taurus.

At first, thrilled and happy at what seems a gift from the gods, they celebrate with a bottle of champagne and a fine dinner at a good restaurant, suggested by her, followed up by a weekend trip to an island resort, his idea. For a few days they float on the bubble of their mutual happiness, but once back in the workaday world, they begin a serious discussion as to how to use the money.

They are sitting in their cozy living room filled with the solid, last-for-life furniture she has selected, decorated with his travel posters of exotic countries they have yet to visit. She has just made a pot of hot chocolate and a batch of homemade cookies, and they settle down to make some serious decisions and do some intelligent planning.

"How about that trip around the world I've always wanted to take?" he says excitedly, mentally already on the next plane to faraway places. He has a somewhat glazed look in his eyes as if already seeing those stirring scenes.

"Well . . ." she says slowly, "let's not be too hasty. A trip would be very expensive and really we should think carefully about the best way to handle the money in the long run."

"Honey," he interrupts exasperatedly, "this is the chance of our lifetime! We don't want to wait until we retire to see all those wonderful places like," he gestures at the posters on the wall, "Machu Picchu and the Hawaiian Islands—Egypt, Morocco. . . ."

"I know, darling," she says, patting his hand and refilling his cup with more hot chocolate, "and there's enough money for a trip of some kind, but let's *do* think it through first, and not rush into anything."

"I guess you're thinking about some sort of investment," he says, from sure knowledge of her, a bit resigned to the idea of a long-drawn-out discussion, which he hates.

"Right!" she replies enthusiastically. "Something really *solid*—you know, blue chip stuff, nothing risky. Something we can depend on for later."

"Okay—I don't mind investing *some* of the money, but let's go with a commodities broker—we could be just a step away from *millions*."

"Or a step away from losing everything we invest," she cautions. "I think we should buy some property—a house or even an income-producing building," she says, mentally toting up future profits.

"Making money's fine," he says thoughtfully, "but we shouldn't be too greedy—I mean we didn't *earn* this money. We ought to give some of it away . . . maybe to an environmentalist group like 'Save the Whales,' or a scholarship for some Third World kid to go to college."

"We'd be much better off *making* some profit off the money before we go *giving* it away," she snaps. "Why are you always so impractical? I'm as much in favor of a good cause as you are, and you know how much I love animals, but I'm talking about *practical reality.*"

"Sometimes I get so damned sick of your practical reality! Can't you ever be a little adventurous and just *let go?* When do we ever really *splurge?* Hey, come on—this is our chance to travel, see the world, expand our horizons, learn things."

"And throw away our *one real chance* at *future security!*"

"Why don't you *ever* want to *experience anything new?*"

As you can see, trouble stalks their formerly happy home, for here we have the makings of a major domestic rift. The windfall has given them the possibility to live out their ideas about life—but these are dramatically different attitudes!

Her Taurus need for material security feels threatened by his flamboyant enthusiasm and devil-may-care attitude. His free-spirited Sagittarius feels like she is tying him down to a life of reading the *Wall Street Journal* to keep track of their investments. She thinks he's an impractical, immature spendthrift, bent only on immediate pleasures. He thinks she's stodgy, a wet blanket, someone whose idea of fun would be living in a bank vault counting the money and never spending it.

In her world view, she places the highest priority on peace and stability; her life purpose is to preserve what she values.

In his world view, he places the highest priority on adventure and learning; his life purpose is to travel, experience other cultures.

She feels she can learn all she needs to know about life at home, with a full stomach and warm toes.

He feels that only by traveling far and wide can he fulfill his deep need to learn and discover life's variety.

Can this marriage be saved?

Well, that depends on other factors in their charts, whether their Moons, Venuses, Marses, and Ascendants reinforce the basic difference or ameliorate it. And that's what this book is all about—showing you how those *other* factors can affect the basic Sun-sign personality and how those in turn affect relationships.

Below are some key words for the twelve signs. In each, the Sun expresses the *inner self* variously:

In ARIES, the SUN expresses the *self* through ACTION.
In TAURUS _____ STABILITY.
In GEMINI _____ THINKING.
In CANCER _____ FEELING.
In LEO _____ CREATIVITY.
In VIRGO _____ PRACTICALITY.
In LIBRA _____ UNITING.
In SCORPIO _____ DESIRING.
In SAGITTARIUS _____ LEARNING.
In CAPRICORN _____ USEFULNESS.
In AQUARIUS _____ HUMANITY.
In PISCES _____ IMAGINATION.

Your Sun sign is that section of the zodiac the Sun appears to transit at the moment of your birth. The Sun takes a year to transit all twelve of the zodiacal signs.

Thus, if you were born on the first day of May, you are a Taurus, because the Sun appeared to be transiting the section of the zodiac identified as Taurus on that day. Some people are born just as the Sun is changing signs. We call that the "cusp," which is the dividing line between signs. Example dates of this are December 23 and May 21. In such cases, you might need an exact chart, prepared either by a professional astrologer or from a computer, to know exactly which sign you are. If you are born on the cusp, you'll have some of the qualities of each of the two signs, but you'll still definitely be one or the other.

The glyph for the Sun (pictured at the beginning of this chapter) is a circle with a dot at the center. The circle is a symbol for that which is without beginning or end, symbolizing unity, and the dot symbolizes individuality. The dot is the point sent forth from the Universal Source (or the All, the One, God, or however you choose to call it). From that center, we come into manifestation, or life.

THE NATURAL ZODIAC

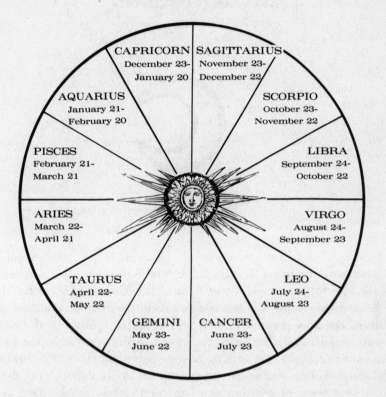

CAPRICORN
December 23-
January 20

SAGITTARIUS
November 23-
December 22

AQUARIUS
January 21-
February 20

SCORPIO
October 23-
November 22

PISCES
February 21-
March 21

LIBRA
September 24-
October 22

ARIES
March 22-
April 21

VIRGO
August 24-
September 23

TAURUS
April 22-
May 22

LEO
July 24-
August 23

GEMINI
May 23-
June 22

CANCER
June 23-
July 23

THAT OLD DEVIL MOON

There is a charming Russian Yiddish folktale about the relative value of the light of the Sun and the light of the Moon to life on Earth.

As you may know, the learned rabbis of the orthodox faith in small villages spend a great deal of time pondering questions of vast and cosmic importance. Basically, theirs is a theoretical rather than practical approach. In this little and very revealing story, the rabbis of a Russian village had spent many years in daily debate over the all-important issue of whether the light of the Sun or the light of the Moon benefits humanity more.

At last, the head rabbi let it be known that a decision had been reached. The excited villagers gathered on the green to receive this long-awaited revelation. There was a hush of expectation as the chief rabbi appeared before the assemblage, robed as befitted such a momentous occasion. Solemnly he announced that the light of the Moon is of greater importance to the human race than the light of the Sun.

There was a moment of stunned silence as the crowd struggled to absorb this information. Then a child asked, "Why?"

With a benign smile, the rabbi answered, "Because, my son, it is dark at night. So we need the light of the Moon more."

We smile at this tale, but it hides an important truth, as do most folktales and legends or fairy tales. The rabbis' conclusion that we need the light of the Moon more because it illumines what is naturally dark, the night, is a metaphor for the unconscious. Though scientifically absurd, the rabbis' conclusion reveals a deep psychological truth about the human psyche—one that, in our busy, almost exclusively Sun-oriented (logical, rational) lives, we often aren't in touch with. Symbolically, the Moon serves to illuminate the less-conscious side of human life, and sometimes in that diffuse light we can see more clearly than in the glare of the noonday sun.

The Moon has been called the "soul of Life." Without it, we would have only the mechanical, an endless efficiency which in the end is soul-less. Without the Moon we would have no poetry, literature, art, music, dance, or dreams. Artists are notorious for being "dreamy," and we dream at night when the Moon reigns over us.

That other half of life, the one that is unseen in the bright light of day, comes alive in us at night, when the Moon sheds her gentle light. Then doors open to magical realms of the imagination and human creativity. Then the wonderful world of the psyche is open to us. Try this experiment to prove this to yourself:

Choose an hour of the day—say, from three to four—and sit quietly in a room by yourself with no distractions. See what comes to your mind, how you feel, what you think, where your awareness goes. Afterward, take that same hour of the night and repeat the procedure. Notice the differences. If you let yourself be in tune with the cosmos, you will *feel* the Moon's energies, for they are not only "out there," they are in you!

Symbolically speaking the Moon gives birth to itself every month as it goes from new moon (black, invisible, just as the fertilized ovum in the womb is at first unknown, even to the mother, and unseen), then grows (as a pregnancy grows) to the full, and then slowly "dies," as it gradually diminishes in the waning period until it is gone from our sight, only to be "reborn" again as it appears the following month as a slender, shining crescent. And how thrilling is that first sight of the newly waxing moon!

The Moon is cyclical and constantly changing. Women "go through phases" in their menstrual cycle. The great flux and flow of life is rhythmical and regular, as the tides come in and go out. Moon terminology everywhere pervades our language. Lovers go for moonlit walks. When in love, the young are moonstruck. Poets go mooning about. The insane are loony, a derivative of *lunar*. Moonlight and roses evokes a romantic mood. Songs by the dozen celebrate the Moon—can you think of a song with the Sun in its title? Surely, no one alive has not at some time or other been impressed by the magical power of the Moon, perhaps newly risen and still red in a Mediterranean sky, or hanging huge and golden as the harvest moon, or

Moon Goddess wearing the newborn crescent Moon in her hair

silvering the snow of a winter's night. In contrast to the Sun's powerful gaze, even the brightest light of the fullest Moon only serves to gleam and soften what it touches. That's how the Moon works in you as well.

The astrologers' pictorial representation (glyph) of the Moon, a semicircle (shown at the beginning of this chapter), represents the finite and manifested. Each day, the Moon absorbs the Sun's rays, returning them to us at night. Thus, the Moon symbolizes all that is receptive in human nature—the unconscious, the emotions, the behavioral instincts. It represents the classic maternal feminine side of the personality (which, of course, exists in men as well as in women). It is *yin* to the Sun's *yang*—receptive, feeling, nurturing. It speaks to us of the deepest, darkest, most interior place where all is gestated before birth, be it a child or a work of art.

People connect intimately with another human being for many reasons—not the least of them to fulfill either what was wonderful in childhood (attempting to duplicate it, as in mother's cooking) or desperately trying to get what was missing. There's a resonance that we're always seeking—a *felt* resonance.

Let's look at two hypothetical scenarios. You are about to make the Big Presentation for the Big Account. For weeks you've been in a state of high anxiety, wrapped up in the project, sometimes unable to sleep through the night. This is IT. Sure, your partner is supportive, listening to your daily litany of how things are going, but how does he or she behave on the Big Day?

· · ·

Scene One: The Big Day arrives. You are dressed for success. And an early start. Outside it's cold and the driveway is decorated with the first snowfall of winter. You check to see that you've got it all together and, just as you are about to walk out the front door, your sleepy spouse, still warm from the bed, wanders in on the way to the kitchen for a cup of the coffee you've made and says "Good luck with the presentation." You get a quick hug.

Scene Two: The Big Day arrives. Last night, your partner suggested dinner out as an advance celebration of your success. Next morning, you waken to the smell of freshly brewed coffee and the tantalizing smell of food cooking. There's even a fresh rose on the breakfast table. Your car is idling in the cleared driveway, getting warmed up. During breakfast, the two of you chat and make plans for the evening ahead with the emphasis on whatever *you* want to do.

Which scenario would you prefer? That's your *lunar response.* Neither is right or wrong. The point is, you have to know yourself *and* your man or woman.

Review the scenarios again. How would *you* likely behave in the situation if it were your partner's presentation? And how would your *partner* want you to behave? You'll learn a lot from this single exercise.

One of the giant pitfalls in any relationship is assuming someone else's needs are the same as your own. This is known as *projecting.* It means assigning your own needs and desires to the other person. Just because you need closeness to feel comfortable doesn't mean that he or she does. And this is what the Moon in the charts can tell us. Your Moon tells you what makes *you* feel loved. Sometimes, all the words in the world won't do it—being told "I love you" a thousand times won't have the same impact as a right, single gesture. That's because the Moon is about *feeling.*

In days mostly past, maybe gone forever, men and women took care of each other in prescribed and socially ordained ways—Mom prepared Dad's favorite meal, washed and ironed his shirts, sorted and rolled his socks. She minded the home atmosphere with his comfort in mind. In return, he did things for her—he dug up her garden in the spring, mowed the lawn, did repairs around the house, built her a new cabinet or a sewing room. Together, through these demonstrations of caring, gradually they wove a life out of the stuff that keeps relationships alive and together—or didn't, as the case may be. A badly cooked meal deliberately served late or the irritation of a constantly leaking faucet might have been covert messages that said, "I'm mad at you," or "You hurt my *feelings*," or, even, "I really don't care about your comfort." These are Moon things.

In these harassing times, with both people in a couple often working, there is less and less time and motivation for the sort of obvious, physical (and automatic) gestures of caring as those assumed to be natural and required by earlier generations. This makes relating harder today than it ever was before. With the new freedoms comes a less structured way of life and fewer sure ways of being together. Moon needs—and remember, the Moon is what makes you feel comfortable and safe—often go unmet.

When this happens, it can create all sorts of relationship troubles: resentment (often unacknowledged); anger (guilt producing); frustration (dissatisfaction at a basic level), and so on. When your Moon needs are not being met, you become unhappy at the deepest level of your being, the place where you were in the cradle when you were dependent on others for your survival needs: nourishment, warmth and cleanliness, a sense of safety and well-being, and, most importantly, love and affection.

The Moon in your chart is the area of your life where old conditioning from childhood resides. It symbolizes what comforts you. It shows patterns that are as old as you are, from the days when you were rocked and held as a baby—or not. The Moon is that part of you having everything to do with what makes you feel good: comfortable, safe, *at home*.

Thus, the Moon is a knee-jerk place within us that ticks off deepset needs . . . we could call these "mommy needs." They are terribly important to our continuing sense of security. When you wake up from a night of depressing thoughts or bad dreams and you go to the refrigerator for a nice glass of milk, that's your Moon. You don't consciously think, "A glass of milk is what makes me feel comfortable, cozy, and cared for." No. You just do it. Automatically.

Even as adults, we all need to be nurtured, to feel cared for, to think we are connected and protected. Unfortunately, some of us didn't get that caring when we should have. And this causes problems later, because those basic unmet childhood needs go underground where they remain alive and well—and *very, very* needy. So, if you were a person who suffered a deprived childhood, lacking in nurturing and being made to feel loved, you will be trying to get this—all your life until you understand it—from a relationship. Often, this deep well of unfulfilled needs can be too much of a weight for a relationship to carry—your partner can't be your mommy or daddy.

The act—and fact—of mating is very much psychologically tied into our childhoods, and though we may think ourselves totally adult when we have sex, live together, or marry, the truth is we're usually looking to fulfill our Moon needs, whether we know it or not.

The Moon tells us what in the long term, over time, is really important to our feeling comfortable, both with ourselves and with another person on an intimate basis.

In our opinion, the Moon is the most important point of compatibility—or incompatibility—between people. The Moon shows how we react when upset, how we comfort ourselves, what is most basic, and, often, what is most unconscious—sometimes uncontrollable, as in bouts of binge eating.

The Moon is how you take care of yourself and others, and how you want to be taken care of. Thus, the Moons in two people's charts indicate *how they will take care of each other*—an essential factor in the cementing of any relationship. Incompatible Moons can cause a lot of trouble at the deepest level of being, where those old patterns set in childhood live.

Let's look at a typical interaction between a couple with difficult Moon placements between them. She's a Leo Moon. He's a Capricorn Moon:

Our couple is sitting in their TV room. He is reviewing his day's work as a writer (he works at home). She's just come in from her work and is relaxing—he doesn't relax. In a playful mood, she turns on the TV to see if there's anything amusing to watch. The noise bothers him, but he keeps on reading. Sitting on the floor, her legs stretched out in front of her, she suddenly notices that her foot is just the same size as his and calls this interesting fact to his attention. He looks and is also astonished. They discuss this for a few moments and then he abruptly says, "That's enough!" and goes back to his papers.

Crushed, she crumples down into a corner of the couch in the fetal position, close to tears, feeling totally rejected. Now she is engulfed by feelings of being unwanted and unloved, thinking bitterly about all the other times he has been cold and indifferent to her.

We have here the ingredients for a major domestic discord. Without applause, the Leo Moon's natural inwardness will surface—*go away and leave me alone to lick my wounds*, it says. Feelings of being

unappreciated and unloved, harking all the way back to childhood lacks, come hurtling to the surface as a result of this—to him—unimportant incident. We call this the "nobody loves me" syndrome.

Like a house of cards, one slight (unintended) reactivates all the old wounds, from the time your mother let your diapers go dirty while she was yacking on the telephone, to the unfeeling aunt who criticized the size and shape of your legs when you were twelve, to the first time you didn't have a date for an important school function, to the last time you got fired. . . . On and on, the whole business leaps into the feeling field. These feelings can cripple a person emotionally. Like sludge in a carburetor, everything stops running until a cleanout occurs.

It does no good, an hour later, when he casually suggests that, since they are both tired, they go out for dinner. Her pleasure has been spoiled. For her, life with him (at least for the time being) is empty and pointless, flat, stale, not worth having. The Moon, you see, isn't logical or rational. She *feels*. That's her function.

Both of these people think (more or less unconsciously) that their behavior will make them more lovable and gain them approval. It's just that they were quite differently programmed in childhood as to what makes a person lovable and acceptable. She was praised for performing—applauded whenever she entertained the family or the public. The more cute tricks she did, the more attention she got. He, on the other hand, was given strokes for diligence and ambition and hard work. The more productive he was, the more he gained his parents' approval. Different folks, different strokes.

Are we stuck with our Moon selves forever? Are those patterns established in our earliest days set in concrete in our psyches? Yes and no. Astrology is a tool that can make things better. You are who you are, of course, but it's only when your Moon energies are operating unconsciously (that is, you don't know you're behaving a certain way because it's automatic) that problems arise. Understanding your own Moon and the other person's is a major step toward creating successful relationships.

Your Moon sign indicates your immediate reactions at the instinctual or gut level. It shows what is going on underneath, which sometimes you're not even aware of. The Moon *reacts*.

It is your personal atmosphere, operating in the background of your more focused Sun sign, rather like a subliminal tape. You pay no attention but it is still giving your mind information. The Moon picks up from the environment and reacts. It's your feelings, moods, the rhythms in your body's sympathetic and autonomous nervous systems, and other bodily processes, such as digestion.

As a child, you probably exhibited your Moon sign more visibly— you hadn't yet learned to express yourself other than through your feelings and bodily processes! Later on, as you discovered the ways of the world—how to be rational and declare yourself an individual— you became more like your Sun sign.

But the Moon is always *there*, lying under the surface, and it becomes more evident when we are relaxed, tired, or ill. That's when those "mommy needs" surface, sometimes very demandingly. Think of how you feel or react when you are really very hungry or completely exhausted. That's your Moon talking.

Below are some key words for the twelve signs. In each, the Moon expresses *needs* variously:

In ARIES, the MOON expresses *need* for ACTION.
In TAURUS _____ STABILITY.
In GEMINI _____ LIGHTNESS.
In CANCER _____ SECURITY.
In LEO _____ ATTENTION.
In VIRGO _____ ORDER.
In LIBRA _____ HARMONY.
In SCORPIO _____ INTENSITY.
In SAGITTARIUS _____ FREEDOM.
In CAPRICORN _____ RESULTS.
In AQUARIUS _____ FRIENDS.
In PISCES _____ SENSITIVITY.

How do the Sun and Moon relate to each other in your and your partner's charts?

The Moon is a feminine sign, so we read it a bit differently in a man's or a woman's chart, but it serves the same function. The basic difference is that in a man's chart it often is a strong clue to the type of woman he will choose for a mate. This doesn't necessarily mean he will choose a woman whose Sun is in the same sign as his Moon. More likely, he'll be attracted to a woman whose Moon is in the same sign as *his* Moon or *his* Sun. The psychologist Carl G. Jung did a well-known statistical experiment in which he examined the charts of married couples. The most frequent combination was the husband's and wife's Moons *in the same sign.* The second most frequent placement was the Sun in the man's chart *exactly opposite* the Moon in the woman's chart. The third most frequent placement was the Sun in the man's chart in the same sign as the Moon in the woman's chart. Jung's experiment went no further, but a man will be attracted to a woman whose Venus is in the same sign as his Moon.

Solar King and Lunar Queen, the "Royal Pair"

Astronomically, we know that the Moon reflects the light of the Sun. The Sun, with its life-giving, yet scorching, light is the Eye of Consciousness. The gentler Moon, with its reflected glory, shines all the brighter because it is the handmaiden to the forces of night, the nonrational—what today we call *right brain*. Intuitive. Creative. Psychic. Artistic.

The Sun, the logical, rational, thinking part of us, corresponds to *left-brain* functions. It is our conscious purpose. It is what we feel we are here on earth to accomplish. It is linear, going neatly from *A* to *B* to *C*, and so on. It *thinks* consciously. Since traditionally men are supposed to do the thinking and women the feeling, old-time astrologers felt that the Sun in a man's chart should be in the same sign as the Moon in the woman's chart. That way, his thinking faculty was in harmony with (and dominated) her feeling capacity. Today, things are different, but solar and lunar placements between charts are still valid and important in judging how a relationship will function. Together, the Sun and Moon form the "royal pair"—masculine-feminine, outer-inner, light-dark, hot-cold. They are opposites, but opposites that depend upon each other for existence and meaning. It is only in the mirror of a relationship that we truly see ourselves.

Sun and Moon as equals

A word of caution: if we become too involved with our Sun energies (that is to say, the conscious mind) and we neglect our Moon energies, we are out of balance. Sadly, too many of us suffer from this condition because we live in a solar-dominated (Sun = masculine) world. Men especially are out of touch with their lunar selves. A wonderful astrologer friend of ours has written a book* about this very thing. As a social worker, she has observed that many people are disconnected from their lunar selves because of pressures to conform to the solar world around them. Lunar types especially have this problem, and it is important to remember that either a man or a woman can be a lunar type.

In our society, we give far much more weight to the Sun, or masculine-rational, functions of ourselves than we do to the Moon, or creative-nonrational. It is interesting to note that, from the astrologer's point of view, the Sun and the Moon *appear* to be exactly the same size when measured from the vantage point of the earth! We know they're not, of course, but, as we said earlier, it is what we see that guides our interpretations.

Being a Lunar Type in a Solar World, by Donna Cunningham (Weiser).

chapter three

YOU'RE IN THE ASCENDANT

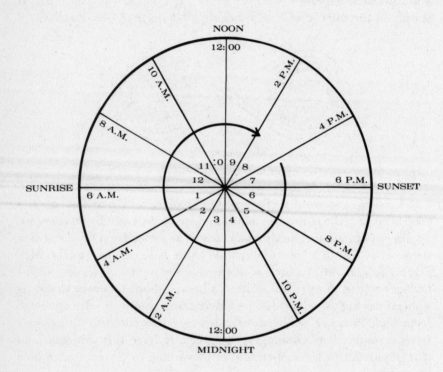

Astrology connects us to the universal energy of the cosmos, both in time and in space. The twelve signs of the zodiac are like an ever-turning wheel. This celestial clock contains all twenty-four hours of the day-night cycle. It is constantly revolving, with a new sign appearing on the horizon every two hours (and a different degree of the same sign every four minutes). Just knowing what *sign* was rising at the time of your birth will give you an entirely new perspective on who you are, astrologically speaking.

The Ascendant, or ASC, most obviously is our first line of social behavior—how we respond and react, who we present ourselves to be. Imagine that you are behind a tinted glass, like the colored filter in a camera, and that you always view the world from behind this screen. And, if you are behind it, then the world has no option but to view you *through* it as well.

This, however, is *not* something coming from the surface. Though most *evident* on the surface, it originates in a deeply internal individuality imprinted at birth. The ASC is the gateway to life on the material plane: it is the Door through which you enter life on this earth. Prior to birth, the unborn infant carries all the energies of the planets within, but it is only at birth that the lifelong imprint of the ASC is received. That moment in time and its particular attributes

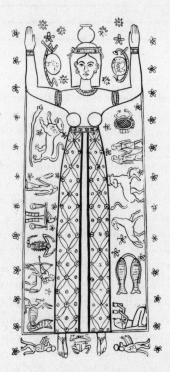

Nut, the Egyptian Sky Goddess, with the symbols of the signs of the zodiac circulating around Her, rising in their Cosmic Order.

are forever a part of you, because, at birth, these qualities symbolized by your ASC permeate your entire being, just as a single drop of dye colors a whole container of water.

Below are some key words for the twelve signs. In each, the ASC
expresses its *first response* variously:

In ARIES, the ASC expresses its *first response* by ACTING.
In TAURUS ———————————————————— WAITING.
In GEMINI ———————————————————— TALKING.
In CANCER ———————————————————— NURTURING.
In LEO ———————————————————— LEADING.
In VIRGO ———————————————————— ANALYZING.
In LIBRA ———————————————————— HARMONIZING.
In SCORPIO ———————————————————— CONTROLLING.
In SAGITTARIUS ———————————————————— ENJOYING.
In CAPRICORN ———————————————————— MANAGING.
In AQUARIUS ———————————————————— SOCIALIZING.
In PISCES ———————————————————— FLOWING.

Put another way, the ASC is the mask that we wear in public. It
is what comes naturally when we deal with any social situation. We've
all known people who are excessively polite and carefully mannered
in public but who can turn into rude slobs in private. Or conversely,
people who can be abrupt and hurried in public and pussycats at
home. Not everything is so extreme, of course, and sometimes at home
we behave as if we were in public, either because we are insecure
about who we are or because we are "putting on a front." The ASC
is that front, but that is not to say it is a false front. It is, as much
as the Sun and Moon and other planets, an innate part of who we
are. It's just that the ASC is the most *visible* part. A person might
very well be able to conceal his or her Moon nature (because that's
the most sensitive, innermost area of life) or have a hard time revealing
the Sun nature (because that's the true core of the self), but the ASC
will always be up front and right there for all to see. Sometimes a
strong ASC (that is, one with major planets configurated with it) can
overshadow the Sun and make it hard for a person to get in touch
with his or her core personality.

Psychologically speaking, the ASC also serves as our first line of
defense against the realities of life and its difficulties. It can be our
most easily accessible and effective coping mechanism and one so
polished with use it becomes almost automatic. For example, someone
with Libra ASC might discover that politeness, good manners, and

an ability to make compromises function as a way to get along in a very competitive family or at school.

Let's see how the foregoing might act when first introduced to someone. You can see each ASC's *first response* to a new situation:

ARIES   would be open and direct, taking the initiative, and talking first. ARIES would display energy, enthusiasm, ambition.

TAURUS   would be pleasant and responsive, but would wait for the other's reaction. TAURUS would display sensuality, substance, and earthiness.

GEMINI   would be talkative, quickly initiating conversation. GEMINI would display intelligence, wit, and curiosity.

CANCER   would be shy but receptive to the other person's feelings. CANCER would display sensitivity, humor, and caring.

LEO   would be warm and engaging, talking freely about him- or herself. LEO would display generosity, taste, and style.

VIRGO   would be restrained, and analyze the other person. VIRGO would display intelligence, seriousness, and practicality.

LIBRA   would dazzle with a smile and encourage the other person to talk about him- or herself. LIBRA would display niceness, intellect, and good manners.

SCORPIO   first would make strong eye contact, then take control of the interaction. SCORPIO would display mystery, magnetism, and perception.

SAGITTARIUS   first would get the person laughing, then pique his or her interest. SAGITTARIUS would display high spirits, wisdom, and playfulness.

CAPRICORN   would be matter-of-fact and reticent while discovering the other person's status. CAPRICORN would display ambition, capability, and integrity.

AQUARIUS   would be interesting and open, and seem fascinated with the other person. AQUARIUS would display intelligence, eccentricity, and humanitarianism.

PISCES   would tune in to the other person, to the extent of mirroring his or her movements. PISCES would display compassion, sensitivity, and creativity.

THE NATURAL ORDER OF THE SIGNS IN THE HOUSES

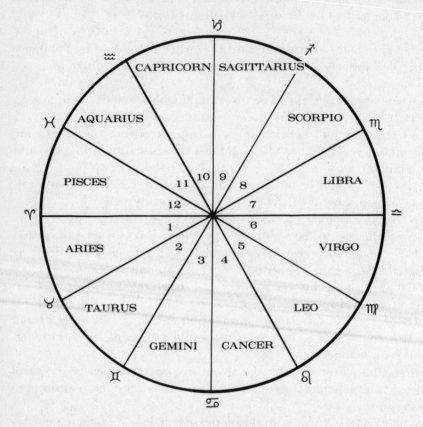

Whatever the Sun sign or signs that the other planets occupy, the ASC will always be the most up-front, obvious factor and will be expressed most immediately in the person's environment.

Unlike the planets (and it's important to remember that the ASC is *not* a planet but a point on the space and time continuum of the Universal round), each of which has its own particular characteristics, the ASC *always* takes on some of the qualities of Aries, the first sign of the zodiac, which begins the vernal (or spring) equinox and therefore is the first sign of the "natural" zodiac.

As it is Aries nature to be the initiator, it is the nature of the ASC to be the most up-front part of your personality. Astrologers call the ASC point the cusp of the first house.

The "houses" are twelve pie-shaped slices of the chart wheel. According to which sign falls on the ASC, or cusp, of the first house, the chart is organized by placing a different sign of the zodiac, in the order just given, on each of the following eleven house cusps (dividing lines between the houses). For example, if you have Cancer on the cusp of the first house, which is to say a Cancer ASC, you would have Leo on the second house cusp, Virgo on the third, and so on.

THE MEANING OF THE HOUSES

The houses describe the various areas of life's activities and needs, what we call the "stage settings," where the different planetary energies operate. Once you have looked up your ASC sign in the tables provided in Part Two, you will be able to determine in which house your Sun, Moon, Venus, and Mars are placed. As the organizer of your chart, the ASC determines which signs are on the other eleven house cusps, and into which houses the planets fall. The diagram above shows the meanings of the twelve houses. For example, a planet in the second house, of money and possessions, expresses its energies somewhat differently from the same planet in the seventh house, of one-to-one relationships. So the houses are important in terms of where in our lives each planetary energy is highlighted.

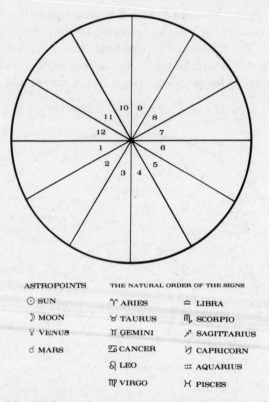

ASTROPOINTS	THE NATURAL ORDER OF THE SIGNS	
☉ SUN	♈ ARIES	♎ LIBRA
☽ MOON	♉ TAURUS	♏ SCORPIO
♀ VENUS	♊ GEMINI	♐ SAGITTARIUS
♂ MARS	♋ CANCER	♑ CAPRICORN
	♌ LEO	♒ AQUARIUS
	♍ VIRGO	♓ PISCES

Above is a blank chart form you can use as a visual tool. After looking up your ASC sign in the tables provided, write it at the left horizontal angle of the blank chart and then, following the "natural" order of the signs listed on the chart, write the rest of the signs on the other house cusps around the wheel. If, for example, you have Aquarius rising, Pisces will be on the second house cusp, Aries on the third, and so on.

Place your Sun (using the glyph shown on the chart form) in the house with its sign on the cusp. Then place the Moon in the same fashion, and your Venus and Mars as you read on and look them up.

To summarize, the ASC is determined from the time and place of birth. It *begins* the chart because it is on the cusp of the first house. It *organizes* the chart because it determines what signs fall on the other eleven house cusps. It *personalizes* the chart and makes it unique to you. It *describes* how you first react in a social situation, and it indicates how others will perceive your behavior. It *reveals* psychologically your preferred method of coping with the outside world. It *functions* as your exterior mask or "personality"—how you choose to let others perceive you first before you reveal your inner dimensions and interior nature.

The ASC, therefore, has a great deal to do with how we react in a social situation (that is, outside ourselves, whether to family, work, or friends and associates), how we present ourselves to others, and how they perceive us. It has been described as the "personality" point.

A person might be observed to exhibit hardly any of his or her Sun sign's characteristics, until you got to know that person very well. Then, of course, the "core" Sun of the person becomes apparent.

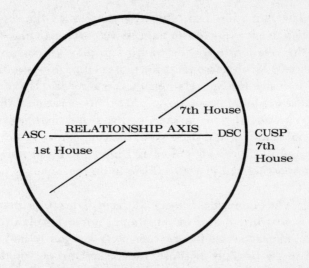

The next most important thing the ASC does, in the context of relationships, is describe the Descendant (DSC). This point, at the sunset position of the chart, *begins your seventh house, that of one-to-one relationships*.

The ASC-DSC axis, the line that slices the chart in half horizontally, is what we call the Relationship Axis. The sign falling on the cusp of the seventh house, or the DSC, is always in exact opposition to your ASC. Opposites do attract!

There are six pairs of opposites:

ARIES/LIBRA	LIBRA/ARIES
TAURUS/SCORPIO	SCORPIO/TAURUS
GEMINI/SAGITTARIUS	SAGITTARIUS/GEMINI
CANCER/CAPRICORN	CAPRICORN/CANCER
LEO/AQUARIUS	AQUARIUS/LEO
VIRGO/PISCES	PISCES/VIRGO

In addition to the sign found on the DSC, any planets placed in the Seventh House will signify important qualities you seek in a life partner. These qualities might be ones which you feel lacking in yourself, which may or may not be consciously acknowledged. For example, someone might seek a powerful, protective partner because of feeling helpless, unprotected, and alone.

Following is a brief review of the four planets this book deals with—Sun, Moon, Venus, and Mars—describing their effects as related to your partner when they are found in the seventh house:

SUN   The Sun rules Leo, and with the Sun in the seventh house you are looking for an impressive partner to play a dominant role in the relationship while wanting to play an equally dominant role yourself. Much personal pride in a relationship is indicated, and there is a desire for the relationship to succeed in the public eye as well. There is a lot of dramatic flair here. Cooperation is the principle quality you want in your partner, and you want marriage to improve your social standing and prestige in the community. Your ideal mate is interested in expressing power and individuality through the marriage, supporting you in your efforts to do the same.

MOON   The Moon rules Cancer, the sign of devotion and nurturing. A strong desire for emotional nurturing, both giving and receiving, characterizes this placement. You want to be "mothered" at some level, possibly because you lacked proper mothering and nurturing in your childhood. You crave affection and you want a close emotional bond that enables you to be yourself without criticism or makeover efforts. Your mate must be sympathetic to the inner child that still lives in your psyche. He or she needs patience and understanding, for you can be moody when upset. A seventh house Moon can be an indicator of more than one marriage and "changeability" within the marriage.

VENUS   Venus rules Libra, the natural occupant of the seventh house. This is a fortunate placement, for Venus seeks harmony and balance in all things. You may be a "people pleaser" and have a lack of self-esteem regarding your own qualifications, and you feel that the appropriate partner will somehow fill in the blanks and balance the scale for you. Depending on the rest of the chart, Venus in the seventh house might be an indicator that you focus too much on outward appearances, such as material possessions or social standing. You seek marriage for the romantic fulfillment and happiness it can bring, usually marrying early. You express love in your personal relationships and expect to receive it in return.

MARS   Energetic Mars rules the action sign of Aries, and you are likely to be quite aggressive about relationships, even combative. You are powerfully attracted to your partner and equally influenced by him or her. You tend to get into a relationship impulsively, without sufficient preparation, which comes from your need to prove yourself in all things. Disappointment in love is not uncommon, owing to the "marry in haste and repent in leisure" rule. In some cases, you are domineering and engage in shouting matches if thwarted. It is quite possible that both you and your partner indulge in impulsive behavior, and this can cause marital discord.

A recent article in a popular magazine was entitled "Good Lasting-Love Match: A + B." It went on to say that research shows that "opposites often not only click but stick." What the researcher found was that couples with contrasting personality types were more committed and more optimistic about marrying. The Ph.D. who did the study says, "As long as they are opposites, the relationship tends to function well."*

This is no news to astrologers, who for centuries have known that the sign opposite your ASC reveals a lot about your relationships: who you will attract and who will attract you!

*Self, June 1987, page 36.

chapter four

THE GODDESS OF LOVE

Venus. Mention of the very word conjures up images . . . from that of the classically beautiful Venus di Milo of the Greek sculptors to the artifically induced blondness of a movie sex queen such as Jean Harlow, Marilyn Monroe, or Brigitte Bardot.

Who is this goddess, so familiar yet so elusive? How and why does she strike such chords in our psyches?

Before being given the name Venus by the Romans, the goddess was known as Aphrodite, of Greece. Centuries of artists have tried to capture her essence . . . poets have waxed poetic and sometimes soppy in an effort to do her proper honor, telling eloquently of the beauty of her face and skin, perfect form, enticing locks, eyes of enchantment, and, of course, lovely breasts. Sculptors have represented her ineffable loveliness, as shown by the many classical marble representations of her that have come down to us through the ages. She particularly captured the imagination of the artists of the Renaissance period. To artists and poets, she has been the quintessence of irresistible charm. To Homer, she was a "lover of laughter," thus her association with play and pleasure.

Goddess of Love

There is today a popular concept among astrologers, when inter-preting Venus in the chart, of a slightly overweight, certainly full-blown, lady of leisure, enwrapped in a pink negligee frosted with lace and ruffles, lying on a velvet chaise lounge eating bonbons. As such, she is the representative of love in the hearts-and-flowers manner of all that is languid and self-indulgent.

But Venus is much more than that. As Aphrodite, she is a goddess of great power, also the Great Mother. Not someone to fool around with, as Psyche discovered!

In this tale, the beautiful and innocent Psyche is the third and last daughter of a king, and word spreads far and wide of her unusual and appealing beauty. Someone has the unspeakable effrontery to compare Psyche's beauty to that of the goddess herself! Needless to say, Aphrodite gets wind of this insult and, not one to suffer in silence, for she can be vengeful (jealousy is one of Venus's negative traits), the goddess immediately wastes the king's land, putting the people into a panic, whereupon they demand that a sacrifice be made and, seeing the wrath of Aphrodite behind the famine, lay it all at poor Psyche's door, cursing her now troublesome beauty and blaming the girl for what was not her fault at all.

Psyche is led atop a barren hill and left for the wild beasts to devour. Everybody goes home, dusting their hands, figuring, "That's that." Just as she is about to despair, alone and cold with night fast coming on, missing her family terribly and, of course, feeling guilty for being so beautiful, she is magically transported by an invisible force to an island of great beauty and luxury, and installed in a magnificent palace. There, an invisible lover treats her to divine rapture, and he is none other than Aphrodite's son, the god Eros himself.

Eros has cautioned her never, never to ask to see him (it is very, very dangerous for mortals to look upon a god or goddess, though one can safely make love with them so long as this prohibition is kept) and, of course, Psyche never has, being quite satisfied with things just the way they are.

But her jealous and meddlesome sisters, having discovered her enviable situation, nag at her, asking how can she be sure that her lover isn't some horrible, foul beast with evil powers of black magic? Torn between wanting to please her family and her loyalty to her unseen lover, Psyche wavers. The sisters wrest a promise from her to hold up the lamp and get a look at him the next time he visits her. They instill the worm of doubt into her young and pure heart. Sighing, she promises, thinking that perhaps a peek won't hurt, just to be sure. A greater mistake was never made.

When Eros again arrives, after their always exquisite lovemaking, he falls asleep on the couch beside Psyche and she timidly lifts the burning lamp over him, spilling the hot oil on him, waking him. For a flash she sees the most beautiful man in creation, and then it is all over. Everything vanishes—Eros, palace, lake, all, and she is once more upon the barren plain, unprotected from the elements. What to do? She is alone, with no resources (certainly no job training!). In a situation like this, one finds the nearest goddess and asks for help. Coming upon a little shrine of the goddess Demeter, the Earth Mother, which is in a sad state of neglect, and being conscientious, she begins to tidy up, sweeping the floor and gathering fresh flowers and herbs to honor the goddess. Demeter, like any mother, feels sympathy for the poor child and tells her that she has managed to offend great Aphrodite.

Confronted with this knowledge, Psyche has no choice left but to seek out the angry goddess and ask her forgiveness. Aphrodite then assigns to her four impossible tasks, each more difficult than the last, but at each turn Psyche finds helpers in the plant and animal world who make it possible for her to complete the task. The final task includes a trip to Hades. (As anyone who has ever been in love can attest, at some point there is a trip to hell!) At last, at great peril and risking her life every step along the way, she finishes the tasks, and through the overcoming of these obstacles she attains a maturity that frees her of the goddess's rage. When the last task is successfully completed, Aphrodite amazingly turns into the most charming mother-in-law you could imagine, restoring her to Eros and giving the couple her blessing!

The point to this briefly told story is that love, or Aphrodite-Venus, is the *transformer*. It not only transforms the innocent who has no knowledge of sex, giving him or her "carnal knowledge," but it transforms the person psychologically. Who has not seen a young person become suddenly aware that there is an opposite sex. Full of mystery, he or she goes mooning about, even discarding jeans for more formal wear. Previously "icky" matters such as personal hygiene, clothes, and cosmetics become all-important. He or she spends countless hours examining him- or herself in the mirror to see if the felt inner changes are visible to others. *Hours* are spent in the bathroom and on the telephone.

This is the process of transformation initiated by love, which is symbolized by Venus. The goddess initiates the hero or heroine in our story. She makes demands that seem quite out of the question, but help comes from the instinctual sphere (represented by animals, plants, and the natural world), and lo! the task gets done. And the goddess is pleased. When that happens, we are using our Venus energy correctly, flowingly, not damming it up with repressions.

Love, as anyone over thirty certainly knows—and many much younger—is not an unmixed blessing. Like the hot oil that burned Eros, love can bring pain. And abandonment, such as Psyche suffered. Great hearts risk all, and take the consequences. Timid hearts risk little and concomitantly achieve little. Love demands risks, but, oh, the rewards can be great indeed! Not only the reward of physical pleasure, but the much more important reward of personal growth. It is the experience of love that separates the girls from the women, the men from the boys.

So how do we interpret this goddess in the chart?

Venus represents the *affections*, tells you about what you value, describes your social nature—that is, how you like to be sociable.

Her process is *relating*. She shows how you reach out to others through the act of relating to them. For most of us, relationships—the having of them or the lack of them—are what cause us the most trouble in life.

Venus and Eros actually are two sides of the same principle—Venus draws us toward her by means of eros, or sexual attraction, and once in the realm of the goddess we undergo her process of transformation-through-love whether we will or no.

Thus, Venus represents not only what qualities in you attract other people, but, more importantly, what you find attractive in another, or "what turns you on." Venus tells what you *want*.

In the chart, Venus represents the deeply feminine part of each of us, men as well as women, in our capacity to reach out to others in a loving and affectionate way, not only sexually or erotically. Where she resides is where we have, or are inhibited about, magnetic qualities of personality—what is called *personal magnetism*. Venus's glyph (shown at the beginning of this chapter) is a cross topped by a circle. The cross is known as the "cross of matter" and the circle represents the spiritual element that precedes coming into the material realm. These two elements making up the symbol for Venus in the language of astrology indicate that Spirit informs Matter, inspiring it to ever-higher states.

The Venus placement governs not only the creation of beauty, but the enjoyment of it, for she is appreciation as well as creation. Venus indicates how we enjoy or appreciate the sensual, the sexual, the romantic, and the beautiful. Venus tells how we fulfill both the creative and the procreative urges and, whether we manifest a baby or a work of art, we are watched over by her benevolent eye, for she is protectoress and healer, too.

It is in this role that she serves to bind us to another, with the force that we experience as love. Yet, love is never coercive, it is always voluntary. Love can be *given*, it cannot be *taken*.

Venusian energies are experienced spontaneously—and it is this that makes us think of "attraction," but these attractions must be a genuine expression of the Self, what you truly want, not what your parents or society has brainwashed you to think you want! Love is an attraction that only comes about through self-expression, and only an individual can express the Self.

Thus, the purpose of Venus in the chart is to attract us to others, and others to us, in order to allow the process of relationship, which enables us to become more fully developed and self-realized people. It is for our personal growth. Not only that, but Venus and the Venusian type of person recognize that there is great power in relationship. One based on love and voluntary compliance yields the ability to cope with life creatively and with less stress.

Below are some key words for the twelve signs. In each, Venus expresses *love* variously:

In ARIES, VENUS expresses *love* ENTHUSIASTICALLY.
In TAURUS ———————— MATERIALISTICALLY.
In GEMINI ———————— SUPERFICIALLY.
In CANCER ———————— NURTURINGLY.
In LEO ———————— DRAMATICALLY.
In VIRGO ———————— DISCRIMINATINGLY.
In LIBRA ———————— HARMONIZINGLY.
In SCORPIO ———————— INTENSELY.
In SAGITTARIUS ———————— OBJECTIVELY.
In CAPRICORN ———————— CAUTIOUSLY.
In AQUARIUS ———————— DETACHEDLY.
In PISCES ———————— INTUITIVELY.

There are two ways in which Venus comes to birth in the human consciousness.

The first is that overwhelming, spontaneous attraction that fairly knocks everything else out of its way—and out of your mind and senses. This kind of attraction is "just there." You didn't expect it, you didn't ask for it. And now you have to cope with it. This level of experience is a dramatic initiation into the mysteries of the great love goddess. Sexuality is immediately to the fore, and it is usually acted upon immediately. Even shy persons can be caught and carried away upon this tide of love emanating from the goddess at their own center. It takes your breath away.

The second is a gradual pull into a relationship. First, there is a newborn attraction, but it needs nurturing and time to grow before it culminates. Love and trust must be built up slowly, tested, and sometimes retested, before the barrier of inhibition can be removed and physical closeness initiated and enjoyed.

Whichever way you experience her, you will recognize Venus operating in your chart, and the more contact you have with the love goddess within you, the happier you will be!

Obstacles to Venus arise when her energies are repressed, either by externally imposed prohibitions (such as a strict religion which considers not only sex but all sensory pleasures sinful or harmful) or by the person whose Venus is restricted in the chart. Though Venus is considered by astrologers to be the most beneficent of planets, as with any other planetary energy, there is a negative side to Venusian energies. Here's how these operate through the signs:

IN ARIES   Venus is the energy inside us that wants to reach out to others. In Aries, Venus has a tendency to be aggressive in emotional expression. Aries is concerned with self-gratification above all, and although an outgoing nature makes for enthusiasm, Venus in Aries is quick to take the initiative and will pursue the object of desire relentlessly. This often makes for competition where love and sex are concerned and a blunt and outspoken approach when sexual interest is aroused.

IN TAURUS   Venus rules Taurus and is well placed here, but Taurean stability can cause possessiveness, resulting in jealousy when threatened. The innate sensuality can go overboard, becoming gross, and Taurean love of beauty can turn to crude opulence for its own sake. Appreciation of material things, when not tempered by development of the spiritual nature, tends toward mere accumulation of possessions. Because of her great strength, Venus in Taurus can dominate lesser personalities.

IN GEMINI   The desire for variety of experiences in love makes it difficult for Venus in Gemini to settle on just one lover or mate. Permanence just isn't her long suit. Gemini's love of wit and conversation makes this person more interested in talking about love than in actually experiencing it at a deep level. As the saying goes, "he talks a good game, but plays a bad one." The need for constant stimulation makes Gemini travel frequently in pursuit of new and different romantic adventures, which can emphasize an innate fickleness.

IN CANCER   Deeply sensitive, Venus in Cancer can be hurt so easily that it makes any relationship difficult unless there is much self-knowledge and an ability to be objective. Cancer takes everything personally, which makes for moodiness and unpredictability. The great need for security can put off others who get tired of the constant reassurance required. Because of a watery feeling-nature, Cancer can become maudlin, have unstable emotional reactions to ordinary social situations, and indulge in sulking.

IN LEO   The most extravagant of the signs, Leo wants admiration and pursues love with great zest. This need for dramatics can be overblown to the point of gaudiness, and a love for the lavish gesture can become just a case of gilding the lily. Venus in Leo's romantic nature and need for excitement can make for overdoing everything, from the sending of unwanted gifts to praise so excessive it seems insincere. Leo is prone to compete for the center of attention socially—to the point of being obnoxious.

IN VIRGO   Venus in Virgo tends to be critical and analytical about romantic matters, which makes others feel ill at ease, self-conscious, unsure how to please. This analytical approach serves to cut off the natural flow between people, damming up feeling response. It's as if Virgo attempts to appreciate the beauty of a painting by dissecting the composition and understanding how the painter mixed the colors! Venus in Virgo produces more unmarried people than any other Venus position, because they are so picky.

IN LIBRA   Libra rules marriage, and Venus in Libra wants marriage for its own sake, often not taking too much care who the spouse is! Though well-placed here, an aversion to discord and disagreements makes Libra hang on to a relationship just to be in a relationship, at any cost. An inability to deal with confrontation can make Libra upset and nervous, going along with the crowd just to avoid unpleasantness, even to personal detriment. This can make Libra seem conformist and lacking integrity.

IN SCORPIO   The intensity of Scorpio makes this Venus position preoccupied with sex. There is intense emotion around it, and desire is strong, sometimes tending toward the kinky. Scorpio takes everything romantic extremely seriously and can lack objectivity. Pride can lead to an all-or-nothing approach, and if jilted or betrayed, Scorpio can become bitter and seek revenge. Venus in Scorpio has an ability to cut off a relationship abruptly, severing it forever, never looking back. The offending person is effectively dead.

IN SAGITTARIUS   Idealism is the hallmark of Sagittarius, and Venus here can lead to an impractical image of the desired loved one. A natural frankness about inner feelings can become a bluntness that wounds, and Sagittarius can be insensitive to the nuances of others' feelings. Seeking personal ethics, Sagittarius can become dogmatic in efforts to impose personal moral standards on a partner, becoming disappointed when the partner can't live up to them, which then frees Sagittarius to go on seeking the impossible ideal!

IN CAPRICORN Material wealth and status are necessary to Venus in Capricorn, to the point where this position can quite openly marry for money. When courting, Capricorn will want to appear superior, and this can make for a reserve that seems cold and unemotional, though as a rule it is a deep shyness, which unfortunately comes across as snobbishness. Since Capricorn is not easily affectionate, concern for the material side of life can create ulterior motives regarding love and marriage, resulting in a loveless liaison contracted for status.

IN AQUARIUS Venus here is friendly to all in an impersonal way. Aquarius likes to have lots of friends, none too close, however, for this inhibits freedom. Romantic attractions are often undertaken just for the sake of diversion and the lure of something different. Often these are casual, for the messiness of true intimacy doesn't appeal to Venus in Aquarius. Because commitment restricts social freedom—the need for new and unusual experiences—it may be hard to function in a conventional marriage.

IN PISCES Though highly sensitive, Venus in Pisces can be sloppy because of the inability to discriminate. Fearful of hurting others, Pisces can keep feelings submerged until resentments build to an unbearable level, and then martyrdom becomes a refuge. Pisces is prone to becoming excessively emotionally dependent on others, or to fostering excess emotional dependence on themselves. Because of strong emotions, Pisces often loses touch with reality. Without clearly expressed love, Pisces can become despondent.

Even if you are now expressing the negative side of your Venus, you can learn to cultivate the pleasing and sensuous nature of the love goddess by opening up to her positive energy, thereby enhancing your everyday life and making the enjoyment of love much greater. Ways to do this are to focus on your sensory abilities—to experience touch, taste, sight, smell, and hearing in the "here and now," without reference to goals or goal-setting. Venus is about pleasure, and you can't properly have the experience of pleasure if your mind is occupied with tomorrow's business conference or getting the wash done. Duty most often interferes with pleasure, or inhibits or prohibits it.

If you find you have Venus problems, take heart . . . the goddess is willing to give you the help you need if you but pay attention to her. It is merely necessary to learn to give and receive pleasure.

As the artistic, poetic, romantic aspect of life, Venus shows us how to grow, both spiritually and materially. It is through her powers—of our attracting and being attracted to—that we are led on a path of constantly increasing growth through relationships. She holds up a mirror to us, in the eyes of the other person. And it is there that we see, at last, who we truly are.

Venus/Aphrodite in her dove-drawn pleasure chariot

chapter five

THE GOD OF WAR

Mars is known as the god of war because it is his function to create separateness, just as it is the function of Venus to foster unity. These two are polar opposites. Aries and Scorpio, the signs that Mars rules, fall opposite Libra and Taurus, ruled by Venus. This pair of divinities gave birth to Eros, from whose name we get the word *erotic*. Venus and Mars unite love *and* lust. One without the other is only half the show. Love without lust is tame and tepid, and often unrequited or unfulfilled, dreamy yearning for an unrealizable ideal, or nonphysical and given to headaches when sex is mentioned. On the other hand, lust without love is equally unsatisfying, temporary and totally physical, denying the spiritual center of the person. Mars energy needs to be tempered by Venus, or sex becomes just another ball game.

Before he was known as Mars, this god was known as Ares to the Greeks (note the connection to the sign Aries, which is Mars ruled). Although the Greeks in their wisdom and understanding of human nature had to admit that such energies (we might say Martian, or warlike) did exist in the human psyche, they didn't think much of them, preferring to fight only when their liberty was endangered. Ares actually came into the Greek pantheon by way of Thrace, a barbaric country where making war was the pastime of choice. We see a lot of this negative Mars energy around these days on the nightly news.

Mars' glyph, shown at the beginning of this chapter, is a circle with an arrow extending outward from it. This is the quintessential male symbol, indicative of both the virility and the procreativity of the male animal, representing an erect penis by suggesting the thrusting motion which is the male in action. Mars is the Desire principle, both in its sexual connotation of man desiring woman, or vice versa, and in that what we desire is what we manifest in our lives.

Although Mars is what we feel when we are feeling angry—when we want to kill for whatever reason—present-day astrologers no longer consider Mars a totally bad guy. *All* the energies in the chart, even the difficult ones, are there for a reason. In fact, without the get-up-and-go energy of Mars, we'll all be lying down eating lotuses, with grass growing around our ears. It's the Mars energy in us that gets things done. It not only makes war, it makes love. And it goes exploring, opening up new frontiers and building roads and bridges, cars and airplanes. Wherever Mars is strong in a chart, there is unusual assertiveness—for good or for ill.

Mars also represents courage and forthrightness. He is exemplar of all the traditional aspects that we esteem in the male of the species: sexual prowess, courageousness, energy, action, protectiveness, and valor. Mars' glyph is also emblematic of his sword and shield—as warrior, he is not only aggressor but also protector. In pictorial representations, Mars is a virile and vigorous man, usually bearded, helmeted, and carrying a lance, a shield, a sword, and a spear. As god of war, Mars is the principle of action, in any and all spheres. He was first trained as a dancer, then as a warrior. The war dance was to prepare the spirits of the warriors for the coming physical danger and trial, and it joined them together as a group, in what today is called male bonding.

God of War

In one South Seas tribe today, which is still isolated from civilization, the men can no longer go to war because of environmental conditions, so they have ritual war dancing, in which the man with the most endurance wins the contest for his tribe. This seems to satisfy their aggressive urges much as football or ice hockey sublimates these energies for the so-called civilized world. One might even look upon these ball games as a dance of aggression.

Of Mars' many love conquests, Venus is undoubtedly the most important, though some say *she* was the seducer. Whoever started it, this was one of mythology's most impressive love affairs, which at one time or other embroiled all the gods in turmoil and required them to take sides.

Symbolically, Mars has to learn to love. His aggression must be tempered by the energy of Venus. Love must seduce (or heal) aggression. The life force, which is ruled by the goddess, will always prevail over destruction, just as grass will grow over and cover the most bloodied and scarred battlefield. The goddess always returns us to life, no matter how much destruction we have accomplished. Unlike her impetuous consort, however, she takes her time—and it might be centuries. Think of that the next time you crush a living thing or stamp out an impulse to life!

Mars was a lover as well as a warrior. He represents the masculine side of the sexual equation in both sexes. We make war and we make love, and it is the same basic energy. Mars also tells us about courage and the development of will. Mars says, "I will." And not only did he kill the rapist of his daughter, he intervened in the Trojan War (although the gods were forbidden to meddle in mankind's affairs) because his sons were in trouble. So he represents the protector of loved ones.

Though Mars is the primal male energy, we all have Mars in us, both men and women, just as we all have the Sun, Moon, Venus, and the rest of the planets in our charts. Women as well as men have aggressive feelings, get angry, feel passion. Women can be warriors, leaders, athletes. They can fiercely protect their families from harm. Occasionally, they also kill (think of Jean Harris). It's Mars energy behind all of this, no matter the form it takes. Mars shows your heroic aspect.

By sign and house placement, Mars tells how a person fights, what makes him or her angry, and where and what circumstances do this. In other words, Mars tells how you *act*.

On the following page is a listing of key words indicating how Mars variously expresses *action*:

In ARIES, MARS expresses *action* HEROICALLY.
In TAURUS ———————————— PEACEFULLY.
In GEMINI ———————————— INCONSISTENTLY.
In CANCER ———————————— PROTECTIVELY.
In LEO ———————————— GRANDLY.
In VIRGO ———————————— MODESTLY.
In LIBRA ———————————— DIPLOMATICALLY.
In SCORPIO ———————————— PASSIONATELY.
In SAGITTARIUS ———————————— UNINHIBITEDLY.
In CAPRICORN ———————————— SERIOUSLY.
In AQUARIUS ———————————— UNCONVENTIONALLY.
In PISCES ———————————— IDEALISTICALLY.

On the other side of the equation, negative Mars can be expressed as a lack of force, a tendency to be a victim. As astrologers, one of the perplexing things we are asked is why someone who is an Aries acts like a lamb, not a ram. One way to look at this is to think of war. A brave warrior has to be able to sacrifice his life if necessary, and he must know how to follow orders as well. But some sacrifice themselves unnecessarily. These are people with a difficult Mars placement.

Mars is vulnerable in signs like Cancer and Libra. In Cancer, so family oriented, he feels he must have the enthusiastic support of his family to reach his desired goals. He tends to equate himself with his family, and woe be to anyone who disparages a member of his family! Cancer's propensity to mother all and sundry hooks up with Mars' protectiveness and can easily take in all the strays—both human and animal—on the block or in the world. This can lead to feeling overwhelmed and victimized by outer forces.

Mars in Libra is another case. It is very dicey for Mars the warrior to maintain the balance of harmony so dear to Libra. Mars in Libra may live in the middle of conflict, always mediating between adversaries. Or he may come on like a spineless wimp, because he meets an attack with good manners and graciousness. And if that fails, he may simply retreat, increasing the original impression!

In addition to such weak placements, the person will not have understood the natural Mars energy and, therefore, will not have learned to use it to best advantage.

Mars needs a good relation to the feminine. We all need love. Love first comes in mothering, which can be given by either parent. We all need this mothering love to grow strong and confident in life. When children are at the heroic Mars stage, pulling down the house and running rampant, they need to be made to feel safe. This means not allowing little Susan and Billy to kill themselves trying to fly by leaping off the roof. At the same time, they need to be allowed to experience enough freedom so that they are not fearful of exploring their ever-expanding world. Whichever parent supplies this (ideally, both), it is good mothering energy affecting how a child will grow up to act in the world.

Imagine if every time Susan tries to move away from her mother, Mother freezes up and panics, saying, "No, no! You'll hurt yourself!" After enough of this, little Susan becomes permanently fearful of trying anything new or going out on her own without Mother's approval. Conversely, if Susan is allowed to run, and when she falls is gently brushed off and comforted but allowed to continue running, she will feel safe in experimenting.

And if Billy tries to take his time doing something, but is pushed and told to "Quit being a slowpoke," he may develop a panicky style of doing things, nervous and tense. But if he is encouraged to do things at his own pace and given approval no matter how long he takes, he will develop self-confidence in his natural, methodical style and build on it.

In both examples, the children will develop healthy and happy ways of acting in the world, confident in their ability to make an impact on their environment. They will have a good relation to their Mars.

Today, as the barriers between the sexual roles gradually recede, women are expressing their Mars energies more freely, and men with nonaggressive Mars energy can be thought manly. So it's important to be aware of how Mars operates in your own and in the charts of those with whom you are closely associated.

Since Mars has so much to do with the emergent Self, with that Self expressing itself, and with personal drive to goals, whether strictly materialistic or in the larger interests of humankind, it, more than the other planets, has an obvious negative side. That is because Mars rules Aries, the first sign of the zodiac, and therefore by extension influences our actions.

Mars can mean expenditure of energy—and it can also mean how we spend *too much* energy, by sign placement. Following is how Mars overspends energy in the various signs:

IN ARIES   Here, Mars is the natural ruler and expresses himself as the quintessential "I." He is Caesar saying, "I came,

I saw, I conquered." The Mars in Aries person may find that life is an eternal conflict, that there is always another battle to be fought. Mars in Aries intends to win, no matter what, even at times when a judicious retreat would be the better course. Mars in Aries needs to cultivate Venus in her gentler aspect, and learn that it is more fun to make love than to make war.

IN TAURUS Mars in Taurus is out of his quick-witted, quick-moving element. Taurus is the most earthy of the Earth signs, and fiery Mars is slowed down and restricted here. Mars in Taurus people expend too much energy on material things and physical indulgence, from food and wine to sex. Remember that Venus rules Taurus, and here she can easily overpower Mars, making him fat (with her good cooking) and lazy (with her amorous talents). He needs a good dose of self-discipline to get himself going.

IN GEMINI Mars in Gemini fears boredom above all else. He must be constantly on the move, whether the moves are of any use or not. Mars in Gemini spends lots of time talking, about anything or nothing, that could be put to more productive pursuits. Unless his considerable mental energies are channeled into study of a serious nature, technical or scientific, Mars in Gemini spends endless hours "spinning his wheels," just to keep ennui at bay. He can talk all night and still say nothing. Self-discipline is the key.

IN CANCER Since Cancer is the quintessential emotional sign, Mars placed here gets very aggressive about emotional matters, and its "family," whatever that may represent (even if only a dog and a budgie!). Mars in Cancer tends to spend too much valuable energy in self-designated family situations, defensive emotional reactions, and shifting feelings. He needs to learn that there's a bigger world out there that can use his "mothering" drive, that one has to let go, that overprotection can cripple loved ones.

IN LEO Mars in Leo wastes his energy by seeking applause and popularity, as if it were vital to life. He needs constant approval, even at the cost of his dignity. Craving the limelight, he can go too far, leading himself into notoriety for the sake of press, even if it's awful! He needs to learn moderation in all things, as the philosophers advise. Needless to say, this is not easy for a Mars in

Leo, who wants what he wants when he wants it, and how he wants it—usually very dramatically and publicly!

IN VIRGO   In Virgo, Mars' energy can be consumed with the details of everyday living, especially in work. In fact, Mars in Virgo is frequently a workaholic, even if it's only busywork. There is always one more *i* to dot or one more *t* to cross, or one more detail to check. This can cause a neurotic concern for details or can manifest as the overworked-and-underpaid syndrome. Mars in Virgo needs especially to relate to Venus' softening and self-indulgent ways, and to let up a little.

IN LIBRA   Mars is overly concerned with other's opinions and approval, not using his aggression for himself. Libra's ever-compromising nature is at variance with Mars' survival instincts. Mars in Libra expends too much energy on partnerships, becoming the social butterfly, while the Libran insistence on good manners, fair play, sophistication, beauty, and propriety can make him superficial. He has a hard time confronting others, and although constantly involved in disputes, he may need assertiveness training.

IN SCORPIO   Mars rules Scorpio, and negative Scorpio is somewhat paranoid. In this placement, he can spend much time erecting defenses against some imagined future attack, stockpiling his ammunition and ever-planning his strategy. He is also inclined to take risks, some of them foolish, though they look extremely daring. The Scorpion is known for his stinger, and Mars in Scorpio is the stingingest. Venus' powers of love and tenderness are needed to dissolve fears and relate him to his own positive side of strength.

IN SAGITTARIUS   Freewheeling Sagittarius affects Mars' energy by scattering it to the winds. Unless he practices self-discipline, he is like the wild mustang, all speed and no endurance. That impetuous burst of energy fizzles in exhaustion, accomplishing nothing. He tends to get going in a hurry, but not check to see that his supply of fuel is adequate for the trip, often running out of gas in the middle of nowhere. He needs Venus to teach him to slow down, to pace himself, to pay attention.

IN CAPRICORN   Mars is exalted in the sign of Capricorn, and therefore does not waste his energy here. It is one of the best placements possible, but, like Virgo, it can indicate the workaholic. In this case, however, the workaholic isn't concerned with the unimportant details, being involved with overall strategy, working long and hard to achieve his goals and demanding the highest salary available for his qualifications. Here, he needs Venus to help him to relax, to learn the pleasures of play, to let himself be loved.

IN AQUARIUS   Mars in Aquarius tends to spend too much energy in getting the approval of his peer group. Because he is a natural reformer, he assumes that his reforms are necessary, when in fact the opposite may be true. Because society is important to him, he projects that he is equally important to society! In his zeal, he may become only a mirror image of his group, reflecting its values and not his own, thereby losing his individuality. Here, he needs Venus to bring him back to himself, to orient him on a one-to-one basis.

IN PISCES   Mars in Pisces absorbs everything—the ideas of everyone and all that he reads and hears—and this influences him enormously. It can create a pattern whereby he *becomes* the last person he talked to or the last book he read. Ambition dissolves in this haze of impressions, creating a disjointed life without a sure focus. His idealism denies anger, causing him to be swamped by his feelings and, in turn, to act irrationally, even violently. Here, Venus can help by bringing him back to reality and making him realize he inhabits a mortal body.

Mars in the chart functions as the stamina and energy to cope with the pressures of living. It is the basic urge to succeed, to win over life's trials, to endure testing. In its lower aspect, Mars is sheer animal instinct, what is base and unevolved, brute sexual drive and instinctual territorial aggression. Since Mars is related both to Aries (independent force) and to Scorpio (destruction and rebuilding), he has a higher and a lower level.

Through Aries, the person passes into Selfhood and separates from the collective, sometimes becoming too involved with himself. But, through Scorpio's regenerative powers, he is dissolved (Scorpio is a Water sign while Aries is a Fire sign) and returned to the collective, only in a higher state, having realized that old forms must be destroyed so that more evolved forms can take their place. Scorpio's water can absorb negativity and allow the fire of Aries to bring forth the new forms. Water is the cosmic unconsciousness. The fires of Mars can heat these waters to the boiling point, creating the steam of the spirit which then manifests in the material world as a result of the Desire principle.

Thus is the red planet generator of life on the material plane, the here and now. But he also derives from spirit, and it is spirit that desires form. The Martian heat molds spirit into form just as the smith bends heated metal into the desired shape, creating blunt, practical tools or fine, delicate ornaments. All depends on the individual.

Mars energy is the warmonger, the rapist, the murderer. He is also the healer and physician (an amazing number of doctors are Scorpios).

And he's the cop on the beat—carrying a big stick and wearing a gun, but there to protect the law-abiding citizenry.

chapter six

ELEMENTARY, MY DEAR

The zodiac connects us to the four fundamental principles of life, the *elements*—FIRE, EARTH, AIR, and WATER. They refer to the most basic energies we know, not only as abstract concepts, but as physical realities. We could live without none of them. Understanding these life principles and how they operate through your chart is a major step in gaining self-understanding.

However, it is important to remember that, although the four Elements represent the physical world and our relationship to it and dependence upon it, they also represent inner, spiritual energies deeply embedded in our psyches.

They are, in effect, the flow of energies that comprise the universal life pattern in each individual as well as in the cosmic whole. We can view this as pattern, flow, and transmutation of energy, with each of us relating variously to the four energies symbolized by the Elements, depending on how they are distributed in our charts.

Just as one person is a "natural" swimmer, preferring to exercise in the water, and another is a "natural" runner, most comfortable with his or her feet on the ground, we each express the Elements inherently in us in a way that complements our individual nature. Unless, of course, we are denying them. Sometimes, for example, people who have too great a component of a single Element will feel out of balance, compensating by becoming the opposite vibration. That's why it's important to know yourself elementally, so to speak, and by treating yourself accordingly, let your true nature shine forth.

The twelve signs of the zodiac are each represented by an Element. Since there are four Elements (Fire, Earth, Air, Water), there are three signs in each Element. These are known as "triplicities." The Elements march around the chart in a regular order, as follows:

FIRE Aries

      EARTH Taurus

            AIR Gemini

                  WATER Cancer

FIRE Leo

      EARTH Virgo

            AIR Libra

                  WATER Scorpio

FIRE Sagittarius

      EARTH Capricorn

            AIR Aquarius

                  WATER Pisces

Signs in the same Element are considered to be most compatible, and this is important to remember when studying your own chart or comparing yours to another's. It's also necessary to realize that these Elements symbolize a real energy flow in you, not just an abstract concept.

Each group of three signs occupying the different Elements forms a triangle, as you will see in the diagrams that follow. This triangle is known astrologically as a "trine," the most beneficial of aspects, indicating free-flowing energies. Thus, for example, if you have a planet in a Fire sign, and your partner has a planet in one of the other Fire signs, that is an automatic plus.

FIRE TRIPLICITY

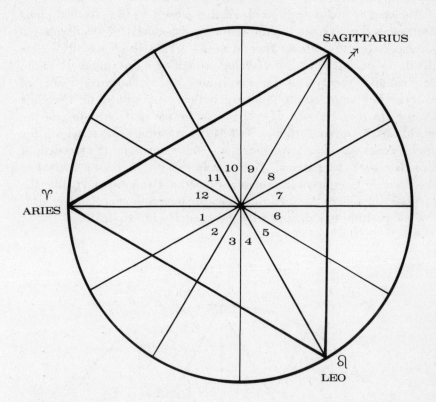

The energy of *Fire* is radiant. It is excitable and enthusiastic. Fire people are spontaneous, quick, full of flowing energy. They can appear to be self-centered, or too objective. They have high spirits, self-esteem, strength that comes in spurts, and a strong desire to express themselves, as well as a great need for freedom. They tend to impatience, especially with the Earth and Water signs, fearing that Water will drench their Fire and Earth smother them with practicality. They are most compatible with themselves or with Air, which fans the flames of their ardor, as well as inspiring them with new ideas for their active natures and minds. But Fire can quickly tire of Air's intellectual speculations unless they can quickly be translated into action.

The energy of *Earth* is solid, related closely to the physical plane and senses. Earth signs are known for hard-headed practicality, based on experience and observance of reality. They don't usually go for the flashy or superficial, preferring something more substantial than inspirations, theoretical considerations, or the intuitive flights of fancy. They want results and are patient and willing to discipline themselves to get them. They have an innate understanding of the world and its many forms as well as the stamina to persist until the goal is reached. They have enormous endurance, and the strength of this gives them persistence. They rarely give up, no matter how hard the road or tiresome the journey. Sometimes slow to start, like the tortoise, they have the fortitude to go the long mile, carrying on after the competition has dropped by the roadside in exhaustion.

EARTH TRIPLICITY

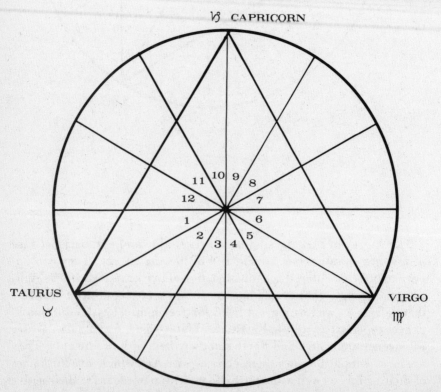

TAURUS ♉   VIRGO ♍

The energy of *Air* is ephemeral, constantly shifting, like the blowing of the winds. The realm of Air is the realm of the mind freed of all physical restrictions (imagine if you could fly!). It is the non-material, where form does not yet exist and is only "in the mind," but it is compelling nonetheless. Ideas must precede manifestation. Every building on earth was once nothing more than air, an idea in the mind of the architect, a set of mere drawings on paper, before it was translated into the hard reality of stone, brick, and mortar. Air signs emphasize theory and concepts, which leads to their finding compatible modes of expressing themselves in words, usually through abstract thoughts. They keep their detachment and don't find it necessary or profitable to become involved in other people's heavy emotions and "messy" lives. Like the air, they like to float above all this!

AIR TRIPLICITY

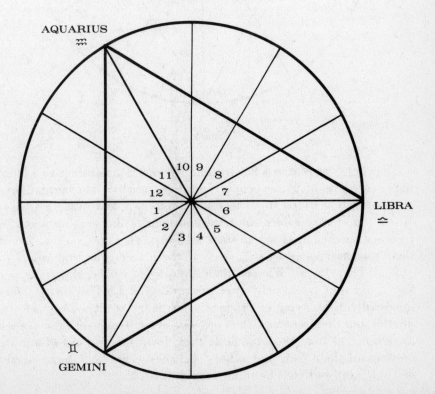

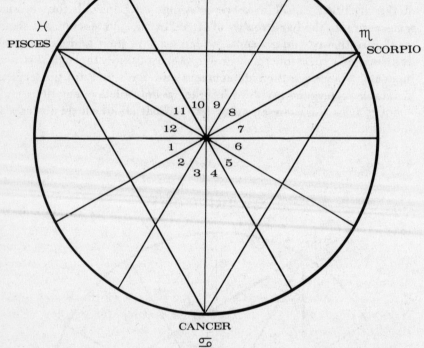

WATER TRIPLICITY

The energy of *Water* is flowing and various intangibles play a large part in the lives of Water people. Intuitive, psychic, imaginative, they are exquisitely tuned in to feelings, their own and other people's. Water signs express deep emotion, and their feeling responses can go from extreme compassion to total self-pity. They are very aware of their unconscious processes, even if these seem dim and weird to others. They *know*. Whence their knowledge comes, they may not know, but they trust their inner promptings and act on them, sometimes willy-nilly, flying in the face of ordinary reality. They are the mystics and the dreamers, the ones who are in touch with the deeper dimensions of life. As water flows they flow, into and out of minute crevices in their own and others' psyches. They are deep, partly invisible, and buffeted by inner currents.

Aries is the most obviously fiery of the Fire signs—quick, impulsive, impatient, driven to action.

In *Leo*, the energy of Fire is more stable—creative, given to the grand gesture, dramatic, ardent.

At *Sagittarius*, Fire becomes more mental and objective—seeking learning and avid to disseminate what it knows.

Taurus is the earthiest of the Earth signs—strongly materialistic, possessive, stolid, stubborn, immovable.

At *Virgo*, Earth becomes more mental and less oppressive—still practical and no dreamer, it is, however, a thinker.

In *Capricorn*, Earth reaches its epitome as the sign of the leader, general, CEO—a mover and a shaker in the world.

Gemini is naturally the airiest of the Air signs—the most abstractly intellectual, feeding on information of all kinds.

At *Libra*, Air energy is translated into balancing relationships of all kinds—weighing, pondering, relating.

When in *Aquarius*, Air reaches its most stable point—building idealism, turning ideas into projects, realizing brotherhood.

Cancer is the Mother of us all—maternal, yielding, caring, guarding—the very bosom of the sea of life.

When in *Scorpio*, Water runs deep and fathomless—mysterious and filled with the unknown. Out of its depths come strange creatures of the unconscious psyche.

At *Pisces*, Water becomes the most watery of the Water signs. Neptune-ruled, Pisces is at home in the eternal ebb and flow of life, the endless susurrating of the feelings.

Fire and Air are always more concerned with getting *out* their expressions. They pour forth energies vitally, without stinting. Fire people use direct action as a vehicle, while Air people use verbal expression or social interaction. Fire's manner is extroverted.

Conversely, Earth and Water are more concerned with their inner worlds. They don't usually project their vital energies outward without thought and reservation. Unlike Fire and Air, Earth and Water are not energy spendthrifts! They may be considered more introspective.

Fire and Air both have the tendency to spread out and diffuse themselves, rising into space, while Earth and Water are gravity-bound, always seeking the common level and collecting there. It is a major difference, one worth noting.

When we find a relationship that is difficult, we often find people of dissimilar elements. A person involved in such a relationship may love but not like the partner, finding the other interesting and exciting, but at the same time irritating and difficult, with constant quarreling. Things continually have to be worked out, and one person seems to do all the compromising. One may be insensitive to the other's needs, or just not comprehend them. That's why understanding the Element characteristics of the signs, and knowing in which signs your planets fall, helps you to understand, even if it is understanding *why* you don't understand!

What the Elements in your chart tell you is how you will tend to use your energies, which ones you are most attuned to consciously, what you're most in touch with naturally. Your dominant Element will show where in your life you are most at ease, what you experience comfortably, and how you can participate spontaneously (or cautiously, as the case may be) in which areas of life.

One great advantage to knowing your elemental makeup is that you can learn a great deal about your natural inner attunement (or lack of attunement) to the physical world. Often this can clear up misunderstandings between people who feel somehow "alien" to another's personality, but don't know it is in the Elements.

As super-sleuth Sherlock Holmes was wont to say, "Elementary, My Dear."

chapter seven

A MODE FOR ALL SEASONS

CARDINAL

FIXED

MUTABLE

"To everything there is a season," we are advised in Ecclesiastes, and this fundamental truth is reflected in another way astrologically, by means of what we call the *modes*.

There are three Modes—CARDINAL, FIXED, and MUTABLE—and these are related to the seasons of the year to which we all instinctively respond at our deepest levels.

Just as the Elements divide the chart into four groups of three each, the Modes divide the chart into three groups of four each. As astrology follows a regular order, the Modes form a regular pattern:

ARIES	CARDINAL
TAURUS	FIXED
GEMINI	*MUTABLE*
CANCER	CARDINAL
LEO	FIXED
VIRGO	*MUTABLE*
LIBRA	CARDINAL
SCORPIO	FIXED
SAGITTARIUS	*MUTABLE*
CAPRICORN	CARDINAL
AQUARIUS	FIXED
PISCES	*MUTABLE*

Examination of the cycle of Earth's seasons shows a close relationship between the Modes and the turning of our planet in relation to our Sun, which of course gives us spring, summer, fall, and winter.

Just as there are three Modes, each of our seasons has three months (with slight variations, of course, depending on where you live).

The first month of any season is naturally the beginning of that season—we might say the *generator* of it. This point is the new phase of the cycle, and its activity is specific to that season alone. For example, Aries, the first sign of the zodiac, represents the vernal equinox, or beginning of spring (about March 21). This is the beginning of the season of renewed life, after its long winter sleep. Astronomically, it is the time when the ecliptic of the Earth crosses the celestial equator, which is our own equator extended into outer space.

The second month of any season is that time when Nature, after the first burst, moves to *conserve* her own energies, concentrating them in leaf and bud, to bring about the fullest possible result. This is the time when life is at its most intense in nature—blossoms hang heavy on the trees, ripe fruit lies still on the branches, or fallen autumn leaves pile up on the ground, protecting the little things underneath from the coming snows of winter.

The third month of each season is a time of *change* into the next season. This is when we feel warm days under spring's cool mantle, when the fruits of summer have all been taken and we feel a crispness in the air telling us summer is over and fall is on the way, or when the first chill breath of winter blows the autumn leaves at the end of a fine, clear day of waning sunshine.

Each of the three months of a season corresponds to a Mode: the first month is Cardinal, the second month is Fixed, and the third month is Mutable.

The Cardinal signs *initiate*, the Fixed signs *conserve*, and the Mutable signs *change*.

CARDINAL QUADRIPLICITY

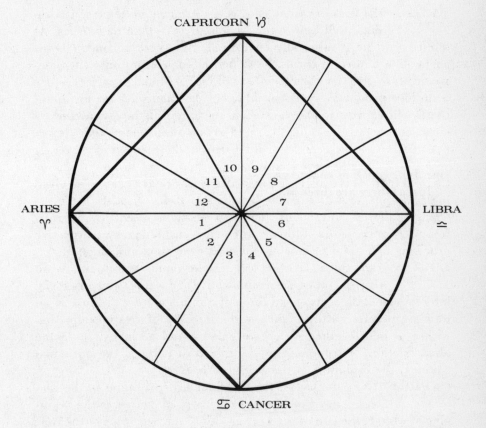

Unlike the Element triplicities, which are compatible with each other, the Modes form what we call a "quadruplicity," or square and opposition aspects. Squares, though dynamic, are the most difficult aspects in a chart, while oppositions require reconciliation of opposing energies. The diagrams illustrate how this pattern forms. For example, in the Cardinal quadruplicity, Aries forms a square to Cancer and Capricorn, and falls opposite Libra. (See Chapter Three for a discussion of opposite signs.)

As they represent the first month of each season, the Cardinal signs—Aries, Cancer, Libra, and Capricorn—are the *initiators*. Active and self-confident, they are usually ambitious and self-motivated. An overabundance of Cardinal signs can give a restless and overactive nature, one that constantly generates new ideas and projects, too many for practicality.

ARIES,   the first Cardinal sign, is the primary initiator of the zodiac, well known for beginning more than he finishes. As a Fire sign, he is especially concerned with creation, and it is his spring-like nature to thrust forth his self-expression onto the environment, to give the world evidence of his first-hand experiences. He is an idea-producer, ever searching out new pathways for his abundantly self-expressive nature. He must be first in all things, and there's considerable ego (meaning "I") underlying all his many activities.

CANCER   is the second Cardinal sign, in the Element of Water. It begins summer. What was bud turns to flower, flower turns to fruit. It is a growing time. All the Cardinal signs are involved in *beginnings*, and as a Water sign Cancer seeks to satisfy her ever-changing desires and moods, her deep emotional needs by initiating feelings. Cancer is the Mother—nurturing, sustaining, ever evocative of feeling and the deep unconsciousness of instinct and emotion.

LIBRA   is the third Cardinal sign, the beginning of autumn. As an Air sign, Libra is communicative and wants to inspire social interactions of all sorts, from those of a public nature to those of an intimate private nature. Libra is the initiator of relationships and wishes to join together, to create balance and harmony, to soothe away friction. Astronomically, Libra's zero point is the autumnal equinox, the beginning of the season of harvest.

CAPRICORN,   the last of the Cardinal signs, is found in the Element of Earth. Capricorn, of course, is the beginning of winter, the end of the year as well as the beginning of the New Year. Like the other Cardinals, Capricorn generates activity, but with an eye to practicality, being earthy. He is concerned with the usefulness of his work, material rewards, and palpable results. Though he can take an overview and doesn't lose sight of the "big picture," he is always aware of the practical nature of what he does.

The Fixed signs c ncentrate energy. They are the conservationists. Extremely strong- illed, they are nearly impossible to move against their wills. Stubborn barely describes this trait. They have almost inexhaustible endurance, patience, and persistence and they rarely give up. They sometimes hold on long past the time to let go, and they can be extremely possessive, to the point of being obsessive.

TAURUS   is the first Fixed sign, and is the most Fixed of the Fixed signs, owing to being an Earth sign. He represents the time when spring is fully manifested and there is great activity in the material realm. Not only are trees bearing fruits and fields growing grain, but animals are gestating their young. Taurus has great appreciation for Nature and all growing things—plants, animals, and babies. Nature's banker, he brings fruition and enables her to concentrate riches for use later. Taurus wants to hold onto material possessions, both increasing and conserving them.

FIXED QUADRIPLICITY

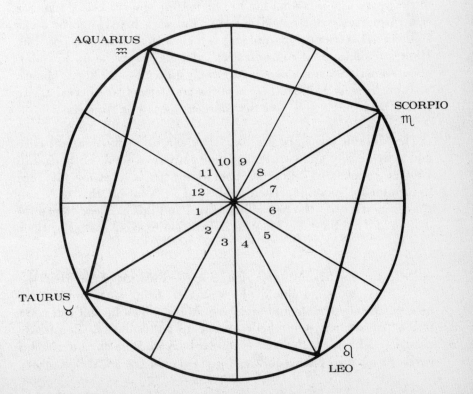

LEO   is the second Fixed sign, in the Element of Fire. In his reign,
we experience the hottest of temperatures—we know that
fixed glaring gaze of the sun only too well. Its intensity tells us a lot
about Leo's powerful strength of purpose. The Sun rules Leo and he
likes to concentrate authority in rulership of some sort. And just as
the Sun rules the Earth during the long, hot summer, Leo seeks to
rule what is around him. But, as summer is a time for children, play,
and family, so Leo is a lover of these things, a protector.

SCORPIO,   the third of the Fixed signs and a Water sign, represents
the concentration of autumn's power, as the trees shed
their leaves so that Nature's powers will be regenerated once again
the following spring. The sign of death and regeneration, Scorpio
presides over the "death" of Nature. While all of the Fixed signs are
of great intensity, Scorpio is the most intense of them, because, as a
Water sign, he is deeply related to the instinctual and unconscious
powers. He seeks to make his feelings and perceptions permanent.

AQUARIUS,   the last of the Fixed signs, is in the Element of Air.
During his time, we experience the coldest weather
of the year, which is opposite to our hottest month, Leo. As an Air
sign, Aquarius is interested in ideas, but as a Fixed sign, he seeks
stability in his friendships and makes them as long-lasting as possible.
He has much mental concentration once he has made up his mind
about something, and it can be extremely difficult to get him to change
it. It might seem a difficult concept for an Element so ethereal as Air
to be Fixed, but this is how the energies operate in Aquarius.

The Mutable signs are flexible. They can do many things at once
and switch easily and swiftly from one activity or mode of thought to
another completely different. They don't get in ruts for they are
tremendously versatile. Their ability to shift means that they can
change course with the prevailing winds, and this can lead to manipulation and double-talk. They need direction to avoid scattering their
energies.

GEMINI,   the first Mutable sign, is in the Element of Air. He is the
most mutable of the Mutables, being airy, and as such
he is extremely flexible and loves versatility, which he cultivates. He
is the transitional point between spring and summer. Constantly
changing behavior is the trait Mutables have in common, and Gemini
revels in his own changeability. He is ever on the go, seeking more

MUTABLE QUADRIPLICITY

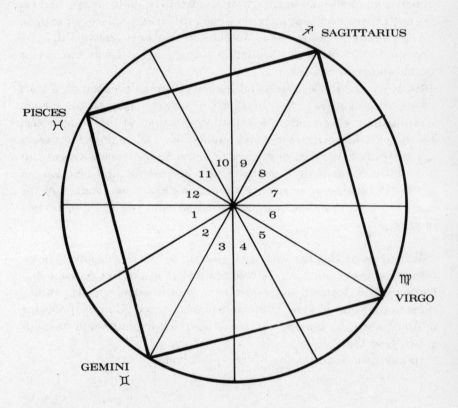

and more change and the stimulation it brings—of mind, ideas, environment, people.

VIRGO, the second Mutable sign, is in the Element of Earth, and is the changeover time between summer and autumn, the harvest time. Virgo is represented as a female figure bearing a sheaf of grain, Mother Earth's service to mankind. Usually multitalented, he seeks to find the right occupation, so he can use his various skills in the service of others and see the results of his meticulous efforts. He does not seek variety for its own sake, like Gemini, but for its practical applications. Being Mutable, he is the most mental of the Earth signs.

SAGITTARIUS   is the third of the Mutable signs, in the Element
                of Fire. Sagittarius is the period of change from
autumn to winter. A seeker, Sagittarius looks for life adventures that
will give him ample opportunity to express his Fire nature, which is
sensual and quick-moving. Sagittarius likes to be on the move, looking
for new experiences that will either enhance his sensual side or expand
his spiritual knowledge. As a Mutable, he is always questioning—his
appetite for intellectual speculation is a goad that keeps him trying
to find the right answer.

PISCES,   the last of the Mutable signs, is in the Element of Water,
            signifying the time when winter changes to spring,
starting the cycle round once again. Most watery of the Water signs,
Pisces' mutability has a flowing quality. Ever-changing, his watery
nature is always trying new ways to adapt to his circumstances, his
own shifting moods and emotions, and the moods and emotions of
others. He can be whimsical, disappearing like some denizen of the
deep, of which you glimpse a mere shadow—did you see it or did you
imagine it?

Having come this far with us, you have acquired considerable information about the basic astrological tenets of the five Astropoints.
On your trek toward understanding yourself astrologically, you've
come to the point of looking up your planets and ASC in the following
tables. Unless, of course, you took the quick-fix route and have already done that.

In any case, it's time for "Places, Everyone."

p a r t   t w o

PLACES, EVERYONE

Below is a form for you to fill out as you look up your planetary placements in the charts that follow. Either photocopy it or copy it onto a separate sheet of paper.

Fill out this Basic Astropoint form and keep it with you as you read the following chapters. You will need it for reference. Also, the scoring system in Chapter 26 will not be accurate unless you have your own and your partner's ASC signs. For this, you will need the time of birth.

BASIC ASTROPOINT FORM

Name: _____

ASTROPOINT	SIGN	ELEMENT	MODE
SUN is in the sign of	_____	_____	_____
MOON is in the sign of	_____	_____	_____
ASC is in the sign of	_____	_____	_____
VENUS is in the sign of	_____	_____	_____
MARS is in the sign of	_____	_____	_____

If you do not already know your Sun sign, turn to the diagram on page 21. If you think that you might be on the cusp, then read the descriptions for *both* signs. You may partake of some of each, but you will definitely be one or the other. Only a computer or a professional astrologer can say for sure.

HOW TO FIND YOUR MOON SIGN

Find the year of your birth in the charts provided. Then find the birth month at the top of the chart. Find your date of birth in the column below it. If it is not listed, then the sign listed for the earlier date is your Moon sign. For instance, if you were born on February 3, 1950, you would see that for February 2, the sign listed is Leo, meaning the moon was in the sign Leo. For February 5, Virgo is listed. This means that the moon is in the sign Leo until February 5 and your Moon is in the sign Leo.

If you are born on a day that starts a new sign (February 5 in this example), your Moon may be in the preceding sign. The only way to be absolutely sure is to have your chart done professionally or by a computer service. In lieu of this, read the text for both signs, and see which seems more like you.

1920

JAN	FEB	MAR	APR	MAY	JUN	JUL	AUG	SEP	OCT	NOV	DEC
1 TAU	1 GEM	1 CAN	1 VIR	1 LIB	1 SAG	1 CAP	1 AQU	1 ARI	1 TAU	1 CAN	1 LEO
3 GEM	2 CAN	2 LEO	3 LIB	3 SCO	4 CAP	4 AQU	2 PIS	3 TAU	3 GEM	3 LEO	2 VIR
5 CAN	4 LEO	4 VIR	5 SCO	5 SAG	6 AQU	6 PIS	5 ARI	5 GEM	5 CAN	5 VIR	5 LIB
7 LEO	6 VIR	7 LIB	8 SAG	8 CAP	9 PIS	8 ARI	7 TAU	8 CAN	7 LEO	7 LIB	7 SCO
10 VIR	8 LIB	9 SCO	10 CAP	10 AQU	11 ARI	11 TAU	9 GEM	10 LEO	9 VIR	10 SCO	9 SAG
12 LIB	11 SCO	11 SAG	13 AQU	13 PIS	13 TAU	13 GEM	11 CAN	12 VIR	11 LIB	12 SAG	12 CAP
14 SCO	13 SAG	14 CAP	15 PIS	15 ARI	15 GEM	15 CAN	13 LEO	14 LIB	13 SCO	15 CAP	14 AQU
17 SAG	16 CAP	16 AQU	17 ARI	17 TAU	17 CAN	17 LEO	15 VIR	16 SCO	16 SAG	17 AQU	17 PIS
19 CAP	18 AQU	19 PIS	20 TAU	19 GEM	19 LEO	19 VIR	17 LIB	18 SAG	18 CAP	20 PIS	19 ARI
22 AQU	20 PIS	21 ARI	22 GEM	21 CAN	21 VIR	21 LIB	20 SCO	21 CAP	21 AQU	22 ARI	22 TAU
24 PIS	23 ARI	23 TAU	24 CAN	23 LEO	24 LIB	23 SCO	22 SAG	23 AQU	23 PIS	24 TAU	24 GEM
26 ARI	25 TAU	25 GEM	26 LEO	25 VIR	26 SCO	26 SAG	25 CAP	26 PIS	26 ARI	26 GEM	26 CAN
29 TAU	27 GEM	27 CAN	28 VIR	27 LIB	29 SAG	28 CAP	27 AQU	28 ARI	28 TAU	28 CAN	28 LEO
31 GEM	29 CAN	29 LEO	30 LIB	30 SCO	30 SAG	31 AQU	30 PIS	30 TAU	30 GEM	30 LEO	30 VIR
		31 LEO		31 SCO			31 PIS		31 GEM		31 VIR

1921

JAN	FEB	MAR	APR	MAY	JUN	JUL	AUG	SEP	OCT	NOV	DEC
1 LIB	1 SCO	1 SAG	1 CAP	1 AQU	1 ARI	1 TAU	1 GEM	1 LEO	1 LIB	1 SCO	1 SAG
3 SCO	2 SAG	4 CAP	3 AQU	2 PIS	4 TAU	3 GEM	2 CAN	2 VIR	4 SCO	2 SAG	2 CAP
6 SAG	4 CAP	6 AQU	5 PIS	5 ARI	6 GEM	5 CAN	4 LEO	4 LIB	6 SAG	4 CAP	4 AQU
8 CAP	7 AQU	9 PIS	7 ARI	7 TAU	8 CAN	7 LEO	6 VIR	6 SCO	8 CAP	7 AQU	7 PIS
11 AQU	9 PIS	11 ARI	10 TAU	9 GEM	10 LEO	9 VIR	8 LIB	8 SAG	11 AQU	9 PIS	9 ARI
13 PIS	12 ARI	14 TAU	12 GEM	11 CAN	12 VIR	11 LIB	10 SCO	11 CAP	13 PIS	12 ARI	12 TAU
16 ARI	14 TAU	16 GEM	14 CAN	14 LEO	14 LIB	13 SCO	12 SAG	13 AQU	16 ARI	14 TAU	14 GEM
18 TAU	17 GEM	18 CAN	16 LEO	16 VIR	16 SCO	16 SAG	15 CAP	16 PIS	18 TAU	17 GEM	16 CAN
20 GEM	19 CAN	20 LEO	18 VIR	18 LIB	19 SAG	18 CAP	17 AQU	18 ARI	20 GEM	19 CAN	18 LEO
22 CAN	21 LEO	22 VIR	21 LIB	20 SCO	21 CAP	21 AQU	20 PIS	21 TAU	23 CAN	21 LEO	20 VIR
24 LEO	23 VIR	24 LIB	23 SCO	22 SAG	24 AQU	23 PIS	22 ARI	23 GEM	25 LEO	23 VIR	22 LIB
26 VIR	25 LIB	26 SCO	25 SAG	25 CAP	26 PIS	26 ARI	25 TAU	25 CAN	27 VIR	25 LIB	25 SCO
28 LIB	27 SCO	29 SAG	27 CAP	27 AQU	29 ARI	28 TAU	27 GEM	27 LEO	29 LIB	27 SCO	27 SAG
31 SCO	28 SCO	31 CAP	30 AQU	30 PIS	30 ARI	31 GEM	29 CAN	29 VIR	31 SCO	30 SAG	29 CAP
			31 PIS				31 CAN	30 VIR			31 CAP

1922

JAN	FEB	MAR	APR	MAY	JUN	JUL	AUG	SEP	OCT	NOV	DEC
1 AQU	1 PIS	1 ARI	1 TAU	1 GEM	1 LEO	1 VIR	1 SCO	1 CAP	1 AQU	1 PIS	1 ARI
3 PIS	2 ARI	4 TAU	2 GEM	2 CAN	2 VIR	2 LIB	2 SAG	3 AQU	3 PIS	2 ARI	2 TAU
6 ARI	4 TAU	6 GEM	5 CAN	4 LEO	5 LIB	4 SCO	5 CAP	6 PIS	6 ARI	4 TAU	4 GEM
8 TAU	7 GEM	8 CAN	7 LEO	6 VIR	7 SCO	6 SAG	6 AQU	8 ARI	8 TAU	7 GEM	6 CAN
10 GEM	9 CAN	11 LEO	9 VIR	8 LIB	9 SAG	8 CAP	9 PIS	11 TAU	11 GEM	9 CAN	9 LEO
13 CAN	11 LEO	13 VIR	11 LIB	10 SCO	11 CAP	11 AQU	12 ARI	13 GEM	13 CAN	11 LEO	11 VIR
15 LEO	13 VIR	14 LIB	13 SCO	12 SAG	13 AQU	13 PIS	15 TAU	16 CAN	15 LEO	14 VIR	13 LIB
17 VIR	15 LIB	17 SCO	15 SAG	15 CAP	16 PIS	16 ARI	17 GEM	18 LEO	17 VIR	16 LIB	15 SCO
19 LIB	17 SCO	19 SAG	17 CAP	17 AQU	18 ARI	18 TAU	19 CAN	20 VIR	19 LIB	18 SCO	17 SAG
21 SCO	19 SAG	21 CAP	20 AQU	20 PIS	21 TAU	21 GEM	21 LEO	22 LIB	21 SCO	20 SAG	19 CAP
23 SAG	22 CAP	23 AQU	22 PIS	22 ARI	23 GEM	23 CAN	23 VIR	24 SCO	23 SAG	22 CAP	22 AQU
25 CAP	24 AQU	26 PIS	25 ARI	25 TAU	25 CAN	25 LEO	25 LIB	26 SAG	25 CAP	24 AQU	24 PIS
28 AQU	27 PIS	28 ARI	27 TAU	27 GEM	28 LEO	27 VIR	27 SCO	28 CAP	28 AQU	27 PIS	26 ARI
30 PIS	28 PIS	31 TAU	30 GEM	29 CAN	30 VIR	29 LIB	30 SAG	30 CAP	30 PIS	29 ARI	29 TAU
31 PIS				31 LEO		31 SCO	31 SAG		31 PIS	30 ARI	31 GEM

1923

JAN	FEB	MAR	APR	MAY	JUN	JUL	AUG	SEP	OCT	NOV	DEC
1 GEM	1 LEO	1 LEO	1 LIB	1 SCO	1 CAP	1 AQU	1 PIS	1 TAU	1 GEM	1 CAN	1 VIR
3 CAN	3 VIR	3 VIR	3 SCO	3 SAG	3 AQU	3 PIS	2 ARI	3 GEM	3 CAN	2 LEO	4 LIB
5 LEO	5 LIB	5 LIB	5 SAG	5 CAP	6 PIS	5 ARI	4 TAU	6 CAN	5 LEO	4 VIR	6 SCO
7 VIR	8 SCO	7 SCO	7 CAP	7 AQU	8 ARI	8 TAU	7 GEM	8 LEO	8 VIR	6 LIB	8 SAG
9 LIB	10 SAG	9 SAG	10 AQU	9 PIS	11 TAU	11 GEM	9 CAN	10 VIR	10 LIB	10 SCO	10 CAP
11 SCO	12 CAP	11 CAP	12 PIS	12 ARI	13 GEM	13 CAN	12 LEO	12 LIB	12 SCO	10 SAG	12 AQU
13 SAG	14 AQU	13 AQU	15 ARI	14 TAU	16 CAN	15 LEO	14 VIR	14 SCO	14 SAG	12 CAP	14 PIS
16 CAP	17 PIS	16 PIS	17 TAU	17 GEM	18 LEO	17 VIR	16 LIB	16 SAG	16 CAP	14 AQU	16 ARI
18 AQU	19 ARI	18 ARI	20 GEM	19 CAN	20 VIR	20 LIB	18 SCO	18 CAP	18 AQU	17 PIS	19 TAU
20 PIS	22 TAU	21 TAU	22 CAN	22 LEO	22 LIB	22 SCO	20 SAG	21 AQU	20 PIS	19 ARI	21 GEM
23 ARI	24 GEM	23 GEM	24 LEO	24 VIR	25 SCO	24 SAG	22 CAP	23 PIS	23 ARI	21 TAU	24 CAN
25 TAU	27 CAN	26 CAN	27 VIR	26 LIB	27 SAG	26 CAP	24 AQU	25 ARI	25 TAU	24 GEM	26 LEO
28 GEM	28 CAN	28 LEO	29 LIB	28 SCO	29 CAP	28 AQU	27 PIS	28 TAU	28 GEM	27 CAN	29 VIR
30 CAN		30 VIR	30 LIB	30 SAG	30 CAP	30 PIS	29 ARI	30 TAU	30 CAN	29 LEO	31 LIB
31 CAN		31 VIR		31 SAG		31 PIS	31 ARI		31 CAN	30 LEO	

1924

JAN	FEB	MAR	APR	MAY	JUN	JUL	AUG	SEP	OCT	NOV	DEC
1 LIB	1 SAG	1 CAP	1 PIS	1 ARI	1 TAU	1 GEM	1 LEO	1 VIR	1 SCO	1 SAG	1 AQU
2 SCO	2 CAP	3 AQU	4 ARI	3 TAU	2 GEM	2 CAN	3 VIR	2 LIB	3 SAG	2 CAP	3 PIS
4 SAG	4 AQU	5 PIS	6 TAU	6 GEM	5 CAN	4 LEO	5 LIB	4 SCO	5 CAP	4 AQU	5 ARI
6 CAP	7 PIS	7 ARI	9 GEM	8 CAN	7 LEO	7 VIR	8 SCO	6 SAG	7 AQU	6 PIS	8 TAU
8 AQU	9 ARI	10 TAU	11 CAN	11 LEO	10 VIR	9 LIB	10 SAG	8 CAP	10 PIS	8 ARI	10 GEM
10 PIS	11 TAU	12 GEM	14 LEO	13 VIR	12 LIB	11 SCO	12 CAP	10 AQU	12 ARI	10 TAU	13 CAN
13 ARI	14 GEM	15 CAN	16 VIR	16 LIB	14 SCO	13 SAG	14 AQU	12 PIS	14 TAU	13 GEM	15 LEO
15 TAU	16 CAN	17 LEO	18 LIB	18 SCO	16 SAG	15 CAP	16 PIS	15 ARI	17 GEM	15 CAN	18 VIR
18 GEM	19 LEO	20 VIR	20 SCO	20 SAG	18 CAP	17 AQU	18 ARI	17 TAU	19 CAN	18 LEO	20 LIB
20 CAN	21 VIR	22 LIB	22 SAG	22 CAP	20 AQU	20 PIS	20 TAU	19 GEM	22 LEO	20 VIR	22 SCO
22 LEO	23 LIB	24 SCO	24 CAP	24 AQU	22 PIS	22 ARI	23 GEM	22 CAN	24 VIR	23 LIB	24 SAG
25 VIR	25 SCO	26 SAG	26 AQU	26 PIS	24 ARI	24 TAU	25 CAN	24 LEO	26 LIB	25 SCO	26 CAP
27 LIB	28 SAG	28 CAP	29 PIS	28 ARI	27 TAU	27 GEM	28 LEO	27 VIR	28 SCO	27 SAG	28 AQU
29 SCO	29 SAG	30 AQU	30 PIS	31 TAU	29 GEM	29 CAN	30 VIR	29 LIB	31 SAG	29 CAP	30 PIS
31 AQU		31 AQU			30 GEM	31 CAN	31 VIR	30 LIB		30 CAP	31 PIS

1925

JAN	FEB	MAR	APR	MAY	JUN	JUL	AUG	SEP	OCT	NOV	DEC
1 PIS	1 TAU	1 TAU	1 CAN	1 LEO	1 VIR	1 LIB	1 SAG	1 AQU	1 PIS	1 TAU	1 GEM
2 ARI	3 GEM	2 GEM	3 LEO	3 VIR	2 LIB	2 SCO	2 CAP	3 PIS	2 ARI	3 GEM	3 CAN
4 TAU	5 CAN	5 CAN	6 VIR	6 LIB	4 SCO	4 SAG	4 AQU	5 ARI	4 TAU	5 CAN	5 LEO
6 GEM	8 LEO	7 LEO	8 LIB	8 SCO	6 SAG	6 CAP	6 PIS	7 TAU	7 GEM	8 LEO	8 VIR
9 CAN	10 VIR	10 VIR	10 SCO	10 SAG	8 CAP	8 AQU	8 ARI	9 GEM	9 CAN	10 VIR	10 LIB
12 LEO	13 LIB	12 LIB	13 SAG	12 CAP	10 AQU	10 PIS	10 TAU	12 CAN	11 LEO	13 LIB	13 SCO
14 VIR	15 SCO	14 SCO	15 CAP	14 AQU	12 PIS	12 ARI	13 GEM	14 LEO	14 VIR	15 SCO	15 SAG
16 LIB	17 SAG	16 SAG	17 AQU	16 PIS	15 ARI	14 TAU	15 CAN	17 VIR	16 LIB	17 SAG	17 CAP
19 SCO	19 CAP	18 CAP	19 PIS	18 ARI	17 TAU	17 GEM	18 LEO	19 LIB	19 SCO	19 CAP	19 AQU
21 SAG	21 AQU	21 AQU	21 ARI	21 TAU	19 GEM	19 CAN	20 VIR	21 SCO	21 SAG	21 AQU	21 PIS
23 CAP	23 PIS	23 PIS	23 TAU	23 GEM	22 CAN	22 LEO	23 LIB	24 SAG	23 CAP	24 PIS	23 ARI
25 AQU	25 ARI	25 PIS	26 GEM	26 CAN	24 LEO	24 VIR	25 SCO	26 CAP	25 AQU	26 ARI	25 TAU
27 PIS	28 TAU	27 TAU	28 CAN	28 LEO	27 VIR	27 LIB	27 SAG	28 AQU	27 PIS	28 TAU	28 GEM
29 ARI		29 GEM	30 CAN	31 VIR	29 LIB	29 SCO	30 CAP	30 PIS	29 ARI	30 GEM	30 CAN
31 TAU		31 GEM			30 LIB	31 SAG	31 CAP		31 ARI		31 CAN

1926

JAN	FEB	MAR	APR	MAY	JUN	JUL	AUG	SEP	OCT	NOV	DEC
1 LEO	1 VIR	1 VIR	1 SCO	1 SAG	1 AQU	1 PIS	1 TAU	1 GEM	1 LEO	1 VIR	1 LIB
4 VIR	3 LIB	2 LIB	3 SAG	2 CAP	3 PIS	2 ARI	3 GEM	2 CAN	4 VIR	3 LIB	2 SCO
6 LIB	5 SCO	4 SCO	5 CAP	5 AQU	5 ARI	4 TAU	5 CAN	4 LEO	6 LIB	5 SCO	5 SAG
9 SCO	8 SAG	7 SAG	7 AQU	7 PIS	7 TAU	7 GEM	8 LEO	7 VIR	9 SCO	7 SAG	7 CAP
11 SAG	10 CAP	9 CAP	10 PIS	9 ARI	9 GEM	9 CAN	10 VIR	9 LIB	11 SAG	10 CAP	9 AQU
13 CAP	12 AQU	11 AQU	12 ARI	11 TAU	12 CAN	12 LEO	13 LIB	12 SCO	14 CAP	12 AQU	11 PIS
15 AQU	14 PIS	13 PIS	14 TAU	13 GEM	14 LEO	14 VIR	15 SCO	14 SAG	16 AQU	14 PIS	14 ARI
17 PIS	16 ARI	15 ARI	16 GEM	15 CAN	17 VIR	17 LIB	18 SAG	16 CAP	18 PIS	16 ARI	16 TAU
19 ARI	18 TAU	17 TAU	18 CAN	18 LEO	19 LIB	19 SCO	20 CAP	18 AQU	20 ARI	18 TAU	18 GEM
21 TAU	20 GEM	19 GEM	21 LEO	20 VIR	22 SCO	21 SAG	22 AQU	21 PIS	22 TAU	20 GEM	20 CAN
24 GEM	22 CAN	22 CAN	23 VIR	23 LIB	24 SAG	24 CAP	24 PIS	22 ARI	24 GEM	23 CAN	22 LEO
26 CAN	25 LEO	24 LEO	26 LIB	25 SCO	26 CAP	26 AQU	26 ARI	24 TAU	26 CAN	25 LEO	25 VIR
29 LEO	27 VIR	27 VIR	28 SCO	28 SAG	28 AQU	28 PIS	28 TAU	27 GEM	29 LEO	27 VIR	27 LIB
31 VIR	28 VIR	29 LIB	30 SAG	30 CAP	30 PIS	30 ARI	30 GEM	29 CAN	31 VIR	30 LIB	30 SCO
		31 LIB		31 CAP		31 ARI	31 GEM	30 CAN			31 SCO

1927

JAN	FEB	MAR	APR	MAY	JUN	JUL	AUG	SEP	OCT	NOV	DEC
1 SAG	1 CAP	1 AQU	1 PIS	1 TAU	1 GEM	1 CAN	1 VIR	1 LIB	1 SAG	1 CAP	1 AQU
3 CAP	2 AQU	4 PIS	2 ARI	3 GEM	2 CAN	2 LEO	3 LIB	2 SCO	4 CAP	2 AQU	2 PIS
6 AQU	4 PIS	5 ARI	4 TAU	5 CAN	4 LEO	4 VIR	5 SCO	4 SAG	6 AQU	5 PIS	4 ARI
8 PIS	6 ARI	7 TAU	6 GEM	8 LEO	7 VIR	6 LIB	8 SAG	6 CAP	8 PIS	7 ARI	6 TAU
10 ARI	8 TAU	10 GEM	8 CAN	10 VIR	9 LIB	9 SCO	10 CAP	9 AQU	10 ARI	9 TAU	8 GEM
12 TAU	10 GEM	12 CAN	10 LEO	13 LIB	12 SCO	11 SAG	12 AQU	11 PIS	12 TAU	11 GEM	10 CAN
14 GEM	13 CAN	14 LEO	13 VIR	15 SCO	14 SAG	14 CAP	14 PIS	13 ARI	14 GEM	13 CAN	12 LEO
16 CAN	15 LEO	17 VIR	15 LIB	18 SAG	16 CAP	16 AQU	16 ARI	15 TAU	16 CAN	15 LEO	15 VIR
19 LEO	17 VIR	19 LIB	18 SCO	20 CAP	19 AQU	18 PIS	19 TAU	17 GEM	19 LEO	17 VIR	17 LIB
21 VIR	20 LIB	22 SCO	20 SAG	22 AQU	21 PIS	20 ARI	21 GEM	19 CAN	21 VIR	20 LIB	20 SCO
24 LIB	22 SCO	24 SAG	23 CAP	25 PIS	23 ARI	22 TAU	23 CAN	21 LEO	24 LIB	22 SCO	22 SAG
26 SCO	25 SAG	27 CAP	25 AQU	27 ARI	25 TAU	24 GEM	25 LEO	24 VIR	26 SCO	25 SAG	25 CAP
29 SAG	27 CAP	29 AQU	27 PIS	29 TAU	27 GEM	27 CAN	28 VIR	26 LIB	29 SAG	27 CAP	27 AQU
31 CAP	28 CAP	31 PIS	29 ARI	31 GEM	29 CAN	29 LEO	30 LIB	29 SCO	31 CAP	30 AQU	29 PIS
			30 ARI		30 CAN	31 VIR	31 LIB	30 SCO			31 ARI

1928

JAN	FEB	MAR	APR	MAY	JUN	JUL	AUG	SEP	OCT	NOV	DEC
1 ARI	1 GEM	1 CAN	1 LEO	1 VIR	1 SCO	1 SAG	1 AQU	1 PIS	1 ARI	1 GEM	1 CAN
2 TAU	3 CAN	3 LEO	2 VIR	2 LIB	3 SAG	3 CAP	4 PIS	2 ARI	2 TAU	2 CAN	2 LEO
5 GEM	5 LEO	6 VIR	4 LIB	4 SCO	5 CAP	5 AQU	6 ARI	4 TAU	4 GEM	4 LEO	4 VIR
7 CAN	7 VIR	8 LIB	7 SCO	7 SAG	8 AQU	7 PIS	8 TAU	6 GEM	6 CAN	6 VIR	6 LIB
9 LEO	10 LIB	11 SCO	9 SAG	9 CAP	10 PIS	10 ARI	10 GEM	9 CAN	8 LEO	9 LIB	8 SCO
11 VIR	12 SCO	13 SAG	12 CAP	12 AQU	12 ARI	12 TAU	12 CAN	11 LEO	10 VIR	11 SCO	11 SAG
13 LIB	15 SAG	16 CAP	14 AQU	14 PIS	15 TAU	14 GEM	14 LEO	13 VIR	13 LIB	14 SAG	14 CAP
16 SCO	17 CAP	18 AQU	17 PIS	16 ARI	17 GEM	16 CAN	17 VIR	15 LIB	15 SCO	16 CAP	16 AQU
18 SAG	20 AQU	20 PIS	19 ARI	18 TAU	19 CAN	18 LEO	19 LIB	18 SCO	17 SAG	19 AQU	18 PIS
21 CAP	22 PIS	22 ARI	21 TAU	20 GEM	21 LEO	20 VIR	20 SCO	20 SAG	20 CAP	21 PIS	21 ARI
23 AQU	24 ARI	24 TAU	23 GEM	22 CAN	23 VIR	23 LIB	24 SAG	23 CAP	23 AQU	23 ARI	23 TAU
25 PIS	26 TAU	26 GEM	25 CAN	24 LEO	25 LIB	25 SCO	26 CAP	25 AQU	25 PIS	26 TAU	25 GEM
28 ARI	28 GEM	28 CAN	27 LEO	27 VIR	28 SCO	28 SAG	29 AQU	27 PIS	27 ARI	28 GEM	27 CAN
30 TAU	29 GEM	31 LEO	29 VIR	29 LIB	30 SAG	30 CAP	31 PIS	30 ARI	29 TAU	30 CAN	29 LEO
31 TAU			30 VIR	31 SCO		31 CAP			31 GEM		31 VIR

1929

JAN	FEB	MAR	APR	MAY	JUN	JUL	AUG	SEP	OCT	NOV	DEC
1 VIR	1 SCO	1 SCO	1 SAG	1 CAP	1 PIS	1 ARI	1 GEM	1 LEO	1 VIR	1 SCO	1 SAG
2 LIB	4 SAG	3 SAG	2 CAP	2 AQU	3 ARI	2 TAU	3 CAN	3 VIR	3 LIB	4 SAG	3 CAP
5 SCO	6 CAP	5 CAP	4 AQU	4 PIS	5 TAU	4 GEM	5 LEO	5 LIB	5 SCO	6 CAP	6 AQU
7 SAG	9 AQU	8 AQU	7 PIS	6 ARI	7 GEM	6 CAN	7 VIR	8 SCO	7 SAG	9 AQU	9 PIS
10 CAP	11 PIS	10 PIS	9 ARI	9 TAU	9 CAN	8 LEO	9 LIB	10 SAG	10 CAP	11 PIS	11 ARI
12 AQU	13 ARI	12 ARI	11 TAU	11 GEM	11 LEO	10 VIR	11 SCO	12 CAP	12 AQU	14 ARI	13 TAU
15 PIS	16 TAU	15 TAU	13 GEM	13 CAN	13 VIR	13 LIB	14 SAG	15 AQU	15 PIS	16 TAU	15 GEM
17 ARI	18 GEM	17 GEM	15 CAN	15 LEO	15 LIB	15 SCO	16 CAP	17 PIS	17 ARI	18 GEM	17 CAN
19 TAU	20 CAN	19 CAN	17 LEO	17 VIR	18 SCO	17 SAG	19 AQU	20 ARI	19 TAU	20 CAN	19 LEO
21 GEM	22 LEO	21 LEO	20 VIR	19 LIB	20 SAG	20 CAP	21 PIS	22 TAU	22 GEM	22 LEO	21 VIR
23 CAN	24 VIR	23 VIR	22 LIB	21 SCO	23 CAP	22 AQU	24 ARI	24 GEM	24 CAN	24 VIR	24 LIB
25 LEO	26 LIB	26 LIB	24 SCO	24 SAG	25 AQU	25 PIS	26 TAU	26 CAN	26 LEO	26 LIB	26 SCO
28 VIR	28 SCO	28 SCO	27 SAG	26 CAP	28 PIS	27 ARI	28 GEM	29 LEO	28 VIR	29 SCO	28 SAG
30 LIB		30 SAG	29 CAP	29 AQU	30 ARI	30 TAU	30 CAN	30 LEO	30 LIB	30 SCO	31 CAP
31 LIB		31 SAG	30 CAP	31 PIS		31 TAU	31 CAN		31 LIB		

1930

JAN	FEB	MAR	APR	MAY	JUN	JUL	AUG	SEP	OCT	NOV	DEC
1 CAP	1 PIS	1 PIS	1 TAU	1 GEM	1 LEO	1 VIR	1 SCO	1 SAG	1 CAP	1 PIS	1 ARI
2 AQU	4 ARI	3 ARI	4 GEM	3 CAN	4 VIR	3 LIB	4 SAG	2 CAP	2 AQU	3 ARI	3 TAU
5 PIS	6 TAU	5 TAU	6 CAN	5 LEO	6 LIB	5 SCO	6 CAP	5 AQU	5 PIS	6 TAU	6 GEM
7 ARI	8 GEM	7 GEM	8 LEO	7 VIR	8 SCO	7 SAG	9 AQU	7 PIS	7 ARI	8 GEM	8 CAN
10 TAU	10 CAN	10 CAN	10 VIR	9 LIB	10 SAG	10 CAP	11 PIS	10 ARI	10 TAU	10 CAN	10 LEO
12 GEM	12 LEO	12 LEO	12 LIB	12 SCO	13 CAP	12 AQU	14 ARI	12 TAU	12 GEM	13 LEO	12 VIR
14 CAN	14 VIR	14 VIR	14 SCO	14 SAG	15 AQU	15 PIS	16 TAU	15 GEM	14 CAN	15 VIR	14 LIB
16 LEO	16 LIB	16 LIB	17 SAG	16 CAP	18 PIS	17 ARI	18 GEM	17 CAN	16 LEO	17 LIB	16 SCO
18 VIR	18 SCO	18 SCO	19 CAP	19 AQU	20 ARI	20 TAU	21 CAN	19 LEO	18 VIR	19 SCO	18 SAG
20 LIB	21 SAG	20 SAG	21 AQU	21 PIS	22 TAU	22 GEM	23 LEO	21 VIR	20 LIB	21 SAG	21 CAP
22 SCO	23 CAP	23 CAP	24 PIS	24 ARI	25 GEM	24 CAN	25 VIR	23 LIB	23 SCO	23 CAP	23 AQU
24 SAG	26 AQU	25 AQU	26 ARI	26 TAU	27 CAN	26 LEO	27 LIB	25 SCO	15 SAG	26 AQU	26 PIS
27 CAP	28 PIS	28 PIS	29 TAU	28 GEM	29 LEO	28 VIR	29 SCO	27 SAG	27 CAP	28 PIS	28 ARI
30 AQU		30 ARI	30 TAU	30 CAN	30 LEO	30 LIB	31 SAG	29 CAP	29 AQU	30 PIS	31 TAU
31 AQU		31 ARI		31 CAN		31 LIB		30 CAP	31 AQU		

1931

JAN	FEB	MAR	APR	MAY	JUN	JUL	AUG	SEP	OCT	NOV	DEC
1 TAU	1 CAN	1 CAN	1 VIR	1 LIB	1 SAG	1 CAP	1 PIS	1 ARI	1 TAU	1 CAN	1 LEO
2 GEM	3 LEO	2 LEO	3 LIB	2 SCO	3 CAP	2 AQU	4 ARI	2 TAU	2 GEM	3 LEO	3 VIR
4 CAN	5 VIR	4 VIR	5 SCO	4 SAG	5 AQU	5 PIS	6 TAU	5 GEM	5 CAN	5 VIR	5 LIB
6 LEO	7 LIB	6 LIB	7 SAG	6 CAP	7 PIS	7 ARI	9 GEM	7 CAN	7 LEO	7 LIB	7 SCO
8 VIR	9 SCO	8 SCO	9 CAP	9 AQU	10 ARI	10 TAU	11 CAN	9 LEO	9 VIR	9 SCO	9 SAG
10 LIB	11 SAG	10 SAG	11 AQU	11 PIS	12 TAU	12 GEM	13 LEO	11 VIR	11 LIB	11 SAG	11 SCO
12 SCO	13 CAP	13 CAP	14 PIS	14 ARI	15 GEM	14 CAN	15 VIR	13 LIB	13 SCO	13 CAP	13 AQU
15 SAG	16 AQU	15 AQU	16 ARI	16 TAU	17 CAN	17 LEO	17 LIB	15 SCO	15 SAG	16 AQU	15 PIS
17 CAP	18 PIS	17 PIS	19 TAU	18 GEM	19 LEO	19 VIR	19 SCO	18 SAG	17 CAP	18 PIS	18 ARI
19 AQU	21 ARI	20 ARI	21 GEM	21 CAN	21 VIR	21 LIB	21 SAG	20 CAP	19 AQU	21 ARI	20 TAU
22 PIS	23 TAU	23 TAU	24 CAN	23 LEO	23 LIB	23 SCO	23 CAP	22 AQU	22 PIS	23 TAU	23 GEM
24 ARI	26 GEM	25 GEM	26 LEO	25 VIR	26 SCO	25 SAG	26 AQU	25 PIS	24 ARI	26 GEM	25 CAN
27 TAU	28 CAN	27 CAN	28 VIR	27 LIB	28 SAG	27 CAP	28 PIS	27 ARI	27 TAU	28 CAN	28 LEO
29 GEM		29 LEO	30 LIB	29 SCO	30 CAP	30 AQU	31 ARI	30 TAU	29 GEM	30 LEO	30 VIR
31 GEM		31 LEO		31 SAG		31 AQU			31 GEM		31 VIR

1932

JAN	FEB	MAR	APR	MAY	JUN	JUL	AUG	SEP	OCT	NOV	DEC
1 LIB	1 SAG	1 SAG	1 AQU	1 PIS	1 TAU	1 GEM	1 CAN	1 VIR	1 LIB	1 SAG	1 CAP
3 SCO	4 CAP	2 CAP	3 PIS	2 ARI	4 GEM	4 CAN	2 LEO	3 LIB	2 SCO	3 CAP	2 AQU
5 SAG	6 AQU	4 AQU	5 ARI	5 TAU	6 CAN	6 LEO	4 VIR	5 SCO	4 SAG	5 AQU	4 PIS
7 SCO	8 PIS	6 PIS	8 TAU	8 GEM	9 LEO	8 VIR	7 LIB	7 SAG	6 CAP	7 PIS	7 ARI
9 AQU	11 ARI	9 ARI	10 GEM	10 CAN	11 VIR	10 LIB	9 SCO	9 SCO	9 AQU	10 ARI	9 TAU
12 PIS	13 TAU	11 TAU	13 CAN	12 LEO	13 LIB	12 SCO	11 SAG	11 AQU	11 PIS	12 TAU	12 GEM
14 ARI	16 GEM	14 GEM	15 LEO	15 VIR	15 SCO	15 SAG	13 CAP	14 PIS	13 ARI	15 GEM	14 CAN
17 TAU	18 CAN	16 CAN	17 VIR	17 LIB	17 SAG	17 CAP	15 AQU	16 ARI	16 TAU	17 CAN	17 LEO
19 GEM	20 LEO	19 LEO	19 LIB	19 SCO	19 CAP	19 AQU	17 PIS	19 TAU	18 GEM	20 LEO	19 VIR
22 CAN	22 VIR	21 VIR	21 SCO	21 SAG	21 AQU	21 PIS	20 ARI	21 GEM	21 CAN	22 VIR	21 LIB
24 LEO	24 LIB	23 LIB	23 SAG	23 CAP	24 PIS	23 ARI	22 TAU	24 CAN	23 LEO	24 LIB	24 SCO
26 VIR	27 SCO	25 SCO	25 CAP	25 AQU	26 ARI	26 TAU	25 GEM	26 LEO	26 VIR	26 SCO	26 SAG
28 LIB	29 SAG	27 SAG	28 AQU	27 PIS	29 TAU	28 GEM	27 CAN	28 VIR	28 LIB	28 SAG	28 CAP
30 SCO		29 CAP	30 PIS	30 ARI	30 TAU	31 CAN	30 LEO	30 LIB	30 SCO	30 CAP	30 AQU
31 SCO		31 AQU		31 ARI			31 LEO		31 SCO		31 AQU

1933

JAN	FEB	MAR	APR	MAY	JUN	JUL	AUG	SEP	OCT	NOV	DEC
1 PIS	1 ARI	1 TAU	1 GEM	1 CAN	1 VIR	1 LIB	1 SAG	1 CAP	1 PIS	1 ARI	1 TAU
3 ARI	2 TAU	4 GEM	3 CAN	2 LEO	3 LIB	3 SCO	3 CAP	2 AQU	3 ARI	2 TAU	2 GEM
6 TAU	4 GEM	6 CAN	5 LEO	5 VIR	6 SCO	5 SAG	5 AQU	4 PIS	6 TAU	5 GEM	4 CAN
8 GEM	7 CAN	9 LEO	7 VIR	7 LIB	8 SAG	7 CAP	8 PIS	6 ARI	8 GEM	7 CAN	7 LEO
11 CAN	9 LEO	11 VIR	10 LIB	9 SCO	10 CAP	9 AQU	10 ARI	8 TAU	11 CAN	10 LEO	9 VIR
13 LEO	12 VIR	13 LIB	12 SCO	11 SAG	12 AQU	11 PIS	12 TAU	11 GEM	13 LEO	12 VIR	12 LIB
15 VIR	14 LIB	15 SCO	14 SAG	13 CAP	14 PIS	13 ARI	14 GEM	13 CAN	16 VIR	14 LIB	14 SCO
18 LIB	16 SCO	17 SAG	16 CAP	15 AQU	16 ARI	16 TAU	17 CAN	16 LEO	18 LIB	16 SCO	16 SAG
20 SCO	18 SAG	20 CAP	18 AQU	17 PIS	18 TAU	18 GEM	20 LEO	18 VIR	20 SCO	19 SAG	18 SCO
22 SAG	20 CAP	22 AQU	20 PIS	20 ARI	21 GEM	21 CAN	22 VIR	21 LIB	22 SAG	21 CAP	20 AQU
24 CAP	22 AQU	24 PIS	23 ARI	22 TAU	23 CAN	23 LEO	24 LIB	23 SCO	24 CAP	23 AQU	22 PIS
26 AQU	25 PIS	26 ARI	25 TAU	25 GEM	26 LEO	26 VIR	26 SCO	25 SAG	26 AQU	25 PIS	24 ARI
28 PIS	27 ARI	29 TAU	27 GEM	27 CAN	28 VIR	28 LIB	29 SAG	27 CAP	28 PIS	27 ARI	27 TAU
31 ARI	28 ARI	31 GEM	30 CAN	30 LEO	30 VIR	30 SCO	31 CAP	29 AQU	31 ARI	29 TAU	29 GEM
				31 LEO		31 SCO		30 AQU		30 TAU	31 GEM

1934

JAN	FEB	MAR	APR	MAY	JUN	JUL	AUG	SEP	OCT	NOV	DEC
1 CAN	1 LEO	1 VIR	1 LIB	1 SCO	1 CAP	1 PIS	1 ARI	1 GEM	1 CAN	1 LEO	1 VIR
3 LEO	2 VIR	4 LIB	2 SCO	2 SAG	2 AQU	4 ARI	2 TAU	3 CAN	3 LEO	2 VIR	2 LIB
6 VIR	4 LIB	6 SCO	4 SAG	4 CAP	4 PIS	6 TAU	4 GEM	6 LEO	6 VIR	4 LIB	4 SCO
8 LIB	7 SCO	8 SAG	6 CAP	6 AQU	6 ARI	8 GEM	7 CAN	8 VIR	8 LIB	7 SCO	6 SAG
10 SCO	9 SAG	10 CAP	8 AQU	8 PIS	9 TAU	11 CAN	9 LEO	11 LIB	10 SCO	9 SAG	8 CAP
12 SAG	11 CAP	12 AQU	11 PIS	10 ARI	11 GEM	13 LEO	12 VIR	13 SCO	13 SAG	11 CAP	10 AQU
14 CAP	13 AQU	14 PIS	13 ARI	12 TAU	13 CAN	16 VIR	14 LIB	15 SAG	15 CAP	13 AQU	12 PIS
16 AQU	15 PIS	16 ARI	15 TAU	15 GEM	16 LEO	18 LIB	17 SCO	18 CAP	17 AQU	15 PIS	15 ARI
18 PIS	17 ARI	19 TAU	17 GEM	17 CAN	18 VIR	21 SCO	19 SAG	20 AQU	19 PIS	17 ARI	17 TAU
21 ARI	19 TAU	21 GEM	20 CAN	20 LEO	21 LIB	23 SAG	21 CAP	22 PIS	21 ARI	20 TAU	19 GEM
23 TAU	22 GEM	23 CAN	22 LEO	22 VIR	23 SCO	25 CAP	23 AQU	24 ARI	23 TAU	22 GEM	22 CAN
25 GEM	24 CAN	26 LEO	25 VIR	25 LIB	25 SAG	27 AQU	25 PIS	26 TAU	25 GEM	24 CAN	24 LEO
28 CAN	27 LEO	28 VIR	27 LIB	27 SCO	27 CAP	29 PIS	27 ARI	28 GEM	28 CAN	27 LEO	27 VIR
30 LEO	28 LEO	31 LIB	29 SCO	29 SAG	29 AQU	31 ARI	29 TAU	30 CAN	30 LEO	29 VIR	29 LIB
21 LEO			30 SCO	31 CAP	30 AQU		31 TAU		31 LEO	30 VIR	31 SCO

1935

JAN	FEB	MAR	APR	MAY	JUN	JUL	AUG	SEP	OCT	NOV	DEC
1 SCO	1 CAP	1 CAP	1 PIS	1 ARI	1 GEM	1 CAN	1 LEO	1 LIB	1 SCO	1 CAP	1 AQU
3 SAG	3 AQU	3 AQU	3 ARI	3 TAU	3 CAN	3 LEO	2 VIR	3 SCO	3 SAG	4 AQU	3 PIS
5 CAP	5 PIS	5 PIS	5 TAU	5 GEM	6 LEO	6 VIR	4 LIB	6 SAG	5 CAP	6 PIS	5 ARI
7 AQU	7 ARI	7 ARI	7 GEM	7 CAN	8 VIR	8 LIB	7 SCO	8 CAP	7 AQU	8 ARI	7 TAU
9 PIS	9 TAU	9 TAU	10 CAN	9 LEO	11 LIB	11 SCO	9 SAG	10 AQU	10 PIS	10 TAU	9 GEM
11 ARI	12 GEM	11 GEM	12 LEO	12 VIR	13 SCO	13 SAG	12 CAP	12 PIS	12 ARI	12 GEM	12 CAN
13 TAU	14 CAN	13 CAN	15 VIR	14 LIB	16 SAG	15 CAP	14 AQU	14 ARI	13 TAU	14 CAN	14 LEO
15 GEM	17 LEO	16 LEO	17 LIB	17 SCO	18 CAP	17 AQU	16 PIS	16 TAU	16 GEM	16 LEO	16 VIR
18 CAN	19 VIR	18 VIR	20 SCO	19 SAG	20 AQU	19 ARI	18 ARI	18 GEM	18 CAN	19 VIR	19 LIB
20 LEO	22 LIB	21 LIB	22 SAG	21 AQU	22 PIS	21 TAU	20 TAU	20 CAN	20 LEO	21 LIB	21 SCO
23 VIR	24 SCO	23 SCO	24 CAP	24 PIS	24 ARI	23 GEM	22 GEM	23 LEO	23 VIR	24 SCO	24 SAG
25 LIB	26 SAG	26 SAG	26 AQU	26 ARI	26 TAU	26 CAN	24 CAN	25 VIR	25 LIB	26 SAG	26 CAP
28 SCO	28 SAG	28 CAP	28 PIS	28 TAU	28 GEM	28 LEO	27 LEO	28 LIB	28 SCO	29 CAP	28 AQU
30 SAG		30 AQU	30 PIS	30 TAU	30 GEM	30 LEO	29 VIR	30 SCO	30 SAG	30 CAP	30 PIS
31 SAG		31 AQU					31 VIR		31 SAG		31 PIS

1936

JAN	FEB	MAR	APR	MAY	JUN	JUL	AUG	SEP	OCT	NOV	DEC
1 ARI	1 TAU	1 GEM	1 LEO	1 VIR	1 LIB	1 SCO	1 CAP	1 PIS	1 ARI	1 GEM	1 CAN
4 TAU	2 GEM	2 CAN	4 VIR	3 LIB	2 SCO	2 SAG	3 AQU	3 ARI	3 TAU	3 CAN	3 LEO
6 GEM	4 CAN	5 LEO	6 LIB	6 SCO	5 SAG	4 CAP	5 PIS	5 TAU	5 GEM	6 LEO	5 VIR
8 CAN	7 LEO	7 VIR	9 SCO	8 SAG	7 CAP	7 AQU	7 ARI	8 GEM	7 CAN	8 VIR	8 LIB
10 LEO	9 VIR	10 LIB	11 SAG	11 CAP	9 AQU	9 PIS	9 TAU	10 CAN	9 LEO	10 LIB	10 SCO
13 VIR	11 LIB	12 SCO	13 CAP	13 AQU	11 PIS	11 ARI	11 GEM	12 LEO	12 VIR	13 SCO	13 SAG
15 LIB	14 SCO	15 SAG	16 AQU	15 PIS	14 ARI	13 TAU	13 CAN	14 VIR	14 LIB	15 SAG	15 CAP
18 SCO	16 SAG	17 CAP	18 PIS	17 ARI	16 TAU	15 GEM	16 LEO	17 LIB	17 SCO	18 CAP	18 AQU
20 SAG	19 CAP	19 AQU	20 ARI	19 TAU	18 GEM	17 CAN	18 VIR	19 SCO	19 SAG	20 AQU	20 PIS
22 SCO	21 AQU	22 PIS	22 TAU	21 GEM	20 CAN	19 LEO	21 LIB	22 SAG	22 CAP	23 PIS	22 ARI
25 AQU	23 PIS	24 ARI	24 GEM	23 CAN	22 LIB	22 VIR	23 SCO	24 CAP	24 AQU	25 ARI	24 TAU
27 PIS	25 ARI	25 TAU	26 CAN	26 LEO	24 SCO	24 LIB	26 SAG	27 AQU	26 PIS	27 TAU	26 GEM
29 ARI	27 TAU	28 GEM	28 LEO	28 VIR	27 LIB	27 SCO	28 CAP	29 PIS	28 ARI	29 GEM	28 CAN
31 TAU	29 GEM	30 CAN	30 LEO	31 SAG	29 SCO	29 SAG	30 AQU	30 PIS	30 TAU	30 GEM	30 LEO
		31 CAN			30 SCO	31 SAG	31 AQU		31 TAU		31 LEO

1937

JAN	FEB	MAR	APR	MAY	JUN	JUL	AUG	SEP	OCT	NOV	DEC
1 LEO	1 LIB	1 LIB	1 SAG	1 CAP	1 AQU	1 ARI	1 TAU	1 CAN	1 LEO	1 LIB	1 SCO
2 VIR	3 SCO	2 SCO	4 CAP	3 AQU	2 PIS	4 TAU	2 GEM	2 LEO	2 VIR	3 SCO	3 SAG
4 LIB	5 SAG	5 SAG	6 AQU	6 PIS	4 ARI	6 GEM	4 CAN	5 VIR	4 LIB	5 SAG	5 CAP
6 SCO	8 CAP	7 CAP	8 PIS	8 ARI	6 TAU	8 CAN	6 LEO	7 LIB	7 SCO	8 CAP	8 AQU
9 SAG	10 AQU	10 AQU	10 ARI	10 TAU	8 GEM	10 LEO	8 VIR	9 SCO	9 SAG	10 SCO	10 PIS
11 CAP	12 PIS	12 PIS	12 TAU	12 GEM	10 CAN	12 VIR	10 LIB	12 SAG	12 CAP	13 AQU	12 ARI
14 AQU	15 ARI	14 ARI	14 GEM	14 CAN	12 LEO	14 LIB	13 SCO	14 CAP	14 AQU	15 PIS	15 TAU
16 PIS	17 TAU	16 TAU	16 CAN	16 LEO	14 VIR	17 SCO	15 SAG	17 AQU	16 PIS	17 ARI	17 GEM
18 ARI	19 GEM	18 GEM	19 LEO	18 VIR	17 LIB	19 SAG	18 CAP	19 PIS	19 ARI	19 TAU	19 CAN
20 TAU	21 CAN	20 CAN	21 VIR	20 LIB	19 SCO	22 CAP	20 AQU	21 ARI	21 TAU	21 GEM	21 LEO
22 GEM	23 LEO	22 LEO	23 LIB	23 SCO	22 SAG	24 AQU	23 PIS	23 TAU	23 GEM	23 CAN	23 VIR
25 CAN	25 VIR	25 VIR	26 SCO	26 SAG	24 CAP	26 PIS	25 ARI	25 GEM	25 CAN	25 LEO	25 LIB
27 LEO	28 LIB	27 LIB	28 SAG	28 CAP	27 AQU	29 ARI	27 TAU	27 CAN	27 LEO	28 VIR	27 SCO
29 VIR		29 SCO	30 SAG	31 AQU	29 PIS	31 TAU	29 GEM	30 LEO	29 VIR	30 SCO	30 SAG
31 LIB		31 SCO			30 PIS		31 CAN		31 LIB		31 SAG

1938

JAN	FEB	MAR	APR	MAY	JUN	JUL	AUG	SEP	OCT	NOV	DEC
1 CAP	1 AQU	1 AQU	1 ARI	1 TAU	1 CAN	1 LEO	1 LIB	1 SCO	1 CAP	1 AQU	1 PIS
4 AQU	3 PIS	2 PIS	3 TAU	2 GEM	3 LEO	2 VIR	3 SCO	2 SAG	4 AQU	3 PIS	3 ARI
6 PIS	5 ARI	4 ARI	5 GEM	4 CAN	5 VIR	4 LIB	5 SAG	4 CAP	6 PIS	5 ARI	5 TAU
9 ARI	7 TAU	6 TAU	7 CAN	6 LEO	7 LIB	6 SCO	8 CAP	7 AQU	9 ARI	7 TAU	7 GEM
11 TAU	9 GEM	9 GEM	9 LEO	8 VIR	9 SCO	9 SAG	10 AQU	9 PIS	11 TAU	10 GEM	9 CAN
13 GEM	11 CAN	11 CAN	11 VIR	11 LIB	12 SAG	11 CAP	13 PIS	11 ARI	13 GEM	12 CAN	11 LEO
15 CAN	13 LEO	13 LEO	13 LIB	13 SCO	14 CAP	14 AQU	15 ARI	14 TAU	15 CAN	14 LEO	13 VIR
17 LEO	16 VIR	15 VIR	16 SCO	15 SAG	17 AQU	16 PIS	17 TAU	16 GEM	17 LEO	16 VIR	15 LIB
19 VIR	18 LIB	17 LIB	18 SAG	18 CAP	19 PIS	19 ARI	20 GEM	18 CAN	20 VIR	18 LIB	17 SCO
21 LIB	20 SCO	19 SCO	21 CAP	20 AQU	22 ARI	21 TAU	22 CAN	20 LEO	22 LIB	20 SCO	20 SAG
24 SCO	22 SAG	22 SAG	23 AQU	23 PIS	24 TAU	23 GEM	24 LEO	22 VIR	24 SCO	23 SAG	22 CAP
26 SAG	25 CAP	24 CAP	26 PIS	25 ARI	26 GEM	25 CAN	26 VIR	24 LIB	26 SAG	25 CAP	25 AQU
29 CAP	27 AQU	27 AQU	28 ARI	28 TAU	28 CAN	27 LEO	28 LIB	27 SCO	29 CAP	28 AQU	27 PIS
31 AQU	28 AQU	29 PIS	30 TAU	30 GEM	30 LEO	29 VIR	30 SCO	29 SAG	31 AQU	30 PIS	30 ARI
		31 PIS		31 GEM		31 VIR	31 SCO	30 SAG			31 ARI

1939

JAN	FEB	MAR	APR	MAY	JUN	JUL	AUG	SEP	OCT	NOV	DEC
1 TAU	1 GEM	1 CAN	1 LEO	1 LIB	1 SCO	1 CAP	1 AQU	1 ARI	1 TAU	1 GEM	1 LEO
3 GEM	2 CAN	3 LEO	2 VIR	3 SCO	2 SAG	4 AQU	3 PIS	4 TAU	4 GEM	2 CAN	4 VIR
5 CAN	4 LEO	5 VIR	4 LIB	5 SAG	4 CAP	6 PIS	5 ARI	6 GEM	6 CAN	4 LEO	6 LIB
7 LEO	6 VIR	7 LIB	6 SCO	8 CAP	7 AQU	9 ARI	8 TAU	9 CAN	8 LEO	6 VIR	8 SCO
9 VIR	8 LIB	9 SCO	8 SAG	10 AQU	9 PIS	11 TAU	10 GEM	11 LEO	10 VIR	8 LIB	10 SAG
11 LIB	10 SCO	12 SAG	10 CAP	13 PIS	12 ARI	14 GEM	12 CAN	13 VIR	12 LIB	11 SCO	12 CAP
14 VIR	12 SAG	14 CAP	13 AQU	15 ARI	14 TAU	16 CAN	14 LEO	15 LIB	14 SCO	13 SAG	15 AQU
16 SAG	15 CAP	17 AQU	15 PIS	18 TAU	16 GEM	18 LEO	16 VIR	17 SCO	16 SAG	15 CAP	17 PIS
19 CAP	17 AQU	19 PIS	18 ARI	20 GEM	18 CAN	20 VIR	18 LIB	19 SAG	19 CAP	17 AQU	20 ARI
21 AQU	20 PIS	22 ARI	20 TAU	22 CAN	20 LEO	22 LIB	20 SCO	21 CAP	21 AQU	20 PIS	22 TAU
24 PIS	22 ARI	24 TAU	23 GEM	24 LEO	22 VIR	24 SCO	23 SAG	24 AQU	24 PIS	22 ARI	25 GEM
26 ARI	25 TAU	26 GEM	25 CAN	26 VIR	25 LIB	26 SAG	25 CAP	26 PIS	26 ARI	25 TAU	27 CAN
29 TAU	27 GEM	29 CAN	27 LEO	28 LIB	27 SCO	29 CAP	27 AQU	29 ARI	28 TAU	27 GEM	29 LIB
31 GEM	28 GEM	31 LEO	29 VIR	31 SCO	29 SAG	31 AQU	30 PIS	30 ARI	31 GEM	29 CAN	31 SCO
			30 VIR		30 SAG		31 PIS			30 CAN	

1940

JAN	FEB	MAR	APR	MAY	JUN	JUL	AUG	SEP	OCT	NOV	DEC
1 VIR	1 SCO	1 SAG	1 CAP	1 AQU	1 ARI	1 TAU	1 CAN	1 LEO	1 LIB	1 SCO	1 CAP
2 LIB	3 SAG	3 CAP	2 AQU	2 PIS	3 TAU	3 GEM	4 LEO	2 VIR	3 SCO	2 SAG	4 AQU
4 SCO	5 CAP	6 AQU	4 PIS	4 ARI	5 GEM	5 CAN	6 VIR	4 LIB	5 SAG	4 CAP	6 PIS
6 SAG	7 AQU	8 PIS	7 ARI	7 TAU	8 CAN	7 LEO	8 LIB	6 SCO	8 CAP	6 AQU	8 ARI
9 CAP	10 PIS	11 ARI	9 TAU	9 GEM	10 LEO	9 VIR	10 SCO	8 SAG	10 AQU	9 PIS	11 TAU
11 AQU	12 ARI	13 TAU	12 GEM	11 CAN	12 VIR	11 LIB	12 SAG	10 CAP	12 PIS	11 ARI	14 GEM
14 PIS	15 TAU	16 GEM	14 CAN	14 LEO	14 LIB	14 SCO	14 CAP	13 AQU	15 ARI	14 TAU	16 CAN
16 ARI	17 GEM	18 CAN	16 LEO	16 VIR	16 SCO	16 SAG	16 AQU	15 PIS	17 TAU	16 GEM	18 LEO
19 TAU	20 CAN	20 LEO	19 VIR	18 LIB	18 SAG	18 CAP	19 PIS	18 ARI	20 GEM	19 CAN	20 VIR
21 GEM	22 LEO	22 VIR	21 LIB	20 SCO	21 CAP	20 AQU	21 ARI	20 TAU	22 CAN	21 LEO	23 LIB
23 CAN	24 VIR	24 LIB	23 SCO	22 SAG	23 AQU	23 PIS	24 TAU	23 GEM	25 LEO	23 VIR	25 SCO
25 LEO	26 LIB	26 SCO	25 SAG	24 CAP	25 PIS	25 ARI	26 GEM	25 CAN	27 VIR	25 LIB	27 SAG
27 VIR	28 SCO	28 SAG	27 CAP	26 AQU	28 ARI	28 TAU	29 CAN	27 LEO	29 LIB	27 SCO	29 CAP
29 LIB	29 SCO	30 CAP	29 AQU	29 PIS	30 TAU	30 GEM	31 LEO	29 VIR	31 SCO	29 SAG	31 AQU
31 SCO		31 CAP	30 AQU	31 ARI		31 GEM		30 VIR		30 SAG	

1941

JAN	FEB	MAR	APR	MAY	JUN	JUL	AUG	SEP	OCT	NOV	DEC
1 AQU	1 ARI	1 ARI	1 TAU	1 GEM	1 LEO	1 VIR	1 SCO	1 CAP	1 AQU	1 ARI	1 TAU
2 PIS	4 TAU	3 TAU	2 GEM	2 CAN	3 VIR	2 LIB	2 SAG	3 AQU	3 PIS	4 TAU	3 GEM
5 ARI	6 GEM	6 GEM	4 CAN	4 LEO	5 LIB	4 SCO	5 CAP	5 PIS	5 ARI	6 GEM	6 CAN
7 TAU	9 CAN	8 CAN	7 LEO	6 VIR	7 SCO	6 SAG	7 AQU	8 ARI	7 TAU	9 CAN	8 LEO
10 GEM	11 LEO	10 LEO	9 VIR	8 LIB	9 SAG	8 CAP	9 PIS	10 TAU	10 GEM	11 LEO	11 VIR
12 CAN	13 VIR	12 VIR	11 LIB	10 SCO	11 CAP	10 AQU	11 ARI	13 GEM	12 CAN	14 VIR	13 LIB
14 LEO	15 LIB	14 LIB	13 SCO	12 SAG	13 AQU	13 PIS	14 TAU	15 CAN	15 LEO	16 LIB	15 SCO
17 VIR	17 SCO	17 SCO	15 SAG	14 CAP	15 PIS	15 ARI	16 GEM	17 LEO	17 VIR	18 SCO	17 SAG
19 LIB	19 SAG	19 SAG	17 CAP	17 AQU	18 ARI	17 TAU	19 CAN	20 VIR	19 LIB	20 SAG	19 CAP
21 SCO	21 CAP	21 CAP	19 AQU	19 PIS	20 TAU	20 GEM	21 LIB	22 LIB	21 SCO	22 CAP	21 AQU
23 SAG	24 AQU	23 AQU	22 PIS	21 ARI	23 GEM	22 CAN	23 SCO	24 SCO	23 SAG	24 AQU	23 PIS
25 CAP	26 PIS	25 PIS	24 ARI	24 TAU	25 CAN	25 LEO	25 SAG	26 SAG	25 CAP	26 PIS	26 ARI
27 AQU	28 ARI	28 ARI	27 TAU	26 GEM	27 LEO	27 VIR	28 CAP	28 CAP	27 AQU	28 ARI	28 TAU
30 PIS		30 TAU	29 GEM	29 CAN	30 VIR	29 LIB	30 AQU	30 AQU	30 PIS	30 ARI	31 GEM
31 PIS		31 TAU	30 GEM	31 LEO		31 SCO	31 SAG		31 PIS		

1942

JAN	FEB	MAR	APR	MAY	JUN	JUL	AUG	SEP	OCT	NOV	DEC
1 GEM	1 LEO	1 LEO	1 LIB	1 SCO	1 CAP	1 AQU	1 ARI	1 ARI	1 GEM	1 LEO	1 VIR
2 CAN	3 VIR	3 VIR	3 SCO	3 SAG	3 AQU	3 PIS	4 TAU	2 GEM	2 CAN	4 VIR	3 LIB
5 LEO	6 LIB	5 LIB	5 SAG	5 CAP	5 PIS	5 ARI	6 GEM	5 CAN	5 LEO	6 LIB	6 SCO
7 VIR	8 SCO	7 SCO	7 CAP	7 AQU	8 ARI	7 TAU	9 CAN	7 LEO	7 VIR	8 SCO	8 SAG
9 LIB	10 SAG	9 SAG	10 AQU	9 PIS	10 TAU	10 GEM	11 LEO	10 VIR	9 LIB	10 SAG	10 CAP
12 SCO	12 CAP	11 CAP	12 PIS	11 ARI	13 GEM	12 CAN	14 VIR	12 LIB	12 SCO	12 CAP	12 AQU
14 SAG	14 AQU	13 AQU	14 ARI	14 TAU	15 CAN	15 LEO	16 LIB	14 SCO	14 SAG	14 AQU	14 PIS
16 CAP	16 PIS	16 PIS	17 TAU	16 GEM	18 LEO	17 VIR	18 SCO	16 SAG	16 CAP	16 PIS	16 ARI
18 AQU	18 ARI	18 ARI	19 GEM	19 CAN	20 VIR	20 LIB	20 SAG	19 CAP	18 AQU	19 ARI	18 TAU
20 PIS	21 TAU	20 TAU	22 CAN	21 LEO	22 LIB	22 SCO	22 CAP	21 AQU	20 PIS	21 TAU	21 GEM
22 ARI	23 GEM	23 GEM	24 LEO	24 VIR	25 SCO	24 SAG	24 AQU	23 PIS	22 ARI	23 GEM	23 CAN
24 TAU	26 CAN	25 CAN	26 VIR	26 LIB	27 SAG	26 CAP	26 PIS	25 ARI	25 TAU	26 CAN	26 LEO
27 GEM	28 LEO	28 LEO	29 LIB	28 SCO	29 CAP	28 ARI	29 ARI	27 TAU	27 GEM	28 LEO	28 VIR
30 CAN		30 VIR	30 LIB	30 SAG	30 CAP	30 PIS	31 TAU	30 GEM	30 CAN	30 LEO	31 LIB
31 CAN		31 VIR		31 SAG		31 PIS			31 CAN		

1943

JAN	FEB	MAR	APR	MAY	JUN	JUL	AUG	SEP	OCT	NOV	DEC
1 LIB	1 SAG	1 SAG	1 AQU	1 PIS	1 TAU	1 GEM	1 LEO	1 VIR	1 LIB	1 SAG	1 CAP
2 SCO	2 CAP	2 CAP	2 PIS	2 ARI	3 GEM	2 CAN	4 VIR	2 LIB	2 SCO	3 CAP	2 AQU
4 SAG	4 AQU	4 AQU	4 ARI	4 TAU	5 CAN	5 LEO	6 LIB	5 SCO	4 SAG	5 AQU	4 PIS
6 CAP	6 PIS	6 PIS	7 TAU	6 GEM	7 LEO	7 VIR	8 SCO	7 SAG	6 CAP	7 PIS	6 ARI
8 AQU	9 ARI	8 ARI	9 GEM	9 CAN	10 VIR	10 LIB	11 SAG	9 CAP	9 AQU	9 ARI	8 TAU
10 PIS	11 TAU	10 TAU	11 CAN	11 LEO	12 LIB	12 SCO	13 CAP	11 AQU	11 PIS	11 TAU	11 GEM
12 ARI	13 GEM	12 GEM	14 LEO	14 VIR	15 SCO	14 SAG	15 AQU	13 PIS	13 ARI	13 GEM	13 CAN
14 TAU	16 CAN	15 CAN	16 VIR	16 LIB	17 SAG	16 CAP	17 PIS	15 ARI	15 TAU	16 CAN	16 LEO
17 GEM	18 LEO	17 LEO	19 LIB	18 SCO	19 CAP	18 AQU	19 ARI	17 TAU	17 GEM	18 LEO	18 VIR
19 CAN	21 VIR	20 VIR	21 SCO	21 SAG	21 AQU	20 PIS	21 TAU	20 GEM	19 CAN	21 VIR	21 LIB
22 LEO	23 LIB	22 LIB	23 SAG	23 CAP	23 PIS	22 ARI	23 GEM	22 CAN	22 LEO	23 LIB	23 SCO
24 VIR	25 SCO	25 SCO	25 CAP	25 AQU	25 ARI	25 TAU	26 CAN	25 LEO	24 VIR	26 SCO	25 SAG
27 LIB	28 SAG	27 SAG	27 AQU	27 PIS	27 TAU	27 GEM	28 LEO	27 VIR	27 LIB	28 SAG	27 CAP
29 SCO		29 CAP	30 PIS	29 ARI	30 GEM	29 CAN	31 VIR	30 LIB	29 SCO	30 CAP	29 AQU
31 SAG		31 AQU		31 TAU		31 CAN			31 SAG		31 PIS

1944

JAN	FEB	MAR	APR	MAY	JUN	JUL	AUG	SEP	OCT	NOV	DEC
1 PIS	1 TAU	1 TAU	1 CAN	1 LEO	1 LIB	1 SCO	1 SAG	1 AQU	1 PIS	1 TAU	1 GEM
3 ARI	3 GEM	2 GEM	3 LEO	2 VIR	4 SCO	3 SAG	2 CAP	3 PIS	2 ARI	3 GEM	2 CAN
5 TAU	6 CAN	4 CAN	5 VIR	5 LIB	6 SAG	6 CAP	4 AQU	5 ARI	4 TAU	5 CAN	4 LEO
7 GEM	8 LEO	6 LEO	8 LIB	7 SCO	8 CAP	8 AQU	6 PIS	7 TAU	6 GEM	7 LEO	7 VIR
9 CAN	11 VIR	9 VIR	10 SCO	10 SAG	10 AQU	10 PIS	8 ARI	9 GEM	8 CAN	9 VIR	9 LIB
12 LEO	13 LIB	11 LIB	13 SAG	12 CAP	13 PIS	12 ARI	10 TAU	11 CAN	11 LEO	12 LIB	12 SCO
14 VIR	16 SCO	14 SCO	15 CAP	14 AQU	15 ARI	14 TAU	12 GEM	13 LEO	13 VIR	15 SCO	14 SAG
17 LIB	18 SAG	16 SAG	17 AQU	16 PIS	17 TAU	16 GEM	15 CAN	16 VIR	16 LIB	17 SAG	17 CAP
19 SCO	20 CAP	19 CAP	19 PIS	18 ARI	19 GEM	19 CAN	17 LEO	18 LIB	18 SCO	19 CAP	19 AQU
22 SAG	22 AQU	21 AQU	21 ARI	21 TAU	21 CAN	21 LEO	20 VIR	21 SCO	21 SAG	22 AQU	21 PIS
24 CAP	24 PIS	23 PIS	23 TAU	23 GEM	24 LEO	23 VIR	22 LIB	23 SAG	23 CAP	24 PIS	23 ARI
26 AQU	26 ARI	25 ARI	25 GEM	25 CAN	26 VIR	26 LIB	25 SCO	26 CAP	25 AQU	26 ARI	25 TAU
28 PIS	28 TAU	27 TAU	28 CAN	27 LEO	29 LIB	28 SCO	29 SAG	28 AQU	27 PIS	28 TAU	27 GEM
30 ARI	29 TAU	29 GEM	30 LEO	30 VIR	30 LIB	31 SAG	30 CAP	30 PIS	30 ARI	30 GEM	30 CAN
31 ARI		31 CAN		31 VIR			31 CAP		31 ARI		31 CAN

1945

JAN	FEB	MAR	APR	MAY	JUN	JUL	AUG	SEP	OCT	NOV	DEC
1 LEO	1 VIR	1 LIB	1 SCO	1 SAG	1 AQU	1 PIS	1 TAU	1 CAN	1 LEO	1 VIR	1 LIB
3 VIR	2 LIB	4 SCO	3 SAG	2 CAP	3 PIS	3 ARI	3 GEM	4 LEO	3 VIR	2 LIB	2 SCO
6 LIB	5 SCO	6 SAG	5 CAP	5 AQU	5 ARI	5 TAU	5 CAN	6 VIR	6 LIB	4 SCO	4 SAG
8 SCO	7 SAG	9 CAP	7 AQU	7 PIS	7 TAU	7 GEM	7 LEO	8 LIB	8 SCO	7 SAG	7 CAP
11 SAG	9 CAP	11 AQU	10 PIS	9 ARI	9 GEM	9 CAN	10 VIR	11 SCO	11 SAG	9 CAP	9 AQU
13 CAP	12 AQU	13 PIS	12 ARI	11 TAU	11 CAN	11 LEO	12 LIB	13 SAG	13 CAP	12 AQU	11 PIS
15 AQU	14 PIS	15 ARI	14 TAU	13 GEM	14 LEO	13 VIR	15 SCO	16 CAP	16 AQU	14 PIS	14 ARI
17 PIS	16 ARI	17 TAU	16 GEM	15 CAN	16 VIR	16 LIB	17 SAG	18 AQU	18 PIS	16 ARI	16 TAU
19 ARI	18 TAU	19 GEM	18 CAN	17 LEO	18 LIB	18 SCO	20 CAP	20 PIS	20 ARI	18 TAU	18 GEM
21 TAU	20 GEM	21 CAN	20 LEO	20 VIR	21 SCO	21 SAG	22 AQU	22 ARI	22 TAU	20 GEM	20 CAN
24 GEM	22 CAN	24 LEO	22 VIR	22 LIB	23 SAG	23 CAP	24 PIS	24 TAU	24 GEM	22 CAN	22 LEO
26 CAN	24 LEO	26 VIR	25 LIB	25 SCO	26 CAP	25 AQU	26 ARI	26 GEM	26 CAN	24 LEO	24 VIR
28 LEO	27 VIR	29 LIB	27 SCO	27 SAG	28 AQU	28 PIS	28 TAU	29 CAN	28 LEO	27 VIR	26 LIB
31 VIR	28 VIR	31 SCO	30 SAG	30 CAP	30 PIS	30 ARI	30 GEM	30 CAN	30 VIR	29 LIB	29 SCO
				31 CAP		31 ARI	31 GEM		31 VIR	30 LIB	31 SCO

1946

JAN	FEB	MAR	APR	MAY	JUN	JUL	AUG	SEP	OCT	NOV	DEC
1 SAG	1 CAP	1 AQU	1 PIS	1 TAU	1 GEM	1 LEO	1 VIR	1 SCO	1 SAG	1 CAP	1 AQU
3 CAP	2 AQU	3 PIS	2 ARI	3 GEM	2 CAN	3 VIR	2 LIB	3 SAG	3 CAP	2 AQU	2 PIS
5 AQU	4 PIS	5 ARI	4 TAU	5 CAN	4 LEO	6 LIB	4 SCO	6 CAP	6 AQU	4 PIS	4 ARI
8 PIS	6 ARI	8 TAU	6 GEM	7 LEO	6 VIR	8 SCO	7 SAG	8 AQU	8 PIS	7 ARI	6 TAU
10 ARI	8 TAU	10 GEM	8 CAN	10 VIR	8 LIB	11 SAG	9 CAP	11 PIS	10 ARI	9 TAU	8 GEM
12 TAU	10 GEM	12 CAN	10 LEO	12 LIB	11 SCO	13 CAP	12 AQU	13 ARI	12 TAU	11 GEM	10 CAN
14 GEM	13 CAN	14 LEO	12 VIR	15 SCO	13 SAG	16 AQU	14 PIS	15 TAU	14 GEM	13 CAN	12 LEO
16 CAN	15 LEO	16 VIR	15 LIB	17 SAG	16 CAP	18 PIS	16 ARI	17 GEM	16 CAN	15 LEO	14 VIR
18 LEO	17 VIR	19 LIB	17 SCO	20 CAP	18 AQU	20 ARI	19 TAU	19 CAN	19 LEO	17 VIR	17 LIB
21 VIR	19 LIB	21 SCO	20 SAG	22 AQU	21 PIS	22 TAU	21 GEM	21 LEO	21 VIR	19 LIB	19 SCO
23 LIB	22 SCO	24 SAG	22 CAP	24 PIS	23 ARI	25 GEM	23 CAN	23 VIR	23 LIB	22 SCO	21 SAG
25 SCO	24 SAG	26 CAP	25 AQU	27 ARI	25 TAU	27 CAN	25 LEO	26 LIB	25 SCO	24 SAG	24 CAP
28 SAG	27 CAP	28 AQU	27 PIS	29 TAU	27 GEM	29 LEO	27 VIR	28 SCO	28 SAG	27 CAP	26 AQU
30 CAP	28 CAP	31 PIS	29 ARI	31 GEM	29 CAN	31 VIR	29 LIB	30 SCO	30 CAP	29 AQU	29 PIS
31 CAP			30 ARI		30 CAN		31 LIB		31 CAP	30 AQU	31 ARI

1947

JAN	FEB	MAR	APR	MAY	JUN	JUL	AUG	SEP	OCT	NOV	DEC
1 ARI	1 GEM	1 GEM	1 LEO	1 VIR	1 SCO	1 SAG	1 CAP	1 PIS	1 ARI	1 GEM	1 CAN
3 TAU	3 CAN	2 CAN	3 VIR	2 LIB	3 SAG	3 CAP	2 AQU	3 ARI	3 TAU	3 CAN	3 LEO
5 GEM	5 LEO	4 LEO	5 LIB	5 SCO	6 CAP	6 AQU	4 PIS	5 TAU	5 GEM	5 LEO	5 VIR
7 CAN	7 VIR	7 VIR	7 SCO	7 SAG	8 AQU	8 PIS	7 ARI	8 GEM	7 CAN	7 VIR	7 LIB
9 LEO	9 LIB	9 LIB	10 SAG	9 CAP	11 PIS	11 ARI	9 TAU	10 CAN	9 LEO	10 LIB	9 SCO
11 VIR	12 SCO	11 SCO	12 CAP	12 AQU	13 ARI	13 TAU	11 GEM	12 LEO	11 VIR	12 SCO	11 SAG
13 LIB	14 SAG	13 SAG	15 AQU	15 PIS	15 TAU	15 GEM	13 CAN	14 VIR	13 LIB	14 SAG	14 CAP
15 SCO	17 CAP	16 CAP	17 PIS	17 ARI	18 GEM	17 CAN	15 LEO	16 LIB	15 SCO	17 CAP	16 AQU
18 SAG	19 AQU	18 AQU	19 ARI	19 TAU	20 CAN	19 LEO	17 VIR	18 SCO	18 SAG	19 AQU	19 PIS
20 CAP	21 PIS	21 PIS	22 TAU	21 GEM	22 LEO	21 VIR	20 LIB	20 SAG	20 CAP	22 PIS	21 ARI
23 AQU	24 ARI	23 ARI	24 GEM	23 CAN	24 VIR	23 LIB	22 SCO	23 CAP	23 AQU	24 ARI	24 TAU
25 PIS	26 TAU	25 TAU	26 CAN	25 LEO	26 LIB	25 SCO	24 SAG	25 AQU	25 PIS	26 TAU	26 GEM
28 ARI	28 GEM	27 GEM	28 LEO	27 VIR	28 SCO	28 SAG	27 CAP	28 PIS	28 ARI	28 GEM	28 CAN
30 TAU		30 CAN	30 VIR	30 LIB	30 SCO	30 CAP	29 AQU	30 ARI	30 TAU	30 GEM	30 LEO
31 TAU		31 CAN		31 LIB		31 CAP	31 AQU		31 TAU		31 LEO

1948

JAN	FEB	MAR	APR	MAY	JUN	JUL	AUG	SEP	OCT	NOV	DEC
1 VIR	1 LIB	1 SCO	1 CAP	1 AQU	1 PIS	1 ARI	1 GEM	1 LEO	1 VIR	1 SCO	1 SAG
3 LIB	2 SCO	2 SAG	3 AQU	3 PIS	2 ARI	2 TAU	3 CAN	3 VIR	3 LIB	3 SAG	3 CAP
5 SCO	4 SAG	5 CAP	6 PIS	6 ARI	5 TAU	4 GEM	5 LEO	5 LIB	5 SCO	5 CAP	5 AQU
8 SAG	6 CAP	7 AQU	8 ARI	8 TAU	7 GEM	6 CAN	7 VIR	7 SCO	7 SAG	8 AQU	8 PIS
10 CAP	9 AQU	10 PIS	11 TAU	10 GEM	9 CAN	8 LEO	9 LIB	9 SAG	9 CAP	10 PIS	10 ARI
13 AQU	11 PIS	12 ARI	13 GEM	13 CAN	11 LEO	10 VIR	11 SCO	12 CAP	12 AQU	13 ARI	13 TAU
15 PIS	14 ARI	15 TAU	15 CAN	15 LEO	13 VIR	12 LIB	13 SAG	14 AQU	14 PIS	15 TAU	15 GEM
18 ARI	16 TAU	17 GEM	18 LEO	17 VIR	15 LIB	15 SCO	16 CAP	17 PIS	17 ARI	18 GEM	17 CAN
20 TAU	19 GEM	19 CAN	20 VIR	19 LIB	17 SCO	17 SAG	18 AQU	19 ARI	19 TAU	20 CAN	19 LEO
22 GEM	21 CAN	21 LEO	22 LIB	21 SCO	20 SAG	19 CAP	21 PIS	22 TAU	21 GEM	22 LEO	22 VIR
24 CAN	23 LEO	23 VIR	24 SCO	23 SAG	22 CAP	22 AQU	23 ARI	24 GEM	24 CAN	24 VIR	24 LIB
26 LEO	25 VIR	25 LIB	26 SAG	26 CAP	24 AQU	24 PIS	26 TAU	26 CAN	26 LEO	26 LIB	26 SCO
28 VIR	27 LIB	27 SCO	28 CAP	28 AQU	27 PIS	27 ARI	28 GEM	29 LEO	28 VIR	29 SCO	28 SAG
30 LIB	29 SCO	30 SAG	30 CAP	31 PIS	29 ARI	29 TAU	30 CAN	30 LEO	30 LIB	30 SCO	30 CAP
31 LIB		31 SAG			30 ARI	31 TAU	31 CAN		31 LIB		30 CAP

1949

JAN	FEB	MAR	APR	MAY	JUN	JUL	AUG	SEP	OCT	NOV	DEC
1 CAP	1 PIS	1 PIS	1 TAU	1 GEM	1 CAN	1 VIR	1 SCO	1 SAG	1 CAP	1 PIS	1 ARI
2 AQU	3 ARI	2 ARI	3 GEM	3 CAN	2 LEO	3 LIB	4 SAG	2 CAP	2 AQU	3 ARI	3 TAU
4 PIS	5 TAU	5 TAU	6 CAN	5 LEO	4 VIR	5 SCO	6 CAP	4 AQU	4 PIS	5 TAU	5 GEM
7 ARI	8 GEM	7 GEM	8 LEO	7 VIR	6 LIB	7 SAG	8 AQU	7 PIS	6 ARI	8 GEM	7 CAN
9 TAU	10 CAN	10 CAN	10 VIR	10 LIB	8 SCO	10 CAP	10 PIS	9 ARI	9 TAU	10 CAN	10 LEO
11 GEM	12 LEO	12 LEO	12 LIB	12 SCO	10 SAG	12 AQU	13 ARI	12 TAU	12 GEM	13 LEO	12 VIR
14 CAN	14 VIR	14 VIR	14 SCO	14 SAG	12 CAP	14 PIS	15 TAU	14 GEM	14 CAN	15 VIR	14 LIB
16 LEO	16 LIB	16 LIB	16 SAG	16 CAP	14 AQU	17 ARI	18 GEM	17 CAN	16 LEO	17 LIB	16 SCO
18 VIR	18 SCO	18 SCO	18 CAP	18 AQU	17 PIS	19 TAU	20 CAN	19 LEO	18 VIR	19 SCO	18 SAG
20 LIB	20 SAG	20 SAG	21 AQU	20 PIS	19 ARI	22 GEM	23 LEO	21 VIR	21 LIB	21 SAG	20 CAP
22 SCO	23 CAP	22 CAP	23 PIS	23 ARI	22 TAU	24 CAN	25 VIR	23 LIB	23 SCO	23 CAP	23 AQU
24 SAG	25 AQU	24 AQU	26 ARI	25 TAU	24 GEM	26 LEO	27 LIB	25 SCO	25 SAG	25 AQU	25 PIS
27 CAP	28 PIS	27 PIS	28 TAU	28 GEM	27 CAN	28 VIR	29 SCO	27 SAG	27 CAP	28 PIS	27 ARI
29 AQU		29 ARI	30 TAU	30 CAN	29 LEO	30 LIB	31 SAG	29 CAP	29 AQU	30 ARI	30 TAU
31 PIS		31 ARI		31 CAN	30 LEO	31 LIB		30 CAP	31 PIS		31 TAU

1950

JAN	FEB	MAR	APR	MAY	JUN	JUL	AUG	SEP	OCT	NOV	DEC
1 GEM	1 CAN	1 CAN	1 VIR	1 LIB	1 SAG	1 CAP	1 PIS	1 ARI	1 GEM	1 CAN	1 LEO
4 CAN	2 LEO	2 LEO	3 LIB	2 SCO	2 CAP	2 AQU	3 ARI	2 TAU	4 CAN	3 LEO	2 VIR
6 LEO	5 VIR	4 VIR	5 SCO	4 SAG	4 AQU	4 PIS	5 TAU	4 GEM	6 LEO	5 VIR	5 LIB
8 VIR	7 LIB	6 LIB	7 SAG	6 CAP	7 PIS	6 ARI	8 GEM	7 CAN	9 VIR	7 LIB	7 SCO
10 LIB	9 SCO	8 SCO	9 CAP	8 AQU	9 ARI	9 TAU	10 CAN	9 LEO	11 LIB	9 SCO	9 SAG
13 SCO	11 SAG	10 SAG	11 AQU	10 PIS	12 TAU	11 GEM	13 LEO	11 VIR	13 SCO	11 SAG	11 CAP
15 SAG	13 CAP	12 CAP	13 PIS	13 ARI	14 GEM	14 CAN	15 VIR	13 LIB	15 SAG	13 CAP	13 AQU
17 CAP	15 AQU	15 AQU	16 ARI	15 TAU	16 CAN	16 LEO	17 LIB	16 SCO	17 CAP	15 AQU	15 PIS
19 AQU	18 PIS	17 PIS	18 TAU	18 GEM	19 LEO	19 VIR	19 SCO	18 SAG	19 AQU	18 PIS	17 ARI
21 PIS	20 ARI	19 ARI	21 GEM	20 CAN	21 VIR	21 LIB	21 SAG	20 CAP	21 PIS	20 ARI	20 TAU
24 ARI	23 TAU	22 TAU	23 CAN	23 LEO	24 LIB	23 SCO	23 CAP	22 AQU	24 ARI	22 TAU	22 GEM
26 TAU	25 GEM	24 GEM	26 LEO	25 VIR	26 SCO	25 SAG	26 AQU	24 PIS	26 TAU	25 GEM	25 CAN
29 GEM	28 CAN	27 CAN	28 VIR	27 LIB	28 SAG	27 CAP	28 PIS	26 ARI	29 GEM	28 CAN	27 LEO
31 CAN		29 LEO	30 LIB	29 SCO	30 CAP	29 AQU	30 ARI	29 TAU	31 CAN	30 LEO	30 VIR
		31 VIR		31 SAG		31 PIS	31 ARI	30 TAU			31 VIR

1951

JAN	FEB	MAR	APR	MAY	JUN	JUL	AUG	SEP	OCT	NOV	DEC
1 LIB	1 SCO	1 SAG	1 AQU	1 PIS	1 ARI	1 GEM	1 CAN	1 VIR	1 LIB	1 SCO	1 CAP
3 SCO	2 SAG	3 CAP	3 PIS	3 ARI	2 TAU	4 CAN	3 LEO	4 LIB	3 SCO	2 SAG	3 AQU
5 SAG	4 CAP	5 AQU	6 ARI	5 TAU	4 GEM	6 LEO	5 VIR	6 SCO	5 SAG	4 CAP	5 PIS
7 CAP	6 AQU	7 PIS	8 TAU	8 GEM	7 CAN	9 VIR	7 LIB	8 SAG	8 CAP	6 AQU	7 ARI
9 AQU	8 PIS	9 ARI	11 GEM	10 CAN	9 LEO	11 LIB	10 SCO	10 CAP	10 AQU	8 PIS	10 TAU
11 PIS	10 ARI	12 TAU	13 CAN	13 LEO	12 VIR	14 SCO	12 SAG	12 AQU	12 PIS	10 ARI	12 GEM
14 ARI	12 TAU	14 GEM	16 LEO	15 VIR	14 LIB	16 SAG	14 CAP	14 PIS	14 ARI	13 TAU	15 CAN
16 TAU	15 GEM	17 CAN	18 VIR	18 LIB	16 SCO	18 CAP	16 AQU	17 ARI	16 TAU	15 GEM	17 LEO
19 GEM	17 CAN	19 LEO	20 LIB	20 SCO	18 SAG	20 AQU	18 PIS	19 TAU	19 GEM	17 CAN	20 VIR
21 CAN	20 LEO	22 VIR	22 SCO	22 SAG	20 CAP	22 PIS	20 ARI	21 GEM	21 CAN	20 LEO	22 LIB
24 LEO	22 VIR	24 LIB	24 SAG	24 CAP	22 AQU	24 ARI	22 TAU	24 CAN	24 LEO	22 VIR	24 SCO
26 VIR	24 LIB	26 SCO	26 CAP	26 AQU	24 PIS	26 TAU	25 GEM	26 LEO	26 VIR	25 LIB	27 SAG
28 LIB	27 SCO	28 SAG	28 AQU	28 PIS	26 ARI	29 GEM	27 CAN	29 VIR	28 LIB	27 SCO	29 CAP
30 SCO	28 SCO	30 CAP	30 AQU	30 ARI	29 TAU	31 CAN	30 LEO	30 VIR	31 SCO	29 SAG	31 AQU
31 SCO		31 CAP		31 ARI	30 TAU		31 LEO			30 SAG	

1952

JAN	FEB	MAR	APR	MAY	JUN	JUL	AUG	SEP	OCT	NOV	DEC
1 AQU	1 ARI	1 TAU	1 GEM	1 CAN	1 VIR	1 LIB	1 SAG	1 CAP	1 PIS	1 ARI	1 GEM
2 PIS	2 TAU	3 GEM	2 CAN	2 LEO	3 LIB	3 SCO	3 CAP	2 AQU	3 ARI	2 TAU	4 CAN
4 ARI	5 GEM	5 CAN	4 LEO	4 VIR	5 SCO	5 SAG	5 AQU	4 PIS	5 TAU	4 GEM	6 LEO
6 TAU	7 CAN	8 LEO	7 VIR	7 LIB	8 SAG	7 CAP	7 PIS	6 ARI	8 GEM	6 CAN	9 VIR
8 GEM	10 LEO	11 VIR	9 LIB	9 SCO	10 CAP	9 AQU	9 ARI	8 TAU	10 CAN	9 LEO	11 LIB
11 CAN	12 VIR	13 LIB	12 SCO	11 SAG	12 AQU	11 PIS	12 TAU	10 GEM	12 LEO	11 VIR	14 SCO
13 LEO	15 LIB	15 SCO	14 SAG	13 CAP	14 PIS	13 ARI	14 GEM	13 CAN	15 VIR	14 LIB	16 SAG
16 VIR	17 SCO	18 SAG	16 CAP	15 AQU	16 ARI	15 TAU	16 CAN	15 LEO	17 LIB	16 SCO	18 CAP
18 LIB	19 SAG	20 CAP	18 AQU	17 PIS	18 TAU	18 GEM	19 LEO	18 VIR	20 SCO	18 SAG	20 AQU
21 SCO	21 CAP	22 AQU	20 PIS	20 ARI	20 GEM	20 CAN	21 VIR	20 LIB	22 SAG	21 CAP	22 PIS
23 SAG	23 AQU	24 PIS	22 ARI	22 TAU	23 CAN	23 LEO	24 LIB	23 SCO	24 CAP	23 AQU	24 ARI
25 CAP	26 PIS	26 ARI	25 TAU	24 GEM	25 LEO	25 VIR	26 SCO	25 SAG	26 AQU	25 PIS	26 TAU
27 AQU	28 ARI	28 TAU	27 GEM	27 CAN	28 VIR	28 LIB	29 SAG	27 CAP	29 PIS	27 ARI	29 GEM
29 PIS	29 ARI	30 GEM	29 CAN	29 LEO	30 LIB	30 SCO	31 CAP	29 AQU	31 ARI	29 TAU	31 CAN
31 ARI		31 GEM	30 CAN	31 LEO		31 SCO		30 AQU		30 TAU	

1953

JAN	FEB	MAR	APR	MAY	JUN	JUL	AUG	SEP	OCT	NOV	DEC
1 CAN	1 VIR	1 VIR	1 LIB	1 SAG	1 CAP	1 AQU	1 ARI	1 GEM	1 CAN	1 VIR	1 LIB
2 LEO	4 LIB	3 LIB	2 SCO	4 CAP	2 AQU	2 PIS	2 TAU	3 CAN	2 LEO	4 LIB	3 SCO
5 VIR	6 SCO	5 SCO	4 SAG	6 AQU	4 PIS	4 ARI	4 GEM	5 LEO	5 VIR	6 SCO	6 SAG
7 LIB	9 SAG	8 SAG	6 CAP	8 PIS	6 ARI	6 TAU	6 CAN	8 VIR	7 LIB	9 SAG	8 CAP
10 SCO	11 CAP	10 CAP	9 AQU	10 ARI	8 TAU	8 GEM	9 LEO	10 LIB	10 SCO	11 CAP	10 AQU
12 SAG	13 AQU	12 AQU	11 PIS	12 TAU	11 GEM	10 CAN	11 VIR	13 SCO	12 SAG	13 AQU	13 PIS
14 CAP	15 PIS	14 PIS	13 ARI	14 GEM	13 CAN	13 LEO	14 LIB	15 SAG	15 CAP	15 PIS	15 ARI
16 AQU	17 ARI	16 ARI	15 TAU	16 CAN	15 LEO	15 VIR	16 SCO	17 CAP	17 AQU	18 ARI	17 TAU
18 PIS	19 TAU	18 TAU	17 GEM	19 LEO	18 VIR	18 LIB	19 SAG	20 AQU	19 PIS	20 TAU	19 GEM
20 ARI	21 GEM	20 GEM	19 CAN	21 VIR	20 LIB	20 SCO	21 CAP	22 PIS	21 ARI	22 GEM	21 CAN
23 TAU	23 CAN	23 CAN	21 LEO	24 LIB	23 SCO	22 SAG	23 AQU	24 ARI	23 TAU	24 CAN	23 LEO
25 GEM	26 LEO	25 LEO	24 VIR	26 SCO	25 SAG	25 CAP	25 PIS	26 TAU	25 GEM	26 LEO	26 VIR
27 CAN	28 VIR	28 VIR	27 LIB	29 SAG	27 CAP	27 AQU	27 ARI	28 GEM	27 CAN	28 VIR	28 LIB
30 LEO		30 LIB	29 SCO	31 CAP	29 AQU	29 PIS	29 TAU	30 CAN	30 LEO	30 VIR	31 SCO
31 LEO		31 LIB	30 SCO		30 AQU	31 ARI	31 GEM		31 LEO		

1954

JAN	FEB	MAR	APR	MAY	JUN	JUL	AUG	SEP	OCT	NOV	DEC
1 SCO	1 CAP	1 CAP	1 PIS	1 ARI	1 GEM	1 CAN	1 VIR	1 LIB	1 SCO	1 CAP	1 AQU
2 SAG	3 AQU	3 AQU	3 ARI	3 TAU	3 CAN	3 LEO	4 LIB	2 SCO	2 SAG	4 AQU	3 PIS
5 CAP	5 PIS	5 PIS	5 TAU	5 GEM	5 LEO	5 VIR	6 SCO	5 SAG	5 CAP	6 PIS	5 ARI
7 AQU	7 ARI	7 ARI	7 GEM	7 CAN	8 VIR	7 LIB	9 SAG	7 CAP	7 AQU	8 ARI	7 TAU
9 PIS	9 TAU	9 TAU	9 CAN	9 LEO	10 LIB	10 SCO	11 CAP	10 AQU	9 PIS	10 TAU	9 GEM
11 ARI	11 GEM	11 GEM	12 LEO	11 VIR	12 SCO	12 SAG	13 AQU	12 PIS	11 ARI	12 GEM	11 CAN
13 TAU	14 CAN	13 CAN	14 VIR	14 LIB	15 SAG	15 CAP	16 PIS	14 TAU	13 TAU	14 CAN	13 LEO
15 GEM	16 LEO	15 LEO	16 LIB	16 SCO	17 CAP	17 AQU	18 ARI	16 GEM	15 GEM	16 LEO	16 VIR
17 CAN	18 VIR	18 VIR	19 SCO	19 SAG	20 AQU	19 PIS	20 TAU	18 CAN	18 CAN	18 VIR	18 LIB
20 LEO	21 LIB	20 LIB	21 SAG	21 CAP	22 PIS	21 ARI	22 GEM	20 LEO	20 LEO	21 LIB	21 SCO
22 VIR	23 SCO	23 SCO	24 CAP	24 AQU	24 ARI	24 TAU	24 CAN	23 VIR	22 VIR	23 SCO	23 SAG
25 LIB	26 SAG	25 SAG	26 AQU	26 PIS	26 TAU	26 GEM	26 LEO	25 LIB	25 LIB	26 SAG	26 CAP
27 SCO	28 CAP	28 CAP	29 PIS	28 ARI	28 GEM	28 CAN	29 VIR	27 SCO	27 SCO	28 CAP	28 AQU
30 SAG		30 AQU	30 PIS	30 TAU	30 CAN	30 LEO	31 LIB	30 SCO	30 SAG	30 CAP	30 PIS
31 SAG				31 TAU		31 LEO			31 SAG		31 PIS

1955

JAN	FEB	MAR	APR	MAY	JUN	JUL	AUG	SEP	OCT	NOV	DEC
1 PIS	1 TAU	1 GEM	1 CAN	1 VIR	1 LIB	1 SCO	1 CAP	1 AQU	1 PIS	1 TAU	1 GEM
2 ARI	2 GEM	3 CAN	2 LEO	4 LIB	2 SCO	2 SAG	3 AQU	2 PIS	2 ARI	2 GEM	2 CAN
4 TAU	4 CAN	6 LEO	4 VIR	6 SCO	5 SAG	5 CAP	6 PIS	4 ARI	4 TAU	4 CAN	4 LEO
6 GEM	6 LEO	8 VIR	6 LIB	9 SAG	7 CAP	7 AQU	8 ARI	7 TAU	6 GEM	6 LEO	6 VIR
8 CAN	8 VIR	10 LIB	9 SCO	11 CAP	10 AQU	1O PIS	10 TAU	9 GEM	8 CAN	9 VIR	8 LIB
10 LEO	11 LIB	13 SCO	11 SAG	14 AQU	12 PIS	12 ARI	12 GEM	11 CAN	10 LEO	11 LIB	10 SCO
12 VIR	13 SCO	15 SAG	14 CAP	16 PIS	15 ARI	14 TAU	15 CAN	13 LEO	12 VIR	13 SCO	13 SAG
14 LIB	16 SAG	18 CAP	16 AQU	18 ARI	17 TAU	16 GEM	17 LEO	15 VIR	15 LIB	16 SAG	16 CAP
17 SCO	18 CAP	20 AQU	19 PIS	20 TAU	19 GEM	18 CAN	19 VIR	17 LIB	17 SCO	18 CAP	18 AQU
19 SAG	21 AQU	22 PIS	21 ARI	22 GEM	21 CAN	20 LEO	21 LIB	20 SCO	19 SAG	21 AQU	21 PIS
22 CAP	23 PIS	24 ARI	23 TAU	24 CAN	23 LEO	22 VIR	23 SCO	22 SAG	22 CAP	23 PIS	23 ARI
24 AQU	25 ARI	27 TAU	25 GEM	26 LEO	25 VIR	25 LIB	26 SAG	25 CAP	24 AQU	26 ARI	25 TAU
27 PIS	27 TAU	29 GEM	27 CAN	29 VIR	27 LIB	27 SCO	28 CAP	27 AQU	27 PIS	28 TAU	27 GEM
29 ARI	28 TAU	31 CAN	29 LEO	31 LIB	30 SCO	29 SAG	31 AQU	30 PIS	29 ARI	30 GEM	29 CAN
31 TAU			30 LEO			31 SAG			31 TAU		31 LEO

1956

JAN	FEB	MAR	APR	MAY	JUN	JUL	AUG	SEP	OCT	NOV	DEC
1 LEO	1 LIB	1 SCO	1 SAG	1 CAP	1 PIS	1 ARI	1 TAU	1 CAN	1 LEO	1 LIB	1 SCO
2 VIR	3 SCO	4 SAG	3 CAP	3 AQU	4 ARI	3 TAU	2 GEM	2 LEO	2 VIR	2 SCO	2 SAG
4 LIB	6 SAG	6 CAP	5 AQU	5 PIS	6 TAU	6 GEM	4 CAN	4 VIR	4 LIB	5 SAG	4 CAP
7 SCO	8 CAP	9 AQU	8 PIS	7 ARI	8 GEM	8 CAN	6 LEO	7 LIB	6 SCO	7 CAP	7 AQU
9 SAG	11 AQU	11 PIS	10 ARI	10 TAU	10 CAN	10 LEO	8 VIR	9 SCO	8 SAG	10 AQU	9 PIS
12 CAP	13 PIS	14 ARI	12 TAU	12 GEM	12 LEO	12 VIR	10 LIB	11 SAG	11 CAP	12 PIS	12 ARI
14 AQU	15 ARI	16 TAU	14 GEM	14 CAN	14 VIR	14 LIB	12 SCO	13 CAP	13 AQU	15 ARI	14 TAU
17 PIS	18 TAU	18 GEM	17 CAN	16 LEO	16 LIB	16 SCO	15 SAG	16 AQU	16 PIS	17 TAU	17 GEM
19 ARI	20 GEM	20 CAN	19 LEO	18 VIR	19 SCO	18 SAG	17 CAP	18 PIS	18 ARI	19 GEM	19 CAN
21 TAU	22 CAN	22 LEO	21 VIR	20 LIB	21 SAG	21 CAP	20 AQU	21 ARI	21 TAU	21 CAN	21 LEO
24 GEM	24 LEO	24 VIR	23 LIB	22 SCO	24 CAP	23 AQU	22 PIS	23 TAU	23 GEM	23 LEO	23 VIR
26 CAN	26 VIR	27 LIB	25 SCO	25 SAG	26 AQU	26 PIS	25 ARI	25 GEM	25 CAN	25 VIR	25 LIB
28 LEO	28 LIB	29 SCO	28 SAG	27 CAP	29 PIS	28 ARI	27 TAU	28 CAN	27 LEO	28 LIB	27 SCO
30 VIR	29 LIB	31 SAG	30 CAP	30 AQU	30 PIS	31 TAU	29 GEM	30 LEO	29 VIR	30 SCO	29 SAG
31 VIR				31 AQU			31 CAN		31 LIB		31 SAG

1957

JAN	FEB	MAR	APR	MAY	JUN	JUL	AUG	SEP	OCT	NOV	DEC
1 CAP	1 AQU	1 PIS	1 ARI	1 TAU	1 CAN	1 LEO	1 LIB	1 SAG	1 CAP	1 AQU	1 PIS
3 AQU	2 PIS	4 ARI	2 TAU	2 GEM	3 LEO	2 VIR	3 SCO	3 CAP	3 AQU	2 PIS	2 ARI
6 PIS	5 ARI	6 TAU	5 GEM	4 CAN	5 VIR	4 LIB	5 SAG	6 AQU	6 PIS	4 ARI	4 TAU
8 ARI	7 TAU	9 GEM	7 CAN	6 LEO	7 LIB	6 SCO	7 CAP	8 PIS	8 ARI	7 TAU	7 GEM
11 TAU	9 GEM	11 CAN	9 LEO	9 VIR	9 SCO	9 SAG	10 AQU	11 ARI	11 TAU	9 GEM	9 CAN
13 GEM	11 CAN	13 LEO	11 VIR	11 LIB	11 SAG	11 CAP	12 PIS	13 TAU	13 GEM	12 CAN	11 LEO
15 CAN	14 LEO	15 VIR	13 LIB	13 SCO	14 CAP	13 AQU	15 ARI	16 GEM	15 CAN	14 LEO	13 VIR
17 LEO	15 VIR	17 LIB	15 SCO	15 SAG	16 AQU	16 PIS	17 TAU	18 CAN	18 LEO	16 VIR	15 LIB
19 VIR	17 LIB	19 SCO	18 SAG	17 CAP	19 PIS	18 ARI	20 GEM	20 LEO	20 VIR	18 LIB	17 SCO
21 LIB	20 SCO	21 SAG	20 CAP	20 AQU	21 ARI	21 TAU	22 CAN	22 VIR	22 LIB	20 SCO	20 SAG
23 SCO	22 SAG	24 CAP	22 AQU	22 PIS	23 TAU	23 GEM	24 LEO	24 LIB	24 SCO	22 SAG	22 CAP
26 SAG	24 CAP	26 AQU	25 PIS	25 ARI	26 GEM	25 CAN	26 VIR	26 SCO	26 SAG	24 CAP	24 AQU
28 CAP	27 AQU	29 PIS	27 ARI	27 TAU	28 CAN	27 LEO	28 LIB	28 SAG	28 CAP	27 AQU	27 PIS
30 AQU	28 AQU	31 ARI	30 TAU	29 GEM	30 LEO	29 VIR	30 SCO	30 SAG	30 AQU	29 PIS	29 ARI
31 AQU				31 GEM		31 LIB	31 SCO		31 AQU	30 PIS	31 ARI

1958

JAN	FEB	MAR	APR	MAY	JUN	JUL	AUG	SEP	OCT	NOV	DEC
1 TAU	1 GEM	1 CAN	1 LEO	1 LIB	1 SCO	1 CAP	1 AQU	1 ARI	1 TAU	1 GEM	1 LEO
3 GEM	2 CAN	3 LEO	2 VIR	3 SCO	2 SAG	3 AQU	2 PIS	3 TAU	3 GEM	2 CAN	4 VIR
5 CAN	4 LEO	5 VIR	4 LIB	5 SAG	4 CAP	6 PIS	4 ARI	6 GEM	6 CAN	4 LEO	6 LIB
7 LEO	6 VIR	7 LIB	6 SCO	7 CAP	6 AQU	8 ARI	7 TAU	8 CAN	8 LEO	6 VIR	8 SCO
9 VIR	8 LIB	9 SCO	8 SAG	10 AQU	8 PIS	11 TAU	10 GEM	11 LEO	10 VIR	9 LIB	10 SAG
12 LIB	10 SCO	11 SAG	10 CAP	12 PIS	11 ARI	13 GEM	12 CAN	13 VIR	12 LIB	11 SCO	12 CAP
14 SCO	12 SAG	14 CAP	12 AQU	14 ARI	13 TAU	16 CAN	14 LEO	15 LIB	14 SCO	13 SAG	14 AQU
16 SAG	14 CAP	16 AQU	15 PIS	17 TAU	16 GEM	18 LEO	16 VIR	17 SCO	16 SAG	15 CAP	16 PIS
18 CAP	17 AQU	18 PIS	17 ARI	20 GEM	18 CAN	20 VIR	18 LIB	19 SAG	18 CAP	17 AQU	19 ARI
20 AQU	19 PIS	21 ARI	20 TAU	22 CAN	20 LEO	22 LIB	20 SCO	21 CAP	20 AQU	19 PIS	21 TAU
23 PIS	22 ARI	24 TAU	22 GEM	24 LEO	23 VIR	24 SCO	22 SAG	23 AQU	23 PIS	22 ARI	24 GEM
25 ARI	24 TAU	26 GEM	25 CAN	26 VIR	25 LIB	26 SAG	25 CAP	26 PIS	25 ARI	24 TAU	26 CAN
28 TAU	27 GEM	28 CAN	27 LEO	28 LIB	27 SCO	28 CAP	27 AQU	28 ARI	28 TAU	27 GEM	29 LEO
30 GEM	28 GEM	31 LEO	29 VIR	31 SCO	29 SAG	31 AQU	29 PIS	30 ARI	30 GEM	29 CAN	31 VIR
31 GEM			30 VIR		30 SAG		31 PIS		31 GEM	30 CAN	

1959

JAN	FEB	MAR	APR	MAY	JUN	JUL	AUG	SEP	OCT	NOV	DEC
1 VIR	1 SCO	1 SCO	1 CAP	1 AQU	1 ARI	1 TAU	1 GEM	1 LEO	1 VIR	1 SCO	1 SAG
2 LIB	3 SAG	2 SAG	2 AQU	2 PIS	3 TAU	3 GEM	2 CAN	3 VIR	2 LIB	3 SAG	2 CAP
4 SCO	5 CAP	4 CAP	5 PIS	4 ARI	6 GEM	6 CAN	4 LEO	5 LIB	4 SCO	5 CAP	4 AQU
6 SAG	7 AQU	6 AQU	7 ARI	7 TAU	8 CAN	8 LEO	7 VIR	7 SCO	7 SAG	7 AQU	7 PIS
8 CAP	9 PIS	9 PIS	10 TAU	9 GEM	11 LEO	10 VIR	9 LIB	9 SAG	9 CAP	9 PIS	9 ARI
11 AQU	12 ARI	11 ARI	12 GEM	12 CAN	13 VIR	13 LIB	11 SCO	11 CAP	11 AQU	12 ARI	11 TAU
13 PIS	14 TAU	13 TAU	15 CAN	14 LEO	15 LIB	15 SCO	13 SAG	14 AQU	13 PIS	14 TAU	14 GEM
15 ARI	17 GEM	16 GEM	17 LEO	17 VIR	17 SCO	17 SAG	15 CAP	16 PIS	15 ARI	17 GEM	16 CAN
18 TAU	19 CAN	18 CAN	19 VIR	19 LIB	19 SAG	19 CAP	17 AQU	18 ARI	18 TAU	19 CAN	19 LEO
20 GEM	21 LEO	21 LEO	22 LIB	21 SCO	21 CAP	21 AQU	19 PIS	20 TAU	20 GEM	22 LEO	21 VIR
23 CAN	24 VIR	23 VIR	24 SCO	23 SAG	23 AQU	23 PIS	22 ARI	23 GEM	23 CAN	24 VIR	24 LIB
25 LEO	26 LIB	25 LIB	26 SAG	25 CAP	26 PIS	25 ARI	24 TAU	25 CAN	25 LEO	26 LIB	26 SCO
27 VIR	28 SCO	27 SCO	28 CAP	27 AQU	28 ARI	28 TAU	27 GEM	28 LEO	28 VIR	28 SCO	28 SAG
29 LIB		29 SAG	30 AQU	29 PIS	30 TAU	30 GEM	29 CAN	30 VIR	30 LIB	30 SAG	30 CAP
31 LIB		31 CAP		31 PIS		31 GEM	31 CAN		31 LIB		31 CAP

1960

JAN	FEB	MAR	APR	MAY	JUN	JUL	AUG	SEP	OCT	NOV	DEC
1 AQU	1 PIS	1 ARI	1 GEM	1 CAN	1 LEO	1 VIR	1 SCO	1 CAP	1 AQU	1 ARI	1 TAU
3 PIS	2 ARI	2 TAU	4 CAN	3 LEO	2 VIR	2 LIB	3 SAG	3 AQU	2 PIS	3 TAU	3 GEM
5 ARI	4 TAU	5 GEM	6 LEO	6 VIR	5 LIB	4 SCO	5 CAP	5 PIS	5 ARI	5 GEM	5 CAN
8 TAU	6 GEM	7 CAN	9 VIR	8 LIB	7 SCO	6 SAG	7 AQU	7 ARI	7 TAU	8 CAN	8 LEO
10 GEM	9 CAN	10 LEO	11 LIB	10 SCO	9 SAG	8 CAP	9 PIS	9 TAU	9 GEM	10 LEO	10 VIR
13 CAN	11 LEO	12 VIR	13 SCO	12 SAG	11 CAP	10 AQU	11 ARI	12 GEM	12 CAN	13 VIR	13 LIB
15 LEO	14 VIR	14 LIB	15 SAG	14 CAP	13 AQU	12 PIS	13 TAU	14 CAN	14 LEO	15 LIB	15 SCO
18 VIR	16 LIB	17 SCO	17 CAP	16 AQU	15 PIS	14 ARI	15 GEM	17 LEO	17 VIR	18 SCO	17 SAG
20 LIB	18 SCO	19 SAG	19 AQU	19 PIS	17 ARI	17 TAU	18 CAN	19 VIR	19 LIB	20 SAG	19 CAP
22 SCO	20 SAG	21 CAP	21 PIS	21 ARI	19 TAU	19 GEM	20 LEO	22 LIB	21 SCO	22 CAP	21 AQU
24 SAG	23 CAP	23 AQU	24 ARI	23 TAU	22 GEM	22 CAN	23 VIR	24 SCO	23 SAG	24 AQU	23 PIS
26 CAP	25 AQU	25 PIS	26 TAU	26 GEM	24 CAN	24 LEO	25 LIB	26 SAG	25 CAP	26 PIS	25 ARI
28 AQU	27 PIS	27 ARI	28 GEM	28 CAN	27 LEO	27 VIR	28 SCO	28 CAP	28 AQU	28 ARI	28 TAU
30 PIS	29 ARI	30 TAU	30 GEM	31 LEO	29 VIR	29 LIB	30 SAG	30 AQU	30 PIS	30 TAU	30 GEM
31 PIS		31 TAU			30 VIR	31 SCO	31 SAG		31 PIS		31 GEM

1961

JAN	FEB	MAR	APR	MAY	JUN	JUL	AUG	SEP	OCT	NOV	DEC
1 GEM	1 LEO	1 LEO	1 LIB	1 SCO	1 CAP	1 AQU	1 ARI	1 TAU	1 CAN	1 LEO	1 VIR
2 CAN	3 VIR	2 VIR	3 SCO	3 SAG	3 AQU	3 PIS	3 TAU	2 GEM	4 LEO	3 VIR	3 LIB
4 LEO	5 LIB	5 LIB	5 SAG	5 CAP	5 PIS	5 ARI	5 GEM	4 CAN	6 VIR	5 LIB	5 SCO
7 VIR	8 SCO	7 SCO	8 CAP	7 AQU	7 ARI	7 TAU	8 CAN	7 LEO	9 LIB	8 SCO	7 SAG
9 LIB	10 SAG	9 SAG	10 AQU	9 PIS	10 TAU	9 GEM	10 LEO	9 VIR	11 SCO	10 SAG	10 CAP
11 SCO	12 CAP	11 CAP	12 PIS	11 ARI	12 GEM	12 CAN	13 VIR	12 LIB	14 SAG	12 CAP	12 AQU
14 SAG	14 AQU	13 AQU	14 ARI	13 TAU	14 CAN	14 LEO	15 LIB	14 SCO	16 CAP	14 AQU	14 PIS
16 CAP	16 PIS	16 PIS	16 TAU	16 GEM	17 LEO	17 VIR	18 SCO	16 SAG	18 AQU	17 PIS	16 ARI
18 AQU	18 ARI	18 ARI	18 GEM	18 CAN	19 VIR	19 LIB	20 SAG	19 CAP	20 PIS	19 ARI	18 TAU
20 PIS	20 TAU	20 TAU	21 CAN	21 LEO	22 LIB	22 SCO	22 CAP	21 AQU	22 ARI	21 TAU	20 GEM
22 ARI	23 GEM	22 GEM	23 LEO	23 VIR	24 SCO	24 SAG	24 AQU	23 PIS	24 TAU	23 GEM	23 CAN
24 TAU	25 CAN	24 CAN	26 VIR	26 LIB	27 SAG	26 CAP	26 PIS	25 ARI	27 GEM	25 CAN	25 LEO
26 GEM	28 LEO	27 LEO	28 LIB	28 SCO	29 CAP	28 AQU	28 ARI	27 TAU	29 CAN	28 LEO	27 VIR
29 CAN		29 VIR	30 LIB	30 SAG	30 CAP	30 PIS	31 TAU	29 GEM	31 LEO	30 VIR	30 LIB
31 LEO		31 VIR		31 SAG		31 PIS		30 GEM			31 LIB

1963

JAN	FEB	MAR	APR	MAY	JUN	JUL	AUG	SEP	OCT	NOV	DEC
1 PIS	1 TAU	1 TAU	1 CAN	1 LEO	1 VIR	1 SCO	1 SAG	1 AQU	1 PIS	1 ARI	1 GEM
3 ARI	3 GEM	2 GEM	3 LEO	3 VIR	2 LIB	4 SAG	3 CAP	4 PIS	3 ARI	2 TAU	3 CAN
5 TAU	5 CAN	5 CAN	6 VIR	5 LIB	4 SCO	6 CAP	5 AQU	6 ARI	5 TAU	3 GEM	5 LEO
7 GEM	8 LEO	7 LEO	8 LIB	8 SCO	7 SAG	9 AQU	7 PIS	8 TAU	7 GEM	6 CAN	7 VIR
9 CAN	10 VIR	9 VIR	11 SCO	10 SAG	9 CAP	11 PIS	9 ARI	10 GEM	9 CAN	8 LEO	10 LIB
11 LEO	12 LIB	12 LIB	13 SAG	13 CAP	11 AQU	13 ARI	11 TAU	12 CAN	11 LEO	10 VIR	12 SCO
14 VIR	15 SCO	14 SCO	16 CAP	15 AQU	14 PIS	15 TAU	14 GEM	14 LEO	14 VIR	12 LIB	15 SAG
16 LIB	17 SAG	17 SAG	18 AQU	17 PIS	16 ARI	17 GEM	16 CAN	16 VIR	16 LIB	15 SCO	17 CAP
19 SCO	20 CAP	19 CAP	20 PIS	20 ARI	18 TAU	19 CAN	18 LEO	19 LIB	19 SCO	17 SAG	20 AQU
21 SAG	22 AQU	22 AQU	22 ARI	22 TAU	20 GEM	22 LEO	20 VIR	21 SCO	21 SAG	20 CAP	22 PIS
23 CAP	24 PIS	24 PIS	24 TAU	24 GEM	22 CAN	24 VIR	23 LIB	24 SAG	24 CAP	22 AQU	24 ARI
26 AQU	26 ARI	26 ARI	26 GEM	26 CAN	24 LEO	26 LIB	25 SCO	26 CAP	26 AQU	25 PIS	26 TAU
28 PIS	28 TAU	28 TAU	28 CAN	28 LEO	26 VIR	29 SCO	28 SAG	29 AQU	28 PIS	27 ARI	28 GEM
30 ARI		30 GEM	30 LEO	30 VIR	29 LIB	31 SAG	30 CAP	30 AQU	31 ARI	29 TAU	30 CAN
31 ARI		31 GEM		31 VIR	30 LIB		31 CAP			30 TAU	31 CAN

1962

JAN	FEB	MAR	APR	MAY	JUN	JUL	AUG	SEP	OCT	NOV	DEC
1 SCO	1 SAG	1 SAG	1 AQU	1 PIS	1 TAU	1 GEM	1 LEO	1 VIR	1 SCO	1 SAG	1 CAP
4 SAG	2 CAP	2 CAP	2 PIS	2 AQU	2 GEM	2 CAN	3 VIR	2 LIB	4 SAG	3 CAP	2 AQU
6 CAP	4 AQU	4 AQU	4 ARI	4 TAU	4 CAN	4 LEO	5 LIB	4 SCO	6 CAP	5 AQU	4 PIS
8 AQU	6 PIS	6 PIS	6 TAU	6 GEM	7 LEO	7 VIR	8 SCO	7 SAG	9 AQU	7 PIS	6 ARI
10 PIS	8 ARI	8 ARI	8 GEM	8 CAN	9 VIR	9 LIB	10 SAG	9 CAP	11 PIS	9 ARI	9 TAU
12 ARI	11 TAU	10 TAU	11 CAN	10 LEO	12 LIB	12 SCO	13 CAP	11 AQU	13 ARI	11 TAU	11 GEM
14 TAU	13 GEM	12 GEM	13 LEO	13 VIR	14 SCO	14 SAG	15 AQU	13 PIS	15 TAU	13 GEM	13 CAN
16 GEM	15 CAN	14 CAN	16 VIR	15 LIB	17 SAG	16 CAP	17 PIS	15 ARI	17 GEM	15 CAN	15 LEO
19 CAN	18 LEO	17 LEO	18 LIB	18 SCO	19 CAP	18 AQU	19 ARI	17 TAU	19 CAN	17 LEO	17 VIR
21 LEO	20 VIR	19 VIR	21 SCO	20 SAG	21 AQU	20 PIS	21 TAU	19 GEM	21 LEO	20 VIR	20 LIB
24 VIR	23 LIB	22 LIB	23 SAG	23 CAP	23 PIS	23 ARI	23 GEM	22 CAN	24 VIR	22 LIB	22 SCO
26 LIB	25 SCO	24 SCO	25 CAP	25 AQU	25 ARI	25 TAU	25 CAN	24 LEO	26 LIB	25 SCO	25 SAG
29 SCO	27 SAG	27 SAG	28 AQU	27 PIS	27 TAU	27 GEM	28 LEO	26 VIR	29 SCO	27 SAG	27 CAP
31 SAG	28 SAG	29 CAP	30 PIS	29 ARI	30 GEM	29 CAN	30 VIR	29 LIB	31 SAG	30 CAP	29 AQU
		31 AQU		31 TAU		31 LEO	31 VIR	30 LIB			31 AQU

1964

JAN	FEB	MAR	APR	MAY	JUN	JUL	AUG	SEP	OCT	NOV	DEC
1 LEO	1 VIR	1 LIB	1 SCO	1 SAG	1 AQU	1 PIS	1 TAU	1 GEM	1 LEO	1 VIR	1 SCO
4 VIR	2 LIB	3 SCO	2 SAG	2 CAP	3 PIS	3 ARI	3 GEM	2 CAN	3 VIR	2 LIB	4 SAG
6 LIB	5 SCO	6 SAG	4 CAP	4 AQU	5 ARI	5 TAU	5 CAN	4 LEO	5 LIB	4 SCO	6 CAP
8 SCO	7 SAG	8 CAP	7 AQU	7 PIS	7 TAU	7 GEM	7 LEO	6 VIR	8 SCO	6 SAG	9 AQU
11 SAG	10 CAP	11 AQU	9 PIS	9 ARI	9 GEM	9 CAN	9 VIR	8 LIB	10 SAG	9 CAP	11 PIS
13 CAP	12 AQU	13 PIS	11 ARI	11 TAU	11 CAN	11 LEO	11 LIB	10 SCO	12 CAP	11 AQU	14 ARI
16 AQU	15 PIS	15 ARI	14 TAU	13 GEM	13 LEO	13 VIR	14 SCO	13 SAG	15 AQU	14 PIS	16 TAU
18 PIS	17 ARI	17 TAU	16 GEM	15 CAN	16 VIR	15 LIB	16 SAG	15 CAP	17 PIS	16 ARI	18 GEM
20 ARI	19 TAU	19 GEM	18 CAN	17 LEO	18 LIB	17 SCO	19 CAP	18 AQU	20 ARI	18 TAU	20 CAN
23 TAU	21 GEM	21 CAN	20 LEO	19 VIR	20 SCO	20 SAG	21 AQU	20 PIS	22 TAU	20 GEM	22 LEO
25 GEM	23 CAN	24 LEO	22 VIR	22 LIB	23 SAG	23 CAP	24 PIS	22 ARI	24 GEM	22 CAN	24 VIR
27 CAN	25 LEO	26 VIR	24 LIB	24 SCO	25 CAP	25 AQU	26 ARI	24 TAU	26 CAN	24 LEO	26 LIB
29 LEO	27 VIR	28 LIB	27 SCO	26 SAG	28 AQU	27 PIS	28 TAU	27 GEM	28 LEO	27 VIR	28 SCO
31 VIR	29 VIR	30 SCO	29 SAG	29 CAP	30 PIS	30 ARI	30 GEM	29 CAN	30 VIR	29 LIB	31 SAG
		31 SCO	30 SAG	31 CAP		31 ARI	31 GEM	30 CAN	31 VIR	30 LIB	

1965

JAN	FEB	MAR	APR	MAY	JUN	JUL	AUG	SEP	OCT	NOV	DEC
1 SAG	1 AQU	1 AQU	1 PIS	1 TAU	1 GEM	1 LEO	1 VIR	1 SCO	1 SAG	1 AQU	1 PIS
2 CAP	4 PIS	3 PIS	2 ARI	3 GEM	2 CAN	3 VIR	2 LIB	2 SAG	2 CAP	4 PIS	3 ARI
5 AQU	6 ARI	5 ARI	4 TAU	5 CAN	4 LEO	5 LIB	4 SCO	5 CAP	5 AQU	6 ARI	6 TAU
7 PIS	8 TAU	8 TAU	6 GEM	8 LEO	6 VIR	8 SCO	6 SAG	7 AQU	7 PIS	8 TAU	8 GEM
10 ARI	11 GEM	10 GEM	8 CAN	10 VIR	8 LIB	10 SAG	9 CAP	10 PIS	10 ARI	11 GEM	10 CAN
12 TAU	13 CAN	12 CAN	10 LEO	12 LIB	10 SCO	12 CAP	11 AQU	12 ARI	12 TAU	13 CAN	12 LEO
14 GEM	15 LEO	14 LEO	12 VIR	14 SCO	13 SAG	15 AQU	14 PIS	15 TAU	14 GEM	15 LEO	14 VIR
16 CAN	17 VIR	16 VIR	15 LIB	16 SAG	15 CAP	17 PIS	16 ARI	17 GEM	17 CAN	17 VIR	16 LIB
18 LEO	19 LIB	18 LIB	17 SCO	19 CAP	18 AQU	20 ARI	19 TAU	19 CAN	19 LEO	19 LIB	19 SCO
20 VIR	21 SCO	20 SCO	19 SAG	21 AQU	20 PIS	22 TAU	21 GEM	21 LEO	21 VIR	21 SCO	21 SAG
22 LIB	23 SAG	23 SAG	22 CAP	24 PIS	23 ARI	25 GEM	23 CAN	23 VIR	23 LIB	24 SAG	23 CAP
25 SCO	26 CAP	25 CAP	24 AQU	26 ARI	25 TAU	27 CAN	25 LEO	26 LIB	25 SCO	26 CAP	26 AQU
27 SAG	28 AQU	28 AQU	27 PIS	29 TAU	27 GEM	29 LEO	27 VIR	28 SCO	27 SAG	28 AQU	28 PIS
30 CAP		30 PIS	29 ARI	31 GEM	29 CAN	31 VIR	29 LIB	30 SAG	30 CAP	30 AQU	31 ARI
31 CAP		31 PIS	30 ARI		30 CAN		31 SCO		31 CAP		

1966

JAN	FEB	MAR	APR	MAY	JUN	JUL	AUG	SEP	OCT	NOV	DEC
1 ARI	1 GEM	1 GEM	1 LEO	1 VIR	1 SCO	1 SAG	1 AQU	1 PIS	1 ARI	1 GEM	1 CAN
2 TAU	3 CAN	2 CAN	3 VIR	2 LIB	3 SAG	2 CAP	4 PIS	2 ARI	2 TAU	3 CAN	3 LEO
5 GEM	5 LEO	5 LEO	5 LIB	4 SCO	5 CAP	5 AQU	6 ARI	5 TAU	5 GEM	5 LEO	5 VIR
7 CAN	7 VIR	7 VIR	7 SCO	7 SAG	8 AQU	7 PIS	9 TAU	7 GEM	7 CAN	8 VIR	7 LIB
9 LEO	9 LIB	8 LIB	9 SAG	9 CAP	10 PIS	10 ARI	11 GEM	10 CAN	9 LEO	10 LIB	9 SCO
11 VIR	11 SCO	11 SCO	11 CAP	11 AQU	13 ARI	12 TAU	13 CAN	12 LEO	11 VIR	12 SCO	11 SAG
13 LIB	13 SAG	13 SAG	14 AQU	14 PIS	15 TAU	15 GEM	15 LEO	14 VIR	13 LIB	14 SAG	13 CAP
15 SCO	16 CAP	15 CAP	16 PIS	16 ARI	17 GEM	17 CAN	17 VIR	16 LIB	15 SCO	16 CAP	16 AQU
17 SAG	18 AQU	18 AQU	19 ARI	19 TAU	20 CAN	19 LEO	19 LIB	18 SCO	17 SAG	18 AQU	18 PIS
20 CAP	21 PIS	20 PIS	21 TAU	21 GEM	22 LEO	21 VIR	21 SCO	20 SAG	20 CAP	21 PIS	21 ARI
22 AQU	23 ARI	23 ARI	24 GEM	23 CAN	24 VIR	23 LIB	24 SAG	22 CAP	22 AQU	23 ARI	23 TAU
25 PIS	26 TAU	25 TAU	26 CAN	25 LEO	26 LIB	25 SCO	26 CAP	25 AQU	24 PIS	26 TAU	26 GEM
27 ARI	28 GEM	27 GEM	28 LEO	27 VIR	28 SCO	27 SAG	28 AQU	27 PIS	27 ARI	28 GEM	28 CAN
30 TAU		30 CAN	30 VIR	30 LIB	30 SAG	30 CAP	31 PIS	30 ARI	29 TAU	30 CAN	30 LEO
31 TAU		31 CAN		31 LIB		31 CAP			31 TAU		31 LEO

1967

JAN	FEB	MAR	APR	MAY	JUN	JUL	AUG	SEP	OCT	NOV	DEC
1 VIR	1 LIB	1 SCO	1 SAG	1 AQU	1 PIS	1 ARI	1 GEM	1 CAN	1 LEO	1 LIB	1 SCO
3 LIB	2 SCO	3 SAG	2 CAP	4 PIS	2 ARI	2 TAU	3 CAN	2 LEO	2 VIR	2 SCO	2 SAG
5 SCO	4 SAG	5 CAP	4 AQU	6 ARI	5 TAU	5 GEM	6 LEO	4 VIR	4 LIB	4 SAG	4 CAP
8 SAG	6 CAP	8 AQU	6 PIS	9 TAU	7 GEM	7 CAN	8 VIR	6 LIB	6 SCO	6 CAP	6 AQU
10 CAP	8 AQU	10 PIS	9 ARI	11 GEM	10 CAN	9 LEO	10 LIB	8 SCO	8 SAG	8 AQU	8 PIS
12 AQU	11 PIS	13 ARI	11 TAU	14 CAN	12 LEO	12 VIR	12 SCO	10 SAG	10 CAP	11 PIS	10 ARI
14 PIS	13 ARI	15 TAU	14 GEM	16 LEO	14 VIR	14 LIB	14 SAG	13 CAP	12 AQU	13 ARI	13 TAU
17 ARI	16 TAU	18 GEM	16 CAN	18 VIR	16 LIB	16 SCO	16 CAP	15 AQU	14 PIS	16 TAU	15 GEM
19 TAU	18 GEM	20 CAN	19 LEO	20 LIB	19 SCO	18 SAG	19 AQU	17 PIS	17 ARI	18 GEM	18 CAN
22 GEM	21 CAN	22 LEO	21 VIR	22 SCO	21 SAG	20 CAP	21 PIS	20 ARI	19 TAU	21 CAN	20 LEO
24 CAN	23 LEO	24 VIR	23 LIB	24 SAG	23 CAP	22 AQU	23 ARI	22 TAU	22 GEM	23 LEO	23 VIR
26 LEO	25 VIR	26 LIB	25 SCO	26 CAP	25 AQU	25 PIS	26 TAU	25 GEM	24 CAN	25 VIR	25 LIB
28 VIR	27 LIB	28 SCO	27 SAG	28 AQU	27 PIS	27 ARI	28 GEM	27 CAN	27 LEO	28 LIB	27 SCO
30 LIB	28 LIB	30 SAG	29 CAP	31 PIS	30 ARI	30 TAU	31 CAN	29 LEO	29 VIR	30 SCO	29 SAG
31 LIB		31 SAG	30 CAP			31 TAU		30 LEO	31 LIB		31 CAP

1968

JAN	FEB	MAR	APR	MAY	JUN	JUL	AUG	SEP	OCT	NOV	DEC
1 CAP	1 PIS	1 ARI	1 TAU	1 GEM	1 LEO	1 VIR	1 LIB	1 SAG	1 AQU	1 PIS	1 ARI
2 AQU	3 ARI	4 TAU	3 GEM	3 CAN	4 VIR	3 LIB	2 SCO	2 CAP	4 PIS	2 ARI	2 TAU
4 PIS	6 TAU	6 GEM	5 CAN	5 LEO	6 LIB	5 SCO	4 SAG	4 AQU	6 ARI	5 TAU	4 GEM
7 ARI	8 GEM	9 CAN	8 LEO	7 VIR	8 SCO	7 SAG	6 CAP	6 PIS	8 TAU	7 GEM	7 CAN
9 TAU	11 CAN	11 LEO	10 VIR	10 LIB	10 SAG	9 CAP	8 AQU	9 ARI	11 GEM	10 CAN	9 LEO
12 GEM	13 LEO	14 VIR	12 LIB	12 SCO	12 CAP	11 AQU	10 PIS	11 TAU	13 CAN	12 LEO	12 VIR
14 CAN	15 VIR	16 LIB	14 SCO	14 SAG	14 AQU	14 PIS	12 ARI	13 GEM	16 LEO	15 VIR	14 LIB
17 LEO	17 LIB	18 SCO	16 SAG	16 CAP	16 PIS	16 ARI	15 TAU	16 CAN	18 VIR	17 LIB	16 SCO
19 VIR	19 SCO	20 SAG	18 SCO	18 AQU	19 ARI	18 TAU	17 GEM	18 LEO	20 LIB	19 SCO	18 SAG
21 LIB	22 SAG	22 CAP	20 AQU	20 PIS	21 TAU	21 GEM	20 CAN	21 VIR	23 SCO	21 SAG	20 CAP
23 SCO	24 CAP	24 AQU	23 PIS	22 ARI	24 GEM	23 CAN	22 LEO	23 LIB	25 SAG	23 CAP	22 AQU
25 SAG	26 AQU	26 PIS	25 ARI	25 TAU	26 CAN	26 LEO	24 VIR	25 SCO	27 CAP	25 AQU	24 PIS
27 CAP	28 PIS	29 ARI	28 TAU	27 GEM	29 LEO	28 VIR	27 LIB	27 SAG	29 AQU	27 PIS	27 ARI
30 AQU	29 PIS	31 TAU	30 GEM	30 CAN	30 LEO	30 LIB	29 SCO	29 CAP	31 PIS	29 ARI	29 TAU
31 AQU				31 CAN		31 LIB	31 SAG	30 CAP		30 ARI	31 TAU

1969

JAN	FEB	MAR	APR	MAY	JUN	JUL	AUG	SEP	OCT	NOV	DEC
1 GEM	1 CAN	1 LEO	1 VIR	1 LIB	1 SAG	1 CAP	1 PIS	1 TAU	1 GEM	1 CAN	1 LEO
3 CAN	2 LEO	4 VIR	2 LIB	2 SCO	2 CAP	2 AQU	2 ARI	3 GEM	3 CAN	2 LEO	2 VIR
6 LEO	4 VIR	6 LIB	5 SCO	4 SAG	4 AQU	4 PIS	4 TAU	6 CAN	6 LEO	5 VIR	4 LIB
8 VIR	7 LIB	8 SCO	7 SAG	6 CAP	6 PIS	6 ARI	6 GEM	8 LEO	8 VIR	7 LIB	7 SCO
10 LIB	9 SCO	10 SAG	9 CAP	8 AQU	9 ARI	8 TAU	9 CAN	11 VIR	11 LIB	9 SCO	9 SAG
13 SCO	11 SAG	12 CAP	11 AQU	10 PIS	11 TAU	11 GEM	12 LEO	13 LIB	13 SCO	11 SAG	11 CAP
15 SAG	13 CAP	15 AQU	13 PIS	12 ARI	13 GEM	13 CAN	15 VIR	16 SCO	15 SAG	13 CAP	13 AQU
17 CAP	15 AQU	17 PIS	15 ARI	15 TAU	16 CAN	16 LEO	17 LIB	18 SAG	17 CAP	15 AQU	15 PIS
19 AQU	17 PIS	19 ARI	18 TAU	17 GEM	19 LEO	18 VIR	19 SCO	20 CAP	19 AQU	18 PIS	17 ARI
21 PIS	19 ARI	21 TAU	20 GEM	20 CAN	21 VIR	21 LIB	22 SAG	22 AQU	21 PIS	20 ARI	19 TAU
23 ARI	22 TAU	24 GEM	22 CAN	22 LEO	23 LIB	23 SCO	24 CAP	24 PIS	24 ARI	22 TAU	22 GEM
25 TAU	24 GEM	26 CAN	25 LEO	25 VIR	26 SCO	25 SAG	26 AQU	26 ARI	26 TAU	24 GEM	24 CAN
28 GEM	27 CAN	29 LEO	27 VIR	27 LIB	28 SAG	27 CAP	28 PIS	28 TAU	28 GEM	27 CAN	27 LEO
30 CAN	28 CAN	31 VIR	30 LIB	29 SCO	30 CAP	29 AQU	30 ARI	30 TAU	30 CAN	29 LEO	29 VIR
31 CAN				31 SAG		31 PIS	31 ARI		31 CAN	30 LEO	31 VIR

1971

JAN	FEB	MAR	APR	MAY	JUN	JUL	AUG	SEP	OCT	NOV	DEC
1 AQU	1 ARI	1 TAU	1 GEM	1 CAN	1 VIR	1 LIB	1 SCO	1 CAP	1 AQU	1 ARI	1 TAU
2 PIS	2 TAU	4 GEM	2 CAN	2 LEO	3 LIB	3 SCO	2 SAG	3 AQU	2 PIS	3 TAU	2 GEM
4 ARI	4 GEM	6 CAN	5 LEO	4 VIR	6 SCO	5 SAG	4 CAP	5 PIS	4 ARI	5 GEM	4 CAN
6 TAU	7 CAN	8 LEO	7 VIR	7 LIB	8 SAG	8 CAP	6 AQU	7 ARI	6 TAU	7 CAN	6 LEO
8 GEM	9 LEO	11 VIR	10 LIB	9 SCO	10 CAP	10 AQU	8 PIS	9 TAU	8 GEM	9 LEO	9 VIR
10 CAN	12 VIR	13 LIB	12 SCO	12 SAG	13 AQU	12 PIS	10 ARI	11 GEM	10 CAN	11 VIR	11 LIB
13 LEO	14 LIB	16 SCO	15 SAG	14 CAP	15 PIS	14 ARI	13 TAU	13 CAN	13 LEO	14 LIB	14 SCO
15 VIR	17 SCO	18 SAG	17 CAP	16 AQU	17 ARI	16 TAU	15 GEM	15 LEO	15 VIR	16 SCO	16 SAG
18 LIB	19 SAG	21 CAP	19 AQU	19 PIS	19 TAU	18 GEM	17 CAN	18 VIR	18 LIB	19 SAG	19 CAP
20 SCO	21 CAP	23 AQU	21 PIS	21 ARI	21 GEM	21 CAN	19 LEO	20 LIB	20 SCO	21 CAP	21 AQU
23 SAG	23 AQU	25 PIS	23 ARI	23 TAU	23 CAN	23 LEO	22 VIR	23 SCO	23 SAG	24 AQU	23 PIS
25 CAP	26 PIS	27 ARI	25 TAU	25 GEM	26 LEO	25 VIR	24 LIB	25 SAG	25 CAP	26 PIS	25 ARI
27 AQU	27 ARI	29 TAU	27 GEM	27 CAN	28 VIR	28 LIB	27 SCO	28 CAP	28 AQU	28 ARI	27 TAU
29 PIS	28 ARI	31 GEM	30 CAN	29 LEO	30 VIR	30 SCO	29 SAG	30 AQU	30 PIS	30 TAU	30 GEM
31 ARI				31 LEO		31 SCO	31 SAG		31 PIS		31 GEM

1970

JAN	FEB	MAR	APR	MAY	JUN	JUL	AUG	SEP	OCT	NOV	DEC
1 LIB	1 SCO	1 SAG	1 AQU	1 PIS	1 TAU	1 GEM	1 CAN	1 VIR	1 LIB	1 SCO	1 CAP
3 SCO	2 SAG	3 CAP	4 PIS	3 ARI	4 GEM	3 CAN	2 LEO	3 LIB	3 SCO	2 SAG	3 AQU
5 SAG	4 CAP	5 AQU	6 ARI	5 TAU	6 CAN	6 LEO	4 VIR	6 SCO	5 SAG	4 CAP	5 PIS
7 CAP	6 AQU	7 PIS	8 TAU	7 GEM	8 LEO	8 VIR	7 LIB	8 SAG	8 CAP	6 AQU	8 ARI
9 AQU	8 PIS	9 ARI	10 GEM	10 CAN	11 VIR	11 LIB	9 SCO	10 CAP	10 AQU	8 PIS	10 TAU
11 PIS	10 ARI	11 TAU	12 CAN	12 LEO	13 LIB	13 SCO	12 SAG	12 AQU	12 PIS	10 ARI	12 GEM
13 ARI	12 TAU	13 GEM	15 LEO	15 VIR	16 SCO	15 SAG	14 CAP	14 PIS	14 ARI	12 TAU	14 CAN
16 TAU	14 GEM	16 CAN	17 VIR	17 LIB	18 SAG	18 CAP	16 AQU	16 ARI	16 TAU	14 GEM	16 LEO
18 GEM	17 CAN	18 LEO	20 LIB	19 SCO	20 CAP	20 AQU	18 PIS	19 TAU	18 GEM	17 CAN	19 VIR
20 CAN	19 LEO	21 VIR	22 SCO	22 SAG	22 AQU	22 PIS	20 ARI	21 GEM	20 CAN	19 LEO	22 LIB
23 LEO	22 VIR	23 LIB	24 SAG	24 CAP	24 PIS	24 ARI	22 TAU	23 CAN	23 LEO	22 VIR	24 SCO
25 VIR	24 LIB	26 SCO	27 CAP	26 AQU	26 ARI	26 TAU	24 GEM	25 LEO	25 VIR	24 LIB	26 SAG
28 LIB	27 SCO	28 SAG	29 AQU	28 PIS	29 TAU	28 GEM	27 CAN	28 VIR	28 LIB	27 SCO	29 CAP
30 SCO	28 SCO	30 CAP	31 AQU	30 ARI	30 TAU	30 CAN	29 LEO	30 VIR	30 SCO	29 SAG	31 AQU
31 SCO		31 CAP		31 ARI		31 CAN	31 LEO		31 SCO	30 SAG	

1972

JAN	FEB	MAR	APR	MAY	JUN	JUL	AUG	SEP	OCT	NOV	DEC
1 CAN	1 LEO	1 VIR	1 SCO	1 SAG	1 CAP	1 AQU	1 ARI	1 GEM	1 CAN	1 VIR	1 LIB
3 LEO	2 VIR	2 LIB	4 SAG	3 CAP	2 AQU	2 PIS	2 TAU	3 CAN	2 LEO	3 LIB	3 SCO
5 VIR	4 LIB	5 SCO	6 CAP	6 AQU	4 PIS	4 ARI	4 GEM	5 LEO	4 VIR	5 SCO	5 SAG
8 LIB	6 SCO	7 SAG	8 AQU	8 PIS	7 ARI	6 TAU	6 CAN	7 VIR	7 LIB	8 SAG	8 CAP
10 SCO	9 SAG	10 CAP	11 PIS	10 ARI	9 TAU	8 GEM	8 LEO	9 LIB	9 SCO	10 CAP	10 AQU
13 SAG	11 CAP	12 AQU	13 ARI	12 TAU	11 GEM	10 CAN	11 VIR	12 SCO	12 SAG	13 AQU	13 PIS
15 CAP	14 AQU	14 PIS	15 TAU	14 GEM	13 CAN	12 LEO	13 LIB	14 SAG	14 CAP	15 PIS	15 ARI
17 AQU	16 PIS	16 ARI	17 GEM	16 CAN	15 LEO	14 VIR	16 SCO	17 CAP	17 AQU	18 ARI	17 TAU
19 PIS	18 ARI	18 TAU	19 CAN	18 LEO	17 VIR	17 LIB	18 SAG	19 AQU	19 PIS	20 TAU	19 GEM
22 ARI	20 TAU	20 GEM	21 LEO	21 VIR	19 LIB	19 SCO	21 CAP	22 PIS	21 ARI	22 GEM	21 CAN
24 TAU	22 GEM	22 CAN	23 VIR	23 LIB	22 SCO	22 SAG	23 AQU	24 ARI	23 TAU	24 CAN	23 LEO
26 GEM	24 CAN	25 LEO	26 LIB	26 SCO	24 SAG	24 CAP	25 PIS	26 TAU	25 GEM	26 LEO	25 VIR
28 CAN	27 LEO	27 VIR	28 SCO	28 SAG	27 CAP	27 AQU	27 ARI	28 GEM	27 CAN	28 VIR	27 LIB
30 LEO	29 VIR	30 LIB	30 SCO	31 CAP	29 AQU	29 PIS	29 TAU	30 CAN	29 LEO	30 LIB	30 SCO
31 LEO		31 LIB			30 AQU	31 ARI	31 GEM		31 LEO		31 SCO

1973

JAN	FEB	MAR	APR	MAY	JUN	JUL	AUG	SEP	OCT	NOV	DEC
1 SAG	1 CAP	1 CAP	1 PIS	1 ARI	1 GEM	1 CAN	1 VIR	1 LIB	1 SAG	1 CAP	1 AQU
4 CAP	3 AQU	2 AQU	3 ARI	3 TAU	3 CAN	2 LEO	3 LIB	2 SCO	4 CAP	3 AQU	3 PIS
6 AQU	5 PIS	4 PIS	5 TAU	5 GEM	5 LEO	4 VIR	5 SCO	4 SAG	7 AQU	5 PIS	5 ARI
9 PIS	7 ARI	7 ARI	7 GEM	7 CAN	7 VIR	7 LIB	8 SAG	7 CAP	9 PIS	8 ARI	7 TAU
11 ARI	10 TAU	9 TAU	9 CAN	9 LEO	9 LIB	9 SCO	10 CAP	9 AQU	11 ARI	10 TAU	9 GEM
13 TAU	12 GEM	11 GEM	11 LEO	11 VIR	12 SCO	12 SAG	13 AQU	12 PIS	13 TAU	12 GEM	11 CAN
15 GEM	14 CAN	13 CAN	14 VIR	13 LIB	14 SAG	14 CAP	15 PIS	14 ARI	16 GEM	14 CAN	13 LEO
17 CAN	16 LEO	15 LEO	16 LIB	16 SCO	17 CAP	17 AQU	18 ARI	16 TAU	18 CAN	16 LEO	15 VIR
19 LEO	18 VIR	17 VIR	18 SCO	18 SAG	19 AQU	19 PIS	20 TAU	18 GEM	20 LEO	18 VIR	18 LIB
22 VIR	20 LIB	20 LIB	21 SAG	21 CAP	22 PIS	21 ARI	22 GEM	20 CAN	22 VIR	20 LIB	20 SCO
24 LIB	23 SCO	22 SCO	23 CAP	23 AQU	24 ARI	24 TAU	24 CAN	21 LEO	24 LIB	23 SCO	22 SAG
26 SCO	25 SAG	24 SAG	26 AQU	26 PIS	26 TAU	26 GEM	26 LEO	25 VIR	26 SCO	25 SAG	25 CAP
29 SAG	28 CAP	27 CAP	28 PIS	28 ARI	28 GEM	28 CAN	28 VIR	27 LIB	29 SAG	28 CAP	27 AQU
31 CAP		29 AQU	30 ARI	30 TAU	30 CAN	30 LEO	30 LIB	29 SCO	31 CAP	30 AQU	30 PIS
		31 AQU		31 TAU		31 LEO	31 LIB	30 SCO			31 PIS

1974

JAN	FEB	MAR	APR	MAY	JUN	JUL	AUG	SEP	OCT	NOV	DEC
1 ARI	1 TAU	1 GEM	1 CAN	1 VIR	1 LIB	1 CAP	1 CAP	1 AQU	1 ARI	1 TAU	1 GEM
4 TAU	2 GEM	4 CAN	2 LEO	3 LIB	3 SCO	2 SAG	3 AQU	2 PIS	4 TAU	2 GEM	2 CAN
6 GEM	4 CAN	6 LEO	4 VIR	6 SCO	5 SAG	4 CAP	5 PIS	4 ARI	6 GEM	4 CAN	4 LEO
8 CAN	6 LEO	8 VIR	6 LIB	8 SAG	7 CAP	7 AQU	8 ARI	6 TAU	8 CAN	7 LEO	6 VIR
10 LEO	8 VIR	10 LIB	8 SCO	10 CAP	9 AQU	9 PIS	10 TAU	9 GEM	10 LEO	9 VIR	8 LIB
12 VIR	10 LIB	12 SCO	11 SAG	13 AQU	12 PIS	12 ARI	13 GEM	11 CAN	12 VIR	11 LIB	10 SCO
14 LIB	13 SCO	14 SAG	13 CAP	15 PIS	14 ARI	14 TAU	15 CAN	13 LEO	15 LIB	13 SCO	13 SAG
16 SCO	15 SAG	17 CAP	16 AQU	18 ARI	17 TAU	16 GEM	17 LEO	15 VIR	17 SCO	15 SAG	15 CAP
19 SAG	17 CAP	19 AQU	18 PIS	20 TAU	19 GEM	18 CAN	19 VIR	17 LIB	19 SAG	18 CAP	17 AQU
21 CAP	20 AQU	22 PIS	21 ARI	22 GEM	21 CAN	20 LEO	21 LIB	19 SCO	21 CAP	20 AQU	20 PIS
24 AQU	22 PIS	24 ARI	23 TAU	24 CAN	23 LEO	22 VIR	23 SCO	21 SAG	24 AQU	23 PIS	22 ARI
26 PIS	25 ARI	26 TAU	25 GEM	26 LEO	25 VIR	24 LIB	25 SAG	24 CAP	26 PIS	25 ARI	25 TAU
29 ARI	27 TAU	29 GEM	27 CAN	29 VIR	27 LIB	26 SCO	28 CAP	26 AQU	29 ARI	27 TAU	27 GEM
31 TAU	28 TAU	31 CAN	29 LEO	31 LIB	29 SCO	29 SAG	30 AQU	29 PIS	31 TAU	30 GEM	29 CAN
			30 LEO		30 SCO	31 CAP	31 AQU	30 PIS			30 LEO

1975

JAN	FEB	MAR	APR	MAY	JUN	JUL	AUG	SEP	OCT	NOV	DEC
1 LEO	1 LIB	1 LIB	1 SAG	1 CAP	1 AQU	1 ARI	1 TAU	1 CAN	1 LEO	1 LIB	1 SCO
2 VIR	3 SCO	2 SCO	3 CAP	3 AQU	2 PIS	4 TAU	3 GEM	3 LEO	3 VIR	3 SCO	3 SAG
4 LIB	5 SAG	4 SAG	5 AQU	5 PIS	4 ARI	6 GEM	5 CAN	5 VIR	5 LIB	5 SAG	5 CAP
6 SCO	7 CAP	7 CAP	8 PIS	8 ARI	7 TAU	9 CAN	7 LEO	7 LIB	7 SCO	8 CAP	7 AQU
9 SAG	10 AQU	9 AQU	10 ARI	10 GEM	9 GEM	11 LEO	9 VIR	9 SCO	9 SAG	10 AQU	10 PIS
11 CAP	12 PIS	12 PIS	13 TAU	13 CAN	11 CAN	13 VIR	11 LIB	12 SAG	11 CAP	12 PIS	12 ARI
14 AQU	15 ARI	14 ARI	15 GEM	15 LEO	13 LEO	15 LIB	13 SCO	14 CAP	14 AQU	15 ARI	15 TAU
16 PIS	17 TAU	17 TAU	18 CAN	17 VIR	15 VIR	17 SCO	15 SAG	16 AQU	16 PIS	17 TAU	17 GEM
19 ARI	20 GEM	19 GEM	20 LEO	19 LIB	17 LIB	19 SAG	18 CAP	19 PIS	19 ARI	20 GEM	19 CAN
21 TAU	22 CAN	21 CAN	22 VIR	21 SCO	20 SCO	21 CAP	20 AQU	21 ARI	21 TAU	22 CAN	22 LEO
23 GEM	24 LEO	24 LEO	24 LIB	23 SAG	22 SAG	24 AQU	22 PIS	24 TAU	23 GEM	24 LEO	24 VIR
26 CAN	26 VIR	26 VIR	26 SCO	25 CAP	24 CAP	26 PIS	25 ARI	26 GEM	26 CAN	27 VIR	26 LIB
28 LEO	28 LIB	28 LIB	28 SAG	28 AQU	26 AQU	29 ARI	28 TAU	29 CAN	28 LEO	29 LIB	28 SCO
30 VIR		30 SCO	30 CAP	30 AQU	29 PIS	31 TAU	30 GEM	30 CAN	30 VIR	30 LIB	30 SAG
31 VIR		31 SCO		31 AQU	30 PIS		31 GEM		31 VIR		31 SAG

1976

JAN	FEB	MAR	APR	MAY	JUN	JUL	AUG	SEP	OCT	NOV	DEC
1 CAP	1 AQU	1 PIS	1 ARI	1 TAU	1 CAN	1 LEO	1 LIB	1 SAG	1 CAP	1 PIS	1 ARI
4 AQU	2 PIS	3 ARI	2 TAU	2 GEM	3 LEO	2 VIR	3 SCO	3 CAP	3 AQU	4 ARI	3 TAU
6 PIS	5 ARI	6 TAU	4 GEM	4 CAN	5 VIR	4 LIB	5 SAG	5 AQU	5 PIS	6 TAU	6 GEM
8 ARI	7 TAU	8 GEM	7 CAN	6 LEO	7 LIB	6 SCO	7 CAP	8 PIS	7 ARI	9 GEM	9 CAN
11 TAU	10 GEM	11 CAN	9 LEO	9 VIR	9 SCO	9 SAG	9 AQU	10 ARI	10 TAU	11 CAN	11 LEO
13 GEM	12 CAN	13 LEO	11 VIR	11 LIB	11 SAG	11 CAP	11 PIS	13 TAU	13 GEM	14 LEO	13 VIR
16 CAN	14 LEO	15 VIR	13 LIB	13 SCO	13 CAP	13 AQU	14 ARI	15 GEM	15 CAN	16 VIR	15 LIB
18 LEO	16 VIR	17 LIB	15 SCO	15 SAG	15 AQU	15 PIS	16 TAU	18 CAN	17 LEO	18 LIB	18 SCO
20 VIR	18 LIB	19 SCO	17 SAG	17 CAP	18 PIS	18 ARI	19 GEM	20 LEO	20 VIR	20 SCO	20 SAG
22 LIB	21 SCO	21 SAG	19 CAP	19 AQU	20 ARI	20 TAU	21 CAN	22 VIR	22 LIB	22 SAG	22 CAP
24 SCO	23 SAG	23 CAP	22 AQU	21 PIS	23 TAU	23 GEM	24 LEO	24 LIB	24 SCO	24 CAP	24 AQU
26 SAG	25 CAP	25 AQU	24 PIS	24 ARI	25 GEM	25 CAN	26 VIR	26 SCO	26 SAG	26 AQU	26 PIS
29 CAP	27 AQU	28 PIS	27 ARI	26 TAU	28 CAN	27 LEO	28 LIB	28 SAG	28 CAP	29 PIS	28 ARI
31 AQU	29 AQU	30 ARI	29 TAU	29 GEM	30 LEO	29 VIR	30 SCO	30 CAP	30 AQU	30 PIS	31 TAU
		31 ARI	30 TAU	31 CAN		31 VIR	31 SCO		31 AQU		

1977

JAN	FEB	MAR	APR	MAY	JUN	JUL	AUG	SEP	OCT	NOV	DEC
1 TAU	1 CAN	1 CAN	1 LEO	1 LIB	1 SCO	1 CAP	1 AQU	1 ARI	1 TAU	1 CAN	1 LEO
2 GEM	4 LEO	3 LEO	2 VIR	3 SCO	2 SAG	3 AQU	2 PIS	3 TAU	2 GEM	4 LEO	3 VIR
5 CAN	6 VIR	5 VIR	4 LIB	5 SAG	4 CAP	5 PIS	4 ARI	5 GEM	5 CAN	6 VIR	6 LIB
7 LEO	8 LIB	7 LIB	6 SCO	7 CAP	6 AQU	7 ARI	6 TAU	8 CAN	7 LEO	8 LIB	8 SCO
9 VIR	10 SCO	9 SCO	8 SAG	9 AQU	8 PIS	10 TAU	9 GEM	10 LEO	10 VIR	11 SCO	10 SAG
12 LIB	12 SAG	11 SAG	10 CAP	11 PIS	10 ARI	12 GEM	11 CAN	12 VIR	12 LIB	13 SAG	12 CAP
14 SCO	14 CAP	14 CAP	12 AQU	14 ARI	13 TAU	15 CAN	14 LEO	15 LIB	14 SCO	15 CAP	14 AQU
16 SAG	16 AQU	16 AQU	14 PIS	16 TAU	15 GEM	17 LEO	16 VIR	17 SCO	16 SAG	17 AQU	16 PIS
18 CAP	19 PIS	18 PIS	17 ARI	19 GEM	18 CAN	20 VIR	18 LIB	19 SAG	18 CAP	19 PIS	18 ARI
20 AQU	21 ARI	20 ARI	19 TAU	21 CAN	20 LEO	22 LIB	20 SCO	21 CAP	20 AQU	21 ARI	21 TAU
22 PIS	23 TAU	23 TAU	21 GEM	24 LEO	23 VIR	24 SCO	23 SAG	23 AQU	23 PIS	23 TAU	23 GEM
25 ARI	26 GEM	25 GEM	24 CAN	26 VIR	25 LIB	26 SAG	25 CAP	25 PIS	25 ARI	26 GEM	26 CAN
27 TAU	28 GEM	28 CAN	27 LEO	29 LIB	27 SCO	28 CAP	27 AQU	28 ARI	27 TAU	28 CAN	28 LEO
30 GEM		30 LEO	29 VIR	31 SCO	29 SAG	30 AQU	29 PIS	30 TAU	30 GEM	30 CAN	31 VIR
31 GEM		31 LEO	30 VIR		30 SAG	31 AQU	31 ARI		31 GEM		

1978

JAN	FEB	MAR	APR	MAY	JUN	JUL	AUG	SEP	OCT	NOV	DEC
1 VIR	1 SCO	1 SCO	1 CAP	1 AQU	1 ARI	1 TAU	1 CAN	1 LEO	1 VIR	1 SCO	1 SAG
2 LIB	3 SAG	2 SAG	3 AQU	2 PIS	3 TAU	2 GEM	4 LEO	2 VIR	2 LIB	3 SAG	2 CAP
4 SCO	5 CAP	4 CAP	5 PIS	4 ARI	5 GEM	5 CAN	6 VIR	5 LIB	4 SCO	5 CAP	4 AQU
6 SAG	7 AQU	6 AQU	7 ARI	6 TAU	8 CAN	7 LEO	9 LIB	7 SCO	7 SAG	7 AQU	6 PIS
8 CAP	9 PIS	8 PIS	9 TAU	9 GEM	10 LEO	10 VIR	11 SCO	9 SAG	9 CAP	9 PIS	9 ARI
10 AQU	11 ARI	10 ARI	11 GEM	11 CAN	13 VIR	12 LIB	13 SAG	12 CAP	11 AQU	11 ARI	11 TAU
12 PIS	13 TAU	13 TAU	14 CAN	14 LEO	15 LIB	15 SCO	15 CAP	14 AQU	13 PIS	14 TAU	13 GEM
15 ARI	16 GEM	15 GEM	16 LEO	16 VIR	17 SCO	17 SAG	17 AQU	16 PIS	15 ARI	16 GEM	16 CAN
17 TAU	18 CAN	18 CAN	19 VIR	19 LIB	19 SAG	19 CAP	19 PIS	18 ARI	17 TAU	18 CAN	18 LEO
19 GEM	21 LEO	20 LEO	21 LIB	21 SCO	21 CAP	21 AQU	21 ARI	20 TAU	20 GEM	21 LEO	21 VIR
22 CAN	23 VIR	23 VIR	23 SCO	23 SAG	23 AQU	23 PIS	24 TAU	22 GEM	22 CAN	23 VIR	23 LIB
25 LEO	26 LIB	25 LIB	26 SAG	25 CAP	25 PIS	25 ARI	26 GEM	25 CAN	25 LEO	26 LIB	26 SCO
27 VIR	28 SCO	27 SCO	28 CAP	27 AQU	28 ARI	27 TAU	28 CAN	27 LEO	27 VIR	28 SCO	28 SAG
29 LIB		29 SAG	30 AQU	29 PIS	30 TAU	30 GEM	31 LEO	30 VIR	29 LIB	30 SAG	30 CAP
31 LIB		31 CAP		31 ARI		31 GEM			31 LIB		31 CAP

1979

JAN	FEB	MAR	APR	MAY	JUN	JUL	AUG	SEP	OCT	NOV	DEC
1 AQU	1 ARI	1 ARI	1 GEM	1 CAN	1 LEO	1 VIR	1 SCO	1 SAG	1 AQU	1 PIS	1 TAU
3 PIS	3 TAU	3 TAU	4 CAN	4 LEO	2 VIR	2 LIB	3 SAG	2 CAP	4 PIS	2 ARI	3 GEM
5 ARI	6 GEM	5 GEM	6 LEO	6 VIR	5 LIB	5 SCO	6 CAP	4 AQU	6 ARI	4 TAU	6 CAN
7 TAU	8 CAN	7 CAN	9 VIR	9 LIB	7 SCO	7 SAG	8 AQU	6 PIS	8 TAU	6 GEM	8 LEO
9 GEM	11 LEO	10 LEO	11 LIB	11 SCO	10 SAG	9 CAP	10 PIS	8 ARI	10 GEM	8 CAN	10 VIR
12 CAN	13 VIR	12 VIR	14 SCO	13 SAG	12 CAP	11 AQU	12 ARI	10 TAU	12 CAN	11 LEO	13 LIB
14 LEO	16 LIB	15 LIB	16 SAG	15 CAP	14 AQU	13 PIS	14 TAU	12 GEM	14 LEO	13 VIR	16 SCO
17 VIR	18 SCO	17 SCO	18 CAP	18 AQU	16 PIS	15 ARI	16 GEM	15 CAN	17 VIR	16 LIB	18 SAG
19 LIB	20 SAG	20 SAG	20 AQU	20 PIS	18 ARI	17 TAU	18 CAN	17 LEO	19 LIB	18 SCO	20 CAP
22 SCO	23 CAP	22 CAP	22 PIS	22 ARI	20 TAU	20 GEM	21 LEO	20 VIR	22 SCO	20 SAG	22 AQU
24 SAG	25 AQU	24 AQU	25 ARI	24 TAU	22 GEM	22 CAN	23 VIR	22 LIB	24 SAG	23 CAP	24 PIS
26 CAP	27 PIS	26 PIS	27 TAU	26 GEM	25 CAN	25 LEO	26 LIB	25 SCO	27 CAP	25 AQU	26 ARI
28 AQU	28 PIS	28 ARI	29 GEM	28 CAN	27 LEO	27 VIR	28 SCO	27 SAG	29 AQU	27 PIS	29 TAU
30 PIS		30 TAU	30 GEM	31 LEO	30 SAG	30 LIB	31 SAG	29 CAP	31 PIS	29 ARI	31 GEM
31 PIS		31 TAU				31 LIB		30 CAP		30 ARI	

1980

JAN	FEB	MAR	APR	MAY	JUN	JUL	AUG	SEP	OCT	NOV	DEC
1 GEM	1 LEO	1 VIR	1 LIB	1 SCO	1 CAP	1 AQU	1 ARI	1 TAU	1 CAN	1 LEO	1 LIB
2 CAN	3 VIR	4 LIB	3 SCO	2 SAG	3 AQU	3 PIS	3 TAU	2 GEM	3 LEO	2 VIR	2 LIB
4 LEO	6 LIB	6 SCO	5 SAG	5 CAP	6 PIS	5 ARI	5 GEM	4 CAN	6 VIR	5 LIB	4 SCO
7 VIR	8 SCO	9 SAG	8 CAP	7 AQU	8 ARI	7 TAU	7 CAN	6 LEO	8 LIB	7 SCO	7 SAG
9 LIB	11 SAG	11 CAP	10 AQU	9 PIS	10 TAU	9 GEM	10 LEO	9 VIR	11 SCO	10 SAG	9 CAP
12 SCO	13 CAP	13 AQU	12 PIS	11 ARI	12 GEM	11 CAN	12 VIR	11 LIB	13 SAG	12 CAP	12 AQU
14 SAG	15 AQU	16 PIS	14 ARI	13 TAU	14 CAN	14 LEO	15 LIB	14 SCO	16 CAP	14 AQU	14 PIS
16 CAP	17 PIS	18 ARI	16 TAU	15 GEM	16 LEO	16 VIR	17 SCO	16 SAG	18 AQU	17 PIS	16 ARI
19 AQU	19 ARI	20 TAU	18 GEM	18 CAN	19 VIR	18 LIB	20 SAG	18 CAP	20 PIS	19 ARI	18 TAU
21 PIS	21 TAU	22 GEM	20 CAN	20 LEO	21 LIB	21 SCO	22 CAP	21 AQU	22 ARI	21 TAU	20 GEM
23 ARI	23 GEM	24 CAN	22 LEO	22 VIR	24 SCO	23 SAG	24 AQU	23 PIS	24 TAU	23 GEM	22 CAN
25 TAU	26 CAN	26 LEO	25 VIR	25 LIB	26 SAG	26 CAP	26 PIS	25 ARI	26 GEM	25 CAN	24 LEO
27 GEM	28 LEO	29 VIR	27 LIB	27 SCO	28 CAP	28 AQU	28 ARI	27 TAU	28 CAN	27 LEO	27 VIR
29 CAN	29 LEO	31 LIB	30 SCO	30 SAG	30 CAP	30 PIS	30 TAU	29 GEM	31 LEO	29 VIR	29 LIB
31 CAN				31 SAG		31 PIS	31 TAU	30 GEM		30 VIR	31 LIB

1981

JAN	FEB	MAR	APR	MAY	JUN	JUL	AUG	SEP	OCT	NOV	DEC
1 SCO	1 SAG	1 CAP	1 AQU	1 PIS	1 TAU	1 GEM	1 LEO	1 LIB	1 SCO	1 SAG	1 AQU
3 SAG	2 CAP	4 AQU	2 PIS	2 ARI	2 GEM	2 CAN	2 VIR	3 SCO	3 SAG	2 CAP	2 AQU
6 CAP	4 AQU	6 PIS	4 ARI	4 TAU	4 CAN	4 LEO	5 LIB	6 SAG	6 CAP	5 AQU	4 PIS
8 AQU	6 PIS	8 ARI	6 TAU	6 GEM	6 LEO	6 VIR	7 SCO	8 CAP	8 AQU	7 PIS	6 ARI
10 PIS	9 ARI	10 TAU	8 GEM	8 CAN	9 VIR	8 LIB	10 SAG	11 AQU	11 PIS	9 ARI	9 TAU
12 ARI	11 TAU	12 GEM	10 CAN	10 LEO	11 LIB	11 SCO	12 CAP	13 PIS	13 ARI	11 TAU	11 GEM
14 TAU	13 GEM	14 CAN	13 LEO	12 VIR	13 SCO	13 SAG	14 AQU	15 ARI	15 TAU	13 GEM	13 CAN
17 GEM	15 CAN	16 LEO	15 VIR	15 LIB	16 SAG	16 CAP	17 PIS	17 TAU	17 GEM	15 CAN	15 LEO
19 CAN	17 LEO	19 VIR	17 LIB	17 SCO	18 CAP	18 AQU	19 ARI	19 GEM	19 CAN	17 LEO	17 VIR
21 LEO	19 VIR	21 LIB	20 SCO	20 SAG	21 AQU	20 PIS	21 TAU	21 CAN	21 LEO	19 VIR	19 LIB
23 VIR	22 LIB	24 SCO	22 SAG	22 CAP	23 PIS	23 ARI	23 GEM	24 LEO	23 VIR	22 LIB	21 SCO
25 LIB	24 SCO	26 SAG	25 CAP	25 AQU	25 ARI	25 TAU	25 CAN	26 VIR	26 LIB	24 SCO	24 SAG
28 SCO	27 SAG	29 CAP	27 AQU	27 PIS	28 TAU	27 GEM	27 LEO	28 LIB	28 SCO	27 SAG	27 CAP
31 SAG	28 SAG	31 AQU	30 PIS	29 ARI	30 GEM	29 CAN	30 VIR	30 LIB	30 SAG	29 CAP	29 AQU
				31 TAU		31 LEO	31 VIR		31 SAG	30 CAP	31 PIS

1982

JAN	FEB	MAR	APR	MAY	JUN	JUL	AUG	SEP	OCT	NOV	DEC
1 PIS	1 TAU	1 TAU	1 CAN	1 LEO	1 LIB	1 SCO	1 SAG	1 AQU	1 PIS	1 TAU	1 GEM
3 ARI	3 GEM	3 GEM	3 LEO	2 VIR	3 SCO	3 SAG	2 CAP	3 PIS	3 ARI	4 GEM	3 CAN
5 TAU	5 CAN	5 CAN	5 VIR	5 LIB	6 SAG	6 CAP	4 AQU	6 ARI	5 TAU	6 CAN	5 LEO
7 GEM	7 LEO	7 LEO	8 LIB	7 SCO	8 CAP	8 AQU	7 PIS	8 TAU	7 GEM	8 LEO	7 VIR
9 CAN	10 VIR	9 VIR	10 SCO	10 SAG	11 AQU	11 PIS	9 ARI	10 GEM	9 CAN	10 VIR	9 LIB
11 LEO	12 LIB	11 LIB	12 SAG	12 CAP	13 PIS	13 ARI	12 TAU	12 CAN	11 LEO	12 LIB	12 SCO
13 VIR	14 SCO	14 SCO	15 CAP	15 AQU	16 ARI	15 TAU	14 GEM	14 LEO	14 VIR	14 SCO	14 SAG
15 LIB	17 SAG	16 SAG	17 AQU	17 PIS	18 TAU	17 GEM	16 CAN	16 VIR	16 LIB	17 SAG	16 CAP
18 SCO	19 CAP	18 CAP	20 PIS	19 ARI	20 GEM	19 CAN	18 LEO	18 LIB	18 SCO	19 CAP	19 AQU
20 SAG	22 AQU	21 AQU	22 ARI	22 TAU	22 CAN	21 LEO	20 VIR	21 SCO	20 SAG	22 AQU	22 PIS
23 CAP	24 PIS	23 PIS	24 TAU	24 GEM	24 LEO	23 VIR	22 LIB	23 SAG	23 CAP	24 PIS	24 ARI
25 AQU	26 ARI	26 ARI	26 GEM	26 CAN	26 VIR	26 LIB	24 SCO	26 CAP	25 AQU	27 ARI	26 TAU
28 PIS	28 TAU	28 TAU	28 CAN	28 LEO	28 LIB	28 SCO	27 SAG	28 AQU	28 PIS	29 TAU	28 GEM
30 ARI		30 GEM	30 LEO	30 VIR	30 LIB	30 SAG	29 CAP	30 AQU	30 ARI	30 TAU	30 CAN
31 ARI		31 GEM		31 VIR		31 SAG	31 CAP		31 ARI		31 CAN

HOW TO FIND YOUR ASCENDANT SIGN

Find your birth date in the following tables. If you were born during Wartime or Daylight Saving Time, refer to Appendix III, "How to Figure Time Changes." This also applies if you were born in a foreign country.

The tables here are calculated for 41° N, the median latitude for the United States and Europe. If you were born in either the northern or southern extremities, you will need either a computer chart or a professional to calculate your Ascendant accurately. Please see the Appendix for further information.

Though the ASC sign changes approximately every two hours daily, it does not vary from year to year. So, no matter what year you were born, determine the ASC only from the day and month of birth. If you were born before the half-hour, pick the preceding hour (for example, if you were born at 3:12 A.M., choose 3:00 A.M.). If you were born on or after the half-hour, choose the following hour.

Since there is little variation from day to day within the three-day periods listed, it is necessary only to pay attention to the *exact degree* given in the listing when your birth date falls in the unlisted intermediate date. (This book is concerned only with the ASC sign, not the precise degree, therefore you need only know the sign for your ASC.)

If your birth date is not listed, check the dates on either side. The degrees run from 0 to 29. If the sign is changing over the three-day period in which your birthday falls—that is, if it is in a late degree on one side and an early degree on the other side—you can estimate your ASC sign by adding 2 degrees to the degree of the sign on the day before your birthday. It is also a good idea to read both scripts of the two signs involved.

If your estimated degree is either 0 or 29, only a professional astrologer or a computer chart can tell you for sure which is your ASC sign. (See Appendix II.)

JANUARY 1

AM		PM	
1	21 LIB	1	13 TAU
2	3 SCO	2	3 GEM
3	14 SCO	3	19 GEM
4	26 SCO	4	4 CAN
5	8 SAG	5	17 CAN
6	21 SAG	6	29 CAN
7	4 CAP	7	10 LEO
8	19 CAP	8	22 LEO
9	7 AQU	9	3 VIR
10	28 AQU	10	16 VIR
11	23 PIS	11	28 VIR
12 noon	19 ARI	12 midnight	10 LIB

JANUARY 4

AM		PM	
1	23 LIB	1	17 TAU
2	5 SCO	2	6 GEM
3	16 SCO	3	22 GEM
4	28 SCO	4	6 CAN
5	11 SAG	5	19 CAN
6	23 SAG	6	1 LEO
7	7 CAP	7	13 LEO
8	22 CAP	8	24 LEO
9	11 AQU	9	6 VIR
10	3 PIS	10	18 VIR
11	29 PIS	11	29 VIR
12 noon	25 ARI	12 midnight	12 LIB

JANUARY 7

AM		PM	
1	25 LIB	1	22 TAU
2	7 SCO	2	9 GEM
3	18 SCO	3	25 GEM
4	29 SCO	4	9 CAN
5	12 SAG	5	21 CAN
6	26 SAG	6	3 LEO
7	10 CAP	7	15 LEO
8	25 CAP	8	26 LEO
9	15 AQU	9	8 VIR
10	7 PIS	10	20 VIR
11	4 ARI	11	2 LIB
12 noon	29 ARI	12 midnight	14 LIB

JANUARY 10

AM		PM	
1	28 LIB	1	25 TAU
2	9 SCO	2	12 GEM
3	21 SCO	3	28 GEM
4	3 SAG	4	11 CAN
5	15 SAG	5	23 CAN
6	28 SAG	6	5 LEO
7	13 CAP	7	17 LEO
8	29 CAP	8	29 LEO
9	20 AQU	9	11 VIR
10	14 PIS	10	23 VIR
11	9 ARI	11	4 LIB
12 noon	3 TAU	12 midnight	16 LIB

JANUARY 13

AM		PM	
1	29 LIB	1	29 TAU
2	12 SCO	2	15 GEM
3	24 SCO	3	29 GEM
4	5 SAG	4	13 CAN
5	18 SAG	5	26 CAN
6	1 CAP	6	8 LEO
7	16 CAP	7	19 LEO
8	3 AQU	8	1 VIR
9	23 AQU	9	13 VIR
10	18 PIS	10	24 VIR
11	14 ARI	11	7 LIB
12 noon	8 TAU	12 midnight	18 LIB

JANUARY 16

AM		PM	
1	2 SCO	1	2 GEM
2	14 SCO	2	18 GEM
3	26 SCO	3	3 CAN
4	8 SAG	4	16 CAN
5	20 SAG	5	28 CAN
6	3 CAP	6	10 LEO
7	19 CAP	7	22 LEO
8	7 AQU	8	3 VIR
9	28 AQU	9	15 VIR
10	23 PIS	10	27 VIR
11	19 ARI	11	9 LIB
12 noon	13 TAU	12 midnight	21 LIB

JANUARY 19

AM		PM	
1	5 SCO	1	6 GEM
2	16 SCO	2	21 GEM
3	28 SCO	3	6 CAN
4	10 SAG	4	18 CAN
5	23 SAG	5	1 LEO
6	7 CAP	6	13 LEO
7	22 CAP	7	24 LEO
8	11 AQU	8	6 VIR
9	3 PIS	9	18 VIR
10	29 PIS	10	29 VIR
11	24 ARI	11	12 LIB
12 noon	17 TAU	12 midnight	23 LIB

JANUARY 22

AM		PM	
1	7 SCO	1	9 GEM
2	19 SCO	2	24 GEM
3	29 SCO	3	8 CAN
4	13 SAG	4	21 CAN
5	26 SAG	5	3 LEO
6	10 CAP	6	15 LEO
7	25 CAP	7	26 LEO
8	15 AQU	8	8 VIR
9	8 PIS	9	20 VIR
10	4 ARI	10	1 LIB
11	28 ARI	11	13 LIB
12 noon	20 TAU	12 midnight	25 LIB

JANUARY 25

AM		PM	
1	9 SCO	1	12 GEM
2	21 SCO	2	28 GEM
3	3 SAG	3	11 CAN
4	15 SAG	4	23 CAN
5	28 SAG	5	5 LEO
6	13 CAP	6	17 LEO
7	29 CAP	7	29 LEO
8	19 AQU	8	10 VIR
9	13 PIS	9	22 VIR
10	8 ARI	10	4 LIB
11	3 TAU	11	16 LIB
12 noon	24 TAU	12 midnight	28 LIB

JANUARY 28

AM		PM	
1	12 SCO	1	15 GEM
2	24 SCO	2	29 GEM
3	5 SAG	3	13 CAN
4	18 SAG	4	26 CAN
5	1 CAP	5	7 LEO
6	16 CAP	6	19 LEO
7	3 AQU	7	1 VIR
8	23 AQU	8	13 VIR
9	17 PIS	9	24 VIR
10	14 ARI	10	7 LIB
11	8 TAU	11	18 LIB
12 noon	28 TAU	12 midnight	29 LIB

JANUARY 31

AM		PM	
1	14 SCO	1	18 GEM
2	26 SCO	2	3 CAN
3	8 SAG	3	16 CAN
4	20 SAG	4	28 CAN
5	3 CAP	5	10 LEO
6	19 CAP	6	22 LEO
7	7 AQU	7	3 VIR
8	28 AQU	8	15 VIR
9	23 PIS	9	27 VIR
10	19 ARI	10	9 LIB
11	13 TAU	11	21 LIB
12 noon	2 GEM	12 midnight	2 SCO

FEBRUARY 3

AM		PM	
1	16 SCO	1	21 GEM
2	28 SCO	2	6 CAN
3	10 SAG	3	18 CAN
4	22 SAG	4	1 LEO
5	6 CAP	5	13 LEO
6	22 CAP	6	24 LEO
7	11 AQU	7	6 VIR
8	3 PIS	8	18 VIR
9	29 PIS	9	29 VIR
10	23 ARI	10	12 LIB
11	16 TAU	11	23 LIB
12 noon	6 GEM	12 midnight	5 SCO

FEBRUARY 6

AM		PM	
1	18 SCO	1	24 GEM
2	29 SCO	2	8 CAN
3	12 SAG	3	21 CAN
4	26 SAG	4	3 LEO
5	9 CAP	5	15 LEO
6	25 CAP	6	26 LEO
7	14 AQU	7	8 VIR
8	6 PIS	8	20 VIR
9	2 ARI	9	2 LIB
10	28 ARI	10	14 LIB
11	20 TAU	11	26 LIB
12 noon	9 GEM	12 midnight	7 SCO

FEBRUARY 9

AM		PM	
1	21 SCO	1	27 GEM
2	3 SAG	2	10 CAN
3	14 SAG	3	23 CAN
4	28 SAG	4	5 LEO
5	12 CAP	5	17 LEO
6	29 CAP	6	29 LEO
7	18 AQU	7	11 VIR
8	12 PIS	8	23 VIR
9	8 ARI	9	4 LIB
10	3 TAU	10	16 LIB
11	24 TAU	11	28 LIB
12 noon	12 GEM	12 midnight	9 SCO

FEBRUARY 12

AM		PM	
1	23 SCO	1	29 GEM
2	5 SAG	2	13 CAN
3	17 SAG	3	26 CAN
4	1 CAP	4	8 LEO
5	15 CAP	5	19 LEO
6	2 AQU	6	1 VIR
7	23 AQU	7	13 VIR
8	17 PIS	8	24 VIR
9	14 ARI	9	7 LIB
10	8 TAU	10	18 LIB
11	28 TAU	11	29 LIB
12 noon	15 GEM	12 midnight	12 SCO

FEBRUARY 15

AM		PM	
1	25 SCO	1	3 CAN
2	7 SAG	2	16 CAN
3	20 SAG	3	28 CAN
4	3 CAP	4	10 LEO
5	18 CAP	5	22 LEO
6	5 AQU	6	3 VIR
7	28 AQU	7	15 VIR
8	23 PIS	8	27 VIR
9	17 ARI	9	9 LIB
10	11 TAU	10	21 LIB
11	2 GEM	11	2 SCO
12 noon	18 GEM	12 midnight	14 SCO

FEBRUARY 18

AM		PM	
1	27 SCO	1	6 CAN
2	10 SAG	2	18 CAN
3	22 SAG	3	1 LEO
4	6 CAP	4	13 LEO
5	21 CAP	5	24 LEO
6	9 AQU	6	6 VIR
7	1 PIS	7	18 VIR
8	27 PIS	8	29 VIR
9	23 ARI	9	12 LIB
10	16 TAU	10	23 LIB
11	6 GEM	11	5 SCO
12 noon	21 GEM	12 midnight	17 SCO

FEBRUARY 21

AM		PM	
1	29 SCO	1	8 CAN
2	12 SAG	2	22 CAN
3	25 SAG	3	2 LEO
4	9 CAP	4	13 LEO
5	24 CAP	5	26 LEO
6	14 AQU	6	8 VIR
7	6 PIS	7	20 VIR
8	2 ARI	8	1 LIB
9	28 ARI	9	13 LIB
10	20 TAU	10	24 LIB
11	9 GEM	11	6 SCO
12 noon	24 GEM	12 midnight	18 SCO

FEBRUARY 24

AM		PM	
1	3 SAG	1	10 CAN
2	14 SAG	2	23 CAN
3	27 SAG	3	5 LEO
4	12 CAP	4	17 LEO
5	28 CAP	5	29 LEO
6	16 AQU	6	10 VIR
7	10 PIS	7	22 VIR
8	9 ARI	8	4 LIB
9	5 TAU	9	16 LIB
10	27 TAU	10	28 LIB
11	12 GEM	11	9 SCO
12 noon	27 GEM	12 midnight	21 SCO

FEBRUARY 27

AM		PM	
1	5 SAG	1	13 CAN
2	17 SAG	2	26 CAN
3	1 CAP	3	7 LEO
4	15 CAP	4	19 LEO
5	2 AQU	5	1 VIR
6	22 AQU	6	13 VIR
7	16 PIS	7	24 VIR
8	12 ARI	8	7 LIB
9	7 TAU	9	18 LIB
10	28 TAU	10	29 LIB
11	15 GEM	11	12 SCO
12 noon	29 GEM	12 midnight	24 SCO

MARCH 2

AM		PM	
1	7 SAG	1	16 CAN
2	20 SAG	2	28 CAN
3	3 CAP	3	10 LEO
4	18 CAP	4	22 LEO
5	5 AQU	5	3 VIR
6	26 AQU	6	15 VIR
7	21 PIS	7	27 VIR
8	17 ARI	8	9 LIB
9	11 TAU	9	21 LIB
10	2 GEM	10	2 SCO
11	18 GEM	11	14 SCO
12 noon	2 CAN	12 midnight	26 SCO

MARCH 5

AM		PM	
1	9 SAG	1	18 CAN
2	22 SAG	2	29 CAN
3	6 CAP	3	12 LEO
4	22 CAP	4	24 LEO
5	9 AQU	5	5 VIR
6	1 PIS	6	18 VIR
7	27 PIS	7	29 VIR
8	23 ARI	8	11 LIB
9	16 TAU	9	23 LIB
10	4 GEM	10	5 SCO
11	21 GEM	11	16 SCO
12 noon	6 CAN	12 midnight	28 SCO

MARCH 8

AM		PM	
1	12 SAG	1	20 CAN
2	25 SAG	2	2 LEO
3	9 CAP	3	14 LEO
4	24 CAP	4	26 LEO
5	14 AQU	5	8 VIR
6	6 PIS	6	19 VIR
7	2 ARI	7	1 LIB
8	28 ARI	8	13 LIB
9	20 TAU	9	25 LIB
10	8 GEM	10	7 SCO
11	24 GEM	11	18 SCO
12 noon	8 CAN	12 midnight	29 SCO

MARCH 11

AM		PM	
1	14 SAG	1	23 CAN
2	27 SAG	2	5 LEO
3	12 CAP	3	16 LEO
4	28 CAP	4	29 LEO
5	18 AQU	5	10 VIR
6	12 PIS	6	22 VIR
7	6 ARI	7	4 LIB
8	2 TAU	8	16 LIB
9	24 TAU	9	28 LIB
10	11 GEM	10	9 SCO
11	27 GEM	11	21 SCO
12 noon	10 CAN	12 midnight	3 SAG

MARCH 14

AM		PM	
1	17 SAG	1	25 CAN
2	29 SAG	2	7 LEO
3	15 CAP	3	19 LEO
4	2 AQU	4	29 LEO
5	21 AQU	5	13 VIR
6	15 PIS	6	24 VIR
7	12 ARI	7	7 LIB
8	7 TAU	8	18 LIB
9	27 TAU	9	29 LIB
10	14 GEM	10	12 SCO
11	29 GEM	11	24 SCO
12 noon	13 CAN	12 midnight	5 SAG

MARCH 17

AM		PM	
1	19 SAG	1	28 CAN
2	2 CAP	2	10 LEO
3	18 CAP	3	21 LEO
4	5 AQU	4	3 VIR
5	26 AQU	5	15 VIR
6	21 PIS	6	26 VIR
7	17 ARI	7	8 LIB
8	11 TAU	8	20 LIB
9	1 GEM	9	2 SCO
10	17 GEM	10	14 SCO
11	2 CAN	11	26 SCO
12 noon	15 CAN	12 midnight	8 SAG

MARCH 20

AM		PM	
1	21 SAG	1	29 CAN
2	5 CAP	2	12 LEO
3	21 CAP	3	23 LEO
4	8 AQU	4	5 VIR
5	1 PIS	5	17 VIR
6	27 PIS	6	29 VIR
7	22 ARI	7	11 LIB
8	16 TAU	8	23 LIB
9	4 GEM	9	5 SCO
10	20 GEM	10	16 SCO
11	5 CAN	11	28 SCO
12 noon	18 CAN	12 midnight	10 SAG

MARCH 23

AM		PM	
1	24 SAG	1	2 LEO
2	8 CAP	2	14 LEO
3	24 CAP	3	26 LEO
4	12 AQU	4	8 VIR
5	5 PIS	5	19 VIR
6	1 ARI	6	1 LIB
7	26 ARI	7	13 LIB
8	19 TAU	8	24 LIB
9	8 GEM	9	7 SCO
10	23 GEM	10	18 SCO
11	7 CAN	11	29 SCO
12 noon	20 CAN	12 midnight	12 SAG

MARCH 26

AM		PM	
1	27 SAG	1	4 LEO
2	12 CAP	2	16 LEO
3	28 CAP	3	28 LEO
4	17 AQU	4	10 VIR
5	10 PIS	5	22 VIR
6	6 ARI	6	4 LIB
7	2 TAU	7	16 LIB
8	23 TAU	8	28 LIB
9	11 GEM	9	9 SCO
10	26 GEM	10	21 SCO
11	10 CAN	11	3 SAG
12 noon	23 CAN	12 midnight	15 SAG

APRIL 7

AM		PM	
1	8 CAP	1	14 LEO
2	24 CAP	2	26 LEO
3	12 AQU	3	8 VIR
4	5 PIS	4	19 VIR
5	1 ARI	5	1 LIB
6	26 ARI	6	13 LIB
7	19 TAU	7	25 LIB
8	8 GEM	8	6 SCO
9	23 GEM	9	18 SCO
10	7 CAN	10	29 SCO
11	20 CAN	11	12 SAG
12 noon	2 LEO	12 midnight	25 SAG

MARCH 29

AM		PM	
1	29 SAG	1	7 LEO
2	15 CAP	2	19 LEO
3	2 AQU	3	29 LEO
4	21 AQU	4	13 VIR
5	15 PIS	5	24 VIR
6	12 ARI	6	6 LIB
7	7 TAU	7	18 LIB
8	27 TAU	8	29 LIB
9	14 GEM	9	12 SCO
10	29 GEM	10	23 SCO
11	13 CAN	11	5 SAG
12 noon	25 CAN	12 midnight	18 SAG

APRIL 10

AM		PM	
1	11 CAP	1	16 LEO
2	28 CAP	2	28 LEO
3	17 AQU	3	9 VIR
4	10 PIS	4	22 VIR
5	6 ARI	5	3 LIB
6	2 TAU	6	15 LIB
7	23 TAU	7	27 LIB
8	11 GEM	8	9 SCO
9	26 GEM	9	21 SCO
10	10 CAN	10	3 SAG
11	23 CAN	11	14 SAG
12 noon	4 LEO	12 midnight	27 SAG

APRIL 1

AM		PM	
1	2 CAP	1	10 LEO
2	18 CAP	2	21 LEO
3	5 AQU	3	3 VIR
4	26 AQU	4	14 VIR
5	21 PIS	5	26 VIR
6	17 ARI	6	8 LIB
7	11 TAU	7	20 LIB
8	1 GEM	8	2 SCO
9	17 GEM	9	14 SCO
10	2 CAN	10	25 SCO
11	15 CAN	11	8 SAG
12 noon	27 CAN	12 midnight	20 SAG

APRIL 13

AM		PM	
1	14 CAP	1	19 LEO
2	29 CAP	2	29 LEO
3	21 AQU	3	12 VIR
4	15 PIS	4	24 VIR
5	12 ARI	5	6 LIB
6	7 TAU	6	18 LIB
7	27 TAU	7	29 LIB
8	14 GEM	8	12 SCO
9	29 GEM	9	23 SCO
10	13 CAN	10	5 SAG
11	25 CAN	11	17 SAG
12 noon	7 LEO	12 midnight	1 CAP

APRIL 4

AM		PM	
1	5 CAP	1	12 LEO
2	21 CAP	2	23 LEO
3	9 AQU	3	5 VIR
4	1 PIS	4	17 VIR
5	26 PIS	5	29 VIR
6	21 ARI	6	11 LIB
7	14 TAU	7	23 LIB
8	4 GEM	8	4 SCO
9	20 GEM	9	15 SCO
10	5 CAN	10	28 SCO
11	17 CAN	11	10 SAG
12 noon	29 CAN	12 midnight	22 SAG

APRIL 16

AM		PM	
1	17 CAP	1	21 LEO
2	4 AQU	2	3 VIR
3	26 AQU	3	14 VIR
4	20 PIS	4	26 VIR
5	16 ARI	5	8 LIB
6	10 TAU	6	20 LIB
7	1 GEM	7	2 SCO
8	17 GEM	8	13 SCO
9	1 CAN	9	25 SCO
10	15 CAN	10	7 SAG
11	27 CAN	11	20 SAG
12 noon	9 LEO	12 midnight	3 CAP

APRIL 19

AM		PM	
1	20 CAP	1	23 LEO
2	8 AQU	2	5 VIR
3	29 AQU	3	17 VIR
4	25 PIS	4	29 VIR
5	21 ARI	5	11 LIB
6	14 TAU	6	23 LIB
7	4 GEM	7	4 SCO
8	20 GEM	8	15 SCO
9	5 CAN	9	28 SCO
10	17 CAN	10	10 SAG
11	29 CAN	11	22 SAG
12 noon	11 LEO	12 midnight	10 CAP

APRIL 22

AM		PM	
1	24 CAP	1	26 LEO
2	14 AQU	2	7 VIR
3	5 PIS	3	19 VIR
4	1 ARI	4	1 LIB
5	26 ARI	5	13 LIB
6	19 TAU	6	24 LIB
7	8 GEM	7	6 SCO
8	23 GEM	8	18 SCO
9	7 CAN	9	29 SCO
10	20 CAN	10	13 SAG
11	2 LEO	11	25 SAG
12 noon	14 LEO	12 midnight	9 CAP

APRIL 25

AM		PM	
1	27 CAP	1	28 LEO
2	17 AQU	2	9 VIR
3	10 PIS	3	21 VIR
4	6 ARI	4	3 LIB
5	2 TAU	5	15 LIB
6	23 TAU	6	27 LIB
7	11 GEM	7	9 SCO
8	26 GEM	8	20 SCO
9	10 CAN	9	3 SAG
10	22 CAN	10	14 SAG
11	4 LEO	11	27 SAG
12 noon	16 LEO	12 midnight	12 CAP

APRIL 28

AM		PM	
1	2 AQU	1	29 LEO
2	21 AQU	2	12 VIR
3	15 PIS	3	24 VIR
4	10 ARI	4	6 LIB
5	5 TAU	5	18 LIB
6	27 TAU	6	29 LIB
7	14 GEM	7	11 SCO
8	29 GEM	8	23 SCO
9	12 CAN	9	5 SAG
10	25 CAN	10	17 SAG
11	7 LEO	11	29 SAG
12 noon	19 LEO	12 midnight	15 CAP

MAY 1

AM		PM	
1	4 AQU	1	3 VIR
2	24 AQU	2	14 VIR
3	19 PIS	3	26 VIR
4	16 ARI	4	8 LIB
5	10 TAU	5	20 LIB
6	29 TAU	6	2 SCO
7	17 GEM	7	13 SCO
8	1 CAN	8	25 SCO
9	15 CAN	9	7 SAG
10	27 CAN	10	19 SAG
11	9 LEO	11	3 CAP
12 noon	21 LEO	12 midnight	18 CAP

MAY 4

AM		PM	
1	8 AQU	1	4 VIR
2	29 AQU	2	17 VIR
3	25 PIS	3	28 VIR
4	21 ARI	4	10 LIB
5	14 TAU	5	22 LIB
6	3 GEM	6	4 SCO
7	20 GEM	7	15 SCO
8	5 CAN	8	27 SCO
9	17 CAN	9	9 SAG
10	29 CAN	10	21 SAG
11	11 LEO	11	5 CAP
12 noon	23 LEO	12 midnight	21 CAP

MAY 7

AM		PM	
1	21 AQU	1	7 VIR
2	5 PIS	2	18 VIR
3	1 ARI	3	1 LIB
4	26 ARI	4	13 LIB
5	19 TAU	5	24 LIB
6	7 GEM	6	6 SCO
7	23 GEM	7	18 SCO
8	7 CAN	8	29 SCO
9	20 CAN	9	12 SAG
10	1 LEO	10	25 SAG
11	13 LEO	11	9 CAP
12 noon	25 LEO	12 midnight	24 CAP

MAY 10

AM		PM	
1	16 AQU	1	9 VIR
2	9 PIS	2	21 VIR
3	4 ARI	3	3 LIB
4	29 ARI	4	15 LIB
5	23 TAU	5	27 LIB
6	10 GEM	6	9 SCO
7	26 GEM	7	20 SCO
8	10 CAN	8	2 SAG
9	22 CAN	9	14 SAG
10	4 LEO	10	27 SAG
11	16 LEO	11	11 CAP
12 noon	27 LEO	12 midnight	28 CAP

MAY 13

AM		PM	
1	20 AQU	1	12 VIR
2	14 PIS	2	24 VIR
3	10 ARI	3	6 LIB
4	5 TAU	4	18 LIB
5	26 TAU	5	29 LIB
6	13 GEM	6	11 SCO
7	29 GEM	7	22 SCO
8	12 CAN	8	5 SAG
9	25 CAN	9	17 SAG
10	7 LEO	10	29 SAG
11	18 LEO	11	15 CAP
12 noon	29 LEO	12 midnight	2 AQU

MAY 16

AM		PM	
1	24 AQU	1	14 VIR
2	19 PIS	2	25 VIR
3	16 ARI	3	7 LIB
4	10 TAU	4	19 LIB
5	29 TAU	5	2 SCO
6	16 GEM	6	13 SCO
7	1 CAN	7	25 SCO
8	14 CAN	8	7 SAG
9	27 CAN	9	19 SAG
10	9 LEO	10	2 CAP
11	20 LEO	11	18 CAP
12 noon	2 VIR	12 midnight	5 AQU

MAY 19

AM		PM	
1	29 AQU	1	16 VIR
2	25 PIS	2	28 VIR
3	21 ARI	3	10 LIB
4	14 TAU	4	22 LIB
5	3 GEM	5	4 SCO
6	19 GEM	6	15 SCO
7	4 CAN	7	27 SCO
8	17 CAN	8	9 SAG
9	29 CAN	9	21 SAG
10	11 LEO	10	5 CAP
11	22 LEO	11	21 CAP
12 noon	4 VIR	12 midnight	9 AQU

MAY 22

AM		PM	
1	5 PIS	1	18 VIR
2	29 PIS	2	1 LIB
3	25 ARI	3	13 LIB
4	18 TAU	4	24 LIB
5	7 GEM	5	5 SCO
6	22 GEM	6	18 SCO
7	6 CAN	7	29 SCO
8	20 CAN	8	12 SAG
9	1 LEO	9	25 SAG
10	13 LEO	10	9 CAP
11	25 LEO	11	24 CAP
12 noon	7 VIR	12 midnight	14 AQU

MAY 25

AM		PM	
1	8 PIS	1	21 VIR
2	4 ARI	2	3 LIB
3	29 ARI	3	15 LIB
4	22 TAU	4	27 LIB
5	10 GEM	5	9 SCO
6	25 GEM	6	20 SCO
7	9 CAN	7	2 SAG
8	22 CAN	8	14 SAG
9	4 LEO	9	27 SAG
10	16 LEO	10	11 CAP
11	27 LEO	11	28 CAP
12 noon	9 VIR	12 midnight	17 AQU

MAY 28

AM		PM	
1	14 PIS	1	23 VIR
2	10 ARI	2	6 LIB
3	5 TAU	3	17 LIB
4	26 TAU	4	29 LIB
5	13 GEM	5	10 SCO
6	29 GEM	6	22 SCO
7	11 CAN	7	4 SAG
8	24 CAN	8	17 SAG
9	6 LEO	9	29 SAG
10	18 LEO	10	14 CAP
11	29 LEO	11	2 AQU
12 noon	12 VIR	12 midnight	21 AQU

MAY 31

AM		PM	
1	19 PIS	1	25 VIR
2	16 ARI	2	7 LIB
3	10 TAU	3	19 LIB
4	29 TAU	4	2 SCO
5	16 GEM	5	13 SCO
6	1 CAN	6	24 SCO
7	14 CAN	7	7 SAG
8	27 CAN	8	19 SAG
9	8 LEO	9	2 CAP
10	20 LEO	10	18 CAP
11	2 VIR	11	5 AQU
12 noon	13 VIR	12 midnight	26 AQU

JUNE 3

AM		PM	
1	25 PIS	1	28 VIR
2	19 ARI	2	10 LIB
3	13 TAU	3	22 LIB
4	3 GEM	4	3 SCO
5	19 GEM	5	15 SCO
6	4 CAN	6	27 SCO
7	17 CAN	7	9 SAG
8	29 CAN	8	21 SAG
9	11 LEO	9	5 CAP
10	22 LEO	10	21 CAP
11	4 VIR	11	8 AQU
12 noon	16 VIR	12 midnight	1 PIS

JUNE 6

AM		PM	
1	29 PIS	1	1 LIB
2	25 ARI	2	13 LIB
3	17 TAU	3	24 LIB
4	7 GEM	4	5 SCO
5	22 GEM	5	18 SCO
6	6 CAN	6	29 SCO
7	19 CAN	7	11 SAG
8	1 LEO	8	24 SAG
9	13 LEO	9	8 CAP
10	25 LEO	10	23 CAP
11	7 VIR	11	12 AQU
12 noon	18 VIR	12 midnight	5 PIS

JUNE 9

AM		PM	
1	4 ARI	1	3 LIB
2	29 ARI	2	14 LIB
3	22 TAU	3	27 LIB
4	10 GEM	4	8 SCO
5	25 GEM	5	20 SCO
6	9 CAN	6	2 SAG
7	21 CAN	7	14 SAG
8	4 LEO	8	27 SAG
9	16 LEO	9	11 CAP
10	27 LEO	10	28 CAP
11	9 VIR	11	17 AQU
12 noon	21 VIR	12 midnight	10 PIS

JUNE 12

AM		PM	
1	10 ARI	1	5 LIB
2	3 TAU	2	17 LIB
3	26 TAU	3	29 LIB
4	13 GEM	4	10 SCO
5	28 GEM	5	22 SCO
6	11 CAN	6	4 SAG
7	24 CAN	7	16 SAG
8	6 LEO	8	29 SAG
9	18 LEO	9	14 CAP
10	29 LEO	10	29 CAP
11	11 VIR	11	21 AQU
12 noon	23 VIR	12 midnight	15 PIS

JUNE 15

AM		PM	
1	14 ARI	1	7 LIB
2	8 TAU	2	19 LIB
3	29 TAU	3	1 SCO
4	16 GEM	4	12 SCO
5	29 GEM	5	24 SCO
6	13 CAN	6	6 SAG
7	26 CAN	7	19 SAG
8	8 LEO	8	2 CAP
9	20 LEO	9	17 CAP
10	2 VIR	10	4 AQU
11	13 VIR	11	26 AQU
12 noon	25 VIR	12 midnight	20 PIS

JUNE 18

AM		PM	
1	19 ARI	1	10 LIB
2	13 TAU	2	22 LIB
3	3 GEM	3	3 SCO
4	19 GEM	4	15 SCO
5	3 CAN	5	27 SCO
6	17 CAN	6	8 SAG
7	28 CAN	7	21 SAG
8	10 LEO	8	5 CAP
9	22 LEO	9	20 CAP
10	4 VIR	10	8 AQU
11	16 VIR	11	29 AQU
12 noon	28 VIR	12 midnight	25 PIS

JUNE 21

AM		PM	
1	25 ARI	1	12 LIB
2	17 TAU	2	24 LIB
3	7 GEM	3	5 SCO
4	22 GEM	4	18 SCO
5	6 CAN	5	29 SCO
6	19 CAN	6	11 SAG
7	1 LEO	7	24 SAG
8	13 LEO	8	8 CAP
9	25 LEO	9	23 CAP
10	6 VIR	10	12 AQU
11	18 VIR	11	5 PIS
12 noon	1 LIB	12 midnight	1 ARI

JUNE 24

AM		PM	
1	29 ARI	1	14 LIB
2	22 TAU	2	26 LIB
3	10 GEM	3	8 SCO
4	25 GEM	4	19 SCO
5	9 CAN	5	1 SAG
6	21 CAN	6	14 SAG
7	4 LEO	7	26 SAG
8	16 LEO	8	11 CAP
9	27 LEO	9	27 CAP
10	8 VIR	10	16 AQU
11	20 VIR	11	10 PIS
12 noon	2 LIB	12 midnight	5 ARI

JUNE 27

AM		PM	
1	3 TAU	1	17 LIB
2	25 TAU	2	28 LIB
3	12 GEM	3	10 SCO
4	28 GEM	4	22 SCO
5	11 CAN	5	4 SAG
6	24 CAN	6	16 SAG
7	6 LEO	7	29 SAG
8	18 LEO	8	14 CAP
9	29 LEO	9	29 CAP
10	11 VIR	10	21 AQU
11	23 VIR	11	14 PIS
12 noon	5 LIB	12 midnight	10 ARI

JUNE 30

AM		PM	
1	8 TAU	1	19 LIB
2	29 TAU	2	1 SCO
3	16 GEM	3	12 SCO
4	29 GEM	4	24 SCO
5	13 CAN	5	6 SAG
6	26 CAN	6	18 SAG
7	8 LEO	7	1 CAP
8	20 LEO	8	17 CAP
9	2 VIR	9	4 AQU
10	13 VIR	10	24 AQU
11	25 VIR	11	19 PIS
12 noon	7 LIB	12 midnight	16 ARI

JULY 3

AM		PM	
1	13 TAU	1	22 LIB
2	2 GEM	2	3 SCO
3	18 GEM	3	15 SCO
4	3 CAN	4	27 SCO
5	17 CAN	5	8 SAG
6	28 CAN	6	21 SAG
7	10 LEO	7	5 CAP
8	22 LEO	8	20 CAP
9	3 VIR	9	8 AQU
10	16 VIR	10	29 AQU
11	28 VIR	11	25 PIS
12 noon	9 LIB	12 midnight	21 ARI

JULY 6

AM		PM	
1	17 TAU	1	24 LIB
2	6 GEM	2	5 SCO
3	22 GEM	3	17 SCO
4	6 CAN	4	29 SCO
5	19 CAN	5	11 SAG
6	1 LEO	6	24 SAG
7	13 LEO	7	8 CAP
8	25 LEO	8	23 CAP
9	6 VIR	9	12 AQU
10	18 VIR	10	5 PIS
11	29 VIR	11	1 ARI
12 noon	12 LIB	12 midnight	26 ARI

JULY 9

AM		PM	
1	22 TAU	1	26 LIB
2	9 GEM	2	8 SCO
3	25 GEM	3	19 SCO
4	9 CAN	4	2 SAG
5	21 CAN	5	14 SAG
6	3 LEO	6	26 SAG
7	15 LEO	7	11 CAP
8	26 LEO	8	27 CAP
9	8 VIR	9	17 AQU
10	20 VIR	10	8 PIS
11	2 LIB	11	5 ARI
12 noon	14 LIB	12 midnight	29 ARI

JULY 12

AM		PM	
1	24 TAU	1	28 LIB
2	12 GEM	2	10 SCO
3	28 GEM	3	21 SCO
4	11 CAN	4	3 SAG
5	23 CAN	5	16 SAG
6	6 LEO	6	29 SAG
7	17 LEO	7	14 CAP
8	29 LEO	8	29 CAP
9	11 VIR	9	20 AQU
10	23 VIR	10	14 PIS
11	5 LIB	11	10 ARI
12 noon	17 LIB	12 midnight	5 TAU

JULY 15

AM		PM	
1	28 TAU	1	1 SCO
2	15 GEM	2	12 SCO
3	29 GEM	3	24 SCO
4	13 CAN	4	6 SAG
5	26 CAN	5	18 SAG
6	8 LEO	6	1 CAP
7	20 LEO	7	16 CAP
8	1 VIR	8	4 AQU
9	13 VIR	9	24 AQU
10	25 VIR	10	19 PIS
11	7 LIB	11	16 ARI
12 noon	19 LIB	12 midnight	10 TAU

JULY 18

AM		PM	
1	2 GEM	1	3 SCO
2	18 GEM	2	15 SCO
3	3 CAN	3	27 SCO
4	16 CAN	4	8 SAG
5	28 CAN	5	21 SAG
6	10 LEO	6	4 CAP
7	22 LEO	7	20 CAP
8	3 VIR	8	8 AQU
9	15 VIR	9	29 AQU
10	27 VIR	10	25 PIS
11	10 LIB	11	19 ARI
12 noon	21 LIB	12 midnight	13 TAU

JULY 21

AM		PM	
1	6 GEM	1	5 SCO
2	21 GEM	2	17 SCO
3	6 CAN	3	29 SCO
4	18 CAN	4	11 SAG
5	1 LEO	5	24 SAG
6	13 LEO	6	7 CAP
7	24 LEO	7	23 CAP
8	6 VIR	8	12 AQU
9	18 VIR	9	3 PIS
10	29 VIR	10	29 PIS
11	12 LIB	11	25 ARI
12 noon	23 LIB	12 midnight	17 TAU

JULY 24

AM		PM	
1	9 GEM	1	8 SCO
2	24 GEM	2	19 SCO
3	8 CAN	3	1 SAG
4	21 CAN	4	13 SAG
5	3 LEO	5	26 SAG
6	15 LEO	6	11 CAP
7	26 LEO	7	27 CAP
8	8 VIR	8	16 AQU
9	20 VIR	9	8 PIS
10	2 LIB	10	4 ARI
11	14 LIB	11	29 ARI
12 noon	26 LIB	12 midnight	22 TAU

JULY 27

AM		PM	
1	12 GEM	1	9 SCO
2	27 GEM	2	21 SCO
3	11 CAN	3	3 SAG
4	23 CAN	4	16 SAG
5	5 LEO	5	29 SAG
6	17 LEO	6	13 CAP
7	29 LEO	7	29 CAP
8	11 VIR	8	20 AQU
9	23 VIR	9	14 PIS
10	5 LIB	10	10 ARI
11	16 LIB	11	5 TAU
12 noon	28 LIB	12 midnight	26 TAU

JULY 30

AM		PM	
1	15 GEM	1	12 SCO
2	29 GEM	2	24 SCO
3	13 CAN	3	5 SAG
4	26 CAN	4	18 SAG
5	7 LEO	5	1 CAP
6	19 LEO	6	16 CAP
7	1 VIR	7	3 AQU
8	13 VIR	8	24 AQU
9	24 VIR	9	19 PIS
10	7 LIB	10	15 ARI
11	18 LIB	11	8 TAU
12 noon	1 SCO	12 midnight	29 TAU

AUGUST 2

AM		PM	
1	18 GEM	1	15 SCO
2	3 CAN	2	26 SCO
3	16 CAN	3	8 SAG
4	28 CAN	4	21 SAG
5	10 LEO	5	4 CAP
6	22 LEO	6	20 CAP
7	3 VIR	7	7 AQU
8	15 VIR	8	29 AQU
9	27 VIR	9	25 PIS
10	9 LIB	10	19 ARI
11	21 LIB	11	13 TAU
12 noon	3 SCO	12 midnight	3 GEM

AUGUST 5

AM		PM	
1	21 GEM	1	17 SCO
2	6 CAN	2	28 SCO
3	18 CAN	3	11 SAG
4	1 LEO	4	23 SAG
5	13 LEO	5	7 CAP
6	24 LEO	6	22 CAP
7	6 VIR	7	11 AQU
8	18 VIR	8	3 PIS
9	29 VIR	9	29 PIS
10	12 LIB	10	25 ARI
11	23 LIB	11	17 TAU
12 noon	5 SCO	12 midnight	7 GEM

AUGUST 8

AM		PM	
1	24 GEM	1	19 SCO
2	8 CAN	2	1 SAG
3	20 CAN	3	13 SAG
4	3 LEO	4	26 SAG
5	15 LEO	5	10 CAP
6	26 LEO	6	26 CAP
7	8 VIR	7	15 AQU
8	20 VIR	8	8 PIS
9	2 LIB	9	4 ARI
10	14 LIB	10	29 ARI
11	26 LIB	11	22 TAU
12 noon	7 SCO	12 midnight	10 GEM

AUGUST 11

AM		PM	
1	27 GEM	1	21 SCO
2	10 CAN	2	3 SAG
3	23 CAN	3	15 SAG
4	5 LEO	4	28 SAG
5	17 LEO	5	13 CAP
6	29 LEO	6	29 CAP
7	11 VIR	7	20 AQU
8	22 VIR	8	14 PIS
9	4 LIB	9	10 ARI
10	16 LIB	10	4 TAU
11	28 LIB	11	26 TAU
12 noon	10 SCO	12 midnight	13 GEM

AUGUST 14

AM		PM	
1	29 GEM	1	24 SCO
2	13 CAN	2	5 SAG
3	26 CAN	3	18 SAG
4	7 LEO	4	1 CAP
5	19 LEO	5	16 CAP
6	1 VIR	6	3 AQU
7	13 VIR	7	24 AQU
8	24 VIR	8	19 PIS
9	7 LIB	9	15 ARI
10	18 LIB	10	8 TAU
11	29 LIB	11	28 TAU
12 noon	12 SCO	12 midnight	16 GEM

AUGUST 17

AM		PM	
1	2 CAN	1	26 SCO
2	16 CAN	2	8 SAG
3	28 CAN	3	21 SAG
4	10 LEO	4	4 CAP
5	22 LEO	5	19 CAP
6	3 VIR	6	7 AQU
7	15 VIR	7	28 AQU
8	27 VIR	8	23 PIS
9	9 LIB	9	19 ARI
10	21 LIB	10	13 TAU
11	2 SCO	11	2 GEM
12 noon	14 SCO	12 midnight	19 GEM

AUGUST 20

AM		PM	
1	6 CAN	1	28 SCO
2	18 CAN	2	11 SAG
3	29 CAN	3	23 SAG
4	12 LEO	4	7 CAP
5	24 LEO	5	22 CAP
6	6 VIR	6	11 AQU
7	18 VIR	7	3 PIS
8	29 VIR	8	29 PIS
9	11 LIB	9	25 ARI
10	23 LIB	10	17 TAU
11	5 SCO	11	7 GEM
12 noon	16 SCO	12 midnight	22 GEM

AUGUST 23

AM		PM	
1	8 CAN	1	1 SAG
2	20 CAN	2	13 SAG
3	2 LEO	3	26 SAG
4	15 LEO	4	10 CAP
5	26 LEO	5	25 CAP
6	8 VIR	6	15 AQU
7	20 VIR	7	8 PIS
8	1 LIB	8	4 ARI
9	13 LIB	9	29 ARI
10	25 LIB	10	22 TAU
11	7 SCO	11	9 GEM
12 noon	18 SCO	12 midnight	25 GEM

AUGUST 26

AM		PM	
1	10 CAN	1	3 SAG
2	23 CAN	2	15 SAG
3	5 LEO	3	28 SAG
4	16 LEO	4	13 CAP
5	29 LEO	5	29 CAP
6	10 VIR	6	20 AQU
7	22 VIR	7	14 PIS
8	4 LIB	8	9 ARI
9	16 LIB	9	3 TAU
10	28 LIB	10	26 TAU
11	9 SCO	11	12 GEM
12 noon	21 SCO	12 midnight	28 GEM

AUGUST 29

AM		PM	
1	13 CAN	1	5 SAG
2	26 CAN	2	18 SAG
3	7 LEO	3	1 CAP
4	19 LEO	4	16 CAP
5	1 VIR	5	3 AQU
6	13 VIR	6	23 AQU
7	24 VIR	7	17 PIS
8	7 LIB	8	14 ARI
9	18 LIB	9	8 TAU
10	29 LIB	10	29 TAU
11	12 SCO	11	16 GEM
12 noon	24 SCO	12 midnight	29 GEM

SEPTEMBER 1

AM		PM	
1	16 CAN	1	8 SAG
2	28 CAN	2	21 SAG
3	10 LEO	3	4 CAP
4	21 LEO	4	19 CAP
5	3 VIR	5	7 AQU
6	15 VIR	6	28 AQU
7	27 VIR	7	23 PIS
8	8 LIB	8	19 ARI
9	21 LIB	9	13 TAU
10	2 SCO	10	2 GEM
11	14 SCO	11	19 GEM
12 noon	26 SCO	12 midnight	3 CAN

SEPTEMBER 4

AM		PM	
1	18 CAN	1	10 SAG
2	29 CAN	2	23 SAG
3	12 LEO	3	6 CAP
4	24 LEO	4	22 CAP
5	5 VIR	5	11 AQU
6	17 VIR	6	3 PIS
7	29 VIR	7	29 PIS
8	11 LIB	8	24 ARI
9	23 LIB	9	17 TAU
10	5 SCO	10	6 GEM
11	16 SCO	11	22 GEM
12 noon	28 SCO	12 midnight	6 CAN

SEPTEMBER 7

AM		PM	
1	20 CAN	1	12 SAG
2	3 LEO	2	26 SAG
3	15 LEO	3	10 CAP
4	26 LEO	4	25 CAP
5	8 VIR	5	15 AQU
6	19 VIR	6	8 PIS
7	1 LIB	7	4 ARI
8	13 LIB	8	28 ARI
9	25 LIB	9	20 TAU
10	7 SCO	10	9 GEM
11	18 SCO	11	25 GEM
12 noon	29 SCO	12 midnight	9 CAN

SEPTEMBER 10

AM		PM	
1	23 CAN	1	15 SAG
2	5 LEO	2	28 SAG
3	16 LEO	3	13 CAP
4	28 LEO	4	29 CAP
5	10 VIR	5	19 AQU
6	22 VIR	6	13 PIS
7	4 LIB	7	8 ARI
8	16 LIB	8	3 TAU
9	28 LIB	9	24 TAU
10	9 SCO	10	12 GEM
11	21 SCO	11	28 GEM
12 *noon*	3 SAG	12 *midnight*	11 CAN

SEPTEMBER 13

AM		PM	
1	26 CAN	1	18 SAG
2	7 LEO	2	1 CAP
3	19 LEO	3	16 CAP
4	29 LEO	4	3 AQU
5	13 VIR	5	23 AQU
6	24 VIR	6	17 PIS
7	6 LIB	7	14 ARI
8	18 LIB	8	8 TAU
9	29 LIB	9	28 TAU
10	12 SCO	10	15 GEM
11	23 SCO	11	29 GEM
12 *noon*	5 SAG	12 *midnight*	13 CAN

SEPTEMBER 16

AM		PM	
1	28 CAN	1	20 SAG
2	10 LEO	2	3 CAP
3	21 LEO	3	19 CAP
4	3 VIR	4	7 AQU
5	14 VIR	5	28 AQU
6	26 VIR	6	23 PIS
7	8 LIB	7	18 ARI
8	20 LIB	8	13 TAU
9	2 SCO	9	2 GEM
10	14 SCO	10	18 GEM
11	25 SCO	11	3 CAN
12 *noon*	8 SAG	12 *midnight*	16 CAN

SEPTEMBER 19

AM		PM	
1	29 CAN	1	22 SAG
2	12 LEO	2	6 CAP
3	23 LEO	3	22 CAP
4	5 VIR	4	11 AQU
5	17 VIR	5	3 PIS
6	29 VIR	6	29 PIS
7	11 LIB	7	23 ARI
8	23 LIB	8	16 TAU
9	4 SCO	9	6 GEM
10	16 SCO	10	21 GEM
11	27 SCO	11	6 CAN
12 *noon*	10 SAG	12 *midnight*	18 CAN

SEPTEMBER 22

AM		PM	
1	2 LEO	1	26 SAG
2	14 LEO	2	9 CAP
3	26 LEO	3	25 CAP
4	8 VIR	4	14 AQU
5	19 VIR	5	7 PIS
6	1 LIB	6	2 ARI
7	14 LIB	7	28 ARI
8	25 LIB	8	20 TAU
9	7 SCO	9	9 GEM
10	18 SCO	10	24 GEM
11	29 SCO	11	8 CAN
12 *noon*	12 SAG	12 *midnight*	21 CAN

SEPTEMBER 25

AM		PM	
1	4 LEO	1	28 SAG
2	16 LEO	2	13 CAP
3	28 LEO	3	29 CAP
4	10 VIR	4	18 AQU
5	22 VIR	5	12 PIS
6	3 LIB	6	8 ARI
7	15 LIB	7	3 TAU
8	27 LIB	8	24 TAU
9	9 SCO	9	12 GEM
10	21 SCO	10	28 GEM
11	3 SAG	11	11 CAN
12 *noon*	15 SAG	12 *midnight*	23 CAN

SEPTEMBER 28

AM		PM	
1	7 LEO	1	1 CAP
2	19 LEO	2	16 CAP
3	29 LEO	3	3 AQU
4	12 VIR	4	23 AQU
5	24 VIR	5	17 PIS
6	6 LIB	6	14 ARI
7	18 LIB	7	8 TAU
8	29 LIB	8	28 TAU
9	12 SCO	9	15 GEM
10	23 SCO	10	29 GEM
11	5 SAG	11	13 CAN
12 *noon*	18 SAG	12 *midnight*	26 CAN

OCTOBER 1

AM		PM	
1	9 LEO	1	3 CAP
2	21 LEO	2	18 CAP
3	3 VIR	3	5 AQU
4	14 VIR	4	27 AQU
5	26 VIR	5	23 PIS
6	8 LIB	6	17 ARI
7	20 LIB	7	11 TAU
8	2 SCO	8	2 GEM
9	13 SCO	9	18 GEM
10	25 SCO	10	3 CAN
11	7 SAG	11	16 CAN
12 *noon*	20 SAG	12 *midnight*	28 CAN

OCTOBER 4

AM		PM	
1	11 LEO	1	6 CAP
2	23 LEO	2	21 CAP
3	5 VIR	3	9 AQU
4	17 VIR	4	1 PIS
5	29 VIR	5	27 PIS
6	11 LIB	6	23 ARI
7	23 LIB	7	16 TAU
8	4 SCO	8	6 GEM
9	16 SCO	9	21 GEM
10	27 SCO	10	6 CAN
11	10 SAG	11	18 CAN
12 noon	22 SAG	12 midnight	1 LEO

OCTOBER 7

AM		PM	
1	14 LEO	1	9 CAP
2	26 LEO	2	24 CAP
3	8 VIR	3	14 AQU
4	19 VIR	4	6 PIS
5	1 LIB	5	2 ARI
6	13 LIB	6	28 ARI
7	25 LIB	7	20 TAU
8	6 SCO	8	9 GEM
9	18 SCO	9	24 GEM
10	29 SCO	10	8 CAN
11	12 SAG	11	20 CAN
12 noon	25 SAG	12 midnight	3 LEO

OCTOBER 10

AM		PM	
1	16 LEO	1	12 CAP
2	28 LEO	2	28 CAP
3	10 VIR	3	18 AQU
4	21 VIR	4	12 PIS
5	3 LIB	5	8 ARI
6	15 LIB	6	3 TAU
7	27 LIB	7	24 TAU
8	9 SCO	8	12 GEM
9	21 SCO	9	27 GEM
10	3 SAG	10	10 CAN
11	14 SAG	11	23 CAN
12 noon	27 SAG	12 midnight	5 LEO

OCTOBER 13

AM		PM	
1	19 LEO	1	15 CAP
2	29 LEO	2	2 AQU
3	12 VIR	3	23 AQU
4	24 VIR	4	17 PIS
5	6 LIB	5	12 ARI
6	18 LIB	6	8 TAU
7	29 LIB	7	28 TAU
8	11 SCO	8	15 GEM
9	23 SCO	9	29 GEM
10	5 SAG	10	13 CAN
11	17 SAG	11	26 CAN
12 noon	1 CAP	12 midnight	7 LEO

OCTOBER 16

AM		PM	
1	21 LEO	1	18 CAP
2	3 VIR	2	5 AQU
3	14 VIR	3	26 AQU
4	26 VIR	4	22 PIS
5	8 LIB	5	17 ARI
6	20 LIB	6	11 TAU
7	2 SCO	7	2 GEM
8	13 SCO	8	18 GEM
9	25 SCO	9	2 CAN
10	7 SAG	10	16 CAN
11	19 SAG	11	28 CAN
12 noon	3 CAP	12 midnight	10 LEO

OCTOBER 19

AM		PM	
1	23 LEO	1	21 CAP
2	5 VIR	2	9 AQU
3	17 VIR	3	1 PIS
4	29 VIR	4	27 PIS
5	11 LIB	5	23 ARI
6	22 LIB	6	16 TAU
7	4 SCO	7	6 GEM
8	15 SCO	8	21 GEM
9	27 SCO	9	6 CAN
10	9 SAG	10	18 CAN
11	22 SAG	11	29 CAN
12 noon	6 CAP	12 midnight	12 LEO

OCTOBER 22

AM		PM	
1	26 LEO	1	24 CAP
2	7 VIR	2	14 AQU
3	19 VIR	3	6 PIS
4	1 LIB	4	2 ARI
5	13 LIB	5	28 ARI
6	24 LIB	6	20 TAU
7	6 SCO	7	8 GEM
8	18 SCO	8	24 GEM
9	29 SCO	9	8 CAN
10	11 SAG	10	20 CAN
11	25 SAG	11	2 LEO
12 noon	9 CAP	12 midnight	14 LEO

OCTOBER 25

AM		PM	
1	28 LEO	1	28 CAP
2	9 VIR	2	18 AQU
3	21 VIR	3	12 PIS
4	3 LIB	4	7 ARI
5	15 LIB	5	15 TAU
6	27 LIB	6	24 TAU
7	9 SCO	7	12 GEM
8	20 SCO	8	27 GEM
9	2 SAG	9	10 CAN
10	14 SAG	10	23 CAN
11	27 SAG	11	4 LEO
12 noon	12 CAP	12 midnight	16 LEO

OCTOBER 28

AM		PM	
1	29 LEO	1	2 AQU
2	12 VIR	2	21 AQU
3	24 VIR	3	16 PIS
4	6 LIB	4	12 ARI
5	18 LIB	5	7 TAU
6	29 LIB	6	27 TAU
7	11 SCO	7	14 GEM
8	22 SCO	8	29 GEM
9	5 SAG	9	13 CAN
10	17 SAG	10	25 CAN
11	29 SAG	11	7 LEO
12 *noon*	15 CAP	12 *midnight*	19 LEO

NOVEMBER 9

AM		PM	
1	9 VIR	1	17 AQU
2	21 VIR	2	10 PIS
3	3 LIB	3	6 ARI
4	15 LIB	4	2 TAU
5	27 LIB	5	23 TAU
6	9 SCO	6	1 GEM
7	20 SCO	7	26 GEM
8	2 SAG	8	10 CAN
9	14 SAG	9	23 CAN
10	27 SAG	10	4 LEO
11	11 CAP	11	16 LEO
12 *noon*	28 CAP	12 *midnight*	28 LEO

OCTOBER 31

AM		PM	
1	2 VIR	1	5 AQU
2	14 VIR	2	26 AQU
3	25 VIR	3	21 PIS
4	7 LIB	4	17 ARI
5	19 LIB	5	11 TAU
6	2 SCO	6	1 GEM
7	13 SCO	7	18 GEM
8	25 SCO	8	2 CAN
9	7 SAG	9	15 CAN
10	19 SAG	10	27 CAN
11	2 CAP	11	10 LEO
12 *noon*	18 CAP	12 *midnight*	22 LEO

NOVEMBER 12

AM		PM	
1	12 VIR	1	21 AQU
2	24 VIR	2	15 PIS
3	5 LIB	3	12 ARI
4	17 LIB	4	7 TAU
5	29 LIB	5	27 TAU
6	11 SCO	6	14 GEM
7	22 SCO	7	29 GEM
8	5 SAG	8	13 CAN
9	17 SAG	9	25 CAN
10	29 SAG	10	7 LEO
11	15 CAP	11	19 LEO
12 *noon*	2 AQU	12 *midnight*	29 LEO

NOVEMBER 3

AM		PM	
1	4 VIR	1	9 AQU
2	17 VIR	2	1 PIS
3	29 VIR	3	27 PIS
4	10 LIB	4	22 ARI
5	22 LIB	5	16 TAU
6	4 SCO	6	4 GEM
7	15 SCO	7	20 GEM
8	27 SCO	8	5 CAN
9	9 SAG	9	17 CAN
10	21 SAG	10	29 CAN
11	5 CAP	11	12 LEO
12 *noon*	21 CAP	12 *midnight*	23 LEO

NOVEMBER 15

AM		PM	
1	14 VIR	1	26 AQU
2	26 VIR	2	21 PIS
3	7 LIB	3	17 ARI
4	19 LIB	4	11 TAU
5	2 SCO	5	1 GEM
6	13 SCO	6	17 GEM
7	24 SCO	7	2 CAN
8	7 SAG	8	15 CAN
9	19 SAG	9	27 CAN
10	2 CAP	10	9 LEO
11	18 CAP	11	21 LEO
12 *noon*	5 AQU	12 *midnight*	3 VIR

NOVEMBER 6

AM		PM	
1	7 VIR	1	14 AQU
2	19 VIR	2	6 PIS
3	1 LIB	3	1 ARI
4	13 LIB	4	27 ARI
5	24 LIB	5	20 TAU
6	6 SCO	6	8 GEM
7	18 SCO	7	24 GEM
8	29 SCO	8	8 CAN
9	12 SAG	9	20 CAN
10	25 SAG	10	2 LEO
11	8 CAP	11	14 LEO
12 *noon*	24 CAP	12 *midnight*	26 LEO

NOVEMBER 18

AM		PM	
1	16 VIR	1	1 PIS
2	28 VIR	2	27 PIS
3	10 LIB	3	22 ARI
4	22 LIB	4	15 TAU
5	4 SCO	5	4 GEM
6	15 SCO	6	20 GEM
7	27 SCO	7	5 CAN
8	9 SAG	8	17 CAN
9	21 SAG	9	29 CAN
10	5 CAP	10	12 LEO
11	20 CAP	11	23 LEO
12 *noon*	9 AQU	12 *midnight*	5 VIR

NOVEMBER 21

AM		PM	
1	18 VIR	1	5 PIS
2	1 LIB	2	1 ARI
3	13 LIB	3	26 ARI
4	24 LIB	4	19 TAU
5	6 SCO	5	8 GEM
6	18 SCO	6	23 GEM
7	29 SCO	7	7 CAN
8	11 SAG	8	20 CAN
9	24 SAG	9	2 LEO
10	8 CAP	10	14 LEO
11	24 CAP	11	26 LEO
12 noon	12 AQU	12 midnight	8 VIR

NOVEMBER 24

AM		PM	
1	21 VIR	1	10 PIS
2	3 LIB	2	6 ARI
3	15 LIB	3	2 TAU
4	27 LIB	4	23 TAU
5	9 SCO	5	11 GEM
6	20 SCO	6	27 GEM
7	2 SAG	7	10 CAN
8	14 SAG	8	23 CAN
9	27 SAG	9	4 LEO
10	11 CAP	10	16 LEO
11	27 CAP	11	28 LEO
12 noon	17 AQU	12 midnight	10 VIR

NOVEMBER 27

AM		PM	
1	23 VIR	1	15 PIS
2	5 LIB	2	12 ARI
3	17 LIB	3	7 TAU
4	29 LIB	4	27 TAU
5	10 SCO	5	14 GEM
6	22 SCO	6	29 GEM
7	4 SAG	7	13 CAN
8	16 SAG	8	25 CAN
9	29 SAG	9	7 LEO
10	14 CAP	10	19 LEO
11	29 CAP	11	29 LEO
12 noon	21 AQU	12 midnight	12 VIR

NOVEMBER 30

AM		PM	
1	25 VIR	1	21 PIS
2	7 LIB	2	17 ARI
3	19 LIB	3	11 TAU
4	1 SCO	4	1 GEM
5	12 SCO	5	17 GEM
6	24 SCO	6	2 CAN
7	6 SAG	7	15 CAN
8	19 SAG	8	27 CAN
9	2 CAP	9	9 LEO
10	17 CAP	10	21 LEO
11	4 AQU	11	3 VIR
12 noon	26 AQU	12 midnight	14 VIR

DECEMBER 3

AM		PM	
1	28 VIR	1	25 PIS
2	10 LIB	2	21 ARI
3	22 LIB	3	14 TAU
4	3 SCO	4	4 GEM
5	15 SCO	5	20 GEM
6	27 SCO	6	5 CAN
7	9 SAG	7	17 CAN
8	21 SAG	8	29 CAN
9	5 CAP	9	11 LEO
10	20 CAP	10	23 LEO
11	8 AQU	11	5 VIR
12 noon	1 PIS	12 midnight	17 VIR

DECEMBER 6

AM		PM	
1	1 LIB	1	1 ARI
2	12 LIB	2	26 ARI
3	24 LIB	3	19 TAU
4	5 SCO	4	8 GEM
5	17 SCO	5	23 GEM
6	29 SCO	6	7 CAN
7	11 SAG	7	20 CAN
8	24 SAG	8	2 LEO
9	8 CAP	9	14 LEO
10	23 CAP	10	26 LEO
11	12 AQU	11	7 VIR
12 noon	5 PIS	12 midnight	18 VIR

DECEMBER 9

AM		PM	
1	2 LIB	1	6 ARI
2	14 LIB	2	2 TAU
3	26 LIB	3	23 TAU
4	8 SCO	4	11 GEM
5	20 SCO	5	26 GEM
6	1 SAG	6	10 CAN
7	14 SAG	7	23 CAN
8	26 SAG	8	4 LEO
9	11 CAP	9	16 LEO
10	27 CAP	10	28 LEO
11	16 AQU	11	9 VIR
12 noon	10 PIS	12 midnight	21 VIR

DECEMBER 12

AM		PM	
1	5 LIB	1	11 ARI
2	17 LIB	2	6 TAU
3	28 LIB	3	27 TAU
4	10 SCO	4	14 GEM
5	22 SCO	5	29 GEM
6	4 SAG	6	13 CAN
7	16 SAG	7	25 CAN
8	29 SAG	8	7 LEO
9	14 CAP	9	19 LEO
10	29 CAP	10	29 LEO
11	21 AQU	11	12 VIR
12 noon	15 PIS	12 midnight	24 VIR

DECEMBER 15

AM		PM	
1	7 LIB	1	16 ARI
2	19 LIB	2	10 TAU
3	1 SCO	3	1 GEM
4	12 SCO	4	17 GEM
5	24 SCO	5	1 CAN
6	6 SAG	6	15 CAN
7	18 SAG	7	27 CAN
8	1 CAP	8	9 LEO
9	17 CAP	9	21 LEO
10	4 AQU	10	3 VIR
11	24 AQU	11	14 VIR
12 noon	19 PIS	12 midnight	26 VIR

DECEMBER 18

AM		PM	
1	9 LIB	1	21 ARI
2	21 LIB	2	14 TAU
3	3 SCO	3	4 GEM
4	15 SCO	4	20 GEM
5	27 SCO	5	5 CAN
6	8 SAG	6	17 CAN
7	21 SAG	7	29 CAN
8	5 CAP	8	11 LEO
9	20 CAP	9	23 LEO
10	8 AQU	10	4 VIR
11	29 AQU	11	17 VIR
12 noon	25 PIS	12 midnight	29 VIR

DECEMBER 21

AM		PM	
1	12 LIB	1	26 ARI
2	23 LIB	2	19 TAU
3	5 SCO	3	7 GEM
4	17 SCO	4	23 GEM
5	29 SCO	5	7 CAN
6	11 SAG	6	20 CAN
7	24 SAG	7	2 LEO
8	8 CAP	8	13 LEO
9	23 CAP	9	25 LEO
10	12 AQU	10	7 VIR
11	5 PIS	11	19 VIR
12 noon	1 ARI	12 midnight	1 LIB

DECEMBER 24

AM		PM	
1	14 LIB	1	2 TAU
2	26 LIB	2	23 TAU
3	8 SCO	3	10 GEM
4	19 SCO	4	26 GEM
5	1 SAG	5	10 CAN
6	14 SAG	6	22 CAN
7	26 SAG	7	4 LEO
8	11 CAP	8	16 LEO
9	27 CAP	9	28 LEO
10	16 AQU	10	9 VIR
11	9 PIS	11	21 VIR
12 noon	5 ARI	12 midnight	3 LIB

DECEMBER 27

AM		PM	
1	17 LIB	1	5 TAU
2	28 LIB	2	26 TAU
3	10 SCO	3	13 GEM
4	22 SCO	4	29 GEM
5	4 SAG	5	12 CAN
6	16 SAG	6	25 CAN
7	29 SAG	7	6 LEO
8	14 CAP	8	18 LEO
9	29 CAP	9	29 LEO
10	20 AQU	10	12 VIR
11	14 PIS	11	24 VIR
12 noon	10 ARI	12 midnight	6 LIB

DECEMBER 30

AM		PM	
1	19 LIB	1	10 TAU
2	1 SCO	2	29 TAU
3	12 SCO	3	16 GEM
4	24 SCO	4	1 CAN
5	6 SAG	5	14 CAN
6	19 SAG	6	27 CAN
7	1 CAP	7	9 LEO
8	17 CAP	8	20 LEO
9	4 AQU	9	2 VIR
10	24 AQU	10	13 VIR
11	19 PIS	11	26 VIR
12 noon	16 ARI	12 midnight	7 LIB

HOW TO FIND YOUR VENUS SIGN

Under the year of your birth, find your birth date. For example, if you were born on February 25, 1920, your Venus sign is Aquarius, for Venus was in the sign of Aquarius from February 23 until March 18, 1920.

If you were born on the first or last day of a particular time period, it's possible that your Venus might be posited in the preceding or following sign. For example, if the time period is from August 6 to September 10, and you were born on September 10, then you must consider that your Venus might be in the next sign. The only way to be absolutely sure is to have your chart done by computer (see Appendix II for computer services) or by a professional astrologer. If you're not sure, read the adjacent sign, and you will probably be able to decide which is applicable to you.

1920 VENUS

Jan 1–Jan 3	SCO
Jan 4–Jan 28	SAG
Jan 29–Feb 22	CAP
Feb 23–Mar 18	AQU
Mar 19–Apr 11	PIS
Apr 12–May 6	ARI
May 7–May 30	TAU
May 31–Jun 23	GEM
Jun 24–Jul 18	CAN
Jul 19–Aug 11	LEO
Aug 12–Sep 4	VIR
Sep 5–Sep 28	LIB
Sep 29–Oct 23	SCO
Oct 24–Nov 17	SAG
Nov 18–Dec 11	CAP
Dec 12–Dec 31	AQU

1921 VENUS

Jan 1–Jan 6	AQU
Jan 7–Feb 2	PIS
Feb 3–Mar 6	ARI
Mar 7–Apr 25	TAU
Apr 26–Jun 1	ARI
Jun 2–Jul 7	TAU
Jul 8–Aug 5	GEM
Aug 6–Aug 31	CAN
Sep 1–Sep 25	LEO
Sep 26–Oct 20	VIR
Oct 21–Nov 13	LIB
Nov 14–Dec 7	SCO
Dec 8–Dec 31	SAG

1922 VENUS

Jan 1–Jan 24	CAP
Jan 25–Feb 16	AQU
Feb 17–Mar 12	PIS
Mar 13–Apr 6	ARI
Apr 7–Apr 30	TAU
May 1–May 25	GEM
May 26–Jun 19	CAN
Jun 20–Jul 14	LEO
Jul 15–Aug 9	VIR
Aug 10–Sep 6	LIB
Sep 7–Oct 10	SCO
Oct 11–Nov 28	SAG
Nov 29–Dec 31	SCO

1923 VENUS

Jan 1	SCO
Jan 2–Feb 6	SAG
Feb 7–Mar 5	CAP
Mar 6–Mar 31	AQU
Apr 1–Apr 26	PIS
Apr 27–May 21	ARI
May 22–Jun 14	TAU
Jun 15–Jul 9	GEM
Jul 10–Aug 3	CAN
Aug 4–Aug 27	LEO
Aug 28–Sep 20	VIR
Sep 21–Oct 14	LIB
Oct 15–Nov 7	SCO
Nov 8–Dec 1	SAG
Dec 2–Dec 25	CAP
Dec 26–Dec 31	AQU

1924 VENUS

Jan 1–Jan 19	AQU
Jan 20–Feb 12	PIS
Feb 13–Mar 8	ARI
Mar 9–Apr 4	TAU
Apr 5–May 5	GEM
May 6–Sep 8	CAN
Sep 9–Oct 7	LEO
Oct 8–Nov 2	VIR
Nov 3–Nov 26	LIB
Nov 27–Dec 21	SCO
Dec 22–Dec 31	SAG

1925 VENUS

Jan 1–Jan 14	SAG
Jan 15–Feb 7	CAP
Feb 8–Mar 3	AQU
Mar 4–Mar 27	PIS
Mar 28–Apr 20	ARI
Apr 21–May 15	TAU
May 16–Jun 8	GEM
Jun 9–July 3	CAN
Jul 4–Jul 27	LEO
Jul 28–Aug 21	VIR
Aug 22–Sep 15	LIB
Sep 16–Oct 11	SCO
Oct 12–Nov 6	SAG
Nov 7–Dec 5	CAP
Dec 6–Dec 31	AQU

1926 VENUS

Jan 1–Apr 5	AQU
Apr 6–May 6	PIS
May 7–June 2	ARI
Jun 3–Jun 28	TAU
Jun 29–Jul 23	GEM
Jul 24–Aug 17	CAN
Aug 18–Sep 11	LEO
Sep 12–Oct 5	VIR
Oct 6–Oct 29	LIB
Oct 30–Nov 22	SCO
Nov 23–Dec 16	SAG
Dec 17–Dec 31	CAP

1927 VENUS

Jan 1–Jan 8	CAP
Jan 9–Feb 1	AQU
Feb 2–Feb 26	PIS
Feb 27–Mar 22	ARI
Mar 23–Apr 16	TAU
Apr 17–May 11	GEM
May 12–Jun 7	CAN
Jun 8–Jul 7	LEO
Jul 8–Nov 9	VIR
Nov 10–Dec 8	LIB
Dec 9–Dec 31	SCO

1928 VENUS

Jan 1–Jan 3	SCO
Jan 4–Jan 28	SAG
Jan 29–Feb 22	CAP
Feb 23–Mar 17	AQU
Mar 18–Apr 11	PIS
Apr 12–May 5	ARI
May 6–May 29	TAU
May 30–Jun 23	GEM
Jun 24–Jul 17	CAN
Jul 18–Aug 11	LEO
Aug 12–Sep 4	VIR
Sep 5–Sep 28	LIB
Sep 29–Oct 23	SCO
Oct 24–Nov 16	SAG
Nov 17–Dec 11	CAP
Dec 12–Dec 31	AQU

1929 VENUS

```
Jan   1—Jan  5   AQU
Jan   6—Feb  2   PIS
Feb   3—Mar  7   ARI
Mar   8—Apr 19   TAU
Apr  20—June 2   ARI
Jun   3—Jul  7   TAU
Jul   8—Aug  4   GEM
Aug   5—Aug 30   CAN
Aug  31—Sep 25   LEO
Sep  26—Oct 19   VIR
Oct  20—Nov 12   LIB
Nov  13—Dec  6   SCO
Dec   7—Dec 30   SAG
Dec  31          CAP
```

1930 VENUS

```
Jan   1—Jan 23   CAP
Jan  24—Feb 16   AQU
Feb  17—Mar 12   PIS
Mar  13—Apr  5   ARI
Apr   6—Apr 30   TAU
May   1—May 24   GEM
May  25—June 18  CAN
Jun  19—Jul 14   LEO
Jul  15—Aug  9   VIR
Aug  10—Sep  6   LIB
Sep   7—Oct 11   SCO
Oct  12—Nov 21   SAG
Nov  22—Dec 31   SCO
```

1931 VENUS

```
Jan   1—Jan  3   SCO
Jan   4—Feb  6   SAG
Feb   7—Mar  5   CAP
Mar   6—Mar 31   AQU
Apr   1—Apr 25   PIS
Apr  26—May 20   ARI
May  21—Jun 14   TAU
Jun  15—July 9   GEM
Jul  10—Aug  2   CAN
Aug   3—Aug 26   LEO
Aug  27—Sep 20   VIR
Sep  21—Oct 14   LIB
Oct  15—Nov  7   SCO
Nov   8—Dec  1   SAG
Dec   2—Dec 25   CAP
Dec  26—Dec 31   AQU
```

1932 VENUS

```
Jan   1—Jan 18   AQU
Jan  19—Feb 12   PIS
Feb  13—Mar  8   ARI
Mar   9—Apr  4   TAU
Apr   5—May  5   GEM
May   6—Jul 12   CAN
Jul  13—Jul 27   GEM
Jul  28—Sep  8   CAN
Sep   9—Oct  6   LEO
Oct   7—Nov  1   VIR
Nov   2—Nov 26   LIB
Nov  27—Dec 20   SCO
Dec  21—Dec 31   SAG
```

1933 VENUS

```
Jan   1—Jan 13   SAG
Jan  14—Feb  6   CAP
Feb   7—Mar  2   AQU
Mar   3—Mar 27   PIS
Mar  28—Apr 20   ARI
Apr  21—May 14   TAU
May  15—Jun  8   GEM
Jun   9—Jul  2   CAN
Jul   3—Jul 27   LEO
Jul  28—Aug 21   VIR
Aug  22—Sep 15   LIB
Sep  16—Oct 10   SCO
Oct  11—Nov  6   SAG
Nov   7—Dec  5   CAP
Dec   6—Dec 31   AQU
```

1934 VENUS

```
Jan   1—Apr  5   AQU
Apr   6—May  5   PIS
May   6—Jun  1   ARI
Jun   2—Jun 27   TAU
Jun  28—Jul 23   GEM
Jul  24—Aug 17   CAN
Aug  18—Sep 10   LEO
Sep  11—Oct  4   VIR
Oct   5—Oct 28   LIB
Oct  29—Nov 21   SCO
Nov  22—Dec 15   SAG
Dec  16—Dec 31   CAP
```

1935 VENUS

```
Jan   1—Jan  8   CAP
Jan   9—Feb  1   AQU
Feb   2—Feb 25   PIS
Feb  26—Mar 21   ARI
Mar  22—Apr 15   TAU
Apr  16—May 11   GEM
May  12—Jun  7   CAN
Jun   8—Jul  7   LEO
Jul   8—Nov  9   VIR
Nov  10—Dec  8   LIB
Dec   9—Dec 31   SCO
```

1936 VENUS

```
Jan   1—Jan  3   SCO
Jan   4—Jan 28   SAG
Jan  29—Feb 21   CAP
Feb  22—Mar 17   AQU
Mar  18—Apr 10   PIS
Apr  11—May  4   ARI
May   5—May 29   TAU
May  30—Jun 22   GEM
Jun  23—Jul 17   CAN
Jul  18—Aug 10   LEO
Aug  11—Sep  3   VIR
Sep   4—Sep 28   LIB
Sep  29—Oct 22   SCO
Oct  23—Nov 16   SAG
Nov  17—Dec 11   CAP
Dec  12—Dec 31   AQU
```

1937 VENUS

```
Jan   1—Jan  5   AQU
Jan   6—Feb  1   PIS
Feb   2—Mar  9   ARI
Mar  10—Apr 13   TAU
Apr  14—Jun  3   ARI
Jun   4—Jul  7   TAU
Jul   8—Aug  4   GEM
Aug   5—Aug 30   CAN
Aug  31—Sep 24   LEO
Sep  25—Oct 19   VIR
Oct  20—Nov 12   LIB
Nov  13—Dec  6   SCO
Dec   7—Dec 30   SAG
Dec  31          CAP
```

1938 VENUS

Jan 1—Jan 22	CAP
Jan 23—Feb 15	AQU
Feb 16—Mar 11	PIS
Mar 12—Apr 5	ARI
Apr 6—Apr 29	TAU
Apr 30—May 24	GEM
May 25—Jun 18	CAN
Jun 19—Jul 13	LEO
Jul 14—Aug 9	VIR
Aug 10—Sep 6	LIB
Sep 7—Oct 13	SCO
Oct 14—Nov 15	SAG
Nov 16—Dec 31	SCO

1939 VENUS

Jan 1—Jan 4	SCO
Jan 5—Feb 5	SAG
Feb 6—Mar 5	CAP
Mar 6—Mar 30	AQU
Mar 31—Apr 25	PIS
Apr 26—May 20	ARI
May 21—Jun 13	TAU
Jun 14—Jul 8	GEM
Jul 9—Aug 2	CAN
Aug 3—Aug 26	LEO
Aug 27—Sep 19	VIR
Sep 20—Oct 13	LIB
Oct 14—Nov 6	SCO
Nov 7—Nov 30	SAG
Dec 1—Dec 24	CAP
Dec 25—Dec 31	AQU

1940 VENUS

Jan 1—Jan 18	AQU
Jan 19—Feb 11	PIS
Feb 12—Mar 8	ARI
Mar 9—Apr 4	TAU
Apr 5—May 6	GEM
May 7—Jul 5	CAN
Jul 6—Jul 31	GEM
Aug 1—Sep 8	CAN
Sep 9—Oct 6	LEO
Oct 7—Nov 1	VIR
Nov 2—Nov 26	LIB
Nov 27—Dec 20	SCO
Dec 21—Dec 31	SAG

1941 VENUS

Jan 1—Jan 13	SAG
Jan 14—Feb 6	CAP
Feb 7—Mar 2	AQU
Mar 3—Mar 26	PIS
Mar 27—Apr 19	ARI
Apr 20—May 14	TAU
May 15—Jun 7	GEM
Jun 8—Jul 2	CAN
Jul 3—Jul 26	LEO
Jul 27—Aug 20	VIR
Aug 21—Sep 14	LIB
Sep 15—Oct 10	SCO
Oct 11—Nov 5	SAG
Nov 6—Dec 5	CAP
Dec 6—Dec 31	AQU

1942 VENUS

Jan 1—Apr 6	AQU
Apr 7—May 5	PIS
May 6—Jun 1	ARI
Jun 2—Jun 27	TAU
Jun 28—Jul 22	GEM
Jul 23—Aug 16	CAN
Aug 17—Sep 10	LEO
Sep 11—Oct 4	VIR
Oct 5—Oct 28	LIB
Oct 29—Nov 21	SCO
Nov 22—Dec 15	SAG
Dec 16—Dec 31	CAP

1943 VENUS

Jan 1—Jan 7	CAP
Jan 8—Jan 31	AQU
Feb 1—Feb 25	PIS
Feb 26—Mar 21	ARI
Mar 22—Apr 15	TAU
Apr 16—May 10	GEM
May 11—Jun 7	CAN
Jun 8—Jul 7	LEO
Jul 8—Nov 9	VIR
Nov 10—Dec 7	LIB
Dec 8—Dec 31	SCO

1944 VENUS

Jan 1—Jan 2	SCO
Jan 3—Jan 27	SAG
Jan 28—Feb 21	CAP
Feb 22—Mar 16	AQU
Mar 17—Apr 10	PIS
Apr 11—May 4	ARI
May 5—May 28	TAU
May 29—Jun 22	GEM
Jun 23—Jul 16	CAN
Jul 17—Aug 10	LEO
Aug 11—Sep 3	VIR
Sep 4—Sep 27	LIB
Sep 28—Oct 22	SCO
Oct 23—Nov 15	SAG
Nov 16—Dec 9	CAP
Dec 10—Dec 31	AQU

1945 VENUS

Jan 1—Jan 5	AQU
Jan 6—Feb 1	PIS
Feb 2—Mar 10	ARI
Mar 11—Apr 7	TAU
Apr 8—Jun 4	ARI
Jun 5—Jul 7	TAU
Jul 8—Aug 3	GEM
Aug 4—Aug 30	CAN
Aug 31—Sep 24	LEO
Sep 25—Oct 18	VIR
Oct 19—Nov 11	LIB
Nov 12—Dec 5	SCO
Dec 6—Dec 29	SAG
Dec 30—Dec 31	CAP

1946 VENUS

Jan 1—Jan 22	CAP
Jan 23—Feb 15	AQU
Feb 16—Mar 11	PIS
Mar 12—Apr 4	ARI
Apr 5—Apr 28	TAU
Apr 29—May 23	GEM
May 24—Jun 17	CAN
Jun 18—Jul 13	LEO
Jul 14—Aug 8	VIR
Aug 9—Sep 6	LIB
Sep 7—Oct 15	SCO
Oct 16—Nov 7	SAG
Nov 8—Dec 31	SCO

1947 VENUS

Jan	1–Jan 5	SCO
Jan	6–Feb 5	SAG
Feb	6–Mar 4	CAP
Mar	5–Mar 30	AQU
Mar	31–Apr 24	PIS
Apr	25–May 19	ARI
May	20–Jun 13	TAU
Jun	14–Jul 8	GEM
Jul	9–Aug 1	CAN
Aug	2–Aug 25	LEO
Aug	26–Sep 18	VIR
Sep	19–Oct 13	LIB
Oct	14–Nov 6	SCO
Nov	7–Nov 30	SAG
Dec	1–Dec 24	CAP
Dec	25–Dec 31	AQU

1948 VENUS

Jan	1–Jan 17	AQU
Jan	18–Feb 11	PIS
Feb	12–Mar 7	ARI
Mar	8–Apr 3	TAU
Apr	4–May 6	GEM
May	7–Jun 28	CAN
Jun	29–Aug 2	GEM
Aug	3–Sep 8	CAN
Sep	9–Oct 6	LEO
Oct	7–Oct 31	VIR
Nov	1–Nov 25	LIB
Nov	26–Dec 19	SCO
Dec	20–Dec 31	SAG

1949 VENUS

Jan	1–Jan 12	SAG
Jan	13–Feb 5	CAP
Feb	6–Mar 1	AQU
Mar	2–Mar 25	PIS
Mar	26–Apr 19	ARI
Apr	20–May 13	TAU
May	14–Jun 6	GEM
Jun	7–Jul 1	CAN
Jul	2–Jul 26	LEO
Jul	27–Aug 20	VIR
Aug	21–Sep 14	LIB
Sep	15–Oct 9	SCO
Oct	10–Nov 5	SAG
Nov	6–Dec 5	CAP
Dec	6–Dec 31	AQU

1950 VENUS

Jan	1–Apr 6	AQU
Apr	7–May 5	PIS
May	6–Jun 1	ARI
Jun	2–Jun 26	TAU
Jun	27–Jul 22	GEM
Jul	23–Aug 16	CAN
Aug	17–Sep 9	LEO
Sep	10–Oct 3	VIR
Oct	4–Oct 27	LIB
Oct	28–Nov 20	SCO
Nov	21–Dec 14	SAG
Dec	15–Dec 31	CAP

1951 VENUS

Jan	1–Jan 6	CAP
Jan	7–Jan 30	AQU
Jan	31–Feb 24	PIS
Feb	25–Mar 20	ARI
Mar	21–Apr 14	TAU
Apr	15–May 10	GEM
May	11–Jun 6	CAN
Jun	7–Jul 7	LEO
Jul	8–Nov 7	VIR
Nov	8–Dec 8	LIB
Dec	9–Dec 31	SCO

1952 VENUS

Jan	1	SCO
Jan	2–Jan 26	SAG
Jan	27–Feb 20	CAP
Feb	21–Mar 16	AQU
Mar	17–Apr 8	PIS
Apr	9–May 3	ARI
May	4–May 28	TAU
May	29–Jun 21	GEM
Jun	22–Jul 15	CAN
Jul	16–Aug 8	LEO
Aug	9–Sep 2	VIR
Sep	3–Sep 26	LIB
Sep	27–Oct 21	SCO
Oct	22–Nov 15	SAG
Nov	16–Dec 9	CAP
Dec	10–Dec 31	AQU

1953 VENUS

Jan	1–Jan 4	AQU
Jan	5–Feb 1	PIS
Feb	2–Mar 14	ARI
Mar	15–Mar 30	TAU
Mar	31–Jun 4	ARI
Jun	5–Jul 6	TAU
Jul	7–Aug 3	GEM
Aug	4–Aug 29	CAN
Aug	30–Sep 23	LEO
Sep	24–Oct 18	VIR
Oct	19–Nov 11	LIB
Nov	12–Dec 5	SCO
Dec	6–Dec 29	SAG
Dec	30–Dec 31	CAP

1954 VENUS

Jan	1–Jan 21	CAP
Jan	22–Feb 14	AQU
Feb	15–Mar 10	PIS
Mar	11–Apr 3	ARI
Apr	4–Apr 28	TAU
Apr	29–May 23	GEM
May	24–Jun 17	CAN
Jun	18–Jul 12	LEO
Jul	13–Aug 8	VIR
Aug	9–Sep 6	LIB
Sep	7–Oct 22	SCO
Oct	23–Oct 26	SAG
Oct	27–Dec 31	SCO

1955 VENUS

Jan	1–Jan 5	SCO
Jan	6–Feb 5	SAG
Feb	6–Mar 4	CAP
Mar	5–Mar 29	AQU
Mar	30–Apr 24	PIS
Apr	25–May 19	ARI
May	20–Jun 12	TAU
Jun	13–Jul 7	GEM
Jul	8–Jul 31	CAN
Aug	1–Aug 25	LEO
Aug	26–Sep 18	VIR
Sep	19–Oct 12	LIB
Oct	13–Nov 5	SCO
Nov	6–Nov 29	SAG
Nov	30–Dec 23	CAP
Dec	24–Dec 31	AQU

1956 VENUS

Jan 1–Jan 17 AQU
Jan 18–Feb 10 PIS
Feb 11–Mar 7 ARI
Mar 8–Apr 3 TAU
Apr 4–May 7 GEM
May 8–Jun 22 CAN
Jun 23–Aug 3 GEM
Aug 4–Sep 7 CAN
Sep 8–Oct 5 LEO
Oct 6–Oct 31 VIR
Nov 1–Nov 25 LIB
Nov 26–Dec 19 SCO
Dec 20–Dec 31 SAG

1957 VENUS

Jan 1–Jan 12 SAG
Jan 13–Feb 5 CAP
Feb 6–Mar 1 AQU
Mar 2–Mar 25 PIS
Mar 26–Apr 18 ARI
Apr 19–May 12 TAU
May 13–Jun 6 GEM
Jun 7–Jul 1 CAN
Jul 2–Jul 25 LEO
Jul 26–Aug 19 VIR
Aug 20–Sep 13 LIB
Sep 14–Oct 9 SCO
Oct 10–Nov 5 SAG
Nov 6–Dec 6 CAP
Dec 7–Dec 31 AQU

1958 VENUS

Jan 1–Apr 6 AQU
Apr 7–May 4 PIS
May 5–May 31 ARI
Jun 1–Jun 26 TAU
Jun 27–Jul 21 GEM
Jul 22–Aug 15 CAN
Aug 16–Sep 9 LEO
Sep 10–Oct 3 VIR
Oct 4–Oct 27 LIB
Oct 28–Nov 20 SCO
Nov 21–Dec 13 SAG
Dec 14–Dec 31 CAP

1959 VENUS

Jan 1–Jan 6 CAP
Jan 7–Jan 30 AQU
Jan 31–Feb 24 PIS
Feb 25–Mar 20 ARI
Mar 21–Apr 14 TAU
Apr 15–May 10 GEM
May 11–Jun 6 CAN
Jun 7–Jul 8 LEO
Jul 9–Sep 19 VIR
Sep 20–Sep 24 LEO
Sep 25–Nov 9 VIR
Nov 10–Dec 7 LIB
Dec 8–Dec 31 SCO

1960 VENUS

Jan 1   SCO
Jan 2–Jan 26 SAG
Jan 27–Feb 20 CAP
Feb 21–Mar 15 AQU
Mar 16–Apr 8 PIS
Apr 9–May 3 ARI
May 4–May 27 TAU
May 28–Jun 21 GEM
Jun 22–Jul 15 CAN
Jul 16–Aug 8 LEO
Aug 9–Sep 2 VIR
Sep 3–Sep 26 LIB
Sep 27–Oct 21 SCO
Oct 22–Nov 15 SAG
Nov 16–Dec 9 CAP
Dec 10–Dec 31 AQU

1961 VENUS

Jan 1–Jan 4 AQU
Jan 5–Feb 1 PIS
Feb 2–Jun 5 ARI
Jun 6–Jul 6 TAU
Jul 7–Aug 3 GEM
Aug 4–Aug 29 CAN
Aug 30–Sep 23 LEO
Sep 24–Oct 17 VIR
Oct 18–Nov 10 LIB
Nov 11–Dec 4 SCO
Dec 5–Dec 28 SAG
Dec 29–Dec 31 CAP

1962 VENUS

Jan 1–Jan 21 CAP
Jan 22–Feb 14 AQU
Feb 15–Mar 10 PIS
Mar 11–Apr 3 ARI
Apr 4–Apr 27 TAU
Apr 28–May 22 GEM
May 23–Jun 16 CAN
Jun 17–Jul 12 LEO
Jul 13–Aug 8 VIR
Aug 9–Sep 6 LIB
Sep 7–Dec 31 SCO

1963 VENUS

Jan 1–Jan 6 SCO
Jan 7–Feb 5 SAG
Feb 6–Mar 3 CAP
Mar 4–Mar 29 AQU
Mar 30–Apr 23 PIS
Apr 24–May 18 ARI
May 19–Jun 11 TAU
Jun 12–Jul 6 GEM
Jul 7–Jul 31 CAN
Aug 1–Aug 24 LEO
Aug 25–Sep 17 VIR
Sep 18–Oct 11 LIB
Oct 12–Nov 4 SCO
Nov 5–Nov 28 SAG
Nov 29–Dec 23 CAP
Dec 24–Dec 31 AQU

1964 VENUS

Jan 1–Jan 16 AQU
Jan 17–Feb 9 PIS
Feb 10–Mar 6 ARI
Mar 7–Apr 3 TAU
Apr 4–May 8 GEM
May 9–Jun 16 CAN
Jun 17–Aug 4 GEM
Aug 5–Sep 7 CAN
Sep 8–Oct 4 LEO
Oct 5–Oct 30 VIR
Oct 31–Nov 24 LIB
Nov 25–Dec 18 SCO
Dec 19–Dec 31 SAG

1965 VENUS

Jan 1–Jan 11	SAG
Jan 12–Feb 4	CAP
Feb 5–Feb 28	AQU
Mar 1–Mar 24	PIS
Mar 25–Apr 17	ARI
Apr 18–May 11	TAU
May 12–Jun 5	GEM
Jun 6–Jun 30	CAN
Jul 1–Jul 24	LEO
Jul 25–Aug 18	VIR
Aug 19–Sep 13	LIB
Sep 14–Oct 8	SCO
Oct 9–Nov 5	SAG
Nov 6–Dec 6	CAP
Dec 7–Dec 31	AQU

1966 VENUS

Jan 1–Feb 6	AQU
Feb 7–Feb 25	CAP
Feb 26–Apr 6	AQU
Apr 7–May 5	PIS
May 6–May 31	ARI
Jun 1–Jun 26	TAU
Jun 27–Jul 21	GEM
Jul 22–Aug 15	CAN
Aug 16–Sep 8	LEO
Sep 9–Oct 3	VIR
Oct 4–Oct 27	LIB
Oct 28–Nov 20	SCO
Nov 21–Dec 13	SAG
Dec 14–Dec 31	CAP

1967 VENUS

Jan 1–Jan 6	CAP
Jan 7–Jan 30	AQU
Jan 31–Feb 23	PIS
Feb 24–Mar 20	ARI
Mar 21–Apr 14	TAU
Apr 15–May 10	GEM
May 11–Jun 6	CAN
Jun 7–Jul 8	LEO
Jul 9–Sep 9	VIR
Sep 10–Oct 1	LEO
Oct 2–Nov 9	VIR
Nov 10–Dec 7	LIB
Dec 8–Dec 31	SCO

1968 VENUS

Jan 1–Jan 26	SAG
Jan 27–Feb 20	CAP
Feb 21–Mar 15	AQU
Mar 16–Apr 8	PIS
Apr 9–May 3	ARI
May 4–May 27	TAU
May 28–Jun 21	GEM
Jun 22–Jul 15	CAN
Jul 16–Aug 8	LEO
Aug 9–Sep 2	VIR
Sep 3–Sep 26	LIB
Sep 27–Oct 21	SCO
Oct 22–Nov 14	SAG
Nov 15–Dec 9	CAP
Dec 10–Dec 31	AQU

1969 VENUS

Jan 1–Jan 4	AQU
Jan 5–Feb 2	PIS
Feb 3–Jun 6	ARI
Jun 7–Jul 6	TAU
Jul 7–Aug 3	GEM
Aug 4–Aug 29	CAN
Aug 30–Sep 23	LIB
Sep 24–Oct 17	VIR
Oct 18–Nov 10	LIB
Nov 11–Dec 4	SCO
Dec 5–Dec 28	SAG
Dec 29–Dec 31	CAP

1970 VENUS

Jan 1–Jan 21	CAP
Jan 22–Feb 14	AQU
Feb 15–Mar 10	PIS
Mar 11–Apr 3	ARI
Apr 4–Apr 27	TAU
Apr 28–May 22	GEM
May 23–Jun 16	CAN
Jun 17–Jul 12	LEO
Jul 13–Aug 8	VIR
Aug 9–Sep 7	LIB
Sep 8–Dec 31	SCO

1971 VENUS

Jan 1–Jan 7	SCO
Jan 8–Feb 5	SAG
Feb 6–Mar 4	CAP
Mar 5–Mar 29	AQU
Mar 30–Apr 23	PIS
Apr 24–May 18	ARI
May 19–Jun 12	TAU
Jun 13–Jul 6	GEM
Jul 7–Jul 31	CAN
Aug 1–Aug 24	LEO
Aug 25–Sep 17	VIR
Sep 18–Oct 11	LIB
Oct 12–Nov 5	SCO
Nov 6–Nov 29	SAG
Nov 30–Dec 23	CAP
Dec 24–Dec 31	AQU

1972 VENUS

Jan 1–Jan 16	AQU
Jan 17–Feb 10	PIS
Feb 11–Mar 7	ARI
Mar 8–Apr 3	TAU
Apr 4–May 10	GEM
May 11–Jun 11	CAN
Jun 12–Aug 6	GEM
Aug 7–Sep 7	CAN
Sep 8–Oct 5	LEO
Oct 6–Oct 30	VIR
Oct 31–Nov 24	LIB
Nov 25–Dec 18	SCO
Dec 19–Dec 31	SAG

1973 VENUS

Jan 1–Jan 11	SAG
Jan 12–Feb 4	CAP
Feb 5–Feb 28	AQU
Mar 1–Mar 24	PIS
Mar 25–Apr 18	ARI
Apr 19–May 12	TAU
May 13–Jun 5	GEM
Jun 6–Jun 30	CAN
Jul 1–Jul 25	LEO
Jul 26–Aug 19	VIR
Aug 20–Sep 13	LIB
Sep 14–Oct 9	SCO
Oct 10–Nov 5	SAG
Nov 6–Dec 7	CAP
Dec 8–Dec 31	AQU

1974 VENUS

Jan 1–Jan 29   AQU
Jan 30–Feb 28   CAP
Mar 1–Apr 6   AQU
Apr 7–May 4   PIS
May 5–May 31   ARI
Jun 1–Jun 25   TAU
Jun 26–Jul 21   GEM
Jul 22–Aug 14   CAN
Aug 15–Sep 8   LEO
Sep 9–Oct 2   VIR
Oct 3–Oct 26   LIB
Oct 27–Nov 19   SCO
Nov 20–Dec 13   SAG
Dec 14–Dec 31   CAP

1975 VENUS

Jan 1–Jan 6   CAP
Jan 7–Jan 30   AQU
Jan 31–Feb 23   PIS
Feb 24–Mar 19   ARI
Mar 20–Apr 13   TAU
Apr 14–May 9   GEM
May 10–Jun 6   CAN
Jun 7–Jul 9   LEO
Jul 10–Sep 2   VIR
Sep 3–Oct 4   LEO
Oct 5–Nov 9   VIR
Nov 10–Dec 7   LIB
Dec 8–Dec 31   SCO

1976 VENUS

Jan 1   SCO
Jan 2–Jan 26   SAG
Jan 27–Feb 19   CAP
Feb 20–Mar 15   AQU
Mar 16–Apr 8   PIS
Apr 9–May 2   ARI
May 3–May 27   TAU
May 28–Jun 20   GEM
Jun 21–Jun 14   CAN
Jun 15–Aug 8   LEO
Aug 9–Sep 1   VIR
Sep 2–Sep 26   LIB
Sep 27–Oct 20   SCO
Oct 21–Nov 14   SAG
Nov 15–Dec 9   CAP
Dec 10–Dec 31   AQU

1977 VENUS

Jan 1–Jan 4   AQU
Jan 5–Feb 2   PIS
Feb 3–Jun 6   ARI
Jun 7–Jul 6   TAU
Jul 7–Aug 2   GEM
Aug 3–Aug 28   CAN
Aug 29–Sep 22   LEO
Sep 23–Oct 17   VIR
Oct 18–Nov 10   LIB
Nov 11–Dec 4   SCO
Dec 5–Dec 27   SAG
Dec 28–Dec 31   CAP

1978 VENUS

Jan 1–Jan 20   CAP
Jan 21–Feb 13   AQU
Feb 14–Mar 9   PIS
Mar 10–Apr 2   ARI
Apr 3–Apr 27   TAU
Apr 28–May 22   GEM
May 23–Jun 16   CAN
Jun 17–Jul 12   LEO
Jul 13–Aug 8   VIR
Aug 9–Sep 7   LIB
Sep 8–Dec 31   SCO

1979 VENUS

Jan 1–Jan 7   SCO
Jan 8–Feb 5   SAG
Feb 6–Mar 3   CAP
Mar 4–Mar 29   AQU
Mar 30–Apr 23   PIS
Apr 24–May 18   ARI
May 19–Jun 11   TAU
Jun 12–Jul 6   GEM
Jul 7–Jul 30   CAN
Jul 31–Aug 24   LEO
Aug 25–Sep 17   VIR
Sep 18–Oct 11   LIB
Oct 12–Nov 4   SCO
Nov 5–Nov 28   SAG
Nov 29–Dec 22   CAP
Dec 23–Dec 31   AQU

1980 VENUS

Jan 1–Jan 16   AQU
Jan 17–Feb 9   PIS
Feb 10–Mar 6   ARI
Mar 7–Apr 3   TAU
Apr 4–May 12   GEM
May 13–Jun 5   CAN
Jun 6–Aug 6   GEM
Aug 7–Sep 7   CAN
Sep 8–Oct 4   LEO
Oct 5–Oct 30   VIR
Oct 31–Nov 24   LIB
Nov 25–Dec 18   SCO
Dec 19–Dec 31   SAG

1981 VENUS

Jan 1–Jan 11   SAG
Jan 12–Feb 4   CAP
Feb 5–Feb 28   AQU
Mar 1–Mar 24   PIS
Mar 25–Apr 17   ARI
Apr 18–May 11   TAU
May 12–Jun 5   GEM
Jun 6–Jun 29   CAN
Jun 30–Jul 24   LEO
Jul 25–Aug 18   VIR
Aug 19–Sep 12   LIB
Sep 13–Oct 9   SCO
Oct 10–Nov 5   SAG
Nov 6–Dec 8   CAP
Dec 9–Dec 31   AQU

1982 VENUS

Jan 1–Jan 23   AQU
Jan 24–Mar 2   CAP
Mar 3–Apr 6   AQU
Apr 7–May 4   PIS
May 5–May 30   ARI
May 31–Jun 25   TAU
Jun 26–Jul 20   GEM
Jul 21–Aug 14   CAN
Aug 15–Sep 7   LEO
Sep 8–Oct 2   VIR
Oct 3–Oct 26   LIB
Oct 27–Nov 18   SCO
Nov 19–Dec 12   SAG
Dec 13–Dec 31   CAP

chapter eleven

HOW TO FIND YOUR MARS SIGN

Under the year of your birth, find your birth date. For example, if you were born on February 25, 1920, your Mars sign is Scorpio, for Mars was in the sign of Scorpio from February 1 to April 23, 1920.

If you were born on the first or last day of a particular time period, it is possible that your Mars sign might be posited in the preceding or following sign. For example, if the time period is from August 6 to September 10, and you were born on September 10, then you must consider that your Mars might be in the next sign. The only way to be absolutely sure is to have your chart done by a computer (see Appendix II for computer services) or by a professional astrologer. If you are not sure, read the adjacent signs, and you will probably be able to decide which is applicable to you.

1920 MARS

Jan 1–Jan 31	LIB
Feb 1–Apr 23	SCO
Apr 24–Jul 10	LIB
Jul 11–Sep 4	SCO
Sep 5–Oct 18	SAG
Oct 19–Nov 27	CAP
Nov 28–Dec 31	AQU

1921 MARS

Jan 1–Jan 4	AQU
Jan 5–Feb 12	PIS
Feb 13–Mar 24	ARI
Mar 25–May 5	TAU
May 6–Jun 18	GEM
Jun 19–Aug 2	CAN
Aug 3–Sep 19	LEO
Sep 19–Nov 6	VIR
Nov 7–Dec 25	LIB
Dec 26–Dec 31	SCO

1922 MARS

Jan 1–Feb 18	SCO
Feb 19–Sep 13	SAG
Sep 14–Oct 30	CAP
Oct 31–Dec 11	AQU
Dec 12–Dec 31	PIS

1923 MARS

Jan 1–Jan 20	PIS
Jan 21–Mar 3	ARI
Mar 4–Apr 15	TAU
Apr 16–May 30	GEM
May 31–Jul 15	CAN
Jul 16–Aug 31	LEO
Sep 1–Oct 17	VIR
Oct 18–Dec 3	LIB
Dec 4–Dec 31	SCO

1924 MARS

Jan 1–Feb 19	SCO
Feb 20–Mar 6	SAG
Mar 7–Apr 24	CAP
Apr 25–Jun 24	AQU
Jun 25–Aug 24	PIS
Aug 25–Oct 19	AQU
Oct 20–Dec 18	PIS
Dec 19–Dec 31	ARI

1925 MARS

Jan 1–Feb 4	ARI
Feb 5–Mar 23	TAU
Mar 24–May 9	GEM
May 10–Jun 25	CAN
Jun 26–Aug 12	LEO
Aug 13–Sep 28	VIR
Sep 29–Nov 13	LIB
Nov 14–Dec 27	SCO
Dec 28–Dec 31	SAG

1926 MARS

Jan 1–Feb 8	SAG
Feb 9–Mar 22	CAP
Mar 23–May 3	AQU
May 4–Jun 14	PIS
Jun 15–Jul 31	ARI
Aug 1–Dec 31	TAU

1927 MARS

Jan 1–Feb 21	TAU
Feb 22–Apr 16	GEM
Apr 17–Jun 5	CAN
Jun 6–Jul 24	LEO
Jul 25–Sep 10	VIR
Sep 11–Oct 25	LIB
Oct 26–Dec 7	SCO
Dec 8–Dec 31	SAG

1928 MARS

Jan 1–Jan 18	SAG
Jan 19–Feb 27	CAP
Feb 28–Apr 7	AQU
Apr 8–May 16	PIS
May 17–Jun 25	ARI
Jun 26–Aug 8	TAU
Aug 9–Oct 2	GEM
Oct 3–Dec 19	CAN
Dec 20–Dec 31	GEM

1929 MARS

Jan 1–Mar 10	GEM
Mar 11–May 12	CAN
May 13–Jul 3	LEO
Jul 4–Aug 21	VIR
Aug 22–Oct 5	LIB
Oct 6–Nov 18	SCO
Nov 19–Dec 28	SAG
Dec 29–Dec 31	CAP

1930 MARS

Jan 1–Feb 6	CAP
Feb 7–Mar 16	AQU
Mar 17–Apr 24	PIS
Apr 25–Jun 2	ARI
Jun 3–Jul 14	TAU
Jul 15–Aug 27	GEM
Aug 28–Oct 20	CAN
Oct 21–Dec 31	LEO

1931 MARS

Jan 1–Feb 15	LEO
Feb 16–Mar 29	CAN
Mar 30–Jun 9	LEO
Jun 10–Jul 31	VIR
Aug 1–Sep 16	LIB
Sep 17–Oct 29	SCO
Oct 30–Dec 9	SAG
Dec 10–Dec 31	CAP

1932 MARS

Jan 1–Jan 17	CAP
Jan 18–Feb 24	AQU
Feb 25–Apr 2	PIS
Apr 3–May 11	ARI
May 12–Jun 21	TAU
Jun 22–Aug 3	GEM
Aug 4–Sep 19	CAN
Sep 20–Nov 12	LEO
Nov 13–Dec 31	VIR

1933 MARS

Jan 1–Jul 5	VIR
Jul 6–Aug 25	LIB
Aug 26–Oct 8	SCO
Oct 9–Nov 18	SAG
Nov 19–Dec 27	CAP
Dec 28–Dec 31	AQU

1934 MARS

Jan 1–Feb 3	AQU
Feb 4–Mar 13	PIS
Mar 14–Apr 21	ARI
Apr 22–Jun 1	TAU
Jun 2–Jul 14	GEM
Jul 15–Aug 29	CAN
Aug 30–Oct 17	LEO
Oct 18–Dec 10	VIR
Dec 11–Dec 31	LIB

1935 MARS

Jan	1–Jul 28	LIB
Jul	29–Sep 15	SCO
Sep	16–Oct 27	SAG
Oct	28–Dec 6	CAP
Dec	7–Dec 31	AQU

1936 MARS

Jan	1–Jan 13	AQU
Jan	14–Feb 21	PIS
Feb	22–Mar 31	ARI
Apr	1–May 12	TAU
May	13–Jun 24	GEM
Jun	25–Aug 9	CAN
Aug	10–Sep 25	LEO
Sep	26–Nov 13	VIR
Nov	14–Dec 31	LIB

1937 MARS

Jan	1–Jan 4	LIB
Jan	5–Mar 12	SCO
Mar	13–May 13	SAG
May	14–Aug 7	SCO
Aug	8–Sep 29	SAG
Sep	30–Nov 10	CAP
Nov	11–Dec 20	AQU
Dec	21–Dec 31	PIS

1938 MARS

Jan	1–Jan 29	PIS
Jan	30–Mar 11	ARI
Mar	12–Apr 22	TAU
Apr	23–Jun 6	GEM
Jun	7–Jul 21	CAN
Jul	22–Sep 6	LEO
Sep	7–Oct 24	VIR
Oct	25–Dec 10	LIB
Dec	11–Dec 31	SCO

1939 MARS

Jan	1–Jan 28	SCO
Jan	29–Mar 20	SAG
Mar	21–May 23	CAP
May	24–Jul 20	AQU
Jul	21–Sep 23	CAP
Sep	24–Nov 18	AQU
Nov	19–Dec 31	PIS

1940 MARS

Jan	1–Jan 3	PIS
Jan	4–Feb 16	ARI
Feb	17–Mar 31	TAU
Apr	1–May 16	GEM
May	17–Jul 2	CAN
Jul	3–Aug 18	LEO
Aug	19–Oct 4	VIR
Oct	5–Nov 19	LIB
Nov	20–Dec 31	SCO

1941 MARS

Jan	1–Jan 3	SCO
Jan	4–Feb 16	SAG
Feb	17–Apr 1	CAP
Apr	2–May 15	AQU
May	16–Jul 1	PIS
Jul	2–Dec 31	ARI

1942 MARS

Jan	1–Jan 10	ARI
Jan	11–Mar 6	TAU
Mar	7–Apr 25	GEM
Apr	26–Jun 13	CAN
Jun	14–Jul 31	LEO
Aug	1–Sep 16	VIR
Sep	17–Oct 31	LIB
Nov	1–Dec 15	SCO
Dec	16–Dec 31	SAG

1943 MARS

Jan	1–Jan 25	SAG
Jan	26–Mar 7	CAP
Mar	8–Apr 16	AQU
Apr	17–May 26	PIS
May	27–Jun 6	ARI
Jun	7–Aug 22	TAU
Aug	23–Dec 31	GEM

1944 MARS

Jan	1–Mar 27	GEM
Mar	28–May 21	CAN
May	22–Jul 11	LEO
Jul	12–Aug 28	VIR
Aug	29–Oct 12	LIB
Oct	13–Nov 24	SCO
Nov	25–Dec 31	SAG

1945 MARS

Jan	1–Jan 4	SAG
Jan	5–Feb 13	CAP
Feb	14–Mar 24	AQU
Mar	25–May 1	PIS
May	2–Jun 10	ARI
Jun	11–Jul 22	TAU
Jul	23–Sep 6	GEM
Sep	7–Nov 10	CAN
Nov	11–Dec 25	LEO
Dec	26–Dec 31	CAN

1946 MARS

Jan	1–Apr 21	CAN
Apr	22–Jun 19	LEO
Jun	20–Aug 8	VIR
Aug	9–Sep 23	LIB
Sep	24–Nov 5	SCO
Nov	6–Dec 16	SAG
Dec	17–Dec 31	CAP

1947 MARS

Jan	1–Jan 24	CAP
Jan	25–Mar 3	AQU
Mar	4–Apr 10	PIS
Apr	11–May 20	ARI
May	21–Jun 30	TAU
Jul	1–Aug 12	GEM
Aug	13–Sep 30	CAN
Oct	1–Nov 30	LEO
Dec	1–Dec 31	VIR

1948 MARS

Jan	1–Feb 11	VIR
Feb	12–May 17	LEO
May	18–Jul 16	VIR
Jul	17–Sep 2	LIB
Sep	3–Oct 16	SCO
Oct	17–Nov 25	SAG
Nov	26–Dec 31	CAP

1949 MARS

Jan   1–Jan 3   CAP
Jan   4–Feb 10   AQU
Feb 11–Mar 20   PIS
Mar 21–Apr 29   ARI
Apr 30–Jun 9   TAU
Jun 10–Jul 22   GEM
Jul 23–Sep 6   CAN
Sep 7–Oct 26   LEO
Oct 27–Dec 25   VIR
Dec 26–Dec 31   LIB

1950 MARS

Jan   1–Mar 27   LIB
Mar 28–Jun 10   VIR
Jun 11–Aug 9   LIB
Aug 10–Sep 24   SCO
Sep 25–Nov 5   SAG
Nov 6–Dec 14   CAP
Dec 15–Dec 31   AQU

1951 MARS

Jan   1–Jan 21   AQU
Jan 22–Feb 28   PIS
Mar 1–Apr 9   ARI
Apr 10–May 20   TAU
May 21–Jul 2   GEM
Jul   3–Aug 17   CAN
Aug 18–Oct 3   LEO
Oct 4–Nov 23   VIR
Nov 24–Dec 31   LIB

1952 MARS

Jan   1–Jan 19   LIB
Jan 20–Aug 26   SCO
Aug 27–Oct 11   SAG
Oct 12–Nov 20   CAP
Nov 21–Dec 29   AQU
Dec 30–Dec 31   PIS

1953 MARS

Jan   1–Feb 7   PIS
Feb 8–Mar 19   ARI
Mar 20–Apr 30   TAU
May 1–Jun 13   GEM
Jun 14–Jul 29   CAN
Jul 30–Sep 14   LEO
Sep 15–Nov 1   VIR
Nov 2–Dec 19   LIB
Dec 20–Dec 31   SCO

1954 MARS

Jan   1–Feb 8   SCO
Feb 9–Apr 11   SAG
Apr 12–Jul 2   CAP
Jul   3–Aug 23   SAG
Aug 24–Oct 20   CAP
Oct 21–Dec 3   AQU
Dec 4–Dec 31   PIS

1955 MARS

Jan   1–Jan 14   PIS
Jan 15–Feb 25   ARI
Feb 26–Apr 9   TAU
Apr 10–May 25   GEM
May 26–Jul 10   CAN
Jul 11–Aug 26   LEO
Aug 27–Oct 12   VIR
Oct 13–Nov 28   LIB
Nov 29–Dec 31   SCO

1956 MARS

Jan   1–Jan 13   SCO
Jan 14–Feb 27   SAG
Feb 28–Apr 13   CAP
Apr 14–Jun 2   AQU
Jun 3–Dec 5   PIS
Dec 6–Dec 31   ARI

1957 MARS

Jan   1–Jan 27   ARI
Jan 28–Mar 16   TAU
Mar 17–May 3   GEM
May 4–Jun 20   CAN
Jun 21–Aug 7   LEO
Aug 8–Sep 23   VIR
Sep 24–Nov 7   LIB
Nov 8–Dec 22   SCO
Dec 23–Dec 31   SAG

1958 MARS

Jan   1–Feb 2   SAG
Feb 3–Mar 16   CAP
Mar 17–Apr 26   AQU
Apr 27–Jun 6   PIS
Jun 7–Jul 20   ARI
Jul 21–Sep 20   TAU
Sep 21–Oct 28   GEM
Oct 29–Dec 31   TAU

1959 MARS

Jan   1–Feb 9   TAU
Feb 10–Apr 9   GEM
Apr 10–May 31   CAN
Jun 1–Jul 19   LEO
Jul 20–Sep 4   VIR
Sep 5–Oct 20   LIB
Oct 21–Dec 2   SCO
Dec 3–Dec 31   SAG

1960 MARS

Jan   1–Jan 13   SAG
Jan 14–Feb 22   CAP
Feb 23–Apr 1   AQU
Apr 2–May 10   PIS
May 11–Jun 19   ARI
Jun 20–Aug 1   TAU
Aug 2–Sep 20   GEM
Sep 21–Dec 31   CAN

1961 MARS

Jan   1–Feb 5   CAN
Feb 6–Feb 7   GEM
Feb 8–May 5   CAN
May 6–Jun 27   LEO
Jun 28–Aug 16   VIR
Aug 17–Sep 30   LIB
Oct 1–Nov 12   SCO
Nov 13–Dec 23   SAG
Dec 24–Dec 31   CAP

1962 MARS

Jan   1–Jan 31   CAP
Feb 1–Mar 11   AQU
Mar 12–Apr 18   PIS
Apr 19–May 27   ARI
Mar 28–Jul 8   TAU
Jul 9–Aug 21   GEM
Aug 22–Oct 10   CAN
Oct 11–Dec 31   LEO

1963 MARS

Jan   1–Jun 2   LEO
Jun 3–Jul 26   VIR
Jul 27–Sep 11   LIB
Sep 12–Oct 24   SCO
Oct 25–Dec 4   SAG
Dec 5–Dec 31   CAP

1964 MARS

Jan	1–Jan 12	CAP
Jan	13–Feb 19	AQU
Feb	20–Mar 28	PIS
Mar	29–May 6	ARI
May	7–Jun 16	TAU
Jun	17–Jul 29	GEM
Jul	30–Sep 14	CAN
Sep	15–Nov 5	LEO
Nov	6–Dec 31	VIR

1965 MARS

Jan	1–Jun 28	VIR
Jun	29–Aug 19	LIB
Aug	20–Oct 3	SCO
Oct	4–Nov 13	SAG
Nov	14–Dec 22	CAP
Dec	23–Dec 31	AQU

1966 MARS

Jan	1–Jan 29	AQU
Jan	30–Mar 8	PIS
Mar	9–Apr 16	ARI
Apr	17–May 27	TAU
May	28–Jul 10	GEM
Jul	11–Aug 24	CAN
Aug	25–Oct 11	LEO
Oct	12–Dec 3	VIR
Dec	4–Dec 31	LIB

1967 MARS

Jan	1–Feb 11	LIB
Feb	12–Mar 31	SCO
Apr	1–Jul 18	LIB
Jul	19–Sep 9	SCO
Sep	10–Oct 22	SAG
Oct	23–Nov 30	CAP
Dec	1–Dec 31	AQU

1968 MARS

Jan	1–Jan 8	AQU
Jan	9–Feb 16	PIS
Feb	17–Mar 26	ARI
Mar	27–May 7	TAU
May	8–Jun 20	GEM
Jun	21–Aug 4	CAN
Aug	5–Sep 20	LEO
Sep	21–Nov 8	VIR
Nov	9–Dec 28	LIB
Dec	29–Dec 31	SCO

1969 MARS

Jan	1–Feb 24	SCO
Feb	25–Sep 20	SAG
Sep	21–Nov 3	CAP
Nov	4–Dec 13	AQU
Dec	14–Dec 31	PIS

1970 MARS

Jan	1–Jan 23	PIS
Jan	24–Mar 6	ARI
Mar	7–Apr 17	TAU
Apr	18–Jun 1	GEM
Jun	2–Jul 17	CAN
Jul	18–Sep 2	LEO
Sep	3–Oct 19	VIR
Oct	20–Dec 5	LIB
Dec	6–Dec 31	SCO

1971 MARS

Jan	1–Jan 23	SCO
Jan	24–Mar 12	SAG
Mar	13–May 3	CAP
May	4–Nov 6	AQU
Nov	7–Dec 26	PIS
Dec	27–Dec 31	ARI

1972 MARS

Jan	1–Feb 10	ARI
Feb	11–Mar 27	TAU
Mar	28–May 12	GEM
May	13–Jun 28	CAN
Jun	29–Aug 15	LEO
Aug	16–Sep 30	VIR
Oct	1–Nov 15	LIB
Nov	16–Dec 30	SCO
Dec	31		SAG

1973 MARS

Jan	1–Feb 12	SAG
Feb	13–Mar 26	CAP
Mar	27–May 8	AQU
May	9–Jun 20	PIS
Jun	21–Aug 12	ARI
Aug	13–Oct 29	TAU
Oct	30–Dec 24	ARI
Dec	25–Dec 31	TAU

1974 MARS

Jan	1–Feb 27	TAU
Feb	28–Apr 20	GEM
Apr	21–Jun 9	CAN
Jun	10–Jul 27	LEO
Jul	28–Sep 12	VIR
Sep	13–Oct 28	LIB
Oct	29–Dec 10	SCO
Dec	11–Dec 31	SAG

1975 MARS

Jan	1–Jan 21	SAG
Jan	22–Mar 3	CAP
Mar	4–Apr 11	AQU
Apr	12–May 21	PIS
May	22–Jul 1	ARI
Jul	2–Aug 14	TAU
Aug	15–Oct 17	GEM
Oct	18–Nov 25	CAN
Nov	26–Dec 31	GEM

1976 MARS

Jan	1–Mar 18	GEM
Mar	19–May 16	CAN
May	17–Jul 6	LEO
Jul	7–Aug 24	VIR
Aug	25–Oct 8	LIB
Oct	9–Nov 20	SCO
Nov	21–Dec 31	SAG

1977 MARS

Jan 1	SAG
Jan 2–Feb 9	CAP
Feb 10–Mar 20	AQU
Mar 21–Apr 27	PIS
Apr 28–Jun 6	ARI
Jun 7–Jul 17	TAU
Jul 18–Sep 1	GEM
Sep 2–Oct 26	CAN
Oct 27–Dec 31	LEO

1978 MARS

Jan 1–Jan 26	LEO
Jan 27–Apr 10	CAN
Apr 11–Jun 14	LEO
Jun 15–Aug 3	VIR
Aug 4–Sep 18	LIB
Sep 19–Nov 3	SCO
Nov 4–Dec 12	SAG
Dec 13–Dec 31	CAP

1979 MARS

Jan 1–Jan 20	CAP
Jan 21–Feb 27	AQU
Feb 28–Apr 7	PIS
Apr 8–May 16	ARI
May 17–Jun 26	TAU
Jun 27–Aug 8	GEM
Aug 9–Sep 24	CAN
Sep 25–Nov 19	LEO
Nov 20–Dec 31	VIR

1980 MARS

Jan 1–Mar 11	VIR
Mar 12–May 4	LEO
May 5–Jul 10	VIR
Jul 11–Aug 29	LIB
Aug 30–Oct 12	SCO
Oct 13–Nov 22	SAG
Nov 23–Dec 30	CAP
Dec 31	AQU

1981 MARS

Jan 1–Feb 6	AQU
Feb 7–Mar 17	PIS
Mar 18–Apr 25	ARI
Apr 26–Jun 5	TAU
Jun 6–Jul 18	GEM
Jul 19–Sep 1	CAN
Sep 2–Oct 21	LEO
Oct 22–Dec 16	VIR
Dec 17–Dec 31	LIB

1982 MARS

Jan 1–Aug 3	LIB
Aug 4–Sep 20	SCO
Sep 21–Oct 31	SAG
Nov 1–Dec 10	CAP
Dec 11–Dec 31	AQU

part three
___

YOU ARE THE DIRECTOR

YOUR STAR SELF: THE PLAY WITHIN

Now that you have looked up your Astropoints and found which sign each occupies, you are ready to audition for your role as the Star Self, in your own personal Astroplay.

A major key to successful relationships is the ability *to understand yourself*. Only when you truly understand your *own* aims, needs, wants, and desires can you relate successfully to another person, whose aims, needs, wants, and desires may be different from your own. Though we usually blame our relationship difficulties on the other person, the real culprit often is not knowing ourselves. Or denying who we are.

This is where astrology can be of great help. By revealing you to yourself, it can allow you to be that Self without apology or guilt.

No matter who your mother, father, aunts, uncles, teachers, lovers, spouses, mentors, bosses, colleagues, or whoever, think you are or want you to be, you are *you*. And it's not only okay to be who you naturally are, it's the only way to find any kind of fulfillment in life. That may seem a bit simplistic, but as therapists we find many of our clients unhappily trying to fulfill a model grafted onto them by parents, teachers, siblings, society at large, or some other outside factor.

Therefore, we feel strongly that self-understanding is the primary key to achieving a happy and fulfilling relationship. And that's what this chapter is all about.

You contain within yourself all the components of the *entire zodiac*. There are ten planets in the chart, even though in this book we discuss only the five Astropoints already covered (Sun, Moon, ASC, Venus, and Mars).

You also have read of the Elements and the Modes in Chapters Six and Seven, and, if you've been following along, you have looked up your planet placements (from your birth date) and your ASC sign (from the time of birth, if you know it). In the following paragraphs, you are going to learn how to put the information to work, learning about yourself and your personal cosmic energies.

Though you do contain the energies of all ten planets, you may not contain all four Elements and all three Modes. Nevertheless, this information is important. Learning what's missing as well as what's there helps you know who you are and how your energies flow.

For example, if you're predominately Air, you might find that Earth types drive you bananas. Chances are, you think they are too pokey and boringly practical. They can't *fly*.

But, and this is a big "but," if you don't know that you are mostly Air, and what that means, you might think there's something wrong with *you*, because you're different from those around you. This is especially true if your parents (or one of them) are dominant Earth types who convinced you that theirs was the only right way to do things and that your way was wrong or "flighty."

So, it's crucial to know *you* first. And in knowing and understanding *you*, it will become apparent that there's nothing *wrong* with you. You're just *you*, and that's okay. And the others—the ones who drive you around the bend—are also okay. They are just being who they are naturally. It's like the way oil and water don't mix—except in this case, it's Earth and Air that don't mix!

Armed with information about who you truly are, you will be in a position to influence whether a relationship will be a "hit" or will close after a disastrous first night. And you do this first by understanding your inner script, the one that you are daily playing out in your life, only now you become aware of it.

Following are lists of key words for each of the Astropoints, covering all twelve signs of the zodiac.

SUN KEY WORDS

The Sun is the basic core of anyone. When you think of *why* you are here and *where* you are going in life, *what* makes you feel important, you are in Sun territory.

The Sun is your *purpose in life*, your *direction*, and your *sense of "I AM."*

Sun in Aries

MY LIFE PURPOSE IS TO: move bravely ahead, meeting all challenges.
I AM: courageous, impulsive, innocent, humorous, vital, enthusiastic, aggressive, insensitive, headstrong, inspired, one-pointed.

Sun in Taurus

MY LIFE PURPOSE IS TO: hold onto everything of value by not changing myself.
I AM: stable, security conscious, beauty loving, grounded, sensual, relaxed, immovable, fixated, conservative, materialistic, placid.

Sun in Gemini

MY LIFE PURPOSE IS TO: learn all I can and make connections using the information.
I AM: versatile, witty, verbal, logical, mental, changeable, social, devious, perceptive, inconsistent, amoral.

Sun in Cancer

MY LIFE PURPOSE IS TO: feel deeply, care strongly, and nurture.
I AM: sensitive, shy, domestic, old-fashioned, imaginative, psychic, intimate, security conscious, tenacious, fearful, cranky.

Sun in Leo

MY LIFE PURPOSE IS TO: unself-consciously and creatively express the Self.
I AM: noble, open, warmhearted, demonstrative, unsuspicious, generous, playful, creative, attention-seeking, tyrannical.

Sun in Virgo

MY LIFE PURPOSE IS TO: humbly be of service through exacting discriminations.
I AM: methodical, practical, thorough, modest, hardworking, uptight, perfectionistic, critical, sensible, orderly, exact.

Sun in Libra

MY LIFE PURPOSE IS TO: fairly and gracefully reconcile opposites and see both sides of all issues.
I AM: fair, gracious, beauty loving, mental, kind, sensitive, analytical, vacillating, indecisive, conflict-avoiding, diplomatic.

Sun in Scorpio

MY LIFE PURPOSE IS TO: probe the mysteries by going to the limit, falling apart, and rebuilding.

I AM: intense, sexual, perceptive, private, suspicious, committed, extreme, vengeful, catalytic, magical, healing.

Sun in Sagittarius

MY LIFE PURPOSE IS TO: positively affirm life and hope by shooting for the stars.

I AM: optimistic, adventurous, humorous, philosophical, grandiose, zealous, fanatical, open, metaphysical, clumsy, blunt.

Sun in Capricorn

MY LIFE PURPOSE IS TO: do what I must with discipline and structure.

I AM: responsible, serious, organized, successful, wry, profound, realistic, conservative, materialistic, status-conscious, repressed.

Sun in Aquarius

MY LIFE PURPOSE IS TO: experiment with all established structures, seeking the one truth.

I AM: unconventional, friendly, humanitarian, original, intuitive, analytical, eccentric, objective, scattered, remote, unfeeling.

Sun in Pisces

MY LIFE PURPOSE IS TO: sensitively flow into all things, showing how we are all one.

I AM: kind, imaginative, creative, compassionate, idealistic, healing, sweet, attuned, addicted, evasive, unrealistic.

MOON KEY WORDS

The Moon is the second most basic component. It represents you when you are most relaxed, at home. It is your instinctual self, your "automatic" personality. The Moon shows how and what bonds you to another.

The Moon is your *needs*, your *sense of family and children*, and what makes you feel *comfortable and secure*.

Moon in Aries

I NEED TO BE: active, adventurous, stimulated, direct, competitive, enthusiastic, first, boss, challenged.

I FEEL CARED FOR BY BEING: given room to move, dealt with directly, made to feel unique.

I'M MOST COMFORTABLE IN ENVIRONMENTS WHERE: there is a lot of action.

Moon in Taurus

I NEED TO BE: stable, well fed, comfortable, financially secure, touched, loved, relaxed, peaceful, conservative.

I FEEL CARED FOR BY BEING: given practical help, dealt with honestly, hugged, made physically comfortable.

I'M MOST COMFORTABLE IN ENVIRONMENTS WHERE: it is sensuous, secure, comfortable.

Moon in Gemini

I NEED TO BE: social, intellectual, interactive, versatile, light, mentally stimulated, talkative, busy, informed.

I FEEL CARED FOR BY BEING: appreciated intellectually, freed from routine, communicated with.

I'M MOST COMFORTABLE IN ENVIRONMENTS WHERE: there is mental stimulation, more than one thing going on.

Moon in Cancer

I NEED TO BE: secure, comfortable, well fed, loony, nurturing, intimate, home, sentimental, protective.

I FEEL CARED FOR BY BEING: fed food I love, babied, made to feel secure.

I'M MOST COMFORTABLE IN ENVIRONMENTS WHERE: it's cozy and quiet, I feel safe.

Moon in Leo

I NEED TO BE: creative, playful, heartfelt, noble, loyal, grand, respected, affectionate, noticed.

I FEEL CARED FOR BY BEING: given special attention and feedback, appreciated for my creativity, played with.

I'M MOST COMFORTABLE IN ENVIRONMENTS WHERE: it is elegant, grand, personally self-expressive.

Moon in Virgo

I NEED TO BE: analytic, detailed, modest, perfect, useful, helpful, precise, kind, sensible.

I FEEL CARED FOR BY BEING: noticed for my effectiveness, appreciated for my skill and insight, nursed when sick.

I'M MOST COMFORTABLE IN ENVIRONMENTS WHERE: things are in their proper place and make sense to me.

Moon in Libra

I NEED TO BE: harmonious, artistic, graceful, fair, balanced, social, intellectual, calm, diplomatic.

I FEEL CARED FOR BY BEING: appreciated for my social diplomacy, respected for my judgment, given focused attention.

I'M MOST COMFORTABLE IN ENVIRONMENTS WHERE: there is harmony and beauty.

Moon in Scorpio

I NEED TO BE: intense, committed, emotional, deep, safe, intimate, perceptive, controlled, powerful.

I FEEL CARED FOR BY BEING: appreciated for my intense perceptions, allowed to take my time trusting, seen as deeply fascinating.

I'M MOST COMFORTABLE IN ENVIRONMENTS WHERE: my intensity doesn't drive others away.

Moon in Sagittarius

I NEED TO BE: free, philosophical, adventurous, laughing, traveling, wise, optimistic, playful, zealous.

I FEEL CARED FOR BY BEING: allowed to roam free, noticed for my wisdom, laughed with.

I'M MOST COMFORTABLE IN ENVIRONMENTS WHERE: there is learning, I'm not limited in any way.

Moon in Capricorn

I NEED TO BE: useful, spartan, ambitious, hardworking, organized, down to earth, productive, disciplined, controlled.

I FEEL CARED FOR BY BEING: appreciated for my accomplishments, allowed to take my time trusting, noticed.

I'M MOST COMFORTABLE IN ENVIRONMENTS WHERE: I feel effective and productive.

Moon in Aquarius

I NEED TO BE: unique, analytical, objective, detached, open-minded, sincere, rebellious, knowledgeable, friendly.

I FEEL CARED FOR BY BEING: appreciated for my intellect, seen as unique, respected for my unconventionality.

I'M MOST COMFORTABLE IN ENVIRONMENTS WHERE: I can be as unusual as I like.

Moon in Pisces

I NEED TO BE: sensitive, devoted, escapist, inspired, merged, imaginative, evasive, attuned, compassionate.

I FEEL CARED FOR BY BEING: allowed my dreaminess, appreciated for my sensitivity, understood.

I'M MOST COMFORTABLE IN ENVIRONMENTS WHERE: I can flow into whatever is happening.

ASCENDANT KEY WORDS

The ASC is the third most basic component. It represents your public persona, how people at first perceive you, and how you respond to new circumstances. The ASC is important because we go *out* into the world. It has been compared to a colored filter through which we see the world and it sees us.

The ASC is your *social mask*, your *first response*, and your *appearance*, both physical and the impression you give others.

Aries Ascendant

MY FIRST RESPONSE TO SITUATIONS IS TO: act quickly, take direct, immediate action.

THE SOCIAL MASK I WEAR IS TO BE: heroic, active, vibrant, achieving, pushy, dominant, impulsive.

Taurus Ascendant

MY FIRST RESPONSE TO SITUATIONS IS TO: wait, take my time, keep calm.

THE SOCIAL MASK I WEAR IS TO BE: calm, placid, strong, sensual, grounded, stubborn, materialistic.

Gemini Ascendant

MY FIRST RESPONSE TO SITUATIONS IS TO: talk, network, gather information.

THE SOCIAL MASK I WEAR IS TO BE: verbal, communicative, versatile, friendly, sociable, interesting, witty, superficial, fickle.

Cancer Ascendant

MY FIRST RESPONSE TO SITUATIONS IS TO: nurture and take care, protect myself, remain secure.
THE SOCIAL MASK I WEAR IS TO BE: sensitive, imaginative, moody, indirect, security conscious, tenacious.

Leo Ascendant

MY FIRST RESPONSE TO SITUATIONS IS TO: rule, take center stage.
THE SOCIAL MASK I WEAR IS TO BE: grand, magnanimous, loyal, theatrical, generous, creative, powerful, self-centered, grandstanding.

Virgo Ascendant

MY FIRST RESPONSE TO SITUATIONS IS TO: analyze, identify problems, devise solutions.
THE SOCIAL MASK I WEAR IS TO BE: modest, attentive, helpful, kind, clean, organized, perfectionistic, picky, fussy.

Libra Ascendant

MY FIRST RESPONSE TO SITUATIONS IS TO: react, sense the right way to maintain harmony.
THE SOCIAL MASK I WEAR IS TO BE: gentle, diplomatic, sociable, artistic, graceful, fair, indecisive, inconsistent, judging.

Scorpio Ascendant

MY FIRST RESPONSE TO SITUATIONS IS TO: keep control, test the waters, find out if it is safe to relax.
THE SOCIAL MASK I WEAR IS TO BE: sexual, perceptive, compelling, intriguing, mysterious, watchful, secretive, vindictive, destructive.

Sagittarius Ascendant

MY FIRST RESPONSE TO SITUATIONS IS TO: enjoy the situation, see the big picture.
THE SOCIAL MASK I WEAR IS TO BE: free-spirited, adventurous, playful, optimistic, philosophical, exaggerating, opinionated.

Capricorn Ascendant

MY FIRST RESPONSE TO SITUATIONS IS TO: be realistic, check the bottom line.
THE SOCIAL MASK I WEAR IS TO BE: ambitious, dedicated, hardworking, serious, status-conscious, organized, stiff, restricting.

Aquarius Ascendant

MY FIRST RESPONSE TO SITUATIONS IS TO: be different yet friendly and social.

THE SOCIAL MASK I WEAR IS TO BE: unique, friendly, social, analytic, idealistic, New Age, detached, know-it-all, perverse.

Pisces Ascendant

MY FIRST RESPONSE TO SITUATIONS IS TO: go with the flow, be empathic, feel the currents.

THE SOCIAL MASK I WEAR IS TO BE: sensitive, creative, imaginative, spiritual, romantic, idealistic, impractical, escapist.

VENUS KEY WORDS

Venus is one indicator of how you act and react in a sexual relationship, and therefore it's very important, but when it comes to a showdown, the Sun, Moon, and ASC are ultimately stronger, because they are so basic.

Venus comes into play when you fall in love and are connecting with another person. It's what gives you pleasure or makes you creative, your taste in clothes and entertainment.

Venus is your heart, how you *love*, your *taste*, what you *want*, what gives you *pleasure*, your *sense of beauty*.

Venus in Aries

I WANT: stimulation, energy, challenge, action, vitality, immediate responses, new experiences.

MY TASTE IS: new, loud, colorful, obvious, unique.

I SHOW LOVE BY: enthusiasm, excitement, fighting and making up, being stimulating, playing.

I FEEL LOVED BY: special attention, having time spent with me.

Venus in Taurus

I WANT: security, stability, money, calm, comfort, beauty, luxury.

MY TASTE IS: conservative, classical, natural, practical, solid.

I SHOW LOVE BY: possessiveness, reliability, affection, being sensual and physical, providing grounding.

I FEEL LOVED BY: being made financially and emotionally secure, having plenty of physical and emotional contact.

Venus in Gemini

I WANT: mental stimulation, lightness, repartee, change, freedom, flirtations, communication.

MY TASTE IS: intellectual, literary, changeable, multifaceted, popular.
I SHOW LOVE BY: talking, playing, being witty, doing unusual things, bringing new interesting information.
I FEEL LOVED BY: interacting, being given space.

Venus in Cancer

I WANT: closeness, sensitivity, security, nurturance, home, children, shelter from the storm.
MY TASTE IS: old-fashioned, sentimental, classical, personal, imaginative.
I SHOW LOVE BY: nurturing, remembering little things, holding on, wanting to set up a home and family, introducing you to my mother.
I FEEL LOVED BY: being nurtured, being intimate.

Venus in Leo

I WANT: glamour, affection, excellence, power, self-expression, attention.
MY TASTE IS: stylish, bold, individualistic, expensive, attention getting.
I SHOW LOVE BY: generosity, passion, loyalty, showing you off, being complementary and protective.
I FEEL LOVED BY: adoration, loyalty.

Venus in Virgo

I WANT: perfection, practicality, purity, thoroughness, discernment, cleanliness.
MY TASTE IS: exacting, clean, simple, orderly, detailed.
I SHOW LOVE BY: attention, taking care, noticing small things, not being critical, being useful.
I FEEL LOVED BY: attention, being catered to.

Venus in Libra

I WANT: beauty, harmony, fairness, intimacy, socializing, give and take.
MY TASTE IS: harmonious, balanced, graceful, comfortable, sensual.
I SHOW LOVE BY: accommodating, making things lovely and pleasant, being affectionate, giving attention, discussing matters.
I FEEL LOVED BY: affection, sharing pleasure and beauty.

Venus in Scorpio

I WANT: intensity, sex, commitment, passion, control, power.
MY TASTE IS: extreme, complicated, personal, definite, bizarre.
I SHOW LOVE BY: passion, commitment, renewing, being sexual, trusting.
I FEEL LOVED BY: passion, deep intimacy on all levels.

Venus in Sagittarius

I WANT: freedom, adventure, good times, travel, meaning, growth.
MY TASTE IS: spirited, outdoorsy, learned, classical, exotic.
I SHOW LOVE BY: being joyous and generous, giving space, sharing adventures.
I FEEL LOVED BY: laughter and having fun, being allowed freedom.

Venus in Capricorn

I WANT: status, meaning, organization, results, money, success, usefulness.
MY TASTE IS: conservative, elegant, simple, basic, classical.
I SHOW LOVE BY: being useful, providing security, helping achieve, reliability, dutifulness.
I FEEL LOVED BY: being made secure and able to relax.

Venus in Aquarius

I WANT: objectivity, distance, originality, experimentation, friendship, rebellion, universality.
MY TASTE IS: avant-garde, scientific, ancient, futuristic, humanistic.
I SHOW LOVE BY: friendship, being interesting and interested, sharing unusual ideas, understanding, loyalty.
I FEEL LOVED BY: being given freedom, friendship.

Venus in Pisces

I WANT: love, transcendence, sensitivity, peace, fluidity, merging, the ideal.
MY TASTE IS: romantic, beautiful, sublime, nature oriented, visionary.
I SHOW LOVE BY: romance, sensitivity, self-sacrifice, eroticism, affection.
I FEEL LOVED BY: intimacy, being allowed to shift and change.

MARS KEY WORDS

Mars shows how you respond sexually, but in ways different from Venus. Venus is love and romance, while Mars is action—the rawly sexual in us. Your Mars is evident when you are in motion—doing, making, building, fighting, defending. It shows most when you are making love or pursuing goals.

Mars is how you *act*, what *turns you on*, what *motivates* you, your style of *anger*, your *aggression*.

Mars in Aries

I ACT: heroically, inspired, self-motivated, quickly, punctually, impulsively, selfishly, competitively, rashly.

I'M MOTIVATED BY THE DESIRE FOR: challenge, self-interest, originality.

I GET ANGRY: instantaneously, intensely, actively.

MY SEXUAL STYLE IS: ardent, romantic, dominant, submissive.

Mars in Taurus

I ACT: steadfastly, dogmatically, resistantly, peacefully, slowly, conservatively, possessively, realistically, kindly.

I'M MOTIVATED BY THE DESIRE FOR: security, love, money.

I GET ANGRY: slowly, totally, physically.

MY SEXUAL STYLE IS: earthy, sensual, enduring, affectionate.

Mars in Gemini

I ACT: logically, flexibly, intelligently, light-heartedly, inconsistently, changeably, superficially, socially.

I'M MOTIVATED BY THE DESIRE FOR: information, ideas, communication.

I GET ANGRY: unpredictably, intellectually, logically.

MY SEXUAL STYLE IS: flirtatious, playful, verbal, uncommitted.

Mars in Cancer

I ACT: shyly, protectively, sensitively, ambitiously, imaginatively, moodily, parentally, indirectly, babyishly.

I'M MOTIVATED BY THE DESIRE FOR: safety, nurturance, closeness.

I GET ANGRY: emotionally, sullenly, privately.

MY SEXUAL STYLE IS: romantic, intimate, nurturing, imaginative.

Mars in Leo

I ACT: grandly, honorably, openly, romantically, courageously, playfully, affectionately, egocentrically, temperamentally.

I'M MOTIVATED BY THE DESIRE FOR: power, love, loyalty.
I GET ANGRY: dramatically, loudly, vehemently.
MY SEXUAL STYLE IS: romantic, passionate, demonstrative, playful.

Mars in Virgo

I ACT: intelligently, properly, helpfully, practically, thoroughly, manipulatively, uptightly, detailedly, healthfully.
I'M MOTIVATED BY THE DESIRE FOR: perfection, practicality, health.
I GET ANGRY: logically, analytically, critically.
MY SEXUAL STYLE IS: knowledgeable, earthy, repressed, bawdy.

Mars in Libra

I ACT: well-balanced, well-mannered, diplomatically, fairly, gracefully, conciliatorially, indecisively, passive-aggressively, selflessly.
I'M MOTIVATED BY THE DESIRE FOR: fairness, beauty, affection, approval.
I GET ANGRY: inconsistently, verbally, with difficulty.
MY SEXUAL STYLE IS: unselfish, gentle, conventional, affectionate.

Mars in Scorpio

I ACT: passionately, seductively, intensely, covertly, dedicatedly, bravely, suspiciously, obsessively, with discipline.
I'M MOTIVATED BY THE DESIRE FOR: power, self-discipline, transcendence.
I GET ANGRY: vengefully, lethally, destructively.
MY SEXUAL STYLE IS: passionate, feeling, controlled, committed.

Mars in Sagittarius

I ACT: freely, positively, zealously, bluntly, grandiosely, extravagantly, humorously, uncommittedly, spiritedly.
I'M MOTIVATED BY THE DESIRE FOR: knowledge, freedom, the big picture.
I GET ANGRY: philosophically, energetically, in a big way.
MY SEXUAL STYLE IS: open, adventurous, playful, uncommitted.

Mars in Capricorn

I ACT: well-organized, responsibly, ethically, seriously, ambitiously, conservatively, dutifully, politically, practically.
I'M MOTIVATED BY THE DESIRE FOR: success, security, integrity.
I GET ANGRY: purposefully, sarcastically, with guilt.
MY SEXUAL STYLE IS: conservative, earthy, puritanical, wild.

Mars in Aquarius

I ACT: unprejudicially, objectively, analytically, coolly, unpredictably, unconventionally, rebelliously, humanely, intuitively.
I'M MOTIVATED BY THE DESIRE FOR: truth, world peace, originality.
I GET ANGRY: unpredictably, coldly, analytically.
MY SEXUAL STYLE IS: unconventional, changeable, detached, friendly.

Mars in Pisces

I ACT: with inspiration, psychically, kindly, sensitively, passively, idealistically, evasively, compassionately, shyly.
I'M MOTIVATED BY THE DESIRE FOR: union, creativity, idealism.
I GET ANGRY: passively, overwhelmingly, emotionally.
MY SEXUAL STYLE IS: flowing, erotic, adoring, sensitive.

You have now read the key words for your planets in the signs and you are ready for Step Two. You will next determine your Element Theme and Mode Theme.

Refer to the Table of Signs, Elements, and Modes, and using your Basic Astropoint form from page 79, filled in with the Astropoints and their signs, look up the Element and Mode of each and fill in the appropriate blanks, reading the table across, from left to right. Example: Sun—Virgo, Element—Earth, Mode—Mutable.

Throughout the following discussion of Astroanalysis, we will be using a famous Sample Couple as examples of how our method works. Their identity will be revealed in the last chapter (no fair peeking!).

TABLE OF SIGNS, ELEMENTS, AND MODES

SIGN	ELEMENT	MODE
ARIES	FIRE	CARDINAL
TAURUS	EARTH	FIXED
GEMINI	AIR	MUTABLE
CANCER	WATER	CARDINAL
LEO	FIRE	FIXED
VIRGO	EARTH	MUTABLE
LIBRA	AIR	CARDINAL
SCORPIO	WATER	FIXED
SAGITTARIUS	FIRE	MUTABLE
CAPRICORN	EARTH	CARDINAL
AQUARIUS	AIR	FIXED
PISCES	WATER	MUTABLE

Below is the completed Basic Astropoint form for Mrs. X, our sample woman:

Name: <u>Mrs. X</u>

ASTROPOINT	SIGN	ELEMENT	MODE
SUN is in the sign of	CANCER	Water	Cardinal
MOON is in the sign of	AQUARIUS	Air	Fixed
ASC is in the sign of	SAGITTARIUS	Fire	Mutable
VENUS is in the sign of	TAURUS	Earth	Fixed
MARS is in the sign of	VIRGO	Earth	Mutable

Count up the total number of your Astropoints in each Element and Mode and fill in the blanks below.

I have _____ Fire-sign Astropoint(s).
I have _____ Earth-sign Astropoint(s).
I have _____ Air-sign Astropoint(s).
I have _____ Water-sign Astropoint(s).

I have _____ Cardinal-sign Astropoint(s).
I have _____ Fixed-sign Astropoint(s).
I have _____ Mutable-sign Astropoint(s).

To determine your Element and Mode Theme, choose the *highest* number you have listed in each category:

My Element Theme is _____.

My Mode Theme is _____.

In the example above, our sample woman has one Astropoint in a Fire sign (ASC in Sagittarius), one Astropoint in an Air sign (Moon in Aquarius), two Astropoints in Earth signs (Venus in Taurus, Mars in Virgo), and one Astropoint in a Water sign (Sun in Cancer).

She has one Astropoint in a Cardinal sign (Sun in Cancer), two Astropoints in Fixed signs (Venus in Taurus, Moon in Aquarius), and two Astropoints in Mutable signs (Mars in Virgo, ASC in Sagittarius).

So, adding up her points, we find she has:

1	Fire-sign Astropoint(s).
1	Air-sign Astropoint(s).
2	Earth-sign Astropoint(s).
1	Water-sign Astropoint(s).
1	Cardinal-sign Astropoint(s).
2	Fixed-sign Astropoint(s).
2	Mutable-sign Astropoint(s).

Since her highest number in the Element column is 2, she has an Earth Element Theme. But, since she does not have a "highest" number in her Mode column, she has *two* Mode Themes. So we say she has a Fixed and Mutable Mode Theme, or a Mixed-Mode Theme.

In the event that you do not have a highest number in either or both Elements and Modes, then you also have two themes, or a mixed theme. We'll explain what this means later on.

ELEMENT THEMES

Following is a listing of the Themes for the Elements and Modes, along with an explanation of what these signify in terms of how you approach your most intimate relationships. Bear in mind that the theme you have scored does not include all ten planets, only the four we are discussing, plus your ASC. Thus, this theme has to do mainly with your relationships.*

Find your Element Theme (Fire, Earth, Air, Water) in the explanations that follow. If you have two themes, then turn to the explanations that follow these, the Mixed-Element Themes (Fire/Earth, Fire/Water, Fire/Air, Earth/Air, Earth/Water, and Air/Water).

*If you had your chart done professionally, or had it calculated by computer, you might find that the other planets—the ones we are not dealing with in this book on relationships—would color or modify your overall life theme, in terms of the Elements and Modes.

SINGLE ELEMENT THEMES

FIRE   You are a vital, alive person who likes to get out there and
         do things. Spontaneous, expressive, active, and vibrant—
you are fun to be around and are always excited about something.
You're fiery, no two ways about it, and there is a glow or sparkle
about you, a warmth everyone feels. Very independent, you also have
a temper. You are a person who needs a vision, a quest to fulfill in
life, and you languish without inspiration. Although you are stimulating, you're not always practical or sensitive. Generally, you're not
introspective, for you need to take action. With other Fire types,
there is dynamism and energy, although things *can* get too spicy and
competitive. You get on easily with Air types, because Air feeds your
fire; Earth types are attractive, but difficult because they ground
your wildness and you resent restriction. With Water types, things
get emotionally steamy, but they can douse your fire with clinging
and insecurity. You are passionate and exciting to be with, but you
sometimes run over other people in your ardor.

EARTH   The salt of the earth, you are sensible, grounded, prac-
          tical. You always use common sense. Conservative by na-
ture, you appreciate material things: nature, money, art. You have
a good sense of reality. Often mature before your time, you're the
one who is always aware of the bottom line. You don't fool around
with abstractions, for you like to see the practical results of your
investments of time and energy. People can rely on you to deal with
the concrete stuff that needs to be done or organized. You want to

feel needed and useful. Often you have a green thumb and are good at making things grow. Other Earth types are familiar and reliable, a solid match, although together you can get too materialistic or bore each other. Water types are easy for you, for water fertilizes your Earth with feeling. Difficult-but-attractive Fire types have the imagination and spontaneity your sensible nature craves. Air types can seem like they're from another planet, although you do appreciate their logic and imagination. You are responsible in relationships, but can be very dense about feelings and resist change.

AIR Like air, you need to flow and circulate. Socializing comes naturally. Friendly and interested, ideas turn you on and you analyze everything. You don't need to know if things will work out practically, because concepts are as real to you as concrete reality. Imaginative and idealistic, your mind soars, so there's something otherworldly about you. Yet, this objective distance makes you the most logical of all people. Your clarity is amazing, and you can be counted on to be a haven of rationality. This can make you seem cool and distant. Other Air types give you space and are as interesting as you are. But together you can space out and never actually *do* anything. Fire types are easy because they warm you up and keep you moving; Water types are difficult, but attractive because they supply the feeling and emotion your dazzling brilliance sometimes lacks. Earth types can bore you and leave you cold, although you appreciate how they get things done. A communicative and interesting companion, you can lack empathy.

WATER   You are the most sensitive of people. You feel everything
and absorb the moods of those around you. Having the
ability to flow into whatever you do, you intuit undercurrents immediately. Often psychic, always perceptive, you are imaginative and
creative, but not always rational. You may not have intellectual reasons for what or why you do what you do, even though you are
frequently right.

Sympathetic and understanding, you like to be intimate. You have
to be careful not to cling or become possessive. Earth types are easy
for you because they give form to your feeling, security for your
sensitivity. Water types match your depth, imagination, and intuition,
but together you can get too insular and stay in your own safe world.
Air types are difficult but draw you because they have the cool objectivity and mental clarity you lose with your subjectivity. Fire types
get you boiling with passion and excitement, sometimes uncomfortably
so. You are a loving and kind companion, but you can smother with
your insecurity.

MIXED-ELEMENT THEMES

If you have a Mixed-Element Theme, read the descriptions that
follow. You can compare how each of the two Elements relates to each
of the other Elements by referring to the previous discussions of the
individual Elements and how they relate to each other.

For example, if you are Fire/Earth and you wanted to know more
about how you get along with Air, you would look at Fire and read
the description of how Fire relates to Air; then you would read the
discussion of Earth and see how Earth relates to Air, combining the
two to understand how a Fire/Earth person would relate to an Air
person.

FIRE/EARTH　You mix practicality with impracticality, impulsiveness with patience. You can be the most reliable person around, then unexpectedly go off on a major exploit. You're a person who can make visions real, mixing strength and courage. A committed and exciting companion, you need to be careful of insensitivity, self-centeredness, and the possibility of bulldozing everyone around you.

FIRE/AIR　You put ideas into action, join vision to logic. You have warmth, yet can be objective. You are knowledgeable, fun, and exciting. Inspired and idealistic, you make things happen. A passionate and communicative companion who ignites quickly, you need to watch for restlessness, being unfocused, getting in tizzies, and grabbing at one unrealistic venture after another.

FIRE/WATER　You are the most intuitive of all people. You're very fluid and your hunches are amazing. Impressionable and sensitive, you can turn the other way and be completely blunt. You also can be extremely patient or act impulsively. A passionate and feeling companion, you need to be careful about selfishness, hysteria, and being unconcerned with anything but your own universe.

EARTH/AIR　You are one of the most efficient people around, combining objectivity with practicality. In you, the ideal and the real meet and you plan and execute well. You can go off on flights of fancy, then return and get to work. An interesting, intelligent, and solid companion, you should watch for skepticism, lack of empathy, and being dryly cynical about life.

EARTH/WATER　You are a productive person. Being simultaneously sensitive and grounded makes you both intuitive and practical. You are able to give your compassion and feeling form in the real world. You have a talent for accepting life and making it work. A reliable and emotional companion, you have to watch for self-satisfaction and being limited to your own little world.

AIR/WATER   You are extremely sensitive, combining compassionate feeling with objectivity. You may wax sympa-
thetic and kind, then detach and analyze what you just experienced,
or vice versa. You're conceptual, but your logic is humanized by your
ability to feel. A responsive and perceptive companion, you need to
avoid being high-strung, nervous, and impractical.

MODE THEMES

SINGLE MODE THEMES

The listing that follows describes the Modes and how they operate.
If you have a single theme, read Cardinal, Fixed, or Mutable. If you
have a mixed theme, look for Cardinal/Fixed, Cardinal/Mutable, or
Fixed/Mutable.

CARDINAL   Your relationships happen quickly and intensely.
When you're attracted, it's immediate. Since you are
ardent, you go in and out of relationships quickly. Impulsive, proud,
and enthusiastic, you are rarely shy about initiating. Some may not
do this obviously, being adept at getting others to do the approaching
(especially Libran types). Because you give totally, you can burn out
if you leap into a relationship before you look at its true reality. You,
more than most, think it is important to take risks. You can be pushy,
impatient, and concerned with power, making power struggles com-
monplace. They may be waiting games, or a war of wits, or out-and-
out battles, but power struggles they are. And you love them!

Other Cardinal types stimulate you for they're as original as you
are, but you can compete with them and fight over who leads the

pack. With Fixed types you are productive, for they make your ideas happen, but they are slow and at first may resist you. Mutable types adjust to your myriad new ideas easily, but often avoid the real issues by sliding away when you want to have it out.

Since you're better at starting things than finishing them, you don't always stick around very long. Try staying to see how the new relationship will work out—don't leave after the first few hard times.

FIXED   You go slowly and deeply. You can spend intense hours with your special person. Once you have given your heart, it remains given. Loyalty is important to you, so your love can be total to the point of obsession. Though not flexible, you are steady and reliable, concerned with real values, principles, and meaning. A strong person, you stand up for yourself and those you love. You know how to be there for your loved ones, and love is a high priority. You are a one-man or one-woman person.

Which means you can get dangerously fixated on the one you want, and then you can't or won't let go. Your intensity may cause battles of will or raise issues of control. You're good at carrying through, less good at initiating. Other Fixed types have the depth and substance you need, but together you can get too rigid, never able to compromise on anything. Cardinal types excite you, supplying get-up-and-go, but their speed and their ability to start new things scares you. Your strong wills clash. Mutable types flow around your fixity and adjust to it, but they seem to you to be will o' the wisps, insubstantial and hard to get a hold on.

Because it is hard for you to initiate, you tend to get in a rut, not saying what needs to be said or doing what needs to be done. Take a risk sometime and try going first, or you may miss out on love.

MUTABLE You have the ability to handle more than one relationship at a time—fortunate, because you like to keep your options open until you are sure that a relationship is just right. Since you are always flexible, you don't mind waiting until the last minute to make a date. But you can be *so* flexible that it's impossible to pin you to a commitment about anything. A master at convoluted, logical arguments (with which you can manipulate your lovers into saying anything or believing anything you say), you feel most loved when appreciated for your verbal skills and communicative abilities, whatever their nature. You have a talent for stringing facts, incidents, and ideas together in such a way as to appear to make sense, or you use so much extravagant detail that no one but you knows what you're talking about. But, whatever it is, *you* seem to know a lot about it. You find other mutable types fun, for they are as varied and changeable as you are. However, together you may never do anything real because you keep shifting what you want to do and must constantly adjust to each other. You find Cardinal types interesting and dynamic. They supply you with direction but they may run right over you. Fixed types provide the stability you need but frustrate you because they are so hard to change.

You need to focus on what you want and learn to use your wonderful versatility to help move you forward in your life, rather than around and around, back and forward, going nowhere.

MIXED-MODE THEMES

If you have a Mixed-Mode Theme, read the descriptions that follow. You can also compare how each of the two Modes relates to each of the other Modes by referring to the previous discussions of the individual Modes and how they relate to each other.

For example, if you are Cardinal/Mutable and you wanted to know how you get along with Fixed, you would look at Cardinal and read the description of how it relates to Fixed, and then you would read the discussion of Mutable and see how it relates to Fixed, combining the two to understand how a Cardinal/Mutable person would relate to Fixed.

CARDINAL/FIXED   You are a dynamic person with strong opinions, a force to be reckoned with. You drive yourself and others. Sometimes you are a creative starter, generating new ideas, but at other times you get stuck in a rut. You need to develop flexibility to complement your intensity.

CARDINAL/MUTABLE   You are an interesting person, full of new ideas and a myriad of projects. There's never a dull moment when you are around because of your many inspirations and lightninglike changes. However, to actualize your ideas and make positive use of your changeability, you need to develop staying power.

FIXED/MUTABLE   A curious contradiction, you are sometimes the most flexible of people, sometimes the most stubborn. You can be inwardly consistent and outwardly changeable, or vice versa. Getting yourself started is a problem for you often need outer energy to get your staying power and flexibility in gear. Then you're on a roll.

You are now a major way along in your self-audition process. You know the Signs, Elements, and Modes of all your Astropoints, and you've read your key words for your individual placements of the Sun, Moon, ASC, Venus, and Mars.

You've also determined your themes for the Elements and the Modes of your Astropoints and read about how those operate in you and your approach to your relationships.

You've now got all the ingredients assembled for a solo performance. As we've been going along so far, we have used a sample woman to show you how to fill in your worksheets and to serve as a guidepost. Let's continue, with Step Three: *Astroanalysis*.

ASTROANALYSIS OF SAMPLE WOMAN

First, we will tell you a little of her history. She married young—age nineteen—in what seemed a perfect match. Her older husband, by twelve years, was her Prince Charming. After two sons and lots of problems in her marriage, she needs to get a better sense of just what is going on, both in herself and in her husband, so that she can assess the possibility of working things out satisfactorily.

Let's take a look at her Sun and Moon first.

With her Cancer Sun (Cardinal, Earth) and her Aquarius Moon (Fixed, Air), there is quite a difference between her sense of her life's direction and what makes her feel comfortable. You can look back at the key words and read those applicable to her.

In her personal Astroplay, the "characters" of the Sun (life purpose) and the Moon (needs) are quite at odds.

Her Cancer Sun character is happiest at home with her children clustered around her, being loving and motherly, nurturing all and sundry, including the dogs and cats, birds and fishes. In this role, she is sensitive and protective of her loved ones, and she does not particularly like leaving home for the outside world.

But her Aquarius Moon character is a wild-eyed radical who breaks rules for the fun of it and damn the consequences! This component of her nature wants to be into the newest, trendiest, most interesting things around, literally *craving* this kind of stimulation. Her Moon's idea of intimacy is a transatlantic phone call.

Her Ascendant is in the freedom-loving, devil-take-the-hindmost sign of Sagittarius (Mutable, Fire). That means that her public persona is free and unfettered, spirited and adventurous. Her first response to any situation is a little wild, often blunt to the point of being shocking.

This character runs around like a wild woman, kicking up her heels, dancing all night, catching planes for exotic places on the spur of the moment, telling anyone and everyone exactly what she thinks of them, not caring a fig for their opinions as she goes on her merry way.

By referring to the key words, you can see that her Aquarius Moon and her Sagittarius ASC have a lot in common. Her basic comfort needs and her first response to situations get along quite easily and harmoniously. Neither one is concerned with practicality, for they constantly seek new and exciting experiences. Both are inspired and tend toward the philosophical approach to life, unconcerned with the past, which is definitely old-hat.

Her love nature (Venus) is found in the solid and practical sign of Taurus (Fixed, Earth). This character is totally grounded and would *never* think of leaving home on the spur of the moment and would plan a long-distance trip with care before packing her suitcase. This component of Mrs. X's nature wants security and is practical and sensual. A woman who knows what she wants, she is happy in nature and in solid, comfortable surroundings. She likes good food and finds change disturbing, so she keeps it at a minimum. An Earth Mother, she could sit all day in the meadow and smell the flowers while watching her children frolic through the grass. Peaceful and kind, it takes a stick of dynamite to blast her out of her routines. She prefers the tried-and-true.

Her Mars character, representing how she acts, is found in Virgo (Mutable, Earth). This character dots the *i*'s and crosses the *t*'s. She organizes her drawers and keeps regular habits. Very meticulous and detail oriented, she is sensible and practical.

We see here another conflict. Her Mars character and her Moon character don't get along at all. And her ASC character always sides with the Moon in her. Poor Mars sometimes takes a beating from these two! A "regular habit" to her Sagittarius ASC would be to change clothes just before rushing out to catch a plane to god-knows-where. Her Aquarius Moon's idea of practicality is to book first-class seats now on the first flight to the farthest planet.

Is there any hope for her to resolve these internal conflicts between her not-so-compatible inner characters and get her show on the road?

Let's analyze a bit further.

Mrs. X's overall conflict is shown by the difference between her Sun, Mars, and Venus, and her Moon and ASC. The issues are of conformity vs. freedom, tradition vs. experimentation; safety vs. adventure; domesticity vs. wanderlust; stability vs. wildness; practicality vs. spontaneity; emotional closeness vs. emotional distance; sensual vs. sexual; being able to take it vs. leaving it.

It might seem an irreconcilable cast, mightn't it? But remember the title of this part, "You Are the Director." That's important. *You* are in charge of your own performance, and you alone can whip your cast into shape so that you have a hit run of your own personal Astroplay.

Going a bit further, we see that three of her Astropoints—Sun in Cancer (life purpose), Venus in Taurus (way of loving), and Mars in Virgo (way of acting)—are in complete harmony with each other. That's now three against five! A majority can rule.

In addition, she has an Earth Element Theme and a Fixed/Mutable Mode Theme. This information tells us that her Earth Theme will contribute quite a lot to the more domestic, stable, and practical parts of her. The Mixed-Mode Theme seems to reflect the conflict between her Moon and ASC and the other characters.

Overall, it would seem that the more stable and conservative characters in her cast will eventually take charge and run the show. They will demand and get more say and will play more important roles in her inner Astroplay.

But she has also cast her Moon and her ASC in her life, and she can't fire them or replace them. She may have to go back into rehearsal quite a few times to get their parts smoothed out and integrated into the whole, but she doesn't have any choice if she wants a successful life and relationship—a hit run.

It is of particular importance to her to give these two rebellious characters appropriate roles to play because they are both basic to her nature. She would never be happy solely in the role of wife and loving mother, despite her Cancer, Taurus, and Virgo. If she tried to repress her deep *need* for freedom (Moon), or muzzle her freedom-loving, blunt-speaking (Sagittarius) ASC, she'd be cutting off her nose to spite her face. And it wouldn't work anyway, because those components of us that we try to repress or ignore will find other ways of getting onto our life stage, some of them not very pleasant. Imagine if you were in the theatre watching a nice play about a happy family at home. Suddenly this wild-eyed, peculiarly dressed woman comes rushing onto center stage, screaming and shouting and calling the happy family obscene names. That's what might happen in Mrs. X's life if she tries to force her Moon and her ASC into the wings or tries to keep them quiet backstage.

These characters need to live and play out their roles, somehow. What is she to do? How can her rebellious youth-quake characters be kept from blowing up her happy home and her child-loving, old-fashioned, sweet-natured characters?

One common way for people of both sexes to express the "un-wanted" parts of themselves is to have a person in their lives, most often their spouse or lover, to act like the Astropoint that gives the person trouble. This happens when they don't know consciously that they are splitting off the parts of themselves they find difficult or embarrassing. Psychologists call this "projection." We "project" the undesired quality on someone else and give them the energy we refuse to use or integrate into ourselves.

It is this mechanism that lets a man choose a woman who is an exact description of his own Moon or Venus, or both, while he himself displays none of these qualities, even though they are in him. Conversely, a woman may choose a man who expresses her unwanted Sun or Mars (traditionally masculine) qualities, while she herself seems not to have them at all.

Our Mrs. X might choose a traditional, home-loving man and then feel free to express her more radical, freedom-loving self. Or she might have a woman friend who is a wild radical, "here today–gone tomorrow" type of person. Then Mrs. X could tend the home fires and wait for her friend to come back from a safari and tell of her exploits, feeding vicariously on her friend's experiences while frowning slightly on the despised "frivolousness."

Although this is one way for Mrs. X to solve her difficulties, she is better advised to understand that all these different and contradictory characters exist in her own life script, and that she is the director. She can't write the roles out, but she *can* decide how they are to be played in her life production.

If you are constantly projecting your unconscious parts onto others, you won't ever know those people for who they truly are. If your close relationships are mainly speaking parts for your discarded Astroplay characters, they won't ever come into focus as real persons to you. Eventually, these relationships will break down.

It's important for Mrs. X, you, and all of us to realize that we are *not* the role our parents or society may have given us. We are *ourselves*, and we can be no other without serious repercussions. If we project our inner characters onto somebody else, they will then have a difficult time being who they are as well. Eventually, our inner conflicts, if not resolved and allowed to play out their parts, will take over and ruin the show. Our relationships will break up.

You hear people say, "I lived with him [or her] for twenty years and never really knew him [her]." This can be disappointing at best, devastating at worst. What a waste of time! Infinitely sadder, however, is to spend a lifetime with yourself and never really know *you*. But if you work to understand your inner scripts—the roles your characters are playing whether you know it or not—you can avoid having part of your life lived out through another person.

How might Mrs. X *appropriately* allow her conflicting characters to play roles in her Astroplay?

Her Sun could concentrate on being a homebody and raising her children, nurturing all and sundry, being sensitive and expressing feelings fully, or she might do some kind of work that relates to the domestic side of life, such as taking care of little children.

Her Moon could engage in the study of scientific theories and esoteric concepts and relate these to the domestic scene, or she could invite groups to her home (groups = Aquarius; home = Moon) to discuss these far-out topics. She needs to be intellectual in some way.

Her ASC wants to travel, kick up its heels, and have fun while learning new things. She could take trips by herself to let off steam and use up this abundant energy, going to places where she could feel free to be this side of herself without causing a public rumpus.

Her Venus wants to plop down and self-indulge, be sexy and pampered, stay put, and enjoy nature in comfortable and secure surroundings. She could schedule time at home, uninterrupted by outside demands, where she could attend to her routines, play with her children, enjoy her garden.

Her Mars concurs with Venus but wants her to do something to express her organizational ability. She needs to find an outlet that will let her be methodical, and she could do this as a volunteer, organizing for a cause or executing the details for a fund-raiser.

We are all a mélange of different characters inside ourselves. The fun of becoming an interesting and fulfilled human being is getting to know all these individual characters—the actors in the play of our lives. We work out our relationship with each one by letting each have its say, in an appropriate and positive manner. Remember the song, "Getting to know you, getting to feel free and easy. . . ." It's like that. As you get to know *you*, you will become more free and easy with who you are, with your many components. And what was once perhaps a source of shame or embarrassment, difficulty or trouble, will become a source of joy and fulfillment. Our inner characters demand only that we recognize who and what they are, and then let them act out their natures on the stage of our life.

Once you fully comprehend your Star Self and the Play Within, you will have the best chance of finding a meaningful, lasting, and deeply enjoyable relationship with your Co-Star and with the members of the supporting cast who are your friends, relatives, co-workers, and others who play major or minor roles to your leading one.

YOUR CO-STAR: WHO'S PLAYING OPPOSITE?

In Chapter 12 we took you through the steps of understanding your Star Self, pointing out that finding fulfillment means knowing and accepting who you are, changing what needs to be changed, and having the wisdom to know when to leave yourself alone.

Astrology can help because it gives you real tools—to see who you are and to identify the difficult areas within you. Now that you have done that for yourself, you are ready to evaluate your Co-Star. Because it takes two to make a relationship, it is important to know your Co-Star's cast of characters and how *they* get along together.

Use the form below exactly as you did for your Star Self at the beginning of Part Two:

BASIC ASTROPOINT FORM

Name: _____

ASTROPOINT	SIGN	ELEMENT	MODE
SUN is in the sign of	_____	_____	_____
MOON is in the sign of	_____	_____	_____
ASC is in the sign of	_____	_____	_____
VENUS is in the sign of	_____	_____	_____
MARS is in the sign of	_____	_____	_____

Step One is to look up the key words for your Co-Star, to get a take on how his or her inner characters operate.

Using the Basic Astropoint form you have filled in so far for your Co-Star, you can now proceed to Step Two and look up your Co-Star's Element and Mode Themes. To do this, turn to the Table of Signs, Elements, and Modes on page 159, and reading from left to right, fill in the Element and Mode blanks.

When filled out, your Co-Star's form should look like this one for our sample man:

ASTROPOINT	SIGN	ELEMENT	MODE
SUN is in the sign of	SCORPIO	Water	Fixed
MOON is in the sign of	TAURUS	Earth	Fixed
ASC is in the sign of	LEO	Fire	Fixed
VENUS is in the sign of	LIBRA	Air	Cardinal
MARS is in the sign of	SAGITTARIUS	Fire	Mutable

Now, using the Basic Astropoint form for your Co-Star, total the Astropoints in each Element and Mode.

My Co-Star has _____ Fire-sign Astropoint(s).
My Co-Star has _____ Earth-sign Astropoint(s).
My Co-Star has _____ Air-sign Astropoint(s).
My Co-Star has _____ Water-sign Astropoint(s).

My Co-Star has _____ Cardinal-sign Astropoint(s).
My Co-Star has _____ Fixed-sign Astropoint(s).
My Co-Star has _____ Mutable-sign Astropoint(s).

To determine your Co-Star's Element Theme and Mode Theme choose the *highest* number you have listed in each category.

My Co-Star's Element Theme is: _____.

My Co-Star's Mode Theme is: _____.

In the example above, our sample man has two Astropoints in Fire signs (ASC in Leo and Mars in Sagittarius), one Earth sign (Moon in Taurus), one Air sign (Venus in Libra), and one Water sign (Sun in Scorpio).

He has one Astropoint in a Cardinal sign (Venus in Libra), three in Fixed signs (Sun in Scorpio, Moon in Taurus, and ASC in Leo), and one in a Mutable sign (Mars in Sagittarius).

So, adding up his points, we find he has:

__2__	Fire-sign Astropoint(s).
__1__	Earth-sign Astropoint(s).
__1__	Air-sign Astropoint(s).
__1__	Water-sign Astropoint(s).
__1__	Cardinal-sign Astropoint(s).
__3__	Fixed-sign Astropoint(s).
__1__	Mutable-sign Astropoint(s).

Since his highest number in the Element column is 2, he has a Fire Element Theme. And since his highest number in the Mode column is 3, he has a Fixed Mode Theme. He does not have any Mixed Themes.

Read about *your* Co-Star's Element Theme and Mode Theme in the listings beginning on page 161.

ASTROANALYSIS OF SAMPLE MAN*

Let's first take a look at his Sun and ASC, which are in conflict.

His Scorpio Sun character, representing his sense of Self, is secretive, private, intense, never taking anything at face value. His Sun distrusts flattery and showiness, is always on the lookout for hidden motives. In a relationship, love and intimacy are not enough—his Sun wants his lover's soul joined to his.

His Leo ASC character, on the other hand, craves center stage, is open and flamboyant (Fire), and feels there's no need to hide anything, knowing a true heart and noble spirit will protect him. Passionate and romantic, this character wants a queen to reign beside him, and he wants everyone to know they are a royal couple.

While his ASC is basking in the limelight, his Sun is ever alert for hidden cues indicating danger and is suspicious of everyone's motives, cringing at publicity and exposure—he doesn't want *anyone* to know *anything* about his business!

While his Leo ASC is saying, "Hey—what's to be so uptight about?

*As you study this Astroanalysis, you will find it helpful to read the sample man's key words for his planetary placements and ASC.

This is *great!*" his Scorpio Sun replies, "Things aren't what they seem. We'll wait and see." Often Leo is right, but Scorpio is always ready and willing to blow Leo's social front with a confrontation, taking the whole show down with him.

Leo ASC maintains his dignity, no matter what, in public especially. His sense of nobility would never allow him to fight dirty, but there is *one* thing these two agree on—it's the desire for power and control. So even though they are basically at odds with each other, they make a compact on this issue and tighten up our sample man's already considerable rigidity. Remember that he has a Fixed Theme.

His Scorpio Sun character doesn't want any "buddies," is happiest alone or with his wife and family or a few tried-and-true companions. Although he might want to test his mettle occasionally in a risk-taking way, he wouldn't want to be obvious for this character looks askance at the show-off behavior of the ASC and Mars characters.

His Sagittarius Mars is in league with his Leo ASC, as both are Fire signs. This adds fuel to the fire (literally!) of how he acts (Mars) and activates the wilder side of his personality, which is naturally flamboyant, desires freedom at any cost, and craves the heights of philosophy and metaphysics. His Mars acts bluntly, as if believing he is divinely protected, kicking up his heels and dashing about on exciting adventures. When this part of him is activated, he throws his arms around all and sundry, calling them his buddies, and goes off hunting or fishing, horseback riding or to play sports.

On the other side of the equation, he has a Taurus Moon and a Libra Venus, and both of these characters value peace and calm. But Venus is diplomatic and refined and is put off by Moon's earthiness and ribaldry, preferring the social graces of refinement and tact. Venus is also terrified of Sun's confrontational nature and will always strive to reconcile differences.

His needs (Moon) and his life purpose (Sun), both in Fixed signs, don't bend. They just push and push until shove comes along and something breaks. His Moon would rather see a table laden with plenty of good, solid food than an elegantly appointed tea-table with finger sandwiches, which would delight Venus.

His Moon wants a stable environment, nothing fussy, with soft chairs, comfortable solid furniture, and function before fanciness. Moon also wants children and the traditional home, which is a bastion of conservative values and serves to maintain the status quo. Venus doesn't mind this scenario, but wants it without any mess—and there are no babies without mess. While his Moon longs to get back to nature, Venus wants to go traveling first class, in style. However, even though their tastes are different, they agree on beauty and luxury being necessary to the good life.

His Sagittarius Mars and Libra Venus are in easy alliance, both being intellectual with a liking for the finer things of life. But blunt and outspoken Mars will often shock tactful, diplomatic Venus.

His Leo ASC gets along well with Libra Venus because they share a love of luxury and elegance, are at ease in social situations, and trust in people's better natures.

In sum, our sample man's basic differences are: between being private, closed, complicated, sensitive, and introspective and being open, attention-seeking, trusting, positive, and insensitive—and, between being conservative, sensible, practical, and a homebody, and being adventurous, showy, impractical, and motivated by spiritual concerns.

He also has conflicts between being intense, gutsy, confrontational (Sun), rough and earthy (Moon), and refined and tactful (Venus).

So, what kind of a woman does he need and want?

He *needs* a Taurus-type woman: strong, gentle, an Earth Mother with a practical mind and a sensible approach to life. He *wants* a Libra-type woman: refined and kind, pretty, gracious, tactful, a good conversationalist. Although Taurus and Libra are not mutually exclusive, both being Venus-ruled, this particular combination is as if he wants the traditional wife-mother at home and a lovely geisha-girl for socializing.

What do his themes tell us? He has a Mixed-Element Theme, Earth/Fire. This underlines his complexity and, as Earth and Fire have a tendency to cancel each other out, indicates a need to compromise between being grounded and self-expressive.

His Mode Theme is clearly Fixed. This heightens the intensity of his Scorpio Sun, increases his Taurus Moon's natural fixity and reluctance to change *anything*, and gives impetus to his Leo ASC's desire to take over and rule. With all this, he is deeply committed but inflexible. He has a tendency to get quite fixated on people and ideas. Once he makes up his mind, which might take quite a while, he is very hard to dissuade.

Unlike our sample woman, he's not easy to analyze. His inner alliances shift back and forth and are not clearly delineated. First one set agrees and dominates, then another. There is much more room in his inner play for overlapping roles than in hers. One thing is clear, however—his Fixed characters pretty much run the show with their strength and determination.

Read his key words to compare how his Astropoints relate to each other. See what's similar—these will be the most emphasized characteristics. For example, his Taurus Moon and Libra Venus share gentleness, kindness, handsomeness, harmony, and a love of beauty in nature and in art. They both want to maintain the status quo. These qualities will be most obvious although the others will be evident as well, but in more subtle ways.

Though he has much contradiction in his basic nature, all the parts of him will have to find expression. How might he go about this?

His Sun could go off by itself and brood, thinking deep thoughts, investigating matters metaphysical and arcane. He needs to find ways to express Scorpio's cynicism and sarcasm without harming himself or others, and he needs ways of being intense that are positive.

His Moon wants him to commune with nature, digging in the dirt and growing things, or just hanging out around trees and flowers, being a lump, unmoving, totally grounded. It also wants him to indulge in hearty food and copious amounts of affection from his loved ones.

His ASC is the public character and wants to be seen appearing grand and magnanimous, with his lady on his arm as glamorous and glorious as she can manage to be. It wants them to look good together and make a larger-than-life impression on others from a position at center stage.

His Venus wants a socially adept woman who's conventional in the sense of being proper, would never do anything to shock—a real lady, charming, graceful, and *always* socially appropriate. If he doesn't express this in himself, he will project it onto his wife.

His Mars wants to travel and have adventures and is devil-may-care about public opinion. If he doesn't express this urge, his wife may do it for him, shocking his Libra Venus in the process. The solution, of course, is for him to act out his own characters and not project them onto her.

chapter fourteen

CURTAIN GOING UP!

Now that you have studied your own and your Co-Star's Play Within, and have become acquainted with your key words and themes, you are ready to Astroplay.

The scripts have been written to be read both silently and aloud. First, locate the scripts for your Astropoints in the chapters that follow and read them to yourself. Then, do the same for your Co-Star (or any other person you are comparing Astropoints with). You can then offer your Co-Star his or her segments to read silently, since you both should be familiar with the scripts before attempting to Astroplay them out loud.

Study your scripts seriously, as you would if you were going to read for a part in a play. Give them inflections in your mind, emphasize the parts that are especially meaningful. Remember, you are giving a dramatic reading! Ask you Co-Star to do the same.

An alternative method is to have a friend act out the parts of your Co-Star. Or, to have a group of friends each take a part of one person's different Astropoints to dramatize. Choose the part you want to act and then have the group switch around. As an evening's entertainment, you can have friends over to Astroplay. After everyone's looked up their Astropoint placements, take turns acting out the various roles in each person's chart. You can even make it into a game of charades! Be as imaginative and dramatic as you like, using props and costumes.

Once you are silently familiar with your Astroscripts and those of anyone else with whom you want to Astroplay, you are ready to read aloud. *Do* take the time for silent preparation, because most people will feel slightly shy (unless they're strongly Leo!) about reading "cold."

You can pick out just one script to concentrate on—perhaps the issue that's uppermost on your mind—how you feel or what you need (Moon). You and your Co-Star can read your own Moon scripts, then Astroplay them together, Moon to Moon.

You can Astroplay each one of your Astroscripts against each one of your partner's: Sun to Sun, Sun to Moon, Sun to ASC, Sun to Venus, Sun to Mars, and so forth, through all of each person's Astroscripts.

Another thing to do is to look in Part Five, "The Reviews," and play off your Astropairs from Rave Reviews, Good Reviews, Mixed Reviews, and Bad Reviews. This way, you'll see how your combinations are working in real life, where your issues are, what your strengths are (Rave and Good Reviews), what needs work (Mixed Reviews), and where you have real problems (Bad Reviews). As you read your scripts together, it will most probably become apparent to you not only what works or doesn't work but *why*.

As you work with your Astroscripts, you may feel emotional or somewhat shy about what is being revealed about you. This is natural. Don't let it bother you. Keep going. The results are worth it!

If you choose not to show your Astroscripts to another person (and, remember, this may seem very personal and private to you at first), you can still learn a great deal about *yourself* and another person (or persons) by reading and studying the Astroscripts. If you're a Virgo type, you might want to become familiar and gain confidence before acting out your scripts with others. Still, you can act them out all by yourself with yourself, taking the various parts in turn. Try using a mirror.

Bolder types may want to rush right into Astroplay without any preparation at all. That's okay, but you will derive most benefit if you follow our suggestions. A surface run-through will produce a superficial result (listen, you Geminis!), while a thorough approach will give you more insightful results. Whatever you do and however you do it, it's up to you! Remember, the title of this part is "You Are the Director." It's your life and your own personal Astroplay. You can handle it as you see fit. We've given you the tools and the clues, the information and the Astroscripts. Modify them to suit your needs and what feels best to you. Rewrite if you like, making them even more personal and specific to you and yours. This is just the beginning! And now . . .

Curtain Going Up!

p a r t   f o u r

THE PLAY'S THE THING

chapter fifteen

ASTROSCRIPTS FOR THE SUN

He is the SUN
A lion, and a Ram.
For Life's objective
We live, and die.
Desire is His nature,
Awesome, too.
The very Self,
He is the "I" in You!

SUN IN ARIES WOMAN

I'm strong and I know it. My issues are about strength, power, and achievement—or their absence. I hate wimpishness. I think fast and act forcefully, protecting my vulnerability with speed. Yes, I am vulnerable, despite my obvious courage and appearances to the contrary. Because I hate to wait, I can be the fool that rushes in. But I'm saved from disaster by my optimism and directness.

I look upon life as an adventure. My enthusiasm generates energy, and I have a newborn quality I bring to any situation. I go straight to the heart of the matter and I fire up people to take action and get things done. My individualism makes me a trailblazer. I always have a goal.

I'm a self-starter, but I hate the follow-up details, so don't look to me to carry things through to the finish line. I'm an idea person. I'm always looking for the next challenge. Don't think me irresponsible. I do check back to see how things are progressing. My pioneering spirit and addiction to speedy accomplishment can make me bossy at times, but I don't mind people pushing back. FAST is my key word. "Do it now" is my motto. Sometimes I feel that there is only one way to do things—my way. That's because I have faith in my visions and will fight for them. If I'm wrong, I can laugh about it. I admit I'm headstrong, but I've got a great sense of humor. Under the right circumstances, I can turn into a lamb—until I get restless and need to be off again.

I like men with get-up-and-go, who aren't intimidated by my need for speed. Forget the plodders—I make mincemeat of them! A guy's got to be a man and know it, or I'm not interested. Shy, sensitive types will have to look elsewhere. I need action all the time. My man and I like to be on the go together and we generate a lot of good energy between us. Sure we fight, but we make up and that's a lot of fun, too.

SUN IN TAURUS WOMAN

Don't rock the boat, that's my motto. I like my life to be secure, stable, and reliable—just like me. My life purpose is to *preserve*, and I know a good thing when I see one—whether it's money, investments, a job, a garden, or a man. When I find one I like, I hold on. Both my common sense and my senses let me know. Speaking of senses, touch is one of my most highly developed—I like things to feel right. I'd rather have a big, old comfortable couch to sink back in than a designer original. I prefer mass and solidity. It's got to *feel* good, and that includes feeling secure. And I prefer things to be functional.

I like to live my life with my feet on the ground and comfort surrounding me. When I have my base of operations, I'm naturally a grounding influence for others as well. I've got an automatic nurturing response. I feed others—with food or attention. I'm earthy and honest, with no bullshit about me. I give great advice. I can spot phonies a mile away, and I hate them. My detectors are strong, and if something or someone's not for real I don't waste my time.

I'm a person who wants things that endure and wear well. I respect traditions and I resist change. It takes dynamite to blast me out of my established routines. It also takes a blast to get me out of my old emotional patterns and ways of thinking. I hold on just because I'm used to it, even when I know it's better to let go. I have a long preparation time, but once I'm ready to change, it's total. I can leave my job and my man, and move just like *that*.

I'm basic. I need lots of hugs and touching. Food is a big deal for me: how to prepare it, what it is, how much I eat. I'm an affectionate person and I'll always try to be kind.

The men in my life are usually strong, silent types or else charismatic and intense. Sometimes they're back-to-the-land farmer types. Whatever they are, I prefer men who are solid and responsible, established in what they do. It helps if they have land and money as well, but at least they need to have a good sense of values, and proof of these must show in their work or in their bank books.

SUN IN GEMINI WOMAN

I have a horror of missing anything. Knowledge for me is positively an addiction. I have to know what's going on—the more places and items I hear about, the better. Life is to be learned about, thought about, written about, talked about. I'm a communicator, a born networker. No one is a better or faster talker than I am. I love words and I love using them in any way I can, whether it's conversation or crossword puzzles. I can discuss anything because I know a little about so many things. I live as if I were plugged into a never-ending party line. I notice, hear, and pick up information from many different sources. By getting all the angles, I stay objective and don't get too heavily into anything. Interacting comes easily to me—I understand the art of flirting.

I adjust to circumstances, modify plans, regroup, and reconnoiter easily. I don't get attached to any one plan or point of view. I keep space for new information. I can come up with more suggestions faster on how to do anything than anyone else and I back myself up with logic.

I've got lots of nervous energy. I'll try anything once. In any area of life. Boredom and routine are my greatest enemies. I switch to different personalities as quickly as I change clothes, and almost as often. I can be two people at once, think one thing and say another and feel quite compatible with myself in this dichotomy. I'll consider every possible option, but I actually believe in very little. I know too much to get attached to any one idea.

I can be hard to pin down, but this keeps me young. So does my flexibility. I'm youthful and I like it. I don't want to grow old, so I circulate, experiencing different people and possibilities. I network like I breathe. Social groups are my meat and drink. I love to talk about what happened and who did what! I don't want anything to pass me by.

I'm looking for my ideal relationship, so I always keep my options open. A muscle man may intrigue me for a while, but it won't last unless he's a good talker. My kind of man is brainy and versatile, has scope and a sense of humor, and can keep up with my multiplicity. Since I'm likely to pack up and leave on the spur of the moment, he needs flexibility as well as humor.

SUN IN CANCER WOMAN

I'm sensitive. Many people don't know this when they first meet me, because I protect myself well. If you were total mush inside, would you let everyone in as soon as you met them? I take everything personally because I feel so deeply. I'm never detached or cold. Sometimes I believe my life purpose is to feel for the whole world. As soon as I care for you, I'll start to take care of you. I'll feed you, button your top button, make sure you take your raincoat, and baby you in general. And I like to be babied.

I'm made for motherhood. Even if I don't have children, if I'm a career woman, I'll be a mother hen to my employees or co-workers. I'll make my office a homey environment, or feed everyone. Often I keep a candy dish full. I can be cranky and moody because I'm emotional and take things personally. It's hard for me to detach and leave my work at the office, and it can be hard for me to keep my feelings to myself. I've got a long memory and don't forget anyone who has been good to me, or bad. Once I've attached myself to someone or something I don't give up easily. I hang on.

Security is high on my list of priorities. I want a home, food in the larder, and money saved. I need a solid base beneath me, a fertile garden outside. With that, I make everyone feel at home, and my loony humor, imagination, and psychic sensitivity come out. I'm devoted to those I love, to the point of smothering them. Sometimes I try to make up for the lack of love in my childhood. I can feel deprived easily, and if these feelings get kicked up too much, I get bitter.

I'm sentimental and old-fashioned at heart and I like men who are traditional. I appreciate a gentleman, a man who is kind and courtly, even if he's macho or parental. It's important to me that a man be good father material. I crave security. You can't raise children properly without money. I need someone who at least is trying to establish himself financially, but as I also go for the sensitive types (I respond to the little boy in all men), my men don't always have money. Money or not, once I fall in love and commit to a relationship, I'll stick with it. My tenacity keeps me hanging in there.

SUN IN LEO WOMAN

The show must go on! I think life's the Greatest Story Ever Told, and I love it—every bit of it, the good with the bad. I'm always aware of an audience, even if it's only my dog. I live fully and dramatically, doing everything with Heart. Honor is important to me and I'm proud, sometimes too much. I can light up a room and turn heads with my magnetic warmth, and I know it and am not shy about it. I say if you've got it, flaunt it.

The best is the only thing that is good enough for me. I'd rather be a magnificent failure than a drone or a mediocre success. I like things done on a grand operatic scale—lots of stage settings, music, candlelight, romance, and, yes, even tragedy. Just as long as it's BIG. I can seem larger than life and make my environment larger than life, too. Being common or ordinary is my worst fear, so I strive to be noble in word, deed, thought, and action. I'm reliable and I don't let anyone down if I can help it. That's part of nobility.

Responsibility comes easily to me and I gravitate to the power position, wherever it is. I'm not afraid to run things, to take the blame for what goes wrong. And I operate up front, with no hidden agendas. The details bore me, but I can see the big picture clearly. Subterfuge and intrigue really put me off. I'm a "What you see is what you get" person, totally.

I like a romance that looks good to the outside world: we have to be a "couple." This sometimes trips me up, for I can be susceptible to flattery and external appearances. Even if the relationship's failing, if it still *looks* good, I'll hang on, even when it hurts. My ideal man is a king to my queen. He's strong enough to be my leading man, bigger than life, unique. He's respected and looked up to, but knowing that I love to play, he indulges me in that. He's no slouch in the royalty department either, and he appreciates the finer things in life— like *me!*

SUN IN VIRGO WOMAN

I shy away from anything obtrusive. Modesty, kindness, intelligence, and service are what I value. Anything flashy or loud puts me off. I'm not afraid of work. I willingly do everyday tasks. In fact, I enjoy the details—those little effects that put the finishing touch on things. I confess it's hard for me to live up to my own standards. I can drive myself crazy with my quest for perfection, which first focuses on myself and then on others and things. I can fall into the I-don't-want-to-be-a-member-of-a-club-that-wants-me-for-a-member syndrome. I get into relationships where I don't want those who want me.

A natural editor and critic, I like to organize. I may have dustballs, but my books and drawers will be orderly, my reports meticulously prepared. I can't turn off my critical ability, but I do try to be helpful with my observations. Abstract, theoretical discussions aren't for me. I make distinctions between things by using examples. Bring it down to earth, I say.

Sometimes people see me as prim and proper, a bit old-fashioned, and it's true I value etiquette and manners. I am drawn to purity of line, whether in high tech or handcrafted work. I respect excellence, quality, and simplicity. I believe in being thorough and taking the time to do it right.

I'm naturally health conscious, and I take care of myself both physically and mentally. Taking care is my joy, from making the perfect cup of tea to buying a perfect gift. I need private time for my special rituals.

Appearances to the contrary, I am really not a prude. I enjoy being risqué. I just don't broadcast this, for I appreciate subtlety. Often I get into relationships and find I don't want the person who wants me. But when *he* cools off, it's another story! I start wanting him all over again. My ideal man doesn't let me get into this. He's intelligent, sensitive, honest, kind, and modest. And excellent at what he does. He keeps me interested, knows I really understand the specialness of the moment and the magic of everyday life. I long to share this for the ordinary experiences of living are the most profound. I live by the proposition that what is small can be great!

SUN IN LIBRA WOMAN

I value relationships. Not just the romantic ones, either. Relationships interest me in the abstract, like harmony in art or music. I seek the perfect balance in all things, first swinging one way and then the other in my quest to achieve it. I am always open to another's point of view and wishes, and I comply if possible. I like to get a proper give and take established early on for living in a civilized and gentle way, with grace and refinement, is important to me, as is beauty, which is harmony made visible. I'm offended by ugliness or coarseness. Even if I'm not upper-class by birth, I'm naturally charming, classy, and refined. I try to be considerate and socially appropriate at all times because scenes distress me, especially in public. I can smell strife in the making, and I quickly act to mediate or defuse a potentially difficult situation.

Though I'm exquisitely tuned to other people, it takes me a long time to tune into myself. Since I'm essentially mental, I rationalize, denying my own needs and feelings. As a result, I may let you down or kill you with kindness. When I do get in touch with my anger, I dredge up everything you've ever done that annoyed me, but that I was too civil to mention. When balance is restored, I revert to my natural diplomacy. Look, I'd *always* rather discuss things rationally and compromise. It's easier to get bees with honey than with vinegar, isn't it? Things can be worked out if you listen objectively to both sides.

I'm smart and independent, but I want a man who treats me like a lady. I have a soft spot for the rugged types with gentle ways— cowboys who wash their hands. Sometimes I want a sensitive, artistic man. Other times I'm attracted to the hard-driving businessman type. Whichever he is, nothing means more to me than a relationship and I sometimes stay in unequal situations just to be in one. Fairness and balance are crucial issues for me, and I am always searching for my perfect complement. I can even go for a man with whom I have nothing in common, just because I feel he balances me—especially if he's good-looking.

SUN IN SCORPIO WOMAN

People either love me or hate me, and I have the same instantaneous reactions to them. Whether I mean to or not, I have this *aura*. It comes from knowing about human passions through my struggles to master my own. I'm a very feeling, sensitive person. Whatever I do, I do with intensity. I tune into emotional undercurrents, especially sexual ones. I can be ecstatic or abjectly miserable. It takes time for others to get used to my intensity. Some never do.

Because of my extremes, I've learned to control myself. I've also learned that I can hurt people with my perceptions, so I tend to be secretive, keeping my insights to myself. I have to admit that my X-ray vision gives me an edge that most people don't have. But it is also a responsibility. I know about power and how it can be abused. I also know how it can heal. I see the dark, instinctual side of life and what it contains.

I like that Joni Mitchell song, "Something's lost but something's gained in livin' every day." I've had so many losses and gone through so many changes that I'm good at handling crises. When in deep water, I become a diver and go as deep as possible to where the truth lies. When hurt, I can be obsessed with hatred and have powerful vengeance fantasies, but I can also let go. That's when my greatest moments happen. Something always has to die in order for something better to be born.

Maybe that's why the men in my life are powerful, with charisma, somewhat mysterious. Perhaps even a bit dangerous. Or they deal with danger in some way. They are men comfortable with being on the edge. That's why they're not intimidated by my intensity, which, I confess, flattens lesser souls. A man has to be really his own person to deal with me. I'm not easy and I know it. But I'm rewarding for someone who will take the time and effort to stay with me, go down into my depths, and see the magic and wonder there. I'm a good guide to the inner world. I know my way about in those murky waters. Strange fish, they say, but fascinating—and you can't see them from the surface.

SUN IN SAGITTARIUS WOMAN

Remember that old song, "Don't Fence Me In"? It applies to me. Give me room and lots of it. Expansion is my primary mode. I like to enjoy life, keep interested, and do what comes naturally. I like the out-of-doors and all that's in it. When I'm out there, I feel at home with the limitless horizon and the eternal stars. The universe is a big place and I want to know all of it, or at least as much as possible. My freedom is very important to me, so I respect the freedom needs of others. I feel that life is like a wonderful yellow-brick road, taking us always to new and exciting adventures—and if some of them are scary, well, you learn that way, too!

People always say I'm "too independent for my own good," whatever that means. How can you be TOO independent? I make up my own mind, thanks very much, on the issues, whatever they are, and I'll tell you straight out what I think, even if you don't ask. I'm blunt, it's true, but I mean no harm. I just speak the truth as I see it, and if I'm wrong, I didn't mean anything personal.

Friends know that I'm very concerned with moral and ethical issues, matters of justice and fair play. I'm a truth seeker. When I find my own right path, I stick to it. My problem is that, because I can see the big picture, I often don't get down to the nitty-gritty, and that makes it hard for me to settle on any one thing.

My ideal man is as freedom-loving as I am, but more grounded. I don't mind if he does the laundry and cooks so long as he doesn't get in my way when I need to move. Basically, I'm not particularly monogamous, but I'm searching for the man who will make me feel he's THE ONE. I know there's a *one* out there—somewhere. And I guess I'll just keep riding until I find him. Then we'll ride off into the distance together—like in the movies—and I'll share my big dreams with him because—at last—I can believe in someone.

SUN IN CAPRICORN WOMAN

I may not be the most cheerful person in the world, but you can always depend on me to manage things well. It's hard for me to express my true feelings so I suffer a lot from inner isolation. I didn't have much of a chance to be a carefree child—there were responsibilities and I had to take care of them. I don't say it didn't make me a better person, but people are always telling me to "lighten up." Especially at work. I'm a workaholic, even if it's just housework. "Woman's work is never done," was said for me, and not just traditional woman's work, though I do more than my share of that also. Whatever job there is to be done, I always seem to do the heaviest share. But I don't complain. I like to work hard and I know I'll get my rewards down the line and they'll be substantial. I know Rome wasn't built in one day. Organization is my forte, whether it's the office filing system or my own closets. I'm the best-organized person around.

I don't waste time, money, or my own efforts—everything has to be to a useful purpose. Sometimes I drive myself too hard—but if I don't do it, who will? The race isn't always to the swift and if I occasionally seem to be a plodder, remember the story of the hare and the tortoise! That tortoise was a Capricorn for sure.

The guy for me has to be substantial and serious—no lightweights, thanks. I like a man with a plan. Either he's already firmly established or clearly going places in the world. He's together enough to take care of me (I long for this but fight it), a pillar of society, and something of a daddy. Don't think I don't like sex or fun. When you get to know me, and I shake off my inhibitions, I'm quite a tart underneath this ladylike exterior! I've pleasantly surprised a few men who cataloged me with the office computer. They discovered I am a very down-to-earth, sexy gal! So I'm smart and I like to run things—somebody has to, why not me?

SUN IN AQUARIUS WOMAN

I don't want an ordinary life. I want to live according to my beliefs, my ideals, my principles. I think my personal life shouldn't be that important. It's other people—causes, social issues, art, science—that motivate me. In these areas, the usual doesn't interest me. The offbeat and the unusual turn me on. I like high-tech science, anything New Age, archaeology, anthropology, to name a few. I also subscribe to the maxim that the unexamined life isn't worth living. Analyzing life is one of my favorite pastimes. My aim is always to be objective with myself and others. I consider myself a reasonable and unprejudiced person.

Although I'm friendly, social, and able to talk to people from all walks of life, I always *feel* that I'm different. I've been accused of being not quite human. Sometimes I wonder myself. I'm one of the few people in the world to whom *weird* is a compliment. I pride myself on my individuality.

To really know me, you need to appreciate how special I am, to understand that I'm unique, no matter how I might appear to be. I always have a new and unusual approach to everything. The true New Woman, that's me, and I don't mind combining the male and female in myself. Sometimes, I need to shock people a little just so they don't assume I'll always do the socially approved thing. In fact, I recognize that revolution is sometimes necessary in all things when the reasonable approach doesn't work. I always try to work with other people well and harmoniously, sometimes forgetting myself in the larger picture.

My ideal man is definitely unusual in some way, even if he's a bit weird. Exotic or talented, or both, he's not the ordinary soul. He's got flair and knows that I appreciate his being different. Sometimes I get too caught up in the *idea* of differentness. I intellectualize and analyze instead of feeling or going with the flow and that can get in the way of real intimacy.

SUN IN PISCES WOMAN

People can tell how sensitive I am as soon as they meet me. It's my trademark. My feelings are so acute that I'm like a highly sensitized photographic plate, which registers all it is exposed to. Whatever vibrations are there, I pick them up. I flow into things, and I can flow right into other people and their situations. I overflow with empathy and compassion. Like a fish in the ocean, I ride the currents of life and with my emotions I touch all the ills and sorrows of the world around me. Your pain becomes my pain. This isn't easy to live with, and I have to practice discrimination constantly or I never know the difference between what's coming in to me and what is my own. That's why I often overreact. When I get confused, which is often, I'll make any excuse to get by. My spirit guides said it was okay. The devil made me do it. I was just following orders.

Life's harshness really grates against my super-sensitivity, and I am almost always seeking relief through creative and imaginative efforts. Nature soothes me and I love the sea. It feeds my spiritual needs. I have healing abilities, but when I'm not using my sensitivity positively I can turn to drugs and alcohol for comfort and get into a do-nothing state. I can get addicted to almost anything to flee from the horrible pain of existence. Responsibility scares me, and I evaporate to escape it.

In romance, I'm an idealist. My suggestibility makes me easily erotic, and I like to use my imagination in love. Men who can inspire me are the greatest attraction. I need people I can believe in, who support my visions. When my insecurities take charge, I go for a man who will take over and mesmerize me. I have to be careful of addictive relationships. I like being understanding, and I like soothing people with my presence. It gives me focus, but I can get hooked on men with problems who need my help.

SUN IN ARIES MAN

Battles don't scare *me*. I'm direct and competitive. Impatience is my middle name. I hate to wait. I'm a no-holds-barred guy. I don't beat around the bush or pull punches. Subterfuge isn't my style. I'd rather have it out, shake hands, and get on with things. I take my masculinity for granted, whatever my job.

I'm enthusiastic because I love being alive. Life is great! I pursue adventure and my ideals, like a knight in shining armor. I'm one of the good guys. My heart is pure and my goals—even if beyond my reach—are the highest. I need the challenge of a quest, which is why I'm always in search of new fields to conquer. My boyhood hero was the strong loner, the type who's sensitive on the inside and tough on the outside. I always win by my wits and daring. Just give me room to move!

A natural executive type, I'm onto every new thing in a flash. My ideas come a mile a minute, but I want others to carry them out. There's no time for me to follow up on all my brainstorms. Don't call me irresponsible. I try to be as effective as possible. I work and move fast, and if that means leaving the details to others, so be it. I get things done. I have newborn eyes that can see the fresh approach to any problem. I'm good with people and I inspire them with my en-thusiasm and vision. Okay, so I can get pushy, but I consider myself a pioneer and a leader, and sometimes you've got to push to get others off their duff. Whatever happens, I have to get my ideas across. I'll fight for what I believe in even if I have to ram my way through an obstacle course. If there is a job to be done, I'm your man!

Sure, I have a temper, but it dies down as quickly as it flares up. Later, I can laugh about what made me mad. I don't hold grudges, but my impulsiveness often gets me in hot water. I know I can be rash, but I manage to get myself out of most scrapes one way or the other. Life's a great adventure. You've got to take risks to win.

I want a woman who's not afraid to trust or to risk, someone who feels life is a challenge and welcomes it, a lady who's not afraid of a fight. I don't care if she is difficult—I can handle it.

SUN IN TAURUS MAN

Don't push me. I've been called the immovable object, but why move? I keep my life stable. I hate change. I am constant by nature. I like to preserve all that is valuable, whether it's money, art, nature, or relationships. I don't need show. I use common sense, and whatever I say or do can be backed up with solid facts and real work. Superficial or facile people do not cut it with me. I keep my life simple and, most of all, comfortable. My home is an oasis of calm amid life's madness.

No one knows better than I the joys of being alive on earth—the feel of the sun on my back, the solid ground beneath my feet, the touch of a hand on my shoulder, the smell of fresh bread baking, the sight of a garden in bloom. If you run around all the time like a chicken with its head cut off, how can you enjoy these pleasures?

The best way to get me to do anything is through love. I take care of my own. Some say I'm possessive. I say I'm protective. That's why I understand the value of money.

I'm affectionate, sensual, cuddly, and basically gentle. Touching comes naturally to me. What I can touch, I trust—whether it's my loved ones or my house and land and possessions. Because I appreciate things of the senses, I admire the beautiful. I like lushness in people and in objects. Give me a curvy woman who likes to cook—a down-to-earth, sexy, natural female on the traditional side, so that we can make a home together.

Granted, this may make me seem like a stodgy chauvinist, but I'm a basic man, and I want a basic woman. I'm stubborn. I don't let go of what's mine. I can hang on and on in a relationship just because it's too darned much trouble to change, enduring situations that would wipe others out.

I know this about myself. But I know also that I'm always there for those I love. I have patience and endurance, and I'm good for the long haul. Just *don't push me.*

SUN IN GEMINI MAN

Versatility is my hallmark. I'm quick. I keep it lighthearted and easy. I need the mental stimulation of words, and I enjoy discussing anything. I like to test my wit on puzzles, crosswords, and puns. A born investigator, I feed my insatiably curious mind with information of all sorts. Every detail interests me. I consider all the various possibilities in any idea or piece of information, keeping the flow of communication going by gathering whatever comes my way and then talking about it. I find no difficulty thinking in one way and acting in another. That's because I keep my mental distance with logic and an analytical approach. I generate many theoretical solutions to any given problem, because I like the interesting angles. But, hey, I don't get personally involved! Life is but a mental exercise!

Like a chameleon, I change to match my current environment. I don't want to grow old so I stay youthful by changing constantly. I'm a high flier, a juggler. Physically and conceptually, I'm continually on the move. Circulating, circulating. Social groups are my stage of operations. In them I am a magician—now you see me one way—presto! I'm someone else in a wink!

Better than most, I know life is impermanent. The perfect woman may be right around the corner—and she's Marilyn Monroe and Marie Curie crossed with the Keystone Cops. She's smart—so we can *talk*. Have you seen anyone like that around? No? I guess I'll keep looking. Anyway, I'm flexible, since everything's relative. There's nothing wrong with monogamy with the *right* person. There's no truth for me. I'm an idealist—and a skeptic at the same time. So many different points of view! I believe in very little but ideas and the idea of change thrills me. My life is a search for a mental ideal. Fortunately, thinking of having it is almost the same as having it.

SUN IN CANCER MAN

I may seem to have a tough, strong exterior, but inside I'm mushy and sentimental—even a little loony. I'm an old-fashioned type—I like my home, children, family, traditions. I admit to being overly sensitive emotionally, even though I usually hide it. My sensitivity makes me shy, and I prefer the indirect approach, crabwise so to speak. I like to *sense* the climate, tune into different levels of energy, especially people's feelings. I like to take care of and be taken care of. The Moon fascinates and inspires me—I'm something of a visionary, interested in the unseen. I have my own way of perceiving things.

I'm a worrywart. I tend to be fearful and do not trust what's unfamiliar. I'm protective of myself and those I love. When I must travel, I stay attuned to my home atmosphere, creating a homey environment wherever I am. Maybe it's a few pictures I carry with me and put up wherever I am or a dish of candy on my desk. It's my nesting instinct.

My insecurity adds drive to my ambition. I want to get ahead, be successful, become a community leader. I get attached to things, especially my work, and I do best when I can use my abilities to promote growth of some kind.

Nurturing others comes naturally to me, and I tend to mother everyone around me, like a hen with a brood of chicks. Food is one of the ways that I comfort myself and others. Sometimes I eat too much and gain weight, or I forget entirely about eating and lose weight. I have a basic conviction that a good meal will cure what ails you.

I like a woman with a sense of continuity, who is attached to her

past history and likes intimacy. If she's a good cook, all the better!
Once I get attached, I don't let go easily, for I'm tenacious. I have
staying power. I'll go through a lot of ups and downs before I let go
or give up.

SUN IN LEO MAN

Isn't life wonderful? It's the greatest story ever told! There's no
room for anything small, petty, or insignificant in my life-style. I live
above the common crowd. My honor means a lot to me. I don't let
people down. You can rely on me. I always play to the crowd, for I
see myself as if on stage or in a novel. And I identify with the role of
the loyal, the good-hearted, and the noble. I'm a responsible man,
open about all I do. I naturally gravitate to power and I like being
in control. I'm not afraid to run things or assume authority. But I
disdain subterfuge, and I don't indulge in secretive games. I have
nothing to hide. I put it all out there for everyone to see.

I'm a warm and loving guy and I can always find something to love
about life. When I feel good, I express myself joyfully and I radiate
goodwill to those around me. People feel good about being themselves
with me. I like to play and be creative with drama and style. Give
me pomp and circumstance, flash and fire. I present myself with flair.
When I'm low-keyed or feeling blue, it's very noticeable. I can blow
up, but those I love can cajole me out of it. My sense of humor verges
on the ridiculous and I don't mind being teased if it's in good fun.
After all, it makes me the center of attention and I'm a natural
performer. I like to get and give feedback. The more I'm applauded,
the better I perform. Sometimes, however, I fall for the performance
rather than what's really going on. I can be taken in by appearances
and stay with a situation because it looks good on the outside even if
it isn't good for me.

I'm sincere in my affections and like a creative, special woman with
presence who makes me the center of her world. I'm a romantic. I
love courtship, candlelit dinners, gift giving, passion, and drama, and
I want an individualistic, feminine woman with style. When I love, I
go all the way, showering my lover with all I possess. But I'm susceptible to flattery and you can take advantage of me. If I lose face,
you lose me. To win my loyal lion's heart appreciate me, share your
love with me, and I'll be yours forever.

SUN IN VIRGO MAN

I'm discriminating. I value modesty, kindness, intelligence, and service to others. I don't trust what is loud or flashy. The subtleties are more my style. I don't blow my own horn. I'd rather be useful than in the limelight. My actions speak for themselves, and I'm not afraid of hard work. Routine doesn't bother me as it does some people. In fact, I rather enjoy the little details of getting things right. I'm a very thorough person with a good memory, and I pay attention to the sequence of things. This makes me a good editor and critic, for I like to organize.

My house may not be the cleanest, but it's always well-organized even if there's dust on the floor. I like to make lists of what needs to be done, and I'm analytical if there's something concrete to be gained by it. I don't speculate or get involved with vague abstractions. Be specific, I say, give examples, and then we can get the job done, whatever it is.

People call me a perfectionist, but I don't see anything wrong with wanting things to be right. And, for me, I always know when it's right, even if my standards are sometimes difficult for me to live up to. I have my rituals about health, and I like to be personally clean and organized. It keeps me sane in this mad world.

I admit I'm a sucker for people who need my brain and analytical talents to get them out of their fog, and I can fall for the wounded-bird types who need my help. But generally I like people who are hard workers and competent at what they do. And I like sincerity.

The woman who is my ideal is also sincere and doesn't need a lot of show. She's practical and likes making an effort with those little touches, like the perfect cup of tea, that make all the difference. I'm not unromantic; I understand the magic of everyday life, when it's right.

SUN IN LIBRA MAN

The need to balance relations among all components is innate in me. I always see both sides of every issue and I deal fairly and justly in all situations. I'm forever trying to reconcile opposite points of view in others and in myself in order to find and maintain the pivot point. This shows in different ways. I like debate, the law, socializing, and art. Indecision and argumentativeness both come naturally to me. Two things are clear. One, I see both sides of any issue and, two, I have an artistry about whatever I do. I'm a gentleman with natural charm, grace, and class. I'm fine-tuned to society and I enjoy intimate social gatherings with good conversation. As a social animal, I am very quick to spot discord brewing and I always try to smooth over the rough spots to avoid ugliness or strife, which offend me. I want my environment to look good and contain civilized behavior. Conventional prettiness is fine with me. Nothing should be exaggerated.

Harmony is important to me, and for this reason I am often overly solicitous of others' needs, ignoring my own. This attitude of mine can cause the imbalance that so much upsets me, and then I recall everything the other person has ever done to offend me, which I was too polite to call to attention at the time. I set myself up by being such a nice guy. To be fair, I put such store in relationships that I focus almost totally on the other person at first. I like to get things off on a felicitous start.

I'm happiest in a relationship because it's hard for me to be alone. I'm always searching for the right woman, my perfect complement with whom to share my life. But I vacillate. I like sweet, feminine, pretty women and sharp, smart women as well. Whichever she is she must have social graces. Nothing turns me off faster than crudeness.

Once I'm involved, I'm not into heavy emotional scenes. I'll discuss anything as long as it's a calm, rational conversation. I need harmony and when my relationships are appropriately balanced, life is beautiful!

SUN IN SCORPIO MAN

Mysteries of life, I want to find you! Whatever I feel, I feel intensely. Whatever I do, I do with feeling. Things aren't bad, they're *evil*. They aren't good, they're *ecstatic*. There is always more going on with me than meets the eye, and I know that's true of everybody. Early on, I learned to keep a lid on my perceptions. People don't want to be exposed and I see too much too intensely. I can't help it. The underside of life—what's wrong, hurt, sick, or just plain nasty—is visible to me. It's great when what's under the surface is love, but it's unfortunately not the usual case. Because I'm so aware of the instinctual level of life, I have an edge. Knowing these things gives me great responsibility and makes me need mastery and self-control. It makes me secretive and private. This discipline gives me magnetic power that radiates to others. And it makes me extremely sexy.

All this is because I'm so sensitive. I feel everything deeply. I fight paranoia, jealousy, and vengefulness in myself so that my greatest triumphs occur when I detach emotionally. I go to extremes and test myself and those around me. I long to pierce the superficial aspects of my existence so I am relentless when I have a purpose. If it means giving up what I love best, I'll do it without a qualm. I push myself to the borderline and feel it every step of the way. When things fall apart I rebuild them. Death and rebirth are part of the cyclical nature of life.

Some people see me as destructive, others as healing. By just being around, I'll challenge you. I'm not fazed by your crises because I've been through so much. I know how to survive life's extremes so I'm calm in a storm. No one understands more clearly than I that life goes on after a fall or disaster.

My ideal woman is strong, centered, someone who can take my extremes and go along for the ride. I like women who are seductive while still and deep, like a well. If she has extreme looks, that's fine with me.

SUN IN SAGITTARIUS MAN

I'm an idea man and I like to keep on the move. I need my space, for I'm always involved in a dozen different projects, mostly connected with my ideals. I like action and adventure, especially out-of-doors, and though life may trip me up or I may fall over my own feet, I'm a "cockeyed optimist." If I can't travel physically, I do it in my mind, experiencing possibilities and learning as much as I can. I don't like downers and negativity, for I'm a positive person and I believe we can better our world. I like to study different cultures and peoples. This helps me to understand and expand my mental horizons.

I'm known for "foot-in-mouth" disease, for I don't hesitate to speak my mind, right or wrong. You'll always know where you stand with me. I'm the man who will tell you that you have bad breath or are putting on a few pounds too many. Hey, I don't mind. That's just more of you to love! There's nothing personal in my comments and I don't have hidden agendas. I get right to the point, but I can also laugh at myself and the human condition. Laughter is the best medicine and fun is a necessity, not a luxury in my book.

High-risk situations get my adrenaline going. Though I may seem like a good-time Charlie, ethics are important to me. I seek the right path for myself and when I find it, I'm true to it. I have great zeal for what I believe in, including true love.

I'm not naturally monogamous because I always feel the best is yet to come. My ideal woman is an interesting and high-spirited soul with a sense of adventure, someone I can talk to. When I finally find her, I can stop roaming. We'll stay up all night discussing important matters, buddies seeking the truth by looking for the grand view . . . and having fun while doing it!

SUN IN CAPRICORN MAN

I may be an organization man, but I'm on my way to the top. Ambition is my middle name. I want the best and I intend to get it, no matter how long it takes. I've always known I had a destiny, that I was going to accomplish something important in the world, whether in business, politics, the social world, or the intellectual sphere. Economic security is important to me, and I don't waste my time, my money, or my efforts.

I'm a law-and-order man, and I believe that we can accomplish the most by staying within the bounds of tradition. What's useful from the past needs to be kept, even if some has to be thrown away. I'm called a conservative, and I am—I abhor waste in any form. I've always liked that story about the usefulness of the pig—it's said every part of him is used except his oink.

The world doesn't frighten me for I know how it works, and I know how to make it work for me. I'm a good problem solver, a troubleshooter, an organizer, and a front man. I drive a hard but fair bargain, and I respect myself and demand respect from others. I believe in hard work and the financial rewards that result. Nobody gets anything for nothing in this world—believe me, I know that! But I never ask anyone to do what I wouldn't do myself.

At home I'm a bit of a tyrant, for I like things just so, and I think a home should run just as efficiently as my office. Why not? There's no reason to be sloppy and inefficient just because you are at home, is there?

My ideal woman is a good manager and likes a well-run home. She's also earthy and good in bed without being obvious about being sexy. She appreciates a good dirty joke, but she is a lady in public. She enjoys quality and has an eye for the future. Mainly, though, she loves me and supports my drive for material security.

SUN IN AQUARIUS MAN

I'm not your typical macho male. It simply doesn't interest me. I don't have to prove myself with acts of bravado. I live by my mind and ideals. Nothing means more to me than truth-seeking. I'd much rather work to change society—discover a wonder drug, or invent something mankind can use—than punch someone out. The cry of the French Revolution—Liberty, Equality, Fraternity—speaks to me. I live for this ideal and the time it will be a social reality. Everything new and old fascinates me, from archaeology and the occult to the latest scientific advances. I'm a high-tech buff, for I believe that most advances of the human race are a result of technological evolution. I work hard to be as evolved as I can be.

I relate strongly to ideas of universal brotherhood, and I'm someone who will extend that to extraterrestrials, if and when they come. Maybe that's because I often feel like an alien myself. I've always identified with Spock of "Star Trek." His logical and brilliant mind, unclouded by irrational human emotion, appeals to me. Emotions invariably mess things up. I'm amazingly open minded and very little shocks me. I can be mentally rigid and seem cold because I maintain my objective distance so I can be a humanitarian.

I can be the best, most interesting friend you'll ever have. In fact, I'll often take friends over lovers. Friendship is safer and lasts longer, with none of those murky human passions to confound or scare me.

My ideal woman *has* to be my friend. She is broadminded and intelligent, unusual in some way—whether she's won the Nobel Prize or has a crooked nose. She understands my need for occasional distance.

Love doesn't come easily to me but I'm not immune. I just need to feel free within a committed situation. Then we both can fly high and far, reach the outer boundaries. Who knows? Maybe we'll meet up with an E.T.!

SUN IN PISCES MAN

For a man, I'm probably one of the most sensitive people you'll ever meet. Why? Because I absorb everything around me. Like a sponge, I soak up the entire environment. I take thoughts, feelings, and atmospheres into myself almost by osmosis. That may sound strange, but it's true. I can actually get inside people and situations, and this particular ability gives me great compassion. Because I *become* the *other*, I have empathy way beyond most people's. I am never immune. Sometimes, I admit, I'm thrown by my spongelike quality. It gets to be too much for me. It's like mind-reading, only sometimes I can't tell the difference between what's in my own mind and what I'm picking up from others. That can be a liability, believe me! I can get really confused. I have to work at distinguishing between what is mine and what isn't. And since it's hard for me to avoid the negativity in the air, I like to escape when I can, which is almost all the time. I take flights of fancy in my imagination, work creatively, or immerse myself in spirituality. Drugs and alcohol help me do this, and I use them freely.

Maybe that's why I'm sweet, gentle, kind, loving, and affectionate. I can soothe you with my presence. I'm very suggestible—you have only to *think* of something you want and I respond. I also *use* the power of suggestion and weave powerful illusions, like a magician.

Some say I'm not of this earth, and true, I like dealing with anything that involves vision, where seeing beyond the obvious is required. I like inspiring others. Life isn't simple and things aren't always what they seem, but I believe in miracles and magic of all kinds.

My ideal woman understands and accepts my visionary nature and where it leads me. She is a romantic with a good head on her shoulders and a dream in her heart. She's more practical than I am (which isn't hard to accomplish!), and when I find her and my life's work, there's no one stronger than I am.

chapter sixteen

ASTROSCRIPTS FOR THE MOON

The MOON we call the silver light
Of Selene, the Queen of Night,
But other names she has as well:
Hecate, the Maid of Hell,
And Artemis, the Queen of Bees.
Your feelings She will gently seize,
Fill with doubt, or amply please!

MOON IN ARIES WOMAN

Action is my friend, boredom is my enemy. *Spirited* is the word most people use about me, and rightly so. I've got enough emotional enthusiasm to share and to spare. People who poke around, trying to figure it out, give me a pain. I know I can get pushy, but I'm just trying to get the job done. The best way I know how, which is usually my way! I don't fool around with game-playing. I'm open and direct. Leave the subterfuge to the professionals, I say. The best way is always the fastest, and I don't have time for baloney. Save it for the sandwich. I just lay all my cards on the table and then I deal with whatever occurs. Let the chips—and the confrontations—fall where they may.

If you want my input, leave me alone to do my brainstorming and then let me inspire others. If you need a quick decision, I'm your woman. A natural executive, that's me. I don't shirk from decision-making, whether it's what's for dinner or whether we should withdraw from the United Nations. It's true that I make hasty decisions and have the time to regret them sometimes, but—win a few, lose a few. As long as there's action and I'm part of it.

I'm very affectionate and I don't mind showing it in public. I guess I'm still a tomboy at heart, always testing the limits. But I'm a lady and I can dazzle you with glamour when the mood hits. I want to be appreciated for my ambition, energy, individuality, humor, and zest for life. Give me the chance, and I'll perk up your world.

My mom was a strong lady and I have to admit that she dominated my life. One had to catch her on the run, but she was vivid and expressive with her affections. She liked doing things with me, but the details escaped her. I want a man who plays it straight emotionally, as I do. No games. He's got to like a direct and forceful woman, or I'll run him over. And he has to be able to handle my speed, my passion, my immediacy of feeling. After that, we can make beautiful music together—in a hurry.

MOON IN TAURUS WOMAN

Touch is my watchword. What I can touch, I can trust, whether it's my checkbook or my lover. Tradition is important to me, because I like what has been proved over time. I don't like to hurry; in fact I can be quite immobile, especially when I'm hunkered down in my nest at home. My personal environment is tailored for comfort, has comfy furniture, a well-stocked pantry and fridge, cozy corners with soft pillows, lovely textures, nice smells. And please note that it is *my* environment. I'll welcome you into it, and please you with my sensuality, but what's mine is mine. I'm very sensitive about that, even though I love sharing. That's because I invest a lot of myself in my possessions, so they are like family to me. Even the old sofa.

Emotionally, I'm stable and my feelings are consistent. I show love by being there for people, doing things for them. I'm a practical sort: I'll iron your shirt or cook you a meal, put a cool cloth on your fevered brow, or just hold your hand while you cry. I provide grounding. That's because I'm a calm person who knows how to remain unruffled when things are falling apart. I'm good at handling emergencies, because I get emotionally involved slowly, later. And by then the crisis is over. If I'm hurt, I can hold on to the hurt for years. It's hard for me to let go of anything I cherish. Especially a loved one.

My mother was your fairly standard-issue conventional sort. She didn't go for the new and trendy, and even if she was a bit stodgy at times, it made me feel secure and comfortable. Housekeeping was an art form to her, and she watched the budget carefully. These qualities are still important to me, no matter how much money I have or make. That's why I like a nice, substantial, reliable man to come home to. Nothing fly-by-night, please. Great sex is comfortable sex, familiar, steady. Change for change's sake isn't my style. If it ain't broke, don't fix it!

MOON IN GEMINI WOMAN

My often-brilliant analyses of my feelings are remarkable for their lack of feeling. I'd really rather talk (and talk some more) about my feelings than bother to actually *feel* them. It's so heavy in that emotional morass and I don't want to get stuck there. It's not that I don't have feelings. I do, and plenty of them. It's just that they keep changing, not only from day to day, but from hour to hour. So why get involved? Nothing's permanent anyway. Especially feelings. Mine at least. Do I sound confused? I'm not, truly; it's just that I'm aware of life's myriad possibilities and I need to constantly express myself through a variety of ways. Variety is as essential to me as air to breathe. It's the breath of my mind, so to speak. There are those who call me fickle, but I say I'm versatile in my affections. I don't hold back or hoard. I exchange everything, from my clothes to my lovers.

What I don't like is intensity. My mental gyrations are designed to avoid deep discussions about problems, and even if you corner me and insist, I'll sidetrack you with a dazzling debate over definition of terms. It's easier for me to have a serious relationship with a book author or an ideology than with someone I know. My mind is my home, and home is where my head is. Polarities interest me, and I switch regularly—so fast that it disorients others.

My mom was not your basic chicken-soup type, either. She was okay if a bit nervous and inconsistent, but she had a hard time sitting still long enough to discuss *my* feelings, or even to realize I had feelings. But she was a great talker. She didn't have any set ways of doing anything and neither do I.

Maybe that's why I want a man who's as flexible as I am, who needs rational discussion more than sloppy feelings all over the place, who can deal with my duality. Who wants to be the same all the time anyway? *Quelle* bore!

MOON IN CANCER WOMAN

My feelings are strong, but I'm very moody with a lot of ups and downs. That's because I have a great imagination and my sensitivity tunes me in to other people's feelings. I can get upset because someone else is upset. That's why my home and family are important to me. I feel secure in the bosom of my family, and I'm my happiest there. Even if I don't have a close natural family, I'll create my own out of friends and lovers. I'm not big on going out. I'd rather stay home where it's nice and safe and comfy. I like to cook. The kitchen is probably the most used room in my house. Food is the best medicine for the inevitable bumps life hands out. A good meal can soothe and comfort, and I have a tendency to overeat because food can be a substitute for the love I am missing at the time.

I like to make homemade things—jams and jellies or knitted objects. And I like an assortment of memorabilia from my past, way back to high school and babyhood. I've got pictures everywhere, and little things that remind me of the things I've done, the places I've been, the people I've known. High-tech and stark modern design leave me cold. Cozy collectibles are my style. I like whatever's old-fashioned, homespun, folk, or just plain comfortable. Especially if someone made it just for me. I crowd my home with cherished little things I've been given or discovered somewhere.

My mother was an important person in my life, probably the strongest influence of anyone. Mothering is a theme in my life, and nurturing and caring come naturally to me. I like to have things to care for, even plants or pets. And I love children. I like to hug and pet them and I like to be held and hugged.

Intimacy doesn't frighten me; I crave it. I need a man who's comfortable with intimacy and with providing me with security, especially the emotional kind. I want him to appreciate my femininity, and if he's into bringing flowers and candy, he'll never want for a good, homecooked dinner!

MOON IN LEO WOMAN

Life's a stage, and I know my place on it—dead center! My home is the set and my lovers are the other actors. Of course, I'm the leading lady as well as the director, producer, and casting director. I don't mind sharing the starring role as long as everyone acknowledges that I'm the one with top billing. Pettiness annoys me intensely, and I'll even give up the spotlight to avoid appearing common or ordinary. I hate negative feelings around me. The sun *must* shine on my parade. It's true that I dramatize my life, but that's only because I can always find something to love intensely, even if it's only a new nail-polish color. The grand gesture becomes me, and I make one quite frequently just for effect. The thunder of applause is the greatest high I can imagine.

In matters of the heart, I'm generous and my love knows no bounds. If I have a warm and tasteful environment where I feel really *special*, I can shine like the noonday sun, warming everybody around with my own radiance. I bask in attention and feedback. Tell me I look lovely, act superbly, am wonderful. Several times an hour. It may seem like a lot of trouble, but the rewards are commensurate. There's no glow like my glow, no warmth like mine. You can get an emotional suntan with me.

My mother was into melodrama and succeeded in getting the lioness's share of the family's attention. If she didn't there was always a new scene for her to play. Dad especially catered to her and her whims. But she kept her dignity no matter what the circumstances. And she loved us kids.

The man for me has to be larger than life, with a noble soul and a powerful personality. I have to be able to trust him completely, because I tend to be gullible and can be seduced by flattery. If he appreciates me for my creativity, spontaneity, and executive ability and if he *tells* me of this frequently, I'll be his loyal friend and lover, and cast him as the leading man in my life.

MOON IN VIRGO WOMAN

I'm shy around the edges. I don't feel comfortable when attention is focused on me. I need to be productive and practical, and what means something to me is the results I achieve, not the public acclaim for them. I prefer to be noticed, if at all, after I've done the work and the scores are in. Even then, I'd rather let my work speak for itself. Though I'm as emotionally needy as anyone else, I don't like to impose on others and I've learned how to practice self-discipline. It's only when I get sick that anyone else ever has to take care of me. And even then I'll do for myself if I can.

I'm a perfectionist in all that I do, whether it's sewing a hem, writing a report, or making a purchase, small or large. I get all the details just right, and I pay attention to the minute evidence. If it's wrong, I'll do it over until I get it right. I examine everything, for I believe that the unexamined life isn't worth living, and when I fall short of my own expectations for myself, I really suffer. That's because I always try to be the best I can be. It's one of the responsibilities of having intelligence. I have a tendency to criticize my loved ones, but I don't mean to wound, only to help them to improve.

My home may not be the cleanest, but it will be in order. Order is vital to me. It helps keep me from getting over-anxious, which is a problem for me. I worry a lot, and making lists of things to be done or bought helps me control that nervousness. I also like to make others feel comfortable and I remember the little things they like, like two lumps of sugar in the tea or a favorite brand of cookies.

My mother was devoted to duty, but she confused me when I was growing up. Said one thing and meant another. In her view, children were to be seen and not heard, and the only time this rule was relaxed was when we were sick.

I want a man who will be kind and attentive to me, and appreciate my orderly ways. He doesn't have to be the handsomest, but he has to be clean and reliable. We can have a sensible life, doing things the right way.

MOON IN LIBRA WOMAN

Strife or discord upsets me. I need a peaceful environment, emotionally as well as physically. I want everything to be nice, and everybody to behave rationally and in a civilized manner. I'm sensitive and refined, a natural diplomat, and I want others to be so as well. I will do all in my power to maintain harmony in any situation, do whatever I can to please others. I want to live graciously and with a minimum of stressful confrontations or emotional scenes. I'll *discuss* any problem in any relationship, as long as the discussion remains calm and courteous. I'm capable of being very fair and open to the other person's point of view.

I confess that my desire to bend over backwards to avoid strife often puts me in a bind, for then I ignore my own needs and exhaust myself meeting those of others. Sometimes I'm so concerned about being fair that I end up being unfair to myself. I compromise easily— anything to keep the peace and not fight. Relationships are so important to me that I'll go the long mile to mediate between people if things get hostile. I'm very mental and I can step outside of my personal emotions. I can judge rationally to restore the balance and proportion in situations.

My mom placed a lot of emphasis on proper social behavior and relations. Good manners were an absolute must. So was etiquette. And being ladylike at all times.

I want a man who sees me as an equal, but I vascillate between wanting to be treated like a pre-liberation woman, having chairs pulled out and coats held, or doing something that is entirely mental and totally independent. The martial arts appeal to me, because perfect balance is the goal. Though I want a man who is calm, quiet, and rational, my need for being in a relationship is so strong that I often compromise my needs. And then I'll do anything to keep it going, even if it hurts.

MOON IN SCORPIO WOMAN

I am never detached. Not about sex, not about work, not about friends, not about anything. I'm passionate and intense, even when I keep it to myself, which I often do. I know how to wait and see what comes to me, and I use my aura of mystery to lure what I want to me, even though I am perfectly capable of going after it myself. I'm deeply emotional and extremely sensitive, both to nuances and to slights. I can be very demanding but I'm vulnerable and get hurt easily. I usually hide my hurt feelings and brood about them in private, planning revenge.

The faint of heart get left behind with me. Only the strong can deal with me, because of my emotional intensity. And it doesn't let up. I'm quick to like or dislike, and I usually produce a love-or-hate reaction in others as well. It's hard for me to trust, because I'm always undergoing some kind of inner transformation that's very private and intense, and I don't share easily. You have to prove to me that you're worthy, but, if you do, I'll stick with you through thick and thin. I have staying power. Extremes come naturally to me, from letting go

completely to cutting off completely and never looking back. I had
to survive the hard way. I learned about emotional manipulation—
how to do it and how to avoid being trapped by it.

My mother was a complex person who often intruded on me, with
both her strengths and her weaknesses. My sexuality was a big problem for her and I've had to work hard to clear up my emotional
relationship with her. She had many sides, and could be a charismatic
and compelling person with good insights.

I want a man who is powerful and fearless. Someone who has seen
the dark side of life and coped with it already. He'll have to be able
to dig into his own psyche for treasures and transform what he finds
there.

MOON IN SAGITTARIUS WOMAN

I'm generous with what I have, especially my knowledge. Learning
is important to me, and I invest a lot of emotional energy in it. I like
to teach and share my insights about life and philosophy. My approach
is always free spirited, unfettered. I can go off on peculiar tangents
in my search for wisdom and meaning, but I must follow the intellectual path or I'll go crazy from boredom and the "stir-crazy" feeling.
I need to get away periodically, preferably far away to a foreign
country, where I can kick up the traces and run free. I'm no stay-
at-home housewife. My idea of cleaning house is to move to another
country and start over. But even if I can't do that, I have a house
full of travel catalogs and I can dream. One day . . .

I'm an optimist first and foremost. No matter how down I get or
how bad the world seems, I always have hope. Things *will* get better.
I know what kind of a person I want to be and what I want to do,
and I'll risk all to get to where I need to go. I have vision and this
guides me. If I have to brave the swamps and climb the highest
mountain in order to grow spiritually, I'll do it. Very little scares me
if the end result is to learn. Whether I actually risk myself physically
or not, I'm always on an adventure of the mind and spirit, through
reading, studying, growing. That's what I feel I'm here for—to expand
my horizons as far as they can go.

My mother was a knowledge freak with a moral side to her. She
wasn't a cookie-baker, but she cared about our souls and educations,
being a bit of a teacher-preacher.

I want a man who is on his own spiritual quest—someone who has
traveled far and wide, if only in his mind and heart. He's got to be
a free spirit, not tied down by conventional thinking and a need for

nightly chicken soup. He's a risk-taker with a good sense of humor, who can laugh at life's travails. And if he's from a different country and can teach me another philosophy, so much the better.

MOON IN CAPRICORN WOMAN

My feelings run deep but I'm shy about expressing them. I can seem uptight and reserved because I disapprove of the public display of emotion. In private, I can be very earthy, but my basic nature is to be elegant and proper. Sloppy emotionalism turns me off, as do over-demonstrative people who fawn over you or paw at you. I'm seen as a strong woman, and people depend on me, so my own vulnerability gets put under wraps, making it even more difficult for me to expose my deepest feelings. I'm so used to shoring up my feelings and just *functioning*, doing what needs to be done, that I get to feeling guilty if I impose my feelings on anyone. I'd rather be the one who is helping out and supporting someone else through a crisis. Which often happens, because I'm a stable and reliable person who can take the strain off others.

My behavior is rarely impetuous, for I'm serious about myself and what I do. And I take others seriously. I need respect, and I get it by being productive and organized, a conscientious worker and friend. Discipline comes easily to me, and I can delay instant gratification for long-term goals and ambitions. I'm a planner and a well-planned operation appeals to me, no matter its nature or purpose. Maturity has always been my goal and I achieved it early, not having had much chance to be a child when I was one.

My mother did her best, but she wasn't the warmest mom in town. Our home was reserved, somewhat austere, and emotionally cold. When she wasn't working hard, she was unhappy about something and kept herself distant from my childish needs. I had to learn self-sufficiency early.

I need a man who is solid and reliable, serious about life, with firm goals and strong ambition. I'll be his partner and work as hard as he does for our mutual benefit, and I'll support his aims if they're high. I'm a lady, but I can let down and roust about. Like fine wine, I get better—and more free—with age.

MOON IN AQUARIUS WOMAN

I'm someone whose brain works overtime. I analyze everything, especially my emotions. I get to the point that I understand them so well that I have no feelings left. Although I know it's important to be in touch with feelings, I'd really rather intellectualize them away. And for this reason I often appear cool or emotionless in intimate relationships. Although I'll talk about what I feel, it's something of a monotone that doesn't express much. Usually I prefer just to have friends and function in groups, because the one-to-one situation gets too involved and messy.

Being different is one way I express myself, and I'm prone to shock people with my individualism—not because I want to, just because that's the way I am. I don't compromise my ideals and that can make me a rebel. I take up far-out causes to have a place to attach my feelings, and sometimes I get into reforming my lover, which can cause trouble! I'm very sincere and my idealism can make me subjugate my own feelings to the needs of others.

The flip side of my coolness is that I act immature and am emotionally erratic, using the telephone to take the worry out of being close. I like advanced telecommunications systems. They let me be "in touch" without the bother of touching. With TV systems you can even see the other person without being anywhere near him! What a trip!

My mother was an unusual person, cool rather than warm. Her idea of nurturing was to stuff us full of ideals and thought systems. Forget the oatmeal. In her own way, she was an inventor and a New Age thinker, years ahead of her time. Her causes often took her attention from the family.

I'm not sure what kind of a man I need. I'm a little confused about my own feminine identity. I'm very aware of both my feminine and my masculine sides, but I'm for sure not your standard-issue little woman. What I do know about myself is that I don't play coy games. I'm an interested and interesting person, and I don't like being gender identified.

MOON IN PISCES WOMAN

I find the everyday world harsh and unloving, so I escape to nature, art, spiritual studies, or my rich fantasy life. I love music because I flow right into it and lose myself. I'm in tune with the downtrodden and with being selfless, so I can find meaning in working with unfortunates of any kind. That's because when I feel needed I am inspired, and then I'm indefatigable. On a personal level, this means that I can feel other people's feelings without particularly trying. I'm like a psychic sponge that soaks up the moods, emotions, and thoughts around me; and sometimes it's difficult to sort it all out. I never am sure what is mine and what isn't. Because I'm so sensitive, I get flooded with emotions and I can become dependent on people or substances. It's a way out for me. The difficulty with being so responsive is that I can fall into sensationalism or cynicism if my loving nature is abused or misused.

I'm a visionary woman with great creativity, and I know that if I could channel it properly I could be an artist. But I get distracted by others' needs and then I become a martyr to their cause, ignoring my own needs. Because it's hard for me to be direct about my feelings, I can punish in subtle ways, hardly noticeable but still there. I need kindness and understanding in order to blossom and flow with the universal energies.

My mother was a woman with a vague and dissatisfied air, rather like a ghost. She was hardly there and didn't seem quite real. In fact, I often felt that I was *her* mother, that she needed me to take care of her more than I needed her to take care of me.

My ideal man is a quiet dreamer with a big vision of how to make the world better. I want him to inspire me and to need me. Together we will do something to help the oppressed people of the world, or save the whales, or send food to the hungry. I want to be true giver always.

MOON IN ARIES MAN

Don't fence me in! I need room to move. Patience isn't my long suit. I'm touchy. My feelings flare up quickly and are impossible for me or anyone else to ignore. My impulses are strong and I can get really pushy if I need something. My perceptions are quick and I form opinions immediately, right or wrong. Whatever I feel, I feel it strongly. I want what I want when I want it, and I hate to be frustrated. Some call me willful—I say independent! I don't mind kids. They are naive, charming and innocent—just like me.

I like to clear the air if there's trouble. Come out with the gloves on, fight clean, and shake hands afterward—that's my style. Adventure and action thrill me, even if it's only the ball game on TV (the closer the score the better) or reading about a safari in Africa. I thrive on challenges, and my home environment has to have built-in challenges and action. Any kind of situation that tests me, even if it's dangerous, appeals. I'm a natural fighter.

Number One is my preferred slot and I have no problem taking the leadership role. I have a problem if I'm *not* the leader. That's because I need my independence and I can't be beholden to anyone. When I'm left alone to do my own thing, I can inspire others with my enthusiasm. It's very catching when I'm "on." Energy surges up in me in great spurts and I operate accordingly. Rest doesn't interest me when I get going and I drive straight to the goal. I go until I drop and then I may get a cold or flu.

Mom was a lively and enthusiastic lady who was always running around like a chicken with its head cut off. And she was always fighting mad about something, big or small. Her Irish was always up. But she didn't crowd me or hem me in. She was too busy with her causes. I like women with spunk, the kind who are always involved in something independent on their own. I don't care if she has a temper, even if it's hotter than Hades. Hey, I *like* action!

MOON IN TAURUS MAN

I need my comforts in order to feel relaxed. I don't like to hurry, so I take my time about what I do. I'm a very sensual man and I like the pleasures of the table and the body. And because I like my creature comforts, I like to have enough money to accommodate them. Give me a big, solid easy chair, a good meal with fine wine, a responsive woman, and all's right with the world.

The world's a stressful place, and I like to keep calm in the face of it all. The hustle and the bustle don't get to me because I stay unruffled. I'm accused of being unresponsive or insensitive, but that's not true. I know the value of a peaceful environment. Getting my hands and feet into the dirt helps keep me grounded. I like nature, walking, gardening. And I'm fond of my possessions, whatever they are.

My home's my secure base, and I like touching what's mine, whether it's the cat, the plants, or the people I love. I know I'm possessive, but I don't think there's anything wrong with this, because I protect what I love. When my secure base is threatened, I may resort to excess food and drink and I have a tendency to gain weight.

Money is important to me and I want a good solid bank account. I like to take care of those I love. And I like what feels real—a house, land, good solid possessions.

I'm not a guy who changes easily, and people know they can depend on me. My feelings, once given, don't usually change. I get taken advantage of occasionally because I'm so sturdy and I can take a lot. But I can also dig in my heels and become stubborn if I'm pushed too far.

My mom was dependable and solid, always there when I needed her. She taught me common sense and reliability. The women in my life have a maternal quality about them, good sound values, even if they are artistic in nature. They wear well because they have inner substance.

MOON IN GEMINI MAN

Change is my middle name. I need it like a fish needs water. I'm wired and restless and I've got to spend my energy or I go crazy. Nothing is permanent, and I live with that uppermost in my mind. Life's ups and downs don't faze me, because I myself can be of two minds at the same time: emotional-analytical or involved-detached. Here today and gone tomorrow, that's me. I'll try anything once, even commitment, but I don't want to feel bound to anything or anyone. Life has too many experiences to offer.

Feelings don't scare me, but I'd rather talk about them than have a heavy emotional scene. Keep it light! I am detached about emotions, my own especially. I don't get involved, because tomorrow's another day and I'll be another person then, so what's the sense? Even when there is a serious issue at stake, I don't ever take it all that seriously. In fact, I don't take anything that seriously. Everything changes with time, and with me that time is usually short.

I like to keep my options open, have an alternative plan, or two or three. That way I'm free, and freedom's what it's all about. When you're free, you don't have to get bored. Boredom is the PITS. Give me variety and lots of it. That's how I get the mental stimulation I need. Change, and more change. Especially where I live. Home isn't just where I hang my hat, it's where my head's at.

My mom was not your basic homemaker type. Oh, she was fine in her own indubitable way, a great talker. A real people person. Social. She loved conversation and read a lot of books and magazines and talked about what she read. I learned from her, but she couldn't sit still long enough to hear about my feelings. So I learned not to have them.

Women who are lighthearted and have their heads full of air are my match. They are usually nervous, high-strung types, and they love my wit and banter. Call me Peter Pan—I want to stay young forever. Don't you?

MOON IN CANCER MAN

I love to eat. Plenty of food and provisions in the house make me feel secure, and I need to feel secure, especially at home. I'm a sensitive man with strong feelings and I'm not afraid to show them. I can appear macho when I'm trying to hide my sensitivity, but I've got a sweet, gentle, imaginative side that can be moody and loony. But I cover it up with a tough shell because I'm very protective of myself, and of those I love. Basically, I'm extremely affectionate when I don't feel threatened. I'm a natural-born father and I love children.

I'm very attached to my home and I like a homey atmosphere of the traditional kind. I'll opt for furniture that's comfortable over the fancy designer stuff. I want to be able to relax on the couch and in the chairs. Stark or cold, the high-tech kind of thing doesn't appeal to me at all. I like cozy. Usually I choose a decor similar to what I grew up with.

My mother was a big influence in my life and I'm still deeply connected to her. She was a good mother of the traditional sort, and I look for some of her qualities in the women who attract me. I like feminine women who would be good mothers. I also like women with a psychic, dreamy, or imaginative side. I especially like them if they enjoy cooking. The way to my heart is definitely through my stomach.

My quest for security includes owning land and property, my own home and what's in it. I need to feel that these things are safe and there for me when I come home. My environment has to be a place where I can feel comfortable being close to my lover and my family.

Intimacy doesn't scare me like it does some men, but I do have to overcome a certain amount of shyness and insecurity before I can relate on an intimate level. But once I've attached myself to a woman, I hang in there through thick and thin. Sometimes I hang on too long, for I prefer the familiar to the new and untried.

MOON IN LEO MAN

Wherever I am or whatever I'm doing, I need to be able to express myself and have an impact on the environment. I need to be noticed, and usually I am. I feel cared for when I get attention and I always return the favor. The spotlight becomes me for I'm a natural performer, no matter what my profession. I can make a good show out of recounting what my day was like. In fact, it's hard for me to relinquish the spotlight until I've gotten the recognition and acknowledgment I need.

I'm an honorable man with a high code of honor and ethics. I need respect and I give myself respect. If I don't get it from others, it really bothers me. I do what I can to maintain my dignity, and I despise cheap or tawdry behavior. Less than the best is unacceptable to me. I strive always for the highest, and I put my whole heart into it.

My feelings are warm and I like to express them freely. I'll hug a fellow male and not feel embarrassed about it—bear hugs are my specialty. I'll give you the shirt off my back if I like you or you need it, and I like being the giver rather than the taker. I'm not comfortable with dependence. I'll go to great lengths to avoid it.

My mother was a great lady, at least in her own mind and mine, with taste and style, no matter her circumstances. She was a force to be reckoned with and she always kept up a sunny front, no matter if things weren't going well. She was affectionate and supportive of me even though the price was becoming part of the audience for her dramatics. She was very much into emoting and histrionics at times, and she could upstage the lot of us easily.

I like women with that "special something" that is immediately noticed by others. A lady with me can be as flashy as she likes, for I like drama and flair in women—either in looks or accomplishments. I like to look good with a woman, so the more impressive she is, the better.

MOON IN VIRGO MAN

I want a regular life. I enjoy being just a normal man, with no pretensions. I'm conscientious to a fault because at an early age I was taught that it's vital to be useful in this world. "Actions speak louder than words" is my motto. My intelligence is my only point of pride, but I'm modest even about that. My mind is exacting, and I've got an eye for detail and a talent for simplicity. Nothing fancy, just fine work of all kinds—whatever is beautifully crafted, whether it's an annual report or a piece of handmade furniture. My efficiency causes me to end up doing the little things others ignore or overlook. Most of the time I don't mind that my work goes unnoticed, but when I get peeved I become supercritical, picking at those close to me. Still, I never ask anything of anyone else that I don't ask of myself.

Taking care of other people comes naturally to me, but I tend to pay little attention to my own needs unless I get really sick. I really appreciate it when someone cares about my health, asks me how I am, or urges me to take vitamins. I also like to have my thoroughness and my skills recognized as valuable qualities.

I'm analytical, down to the last inch, always trying to make sense of what's going on around me. Order is very important to me, and I'll do what I can to attain it, even if it's only making lists of what needs to be bought or done. My search for perfection can make me get uptight and rigid at times, and I often punish myself for not being a better person.

My mother was dutiful and efficient and ran an organized home intelligently. She was helpful and kind to others and generally attentive and caring at home. But she could nitpick you to death or be manipulative, saying one thing while meaning another, a classic giver of double messages. Of course, she often wasn't aware of what she was doing. But the message always was: if I were only perfect, things would be fine for everyone.

I like sensible, productive women and don't mind if they are shy or plain. Capability counts and I appreciate a clean, simple style. It's what's underneath that counts.

MOON IN LIBRA MAN

I'm a gentleman, a genuinely nice person, even if I do say so myself. My primary weapon against life's slings and arrows is my charm and my smile. I have a great smile and I can charm the pants off most anyone, so to speak. Call on me when you need a mediator, for I know how to smooth over a situation. Often I do this by giving in and complying with the other person's wishes, just to keep the peace. Even if it's not always in my own best interests. But, then, why not? I'm a very polite person and politeness is the best social lubricant I know.

I function best in a beautiful, well-balanced environment where there is interesting, cultured conversation. I like to discuss feelings as long as there are no extreme or messy scenes, especially in public. Coarse behavior really turns me off.

I can get emotional about theories concerning ideas of justice, law, the arts, and correct behavior. These things matter to me and I appreciate a well-rounded discussion about them in a gracious setting. I'm good at creating such an environment and keeping it peaceful and subdued. Even so, I love debate and paradoxes fascinate me. I can always see both sides of the question and this ability can lead me into the torment of indecision, because I can defend both sides with equal vigor.

My mother was a proper lady and she raised me accordingly. We had a nice home and she encouraged cultivated tastes. She liked everything to be prettily arranged, and so do I. Pretty women appeal to my sense of balance, even if they are conventionally pretty. Unfortunately, as with other matters, I waffle about women, sometimes wanting the lace-and-ruffles, old-fashioned conventional woman and then thinking I'd be happier with a plain-jane, no-nonsense scholar or an independent-minded career woman. Whatever type she is, she must be a lady.

MOON IN SCORPIO MAN

Nothing is quite what it seems. I'm a person who always knows that there's more to a situation than meets the eye. I investigate, probe, and dig beneath the surface. When I get fixed on someone, an idea, or my work, I don't let go. I'm obsessive in my involvements, totally there for whomever or whatever. That's because I have intense and very strong feelings. I always try to understand the motivations of myself and others, for I find this healing. I do best when I can pour my energy into meaningful work, for then I become very dedicated.

It's important for me to have control over my life, and I see money and sex as a means to that end. I only feel secure when I'm in the driver's seat, and because I'm extremely emotional, sex is always very intense. As I don't trust easily, it takes time for me to open up. When I don't want to feel my feelings I can be sexually controlling. I do this by dominating or by being uninterested in sex.

Abuse, abandonment, hatred, and death are all familiar to me, even when not overt. It was all around me when I was growing up. In fact, it was the things that were swept under the rug that hurt the most. My mother had an emotional laundry list a mile long and it affected me deeply. She was attached to me, dedicated, but often she was intrusive and controlling, or she was too busy dealing with her own issues of loss and pain when I was little to pay much attention to my needs. My feelings for her are complex and not easy to talk about.

My ideal woman has a purpose and strong will with a quiet calm covering her complex nature. A *femme fatale*, she is magnetic and tends toward extremes in looks and personality. Emotional yet controlled, she tolerates my need to push things to the hilt. I self-destruct just so I can rebuild. She understands I can be a force for good, because my struggles let me understand other people's grief, and respond to people without regard to their social masks.

MOON IN SAGITTARIUS MAN

Remember the song, "Give me land, lots of land, under starry skies above. Don't fence me in!" That's how I feel. I need the far horizons and the distant shores. I'm forward thinking and positive, with a good sense of humor. I can philosophize like a guru and then laugh at myself. I love travel, even in my armchair. The idea of foreign countries, cultures, and peoples fascinates me. Morals and ethics are high on my list, too, and I like to share my insights about them with others. Somewhere inside me is a teacher, no matter how I make my living. Whatever is educational or uplifting spiritually appeals to me, and my belief system incorporates a love of growth and freedom as well. I need room to move about, and I give others their space without being asked.

At times I have to take off and go somewhere—to the mountains or camping in the woods. Get close to nature. Then I get a different, larger, perspective. Don't expect my home to be neat as a pin. Too much tidiness cramps my style. And I don't like to get involved in the petty, mundane details of everyday living if I can avoid it. They bring me down and I strive to be up all the time.

My mother was a spirited woman, even if she wasn't the most consistent person in the world. She was into books and educational materials and she cared about our moral and intellectual development. She was herself a natural teacher. She showed she loved me by teaching me things.

I'm in search of my ideal woman. She is wise and free, with a soul, and she's dedicated to her soul's growth, whatever that means to her. I think big and feel big, and she has to appreciate that, because when I care I care in a big way. I confess I have a tendency to exaggerate and I'm not always the most realistic of men, but looking at the larger context helps me stay positive about life. I need a woman who can understand this, and if she's from another country and has a different background, hurrah!

MOON IN CAPRICORN MAN

Work, work, and more work. I'm ambitious and I always hold up my end of things. You can rely on me to get the job done. I've been accused of being a workaholic more than once. If trying to get ahead is a crime, then arrest me. I graduated from the school of hard knocks and know how to get results. I prefer to keep things simple—I don't like too much fuss and bother. I'm a disciplined and organized executive type with a spartan approach. I don't feel right unless I'm working hard so I drive myself and others, too.

Down to earth, I know the bottom line. I'm responsible and real about my feelings. I come through for those I care about. I put my money where my mouth is—I'll lend it to you or spend the day helping you move, for I find it easier to work than deal with feelings. They were frowned upon or ignored in our home, and I was taught that people's problems come from idleness. Drying tears or dealing with emotional scenes embarrasses me no end. There was a definite *right way* and a *wrong way* to be in our home. Controlled and proper was the right way. And *proper* was defined according to my father, the ultimate authority.

I always feel deprived. Inside me there is a waiflike Victorian child-of-the-streets. No matter how rich we were, my family feared poverty. We knew everyone's social position.

My mother wasn't there for me—either because of her busy career, or because she had to keep up appearances. There were times she just seemed so *sad*. She relied on me to be a trouper, and I learned that being industrious and enterprising was the best medicine for feeling lonely. Or needy. Or feeling anything. That's how I got good at diverting my emotions before I could start to feel them. When I'm feeling low I go to the office or to my projects.

I like a woman who's competent and responsible. She may or may not be well educated, but she is experienced and wise. She's classy, unaffected, knows how to act in public, and is unconcerned with frivolous trends. She's controlled on the outside but earthy, even bawdy, on the inside, and she gets better with age. I like mature women to start with.

MOON IN AQUARIUS MAN

Let's face it, I'm a bit peculiar but I'm a very interesting fellow. Whatever is new is my thing and I go chasing after every New Age and Space Age idea and product around, from video to cutting-edge science. I'm a free thinker and I have my own thought system, into which I like to fit all things, neatly. That's why I don't like messy and irrational emotions. They're too hard for me to lock into my theoretical system, which is my base for understanding human behavior and relations. I operate best within my thought frame, and that's why I so often champion causes. Working for a humanitarian endeavor lets me express my feelings in a controlled and safe way.

I've many talents but my problem is that it's hard for me to settle down to one thing and I have a tendency to scatter energy. When freedom calls, I can divest myself of all my possessions just to be unencumbered. I confess to having the Peter Pan complex and the idea of growing up repels me. Who needs it? I'm like that guy in the movie who metamorphosed into an adult at age 12 and found himself in the toy business. I'm always looking for new toys to play with, be they ideas or people.

Blame my idealism. I believe in bettering humanity, in working for the welfare for all people. I live for the ideal—world, career, woman, life. But that shining star is sometimes too far away and then I get disappointed and drop whatever it is that I'm experimenting with, including my current love. But we usually become friends in spite of it.

My mom was an original, not too comfortable with being a mom. She nurtured me by exposing me to new ideas and letting me be myself. For her time, she was progressive. I like women like that—high-minded, singular in their own right. My ideal love would be a perfect human being, with no flaws and no messy emotions. And one day I'll find her, right?

MOON IN PISCES MAN

It's a bit embarrassing to me, really, to let anyone know how sensitive I really am. Especially women. I'm afraid they won't understand—or they'll think I'm a wimp. So I hide how scared I am. If I let them know how much I need to know that I'm loved, how sweet I can be, they could hurt me. It's hard for me to let a woman get close. This has something to do with my mother. I'm sure she was a really hurt person, kind of a martyr. She was into helping others before helping herself. There was something magical about her touch.

She had the ability to put fantasy or imagination into the air. She saved me and I saved her.

I have a vision of the perfect romance. My lady will be someone who can inspire me and help me—an angel, an artist, a healer like a nurse. Sometimes I'm drawn to a woman with a problem. Life's wounded birds attract me. That's because I know I can heal them. Or they can heal me. Something magic happens. It's transformative because we need each other so much.

I crave relationships that are so beautiful they're painful. Then I can soar to the heights. There's always a spiritual element in my feelings. I know I'm unreliable at times but it's because I'm so moody. It's hard for anyone to understand just how intense my dreams and fantasies about love are and how agonizing it is for me when reality crushes my vision of the way things should be. Then I need to withdraw from the uncaringness and crudeness of the world. Escape. To nature, art, music, drinking, or drugs. When I've had a few drinks, I can act *macho*. It's easier to hide my sensitivity and not feel as intensely as I usually do. My sensitivity can make me sick physically. Is there anyone who'll truly understand me?

chapter seventeen

ASTROSCRIPTS FOR THE ASCENDANT

The ASCENDANT is who you are,

Near or far.

It's your Place in Time and

Space, only yours.

It shows in your face!

Others will always know,

Even if you don't tell it so.

ARIES ASCENDANT WOMAN

I'm one of the most enthusiastic people you'll ever meet. That's the first thing everyone notices about me. No matter what, I'm all for it. Whether it's a simple task like cooking dinner or a major one like running a corporation, I'll be the most gung-ho woman around. I champion causes and fight for what's right. I love the action, the sense of aliveness, the speed. Whatever I undertake, I do with zeal and involvement. I'm a warrior woman at heart, with courage to spare. I move fast, and I suffer fools impatiently despite my habit of rushing into situations without thinking. I'm always first, whether it's finishing my dinner and getting my coat, or picking up new ideas and trends. When I want to get somewhere, get out of my way! I want new ventures to invest my energy in. I cut through a crowd faster than anyone, in high heels, if necessary.

I'm not afraid to battle for my beliefs, and when I believe in something, I go for it. Competition is my style. I'm something of a jock even if I wear lace undies. With all my femininity, I'm still macho in my own way even though I know how to use those feminine wiles as weapons in my personal arsenal. I love a good fight, but I'm never mean. I just like stimulation.

I'm exciting to be around because I have ideas and I'm not afraid to put them into action. I'm straightforward and direct, and that goes for romance as well as business. I *hate* game-playing. Subterfuge is not my style. I like all the cards on the table. I know what I want and I'm not shy about making the first move.

When I see a man I like, I'll risk rejection and call him first. Win some, lose some, that's my attitude. It hurts if I'm rebuffed, but life goes on. Sure, I love being pursued and courted, but he has to catch me unawares. I'll run into his arms, then realize that I've jumped too soon and run out again. But if he takes care of me (something he'll have to fight me to do), I'll turn into a lamb. At least until I'm on the move again.

TAURUS ASCENDANT WOMAN

I'm an Earth Mother, no doubt about it. I don't go rushing into things I don't understand. First I take a good, long look at the lay of the land. Then I think about it in my innards, slowly and cautiously. I even *like* waiting! No problem. When I take my time, which I always do, I keep myself and those around me from going off the deep end. Stay calm is always my advice. I can always figure a sensible way out of any situation that I have to deal with. Sensible, from the top of my head to the tips of my toes, that's me. I've got a lot of energy because I don't waste it on frivolous nonsense and dashing about for no reason. I've always got something in reserve, in my pocketbook and in my body. I seldom exhaust myself, for I like to conserve my personal energies just as much as I like to conserve my financial resources.

I like things to be solid, especially bank accounts. As "diamonds are a girl's best friend"—my possessions are investments. My clothes are of the best cut and fabric my budget will allow. I buy the best because I expect it to last for years. I enjoy giving gifts, spending time and thought on them. The things I give are a piece of *me*.

I'm not just materialistic. I'm sensuous, and I like the opposite sex—so much so that I prefer male pets! My animals love me to stroke them. So do my friends and lovers. I give great touch. My voice is one of my best assets, and I use it both to soothe and to flirt. My skin is another one of my best features, smooth and fine. And very sensitive.

Men respond to my femininity but I don't feel like the weaker sex. I am a grounding force for my family and friends. It comes with the Earth Mother territory. I like a complex, charismatic man with strong feelings and strong arms. I'm a traditionalist in love and romance.

GEMINI ASCENDANT WOMAN

You'll never guess *my* age! I'm one of the youngest-looking women you'll ever meet. Certain men adore that because they appreciate a young-looking woman, no matter what her actual age. I'm fascinating because I know a lot and I love to talk about it all. In fact, talk is my major way of relating to people, even people I've just met. I'm a regular broadcaster. If you want to get the news out, it's telephone, telegraph, and tell me. There's hardly a waking moment you won't find me in discussion about something—anything, I don't care what; you name it, I'll talk about it. I analyze everything from every different angle just for the fun of playing with the information and the ideas. I love gossip and I'd make a wonderful gossip columnist.

Frivolous? Of course! That's what makes it so much fun. It's vital information about people, but who can take it seriously? Not me. Here today and gone tomorrow. In an hour they'll forget all about it. I forget about it the moment it's said and go on to the next tidbit. It's all grist for the mill and no harm meant. Life is meant to be light and playful, butterflies of the mind. The more the merrier. I can juggle a dozen ideas at a time and will add any others that seem interesting. Just so long as it's not *boring*. Boredom is the pits—a slow, agonizing death. I may seem cool and distant to some, but I pride myself on my objectivity. You may think me not involved, but that's because it's the information that turns me on. I just love to bat the words around, like Ping-Pong balls. It's a game.

I may appear to be the social butterfly—nothing more than a slick talker—but I do have a deeper side. I'm looking for something to believe in. I have collected and analyzed so much information that it's hard for me to believe in anything, even love. After all, there's always *another* point of view. And so I shoot the breeze. Who else could move fast enough to shoot the breeze? Mentally, that is.

My ideal man is smart *and* funny. He gives me room to move and keeps up with my multitudinous ideas. He likes to talk as much as I do and he enjoys verbal sparring. But, guess what? When I fall in love words desert me. Then I understand faith, pure and simple.

CANCER ASCENDANT WOMAN

I'm not the easiest person to deal with because my emotions tend to flare up unexpectedly. I'm very romantic about everything, and my feelings are always on the surface. I like to take care of others in any situation that arises, but sometimes I get flustered, especially if I feel insecure or my family is involved. Self-preservation is a big issue with me, and the impact of the immediate environment on me always affects me personally, even if it isn't meant to. If it rains on my parade, I feel that the heavens have a grudge against me. Perhaps this is why I'm always sympathetic in my approach to any situation. I know how hurtful things can be, and my feelings act as a powerful antenna to guide me through anything. I literally "feel" my way, especially in an unfamiliar or threatening situation. I do get very emotional and subjective, and this affects my attitude and how I respond.

I always want to protect myself and remain secure, no matter what, and this sometimes makes me seem selfish, but I also nurture and take care of others, once I myself feel comfortable. In fact, I can be very creative and enterprising when I don't feel threatened and my emotions aren't being stirred up. I get others into their feelings in a good way, and I can be extremely persistent and even tenacious, which makes me strong in a quiet way.

I'm always indirect and never approach a problem head-on. People make fun of my "intuition," but then they are always a little bit shamefaced when it turns out I'm right. Emotional issues are the most important to me: what I'm feeling, what others are feeling. I express my emotions freely, and in any social situation I initiate the feeling tone for the entire group.

My ideal man has his life together, is good father material, and can give me the security I crave. I'm a sentimental fool, a dyed-in-the-wool romantic. I like the old-fashioned way, with engagement rings, family traditions, and church weddings. I have a strong nesting instinct, and people feel wonderful in my environment.

LEO ASCENDANT WOMAN

I'm a born queen and I know it. There is nothing shy or retiring about me. I fuss with myself a lot, take good care of my health, exercise, watch my vitamins and minerals. It's not that I expect to live forever, I just want to. I like things to be dramatic and larger than life, and I'll expend a lot of effort to make them so. I'm a powerful woman, with a big ego and a big heart. A grand dame. I'd be a wonderful opera diva if I could sing! The stage is my favorite fantasy, with me right at the center of it, but anywhere will do as long as I can be creative and dramatic and put on a show, even if it's only in my own home. I like to dress well and with style, and I admit I like having the money to do it with. Money means a lot to me, not because I'm materialistic, but because I want to be able to indulge my tastes in a high standard of living.

Even though I tend to be flamboyant, I never lose my dignity. I'm like the cat that accidentally falls off the table and hits the floor looking as if she'd planned just that effect, yawning and then delicately licking a paw, but watching closely to see if anyone interpreted her fall as a loss of dignity. My home is my castle, and I don't let anything bother me when I'm there. It's my refuge. I'm vulnerable to rejection and rebuff, but I almost never show it. I just go home and lick my wounds in privacy.

Since I'm creative, I'm attracted to whatever gives me the opportunity to express myself. I enjoy pooling my talents with intelligent and ingenious friends.

My ideal man is a unique individual who doesn't kowtow to others. He isn't threatened by me and appreciates that I stand out in a crowd. I may appear to be immune to criticism, but I'm actually very tender and I can get moody and upset. He understands and knows that praise and admiration soothe me. He tells me I'm wonderful. And I do the same for him. It takes two to tango.

VIRGO ASCENDANT WOMAN

Remember the white glove test? I'm the one who invented it! If there's a speck of dust, I'll see it and comment on it. Oh, it's not that I'm critical—I just can't help seeing all the little details and minor imperfections. If there's a loose thread on your suit, or a run-to-be snag in your stocking, I'll see it and tell you about it. Only trying to be helpful, of course. I'm very mental and analytical, a real systems analyst no matter the topic. No detail escapes my notice. My success comes from my care for the fine points so often overlooked by sloppy people.

I'm naturally frugal, but I sometimes overspend on fine, beautiful things. I like beauty in my life as long as it has a practical application. Sometimes I swing back and forth between penny-pinching and extravagance. I'm resourceful, creative, and analytical in my mental processes. I don't waste words and I choose mine with precision. A well-turned phrase is music to my ears. In my home, everything has a place and everything stays in its place. I can't stand disorder of any kind. And though I'm frugal, I'm generous. I provide for my loved ones and teach them about the higher virtues.

My first response to any situation is to analyze it, breaking everything down and examining it minutely. If there's a problem, I find the solution. But I rarely put myself forward, even when I know I'm right. I practice the simple virtues of cleanliness and attention and try to be helpful and kind.

I'm attracted to the idealistic type of man with a tender, dreamy nature who can sweep me away by tapping the pure romantic inside my modest exterior. He is sensitive enough to recognize that it takes only one small detail—like forgetting to buy the candles for the birthday cake—to ruin a big event. He recognizes the specialness of the moment and is savvy enough to know it's my attention to all the fine details that made it happen.

LIBRA ASCENDANT WOMAN

I want to know you. That's my initial response to any social situation. The ladylike response. I'm a lady first and foremost, even if that's not in style. Being sweet isn't a crime, and because I have a good mind I can also be very analytical. This helps me maintain a balance that I need because I am so sensitive to issues of fairness. I go out of my way to be fair and nice. In fact, I approach my entire life with the ideas of grace, charm, refinement, and harmony in mind. I dress well and have a good sense of color. My natural good taste makes me classy, and I can choose just the right accessories for any outfit, no matter how limited my budget. It's my artistic response.

Sometimes I'm indecisive, but that's only because I am so concerned with finding the perfect solution to anything, whether it's accessories for a dress or the answer to a political problem involving injustice. It's hard for me to deal with any kind of strife, and I have a built-in barometer that measures all sides of a social situation and warns me if discord is in the making. Then I mediate, if I can, to restore the balance. I seek harmony and peace in all things, and that makes me diplomatic. Any kind of negativity is stressful to me and I can't bear ugliness, physically or emotionally. I avoid these at all costs, even if the cost is a compromise that negates my own needs.

Partnerships are crucial to me, whether romantic or not, and I suffer greatly when any of my relationships aren't going well. If not romantically involved, I'm always seeking the perfect partner or the ideal marriage. I vacillate between a liking for a strong man who's on the macho side and the sensitive, artistic type. I can't bear to be alone. I'll go the whole nine yards to avoid it despite my refined sensibilities. I am always willing to discuss problems and work out reasonable, fair solutions. Unless someone becomes abusive, I take the gentle, graceful, considerate way.

SCORPIO ASCENDANT WOMAN

I'm aware of the fact that I have very strong energy around me—although it's sometimes more negative than I would like. People just seem to react to me so strongly, even if I didn't mean to put anything out. In fact, they either love me or hate me on sight. There's no in between. Maybe they pick up on the fact that very little escapes my notice. I can't help seeing the underside of things, the little nuances of interaction, the subtleties, the veiled glances. I *know* things.

My first response is to hold back. I watch and wait, checking things out. I'm opinionated and I have strong feelings. When I do express myself, it's often too much for most people. So I've learned to control myself.

Life is a mystery to be unraveled and I'm good at the unraveling. But I want to be appreciated as a mystery, also. This is probably why people always think I'm sexy even when I'm not in the least coming on to anyone. Often I don't say much at first, but I like to be seen as charismatic, fascinating, a depth to be plunged into. I definitely don't like being obvious about it though. I like to let my magnetism *happen*.

I'm aware of *power* in the world and I respect it. I'm even a little in awe of it because it makes me feel my own power. And I need a man who has equal power. If he's less than I am, he'll be intimidated. I hate being intimidating, but it's hard for me to avoid. Most men are afraid of me.

A man needs to challenge me. I've got to feel I've met my match—otherwise, I'll make mincemeat of him even if I don't mean or want to. It just happens. Admiration turns me on—but I have to know it's *real*. I can spot a phony a mile off. Because of all this, I'm wary when I first meet people. I wish I could be easy and relaxed, but I can't. Not until I realize that they're fascinated by me.

SAGITTARIUS ASCENDANT WOMAN

Hi! Nice to meet you! What's up? I'm a friendly sort of person who's always got a smile on her face, even if it's raining. I like to get a handle on the big picture, whatever it is, whether it's the PTA conference or a sales pitch I've got to give. And I like to develop a theory to fall back on. I enjoy philosophizing and talking about ideas. I'm always interested in what others have to say, as long as it is intelligent and humorous. I like to have a good time with everything I do, even work. Unusual people especially attract me—maybe they are artistic or from a foreign country. Friends are important and I have a lot of them I've known a long time.

My eyes are always on the stars. I like to contemplate what's at a distance, what's higher up so to speak. Though I think ideas need a practical application, I want to let my mind roam free, for that's the best way to encourage my creativity to come out and play. At home, I take it easy, and I like my solitude and privacy. That's because I work hard and play hard, and then I need a retreat.

Beauty and artistry are important to me, but I want to get paid well for what I do. Money makes the world go round, and it is also the means to go round the world. I love to travel, the farther the better. I learn and experience that way and deepen my philosophical outlook. Meeting new and different people excites me.

I'm the original "cockeyed optimist," for I know there's always sunshine after the rain. Often there's a rainbow to boot! I can always see the good in any situation, no matter how bad it seems. I'm flexible and friendly, keeping my options open—especially in the romance department. Talk to me and turn me on to new things but don't fence me in. I want a man who expands my horizons. I can be downright aggressive when I'm attracted, and I don't hesitate to initiate sex, which is a form of play, and I love to play! Life is a great adventure and I want to be in on whatever is free-spirited and adventurous.

CAPRICORN ASCENDANT WOMAN

I like things to be well-organized and neat, whether it's my home or my office. Discipline is important to me, because that's how I get things done. I'm not afraid of hard work, I welcome it. Everything I do is geared to achieve a specific result, whether I'm baking a cake for the PTA bake sale or organizing a press conference for the introduction of a new product line. I don't do things in a hurry. I'm a firm believer that "haste makes waste," and I don't waste anything— not my time, not my energy. I take life seriously, and I take myself seriously. I'm ambitious and out to accomplish firm goals even though I work well financially in group endeavors. I'm very innovative at everything I do, and I can turn my hand to making money off my unusual ideas.

I'm a good manager and I can handle several jobs at once, whether it's icing a cake and cooking a roast or getting out a report while planning for a conference. I don't shirk from anything. You can depend on me to get the job done, no matter how long it takes. I have staying power. And I'm efficient. I get on well with my fellow workers because I am considerate of their needs and abilities. It's not my feminine wiles but my constructive attitude that makes me a good supervisor. People respect me.

I may appear austere and aloof at times, but I have strong emotions and when I get emotionally attached to a man, I'm very tenacious. The problem is that with my strength I tend to attract men who are emotionally dependent. I'm just your standard-issue Earth Mother, I guess. I can't help it. I have lots of friends who are powerful and influential because I like to surround myself with success. Weak individuals—except sometimes lovers—don't appeal to me. I'm told my aspirations are too high, but what you don't reach for you can't get, right? As the poet said, "Ah, but a man's reach should exceed his grasp, / Or what's a heaven for?"

AQUARIUS ASCENDANT WOMAN

I work and function best as part of a group, whether it's a civic or community group or a task force. I have a real talent for group activities, and I can be original and creative within them. I want to make a major—but unique—contribution to the common good. At the same time, I'm out to have a good time. I'm a fun-lover, a "people person," and I'm always friendly and social. When I find myself in a new or strange situation, I always fall back on my natural friendliness and sociability to get me through. I'm the one who will see that everyone is introduced to everyone else. But I do it in an impersonal way. Sometimes, I'm accused of being cold, but it's only my natural modesty and reserve. I don't like to be in the spotlight. I'm more interested in the group and being a part of that. Even if I want to be unique in my contribution, I don't want more than my share of the applause. I have a circle of close friends with whom I share a philosophical detachment. We do things together, usually for some cause or other.

I'm not too careful with money, but I always seem to manage. I love beautiful things but I rarely go overboard. My home is important to me, and I do enjoy creating an elegant personal environment. I like music and art, and at home I can feel very grounded in my own surroundings.

I'm not the most passionate woman in the world, because I get really involved with my intellectual pursuits and I like intelligent companionship above all else. Sometimes my lovers turn into friends and then we have a sort of brother-sister relationship, which is generally fine with me. The more extreme emotional patterns repel me, and I prefer not to get involved with all that emoting all over the place. I'd rather keep it cool and intellectual, for I like to analyze. Also, I'm often surrounded by people—so it's hard to get too intimate. Which I avoid anyway.

PISCES ASCENDANT WOMAN

I like to draw and paint and write poetry, even if only in my head. Sometimes I fantasize about being a famous poet, but it doesn't matter really. What matters is just thinking about it and dreaming about it. And I love music of all kinds, but the music of strings especially appeals to me. So romantic! I love romance, with a man or just by myself. I enjoy the romantic in all things, be it a novel or an idea. I need to be inspired to be at my best, and I seek inspiration wherever I go and from whatever I do. I like to travel for inspiration, and I sometimes find it in religious or philosophical causes. Once I take up a cause, I can be full of zeal and my shy nature vanishes. I'll even go on protest marches for what I believe in and support and risk confrontation.

Though I'm sensitive and creative, spiritual and kind, I can be bossy with my co-workers because my self-sacrificing ways give me a feeling of superiority over them. I usually am attracted to a job or profession that requires some kind of personal sacrifice, like working long or odd hours or doing menial or unpleasant tasks. I'm service-oriented and I have to watch that I don't exhaust myself in taking care of others' needs, even if it's my job. I could be a victim of burn-out. That's because I get so personally involved, and my empathetic nature almost turns me into the suffering person so that I feel the pain myself.

To escape from my own sensitivity and to recover from sensing the pains of others, I like to drink or get high. Then I can float in my own peaceful world where there is no ugliness, no pain, no frustra-tion—where everything is lovely and dreamy. I need a man who can understand this about me, but who will also be more practical than I am and see to it that the details of everyday life—like food in the fridge and clean towels—are taken care of. I tend to forget them. But the world needs us dreamers, too. Wouldn't it be dreary if no one ever dreamed?

ARIES ASCENDANT MAN

I'm a dragon-slayer. I identify with the knights in shining armor who slew dragons and rescued fair damsels. I take the initiative, plunge into life, and don't bother to look both ways—or even one way. Sometimes, I don't look at all, I just go. "Fools rush in where angels fear to tread"—that's yours truly. I'm the fool, not the angel, because I'm not afraid of anything. Well, maybe I would be if I didn't act so fast that I didn't have time to think about being afraid. Or much else, for that matter. Action is my game. And I go with and for the action. I'm an honorable guy with a pure heart, and I have faith that this and right intentions will carry me through the fray. I'm always on the side of the angels.

Whatever needs doing, I go and do it. I'm a real starter person. I may not finish all the things that I start, because I'm so full of ideas, and sometimes I just have to rush off in another direction following another idea before the last one gets finished. I leave it for others to follow up, when my dust settles. Like the knight of old on the charger, I charge. Ahead. I never look back. You may think me selfish or insensitive, but that's only because I go for what I want in a very direct manner. Enthusiasm describes me. There's excitement and joy in living, and I make things happen. Some call me pushy, but I'm really just someone who's involved. When I get into my ideas I forget the other people around me in the heat of the moment.

I go for the Clint Eastwood scenario. You know—lots of action and the lone hero whips the hell out of the bad guys. But it turns out he's deeply sensitive. He does it all to rescue an abandoned kid or to bring back law and order to the simple folk who were terrorized by bandits. Love and life are a great big adventure to me, mentally and physically. When I'm attracted to a woman, I come on strong. I pursue her and win her with my energy and ardor. She can be soft or she can be strong, but she has to appreciate my enthusiasm as I charge ahead, attaining my goals and blazing new trails.

TAURUS ASCENDANT MAN

"What's the hurry?" is the question I'm always asking. I don't like to rush or be rushed into things, especially when I've just encountered them. I like to take my time and size up the situation before I make my move, whether it's at a business conference or when I meet a new woman. Mr. Slow-and-Easy, that's me. I play a waiting game because I like to keep things calm. And all this rushing around that most people do doesn't get them anywhere. They'd be better advised to cool their jets and see what the situation merits before taking any definite action. When I do make my move, I like it to produce some form of concrete results. People call me materialistic, and I suppose I am, but what else is there? You can't *eat* talk and air! If food on the table and a roof over your head is materialistic, then I'm materialistic.

I'm into making money because I like to shore up against the proverbial rainy day. Proverbs can tell you a lot—even though so-called sophisticated people think them clichés. But "a penny saved" really *is* "a penny earned," and if that penny is well-invested it may earn two pennies. I proceed with caution and circumspection. Nobody can accuse *me* of rushing in where angels fear to tread. My energy is constant, like a well-banked fire, and I don't waste it needlessly on emotional displays or unnecessary actions. Conservation is my middle name. I've always got something in reserve, in the bank and in my body.

I don't change my mind readily, so I'm considered stubborn. But I'm the man they call when they need a shoulder and broad chest to lean on. People rely on my strength and calm.

I like to be the man and have my woman lean on me. I want her to be traditional, for I'm conventional in love and romance. I appreciate the beautiful and the sensual. I like comfort and things good to the touch. I'm a hugger and a lover, reliable and steady. Under my tough mask I'm a very sensual, very tender guy.

GEMINI ASCENDANT MAN

Come fly with me! If I seem youthful, and I do, it's because I'm a flyer at heart. My mind is my vehicle, my own personal star ship. In it, I take off and investigate the outer limits. Then I come back to earth and tell everyone who will listen what I've discovered. There are those who accusingly call me a Peter Pan, who say that I don't want to grow up. Maybe they aren't wrong, after all. Who really wants to grow up? It's so dull being grown-up. And boring. Boring is the worst and I'll do anything to get away from it. Mostly, how I do this is to go out and gather information, of all kinds, from any source. I'm an information monger. I get it and I give it out. I could be a terrific journalist, or a talk-show host. As long as there's talking involved, I'd be good at it: public relations, hype, talking to people and getting them listening, then getting them talking to get another story to pass on. It's all people information. Call it gossip. Who could take it seriously? Not me. I'm already gone, on to the next bit of vital statistics, and yesterday is an old story. So is an hour ago. I live in the now.

Life is quicksilver. It runs and sparkles all over the place. I don't try to pin it down and I hate being pinned down. I can work a room like no one you ever saw, because it's natural for me to mix it up with people and situations. My cleverness is a good tool but I don't like to stay in one place for long. I need to circulate. It keeps me young. In spite of my light-footed ways, I'm a skeptic.

I might be too busy reading about all sorts of relationships to actually be in one, but I have the ability to handle several at once because I value versatility and change. The lady who will win my heart permanently will have to be able to match wits with me, keep my mind stimulated, and talk to me as much as I talk to her. I can get caught by a love that lets me soar heavenward while still keeping me connected. Then I can be a believer.

CANCER ASCENDANT MAN

I find direction by indirection. I'm probably one of the most indirect people you'll ever meet. I rarely go head on into a new situation. I like to feel my way first. My emotions are usually right there on the surface and I get upset easily, especially when I feel threatened or misunderstood. That's why I'd rather be in a position of authority than not. Then I can use my feeling nature to make the right decisions. I like to nurture people, and when I feel secure in my position, I can do it well. But first I always have to protect myself. This can result in a subjective attitude that's not always good. My feelings, when agitated or aroused, can get in the way of my judgment. But if I've got a home base, then it's okay.

I'm very good at communications and I can be quite precise in my formulation of just the right phrase. I like to plan my business and vacation trips with care and watch the details. That way I ensure my sense of security and I don't run into too many unfamiliar situations, which tend to upset me emotionally. I love my family, but sometimes my siblings get under my skin and then I can be very critical of them.

My home is important to me and I want it to be beautiful and comfortable, because nurturing myself helps me to keep calm emotionally. And makes me feel secure.

When I'm left to my own devices and people don't come around upsetting me, I'm imaginative and creative. I'm tenacious and stick with a project in spite of my moodiness. My energy comes through feelings, and I often set the feeling tone of a whole group. It's easy for me to sense what others are feeling, because I'm such a feeling person myself.

I'm a romantic and when I fall in love I'm quick to sense her feelings and respond to them. The woman for me is something of a psychic, and she's on the motherly side, loves children and the home. But she has a strong identity also. I need a woman who's organized and together with herself. I want to look dreamily into her eyes, and we are both so sensitive we can communicate without words.

LEO ASCENDANT MAN

I have to admit that my first response to any situation is to dominate it if I can. And I usually can! It's natural for me to rule, or to want to rule. I've got a lot of energy, more than most, and I can come on like Gang Busters when I want to, which is more often than not. This earns me the epithet of "overbearing" at times, but I don't mind. I've got to express myself and I do it the best way I see fit. I don't always wait to be invited, either, before I commandeer center stage. I like to be noticed. There's nothing wrong with that, is there? Of course not. It's just the way I am. I put out good energy, full of fire, and it makes people feel good to be around me. So why shouldn't I ham it up a little if I feel like it?

Don't make the mistake of thinking that I'm selfish. I like teamwork and I even cue my friends in on any good financial deals I get wind of. I don't fool around with my money. I take good care of it. But I'm willing to share with those I care about, give them good advice. That's why I prefer mutual funds. It's a group thing. My feeling is that we're all people, and we're all in this thing called life together, and everybody's a super person in my book until proved otherwise. I think I'm the most terrific, and I think you're the most terrific, and if we get together we can be even more terrific together. Makes sense, doesn't it?

I give off great energy and I pamper those I love. I'm romantic and generous and my parties are the best! I'll spend my last cent to do it up so everyone will remember forever, because a spectacular evening is my idea of an intimate gathering! But don't think I'm not a serious person. Work is important to me. I play hard, but I work equally hard, and I know my business well. I aim to be a big success, in love as well as my career.

My ideal woman has style, class, and presence. She's a real standout in a crowd and she doesn't take any guff from me or anyone else. She's herself all the time—elegant and real.

VIRGO ASCENDANT MAN

Some people think I'm a fuss-budget, but that's okay by me. I know what I'm doing and I know that what I do is important in its own light, even if others think that the "details" don't matter. They do, and no one knows this better than I. In fact, it's my precise attention to details that has made me a success. Perfection is my goal, and no fine point escapes my notice. There aren't any flaws in my work, not because I'm better than the other guy, but because I pay close attention to all those little details. And I enjoy doing it. A job done well is a job I can be proud of putting my name to. In my book, quality is top, and quantity comes afterward.

Maybe I'm too serious for some tastes, but I have an earthy side too and I can tell a dirty joke as well as the next man. I just don't advertise myself. I'm modest and retiring. My goal is to be helpful and ready to get the job done, not to hog the limelight and blow my own horn. There are plenty enough hornblowers out there. I pride myself on quiet efficiency, on being organized, on my perfectionism. Look, what's the point in doing something wrong when you can do it right with a little care? If it's done wrong, it only has to be done over again. My mental processes never stop, even though I don't make a great display. I'm always analyzing everything.

This tendency of mine to analyze can become over-analyzing, and this I know. Because of my analytical nature and my love of cleanliness, I can seem to be prudish about sex and the functions of the body, but in reality I'm a highly sexed guy. It's just that I'm serious about my pleasures as I'm serious about everything I do, and I want it to be as perfect as possible. I work hard at everything, even sex. My partner is important to me, though I frequently get involved with women who aren't very well organized and then I can help them to get organized. I enjoy that.

LIBRA ASCENDANT MAN

I'm the perfect gentleman and this doesn't embarrass me in the slightest. My first response in social situations is a concern with propriety. I do what is proper and I'm always gracious. As a person of refinement, I'll always want to know what you think. It's only good manners to do so and good manners come from being sensitive and responsive to others' needs and wants. A gentleman can anticipate this and act on it. These qualities make me diplomatic and fair. That's why I take care to dress well and in good taste—nothing loud or boisterous, including after-shave. Quiet refinement is what I favor.

I'm like the kid standing in the middle of the seesaw, trying to get it to balance perfectly. First I swing one way, then the other, seeing both sides of the question. It's hard to get in the perfect middle with nothing swaying in either direction, but I try hard to remain objective and rational. Disharmony makes me miserable, whether it is physical or emotional. When my instincts tell me strife is brewing, I step in to mediate and set things right again. Compromise is my middle name, and I don't like to deliberately provoke anyone, ever. I'm a regular "good guy," which is a mixed blessing. Sometimes I go so far out of the way to avoid a scene that I end up creating one by avoiding issues that need to be resolved. My desire for "peace at any price" has its drawbacks.

Relationships are extremely important to me and I'm at my best in partnerships. I suffer terribly when any relationship is in trouble and I work hard to fix it. Even if I am not in a relationship, I always have the ideal one in view and I go searching for my perfect complement. I feel incomplete without someone with whom to share my life. Romantic courtship is my style and I like to do it in the loveliest possible surroundings.

SCORPIO ASCENDANT MAN

I'm not an easy guy to understand or to get a handle on. That's because I'm naturally secretive and hidden inside myself. I don't go around slopping out my innards on all and sundry. I keep myself to myself. That's because I'm always on the alert—for danger, for sexual opportunities. I can intimidate a roomful of people without even trying, just by my intense attitude and air of mystery. I'm the "tall, dark, handsome stranger" even if I'm a 5-foot, 5-inch blonde. It's my aura. Comes with the territory. My eyes are the fix. I can stare down anyone without a flicker of a blink. It's evident to anyone with whom I come in contact that I'm out to accomplish my goals, whatever they are. I don't fool around. My objectives are fixed, and I put all my energy behind getting them achieved. I have within me hidden sources of strength and power that I can draw on at will. Most people don't know about these things, and that gives me a considerable edge. But I keep quiet about it most of the time.

Money isn't a problem for me, because I understand intuitively how these things work. Money multiplies in my hands, and it's rarely an issue. This may be because I'm circumspect. I don't mouth off about my affairs and when I have to put something in writing, I'm careful of what it is and who sees it. I've a well-deserved reputation for secrecy.

Sex is a major influence on me, and it is never very far from my thoughts. In spite of my sexual orientation, I can be sentimental when I'm in love, even selfless. I give of myself, and I'm very deep. This deepness makes me a hard worker. I'm an original thinker and a self-starter. I get a lot done in a short time because I'm efficient and I take charge. I'll help the other guy out, but I then expect him to learn and carry on on his own. Wealthy women find me attractive, and all women are fascinated by my interests in mystery and supernatural events, séances in particular. As Shakespeare said, "There are more things in heaven and earth . . . than are dreamed of. . . ."

SAGITTARIUS ASCENDANT MAN

I'm a friendly person, and I consider myself an optimist. I like to look at the big picture and enjoy myself in so doing. My goals are all large in scale—the smaller things don't interest me. Although I'm usually in a good mood, I confess that I'm rather preoccupied with my own thoughts and projects. Usually I can convince others of my way of thinking, and that's always to my advantage. It's not that I'm devious, for I'm open and aboveboard, but I do have the ability to inspire others with my "infectious optimism." And, when inspired, they just naturally do things my way.

Despite my capacity to see the big picture, I don't miss the financial details. Actually, I'm practical about money and how it's spent, as well as ambitious to accumulate it. I like durable goods and things that have lasting value. I have a practical nature, and although most of my many ideas come to me in flashes of intuition, I can almost always find a practical application for them. I pride myself on being progressive, but I don't throw the baby out with the bathwater. Those ideas that have stood the test of time are welcome in my scheme. Maybe I'm such a practical guy because my family's the other way around. My siblings are downright peculiar—if and when I see them. Which is why I keep my home as peaceful and quiet as possible. I need my privacy.

I can be an original thinker, and I'm good at conceptualizing. Though I'm basically a free spirit, I like to have a theoretical base from which to take off. At heart, I'm a philosopher no matter what I do for a living. I'm careful about my public image, and though I'm independent in my ways, I don't let that interfere with my professional standing.

I'm not much of a romantic, but I've got a roving eye. I can be downright aggressive when I see someone I like, and if she agrees I am very passionate and demanding. We can enjoy some vigorous sexual play together. But I need versatility in my love affairs. So I'm really a loner.

CAPRICORN ASCENDANT MAN

I take life seriously, work hard, and expect to get ahead. Everything I do has a purpose, and I go about things in a systematic and organized way. I'm not in a hurry. There's plenty of time to get everything done, especially if one has self-discipline, which I do. Whatever I do has a practical end in mind, otherwise what's the point? I'm not the most cheerful of men, I admit that, but then the serious-minded rarely are comedians. They see reality and reality isn't funny. It's damned hard work.

Being serious doesn't mean being mentally stodgy. Not at all. Actually, I'm quite a creative thinker and I make money in original ways, usually through group endeavors. I'm a company man as a rule, maybe an inventor, and I can achieve financial success through innovative ideas. Sometimes these ideas come from flashes of intuition. Even though I'm essentially practical minded, I don't downplay intuition, because I've seen it work for me. That's why I like to work alone. It gives more room for these things to happen. I like to plan and plan well, to organize my thoughts and ideas before I tell them to others. That way I don't get distracted. Consistency is important to me, and even if I'm not a lawyer I have a legal mind. I'm a good researcher, and I like to see my work realized in a structured way that is socially appropriate.

I can be quite romantic, but I tend to be a bit aggressive at home and sometimes there are emotional upsets and arguments. But my love and affection are constant, even if we fight on occasion. Whatever my status in life, I want my children to rise higher and enjoy the good things. I like to have well-appointed surroundings for myself and I appreciate fine dining, art, music, and a cultivated environment.

My emotions are strong, and when I get attached, I stay attached. Because I'm a strong person, I do tend to attract the emotionally dependent, and this can cause me problems. But I can handle them.

AQUARIUS ASCENDANT MAN

I function best in a group situation. My first response is always to be friendly and social, even though I'm also different and unusual.

A humanitarian at heart, I'm always looking for ways to contribute to the common good, and usually I feel the best way to do that is through group endeavors. I'm a "people person," and though I really like people and working for the commonweal, I do it in a rather impersonal way. It's the masses that I love, not specific individuals. I enjoy being admired for my personality and my unusualness, and I want to be loved—by the group. If it gets too personal and emotions get involved, then I go the other way. "Keep it cool" is my motto.

Whatever's New Age interests me. The more far out the better. I'm usually lucky with money, though I'm not particularly careful with it. In fact, I'm sometimes not too practical with my funds, but it never seems to matter. The universe provides. What goes around comes around. Go with the flow. I do tend to defend my pet theories and I can get quite argumentative if they are questioned. But what's generated in the heat of combat is new ideas and new avenues of application. So it's all for the good of everybody, which is what I continually strive for.

I don't hog the limelight, because I'd just as soon be one of the gang. I like a close circle of friends with like minds, idealistic and analytical. Detached. If it stays friendly, I stay. If it gets emotional, I split.

Romance is not a big deal to me, but I tend to get involved with ladies who are romantically inclined. As long as they give me my space, it's okay. But if they start trying to dominate me (and, as I said, I'm an easy guy), then there's trouble back at the ranch. I like having a lot of people around me, because I get involved in community and civic affairs, and if my lady resents this she's liable to get left out in the cold. She has to be able to participate in group activities and enjoy them without getting too emotional about it. And she must be intelligent.

PISCES ASCENDANT MAN
I'm a dreamer. I always go with the flow, whatever it is. And I feel out where the flow is going. My first response to any situation is to find out where the currents are leading, and then go with that. My antennae are very sensitive, and I can almost read other people's thoughts. I pick up on the subtleties around me in the environment and act on that, sometimes without even knowing why. I just do it. Sunsets, moonlight on water, the evening coming on, the night sky with stars winking—these things can put me into a trance. Especially if I'm having a few drinks. Then I can just stare out at the apparent

nothingness and see in it a whole other world. I'm poetically and artistically inclined, and I love music whether I make it myself or just listen to it. I can really get carried away with music.

I've an impractical nature, but I'm good at starting money-making projects. I'm always looking for new ways to make money, because I spend impulsively (to excess, I admit) and I'm not too good at dealing with reality. But I can always begin again. Easy come, easy go, as they say. I like the idea of making money out of my artistic endeavors, and I think a lot about that. It takes me a while to get onto something I think will work, but when I do make up my mind, then I stay with that decision. What I change often is where I live. Or I'll live in more than one place and travel between them. Travel, especially over water, inspires me.

My love life is very special to me, and when I find a lady I treat her like a princess. She is always someone very special, unique, deserving to be put on the highest pedestal I can find. I get emotional and sentimental about her, and I like to share tidbits of wonderful food with her, and I don't mind if she has a maternal streak in her. Usually, because I'm not too well organized, I manage to find women who are better at it than I am, and they take over that part of my life. I don't mind. It makes it easier for me to write poetry, or gives me more time to watch the sun set.

chapter eighteen

ASTROSCRIPTS FOR VENUS

VENUS is of Harmony the Queen,
Stern or sweet is all the same—
Bittersweet, her perfumed name.
Love and pleasure she addresses,
With her looks and glamorous tresses.
Know your wants, attend her well.
She knows how to ring your bell.

VENUS IN ARIES WOMAN

I need constant excitement and new outlets for my enthusiasms, of which I've plenty to spare. Whatever is new or avant-garde turns me on. This applies to people as well as things. I like bright colors, lots of sound, great energy, and whatever's conceptually on the cutting edge. That's why I value people with active minds and active lives, dynamic people who challenge me. Their competitive edge is exciting. I tussle about who's first, and I want to win. I like exclusivity and what's unique. I want to be at the source of energy.

When I fall in love, I go off like a rocket—lots of fire and passion simultaneously. If I care, it shows. I give totally and trustingly. I don't play coy games. I'm the original wear-your-heart-on-your-sleeve gal. And why not? How can you find your heart if you don't lose it first? I'm not a wimp in love, I take risks. And I want someone who will push back yet treat me well. Fighting doesn't faze me. A good fight gets my juices going and clears the air like a whiff of smelling salts clears the head. It not only keeps boredom at bay, it lets us start fresh.

A dynamic man is exciting. If he introduces me to new things, so much the better. He should be ambitious and sympathetic to *my* goals and ambitions, demonstrative in his affections, and have a sense of humor. He will have to be strong enough to stand up to me and smart enough to put me first, for I have to be the *first and only woman in his life*. When I fall for him, he's Prince Charming to me. At least in the beginning.

Sure, I'm disappointed when Prince Charming's charm fades and the guy I thought was so dynamic turns out to be a ho-hum experience. That first flush of infatuation often blinds me completely, and I have to come back to everyday realities. When I get bored I pick a fight. Either we start over or I move on. But, if our love remains a constant adventure, we *both* win. And I stay put.

VENUS IN TAURUS WOMAN

My physical environment is important to me. It must be sensual, beautiful, and above all comfortable. I don't go for fanciness—just the natural and simple. Or what's traditional. If I'm conservative, and I am, it is for a good cause. I want what is solid and enduring, be it a piece of furniture or a relationship. My values tend toward the classical. What's new and trendy, the latest fad, just doesn't interest me. Give me what's been proved by time. Touch is my most highly developed sense, and how things feel affects me strongly. I like wonderful textures—silk and velvet, tweeds and leather, and human skin.

The beauties of nature and the pleasures of the table are both parts of life, and they give me much joy. Just give me the basics, thanks. I have common sense and a great need for security, which means I'm very well-grounded. I'm very protective of my surroundings. The same goes for my relationships.

I like to know for sure what's mine, so I'm a committed person. Some say possessive. Once I get into a relationship, I stay. Although I can get really fixated on someone, I don't like to jump into anything too soon. Once I've decided who I want, I am very determined. I will move heaven and earth to get and keep that person.

I can't do without intimacy. I'm very loving and caring. My hugs are the best and I need them returned. I need a solid and dependable man who will be there for me today and all the tomorrows. He has to be affectionate and patient—and *sexual*. If he has money, so much the better. I don't see anything wrong with marrying a rich man. Money is important in this life, don't kid yourself.

I show my love in thoughtful ways, like remembering birthdays and anniversaries and sending gifts with carefully chosen cards. I celebrate with special food, too. I don't flirt and neither should he. I know love is a valuable commodity. I'm in for the long haul. No one's more *there* or better able to weather life's ups and downs.

VENUS IN GEMINI WOMAN

I'd make a great spy. I love intrigue. And collecting information. And wearing disguises. And meeting odd but interesting people who have some tidbit of information to offer me to add to my collection. I keep my life like a variety show, ever changing. I step lightly and keep flexible. My versatility keeps me young and gives me charm. I can talk about anything and usually do. I've a good eye for catching all the fascinating detail and I don't get heavy. My perceptions are mostly mental and come in brilliant flashes of insight.

I'm a social being and you'll find me at occasions where I can circulate, like the air. Parties and openings, games and gatherings— I'll be there stirring things up in my constant battle against boredom. My interests are wide and varied, from baseball to politics, soap opera to grand opera, trivial pursuit to philosophy, fashion trends to gourmet cooking.

I don't deny I'm a flirt. Why not? It's only a game we're playing. Don't pin me down. It kills my feelings. Find the way to my heart through my mind. I'm looking for my ideal love, the man who will take me into the far realms of mind and feeling, where ordinary reality is left behind. And who will still have his feet on the ground. Being versatile is what it's all about. And interesting. He has to be able to pique my interest continually and keep me on my mental toes. A good conversation will turn me on faster than good sex.

I'm an idealist and things are always falling short of my ideal. Maybe that's why I move around so much. It's just so painful when I'm disappointed, so I always keep one eye watching for the ideal man, no matter whom I'm currently with. I hold with a light and sensitive touch and I need the same in return. My man must be able to keep up with my ever-changing nature, laugh at my puns, appreciate my wit, and stay light. "Light" doesn't mean simple. I like life's complexities. They're like a puzzle. And figuring things out keeps me youthful.

VENUS IN CANCER WOMAN

Most of all I want closeness, with my family, my friends, and especially my lover. I'm super-sensitive and very romantic, and sometimes this makes me insecure and very clingy, but it's just the way I am. My feelings are easily hurt and I really need to feel secure with someone I love. I take care of those I love by making them feel secure, because I know how it feels to be insecure and to have your feelings walked all over. My home is terribly important to me and I make it as nice and as cozy as I can, with all sorts of little comforts, good food, and a pleasant atmosphere. I enjoy having my friends and family over for a home-cooked meal. I'd much rather stay home with my lover or my family than go gadding about to public restaurants and nightclubs.

I'm old-fashioned and I admit it without shame or embarrassment. I feel *good* with my traditional things around me—pictures of people I love, mementos of all sorts, personal treasures that may seem irrelevant to others but mean a lot to me. I love children, too, and their childish ways don't bother me a bit. In fact, I like taking care of them, wiping their little faces, comforting them if they skin a knee, washing and petting them. I'm an Earth Mother type underneath, even if I do have a career.

Because I'm so sensitive and I don't want to weep all over people in public, I keep a fairly dignified pose to cover my vulnerability. I know I'm moody and can be unpredictable, so my security is important to me, both financial and emotional.

I want a man who can guarantee me that security, who can be a good, solid provider and father for my children. It would help enormously if he is a romantic and likes the romantic gesture—you know, like bringing flowers and having dinner by candlelight. If he ridicules me and my rather sentimental tastes, I'll be crushed. I bring a lot of imagination to romance as well, even though I tend to express a big part of myself in a maternal way, by taking care of him, remembering the little things he likes, like two spoons of sugar in his coffee. I know when I've met the right man, because I want to introduce him to my mother and I know she'll love him, too.

VENUS IN LEO WOMAN

I'm a bit like the guy who said, "My tastes are simple. I want only the best." Not only the best, but the grandest. Nothing skimpy, please! Shabbiness gets me downright depressed. I like beauty and the best. When I go anywhere, I go first class. Scrimping gives me the willies. My generosity is well-known, and I exercise it with taste and style, as I do all things. Commonness and vulgarity in people or in the environment turn me off.

For me, love is a many-splendored thing, and I give my all to it. Fantasy takes me to the first kiss, the loving embrace, and on to the ideal culmination. Like grand opera, my love life has to be a passionate and dramatic affair of the heart. I must be wined and dined, fawned over and appreciated. But—be warned—I can pick up a false signal a mile off. It must be sincere. I must feel *truly* loved and adored and know the attention is honest, or I wilt or snarl, depending on my mood. Whatever, I will react—and react powerfully. I'm romantic and strong. My feelings are never neutral, they are always larger-than-life. I confess that my pride can step in when I'm hurt. Then I'd die before I'd let anyone know my true feelings.

I can only be happy when my man and I are involved in a deep mutuality. I must see the love light shining in his eyes. I need reassurance. I have to be praised often, and I'll gladly return the favor. The man for me is affectionate and playful. He's strong and noble, with a loyal heart. Whatever he does he's important in some way. He's the best. I want to be the best he's ever had or could imagine having and I want to be told that I am. Because of this, I sometimes fall for a romantic line or my image of us as a couple, staying in an unhappy situation because it looks good to outsiders.

My life's a movie. I'm the writer, director, and star, and my love's my leading man. Together, we can create romance on a grand scale. If our love is true, ours will be the most fabled story ever told.

VENUS IN VIRGO WOMAN

Whatever I do, it's got to be just right. I expect perfection in myself and how I relate to others, and I want the same back. My sense of what should be is very keen, and I do everything thoroughly with great exactness. I know the value of the little things that make the big difference. I'm a very private person and there are many things I keep to myself about. Nothing major, mind you, or secretive, just private. I have my little rituals and they are very important to me. I need my routines and regular habits to stay healthy, and I'm reluctant to share these with others who might not understand. It's the little details that are vital to me, whether it's my special shampoo for washing my hair or my diet of health foods. I'm persnickety about all my ways and I don't want them interrupted by grosser vibrations. Usually I prefer what is traditional, but, even if that's not the case, I live my personal life-style with exactness and purity.

Love isn't easy for me because everything has to be right. I have a clear sense of what should be and I know precisely what kind of man I want. I know how he dresses and the kind of mind he will have. What he does is less important than *how* he does it. He must have a sense of craftsmanship about his work, be intelligent and sincere. Integrity goes a long way with me. My love is true and a man has to respect that. He must be personally fastidious. No dirty fingernails, please.

He's got to know how to court a woman the old-fashioned way, but underneath my prim and proper facade, there beats a passionate heart that longs to be swept off her feet by romance. When the situation is right, I'm very earthy. Once burned, I'd rather be alone for a time than compromise my ideals. I know how to wait. In love, I'm finely tuned to exactly what makes my man happy. I take care of my lover, and others too. Sometimes I get hooked on people who need me and they use me. Since I'm always willing and unafraid to work on the nitty-gritty in a relationship, we can eventually make it right.

VENUS IN LIBRA WOMAN

Sharing is what I'm all about. I like good conversation and artistic pursuits, and I make my lovely home a place for genteel social gatherings where people can communicate and really talk together in gracious surroundings. I gravitate naturally to the good, the true, and the beautiful, whether it's in art or in people. Whatever is graceful and charming attracts me, in the environment or in personalities. Relationships of all kinds take my attention, and I love to discuss them. When there's a problem, I'm good at working out compromises. The whole idea of relationship intrigues me, including the idea of polarity—that we are two halves of the same whole or two sides of the same coin. How things balance out or complement each other interests me, and I like to talk about it.

Mutuality is very important and I'm most at home interacting on an intimate level, one-to-one. Good manners are the core of intimacy, and it's important that intimates treat each other well. This helps keep the balance. If things get out of balance, I'm the first one to do my fair share to restore it.

I am most myself in a relationship but I can swing back and forth as to how I want to be treated. Sometimes, it's the hearts-and-flowers approach—other times, it's the intellectual and rational. No matter what, I am always considerate and cultured. I take pride in myself as a communicator who can talk things out in a peaceful manner.

My ideal man is gentle and refined, cultured and fair. He's also good looking. He understands that in a close relationship it is important to keep the balance between light and dark, sweet and sour. He doesn't like extremes, but he tolerates them when they happen, working with me to restore equilibrium. He doesn't negate the use of sweetness and fair play. He knows, as do I, that relationships take work and discussion, and that just as you have to take the bad with the good, you can take the good with the bad. I love to love. I'm a natural at it. And I always hold up my end of the bargain.

VENUS IN SCORPIO WOMAN

I am a woman of extremes—in my taste, in my sex. I like intricate art with profound themes and dark palettes with murky images. Or the starkness of minimalism or all-white, Japanese severity or high tech. Sometimes I want religious icons around me, things that probe deep into the unconscious. The subject of death fascinates me, as does the possibility of rebirth. I like stories about people being tested in the extreme, of psychic adventures. I even love a good horror tale. And if it involves sex, so much the better. Sex is central to me, whether I'm doing it a lot or not doing it at all. It's always an issue. It's something I take very seriously even when I'm rejecting it, as I can do. For long periods of time. I can go either way, completely. It's all or nothing at all.

I know that sex and love can be the vehicles for transformative experiences, depending on how you use them. For that reason, love is always a danger to me. I can lose myself in my desire to have it take me away and make me over. Kinky or suspicious sex can be a turn-on for me, and I can like it down and dirty. On the other hand, I also go for spiritual sex, where you can have an intense experience without even moving. Whatever I do or however I do it, I know the power of sex, and power is often a theme in my relationships. I can seek revenge when I've been hurt and I've the patience to wait until I get it. Yet, I can also let go entirely of bad feelings.

Love isn't a simple matter for me, and the man I need isn't simple, either. He's intriguing and complex, even if he is the boy next door. He's sexy and in control, maybe slightly dangerous. He sees me as a fascinating puzzle. My depth and the aliveness of my energy field draw him to me. He doesn't flatter me. He senses I don't like superficiality. As I'm suspicious by nature, he's willing to wait for me to be ready to expose my feelings. When it's right, I give my all and let love transform us both.

VENUS IN SAGITTARIUS WOMAN

Whether I talk about it or not, I'm a very spiritual person. No matter what I do for a living, my real quest is to find a philosophy or a religion that I can really believe in and take to my heart. But it has to be one I've worked out for myself, not something that has been crammed down my throat by others. I want my freedom of thought as well as freedom of choice and movement. I like good times and roving, whether it's getting on an airplane for faraway places or just reading about them or studying a foreign language and culture. Anything that will add meaning and growth to my life attracts me. That goes for people as well. I like to meet foreigners and talk to them about their cultures, learn how they do things differently from what I'm used to. And I'm not at all judgmental. I just want to learn.

I like a fairly high style of living, and I'm a spirited woman with good taste. Sometimes I go for the simple and woodsy sort of thing, like camping out, but I can dress to the nines and hit the hotspots as well. It's all an adventure, and I love adventure. I especially like what can teach me something new, even exotic experiences that might put others off—so long as it's fun and open and aboveboard. I hate subterfuge and intrigue and subtlety. I need my space and I give others theirs without question. Nobody ever has to ask me to move over. Some say I'm too generous, "to a fault," but I like giving presents and seeing people react joyfully to a thoughtful gesture.

The man I want has high ideals and high standards. He has a spirit of adventure and takes risks in his life. He's not afraid of the word *god*, whatever that means to him or to me. We don't have to believe the same things, but he's got to be on a spiritual quest of his own or it's no go. Combined with that, he's got to be able and willing to laugh and have fun with me. I can be serious minded, but I want us to have a good time being together, and that includes silly games, laughter, and having fun sexually. Monogamy really isn't my style, but I'm always ethical in my romantic encounters. I never deceive or tease. When it's right, we'll fly away together to some strange land.

VENUS IN CAPRICORN WOMAN

I'm deeply romantic, traditional, and very practical. It's hard for me to show my feelings, and I need someone who can understand the shy and vulnerable side of me underneath all the obvious practicality. I'm sometimes criticized for being too practical because I seem so capable. But I need a man who wants to take care of me, even though I can take care of myself. In fact, it's what I really crave. People don't suspect how I'm longing to feel taken care of.

Reliability is important to me. My ideal man needs to be as reliable as I am. I'm not a starry-eyed type. I have a realistic view of things and I know that relationships need work. If I think the result is worth the effort, then there's no end to the work I'll put into it. I always do my part. Status is another issue with me. I don't say that I must have a relationship with a man who has status in the world at large, but it wouldn't hurt.

People with practical power turn me on. I mean the movers and shakers of the world, not the glitzy stars. Even if my man isn't on that level, he's got to have that kind of inner strength and ability to get things done—and done *well*—even if it's running a gas station. Men who are really together get my juices flowing.

Some people think I'm cold or too businesslike, but they just don't realize that it's my way of showing I care. Also, they'll find out, when they know me better, that once they have proved I can trust them I let down my guard. There's a wonderful part of me that's like a wood nymph—earthy, dancing with the forest sprites to the pipes of Pan. I can even be a little raunchy when it's propitious, but I don't let that out too easily.

Another part of me is very aware of what magic is about. Magic means understanding how to manipulate the material world. I know what it means to be a true magician, whether it's getting by with very little or parlaying a small investment into a large profit. Calculated risks are my home base, and I do that in love, too. Because I truly understand what it means to be *lonely*, I know how to respect another person's deepest inner feelings.

VENUS IN AQUARIUS WOMAN

I'm an eclectic personality and I put myself together from many different sources, from the antique to the futuristic. No one combines things in a more unusual way and gets away with it. I might wear black lace one day and medical scrubs the next. And on the following day I'll mix them together. Whatever's different is my bag, in clothes or in people. The unusual fascinates me, and even if it's really foreign to me I'll be open to it. I'm totally unprejudiced. Race, religion, culture, land of origin, social status, and the like aren't issues for me. I have many friends of all sorts, and I'm one of the best friends I know. All kinds of relationships interest me, at least in theory. I don't think there's any one way to be or live. Monogamy's fine but it isn't natural. Jealousy isn't something I indulge myself in. I just don't believe in it. Maybe that's why I'm a bit shy of intimacy. Too much room there for all kinds of messy and hurtful feelings. They get in the way of our personal growth. Being rational is the only answer.

Freedom is my key word. To most people, love means being tied down, possessed and possessing, but I have a horror of that. It generally degenerates into boredom and I can't stand being bored. Let me fly! I need my space. I'm always on to the next level of experience, and I'll choose the riskier relationship that will give me room over a more stable, conservative one every time. I can't be restricted. I've got to be able to pursue my interests and see my friends.

My man has to be my friend, first and foremost. He can discuss feelings rationally. I've got a lot of the masculine in me, and I want a man who's got a strong feminine side. He doesn't have to be macho to be a real male. Mostly, I find intelligence to be the sexiest quality in any person, male or female. Nice bodies are fine, but a good mind will win out with me. That and openness to new experiences and new ways of doing anything, whether it's sex or dinner. And he gives me space and isn't jealous of my freedom or my friends. Chances are, he's a bit weird. A musician or an artist. We can wear each other's clothes, which are usually unisex anyway.

VENUS IN PISCES WOMAN

Maybe I'm psychic. At any rate, I'm sensitive to the point of being psychic. I know what "transcendence" means, and I can sometimes almost read minds. What I do is just flow into feelings, my own and others', and this gives me information that isn't available through regular channels. It's scary sometimes how fluid I can be, merging with others even if they don't know it. My ideals are the highest, and I feel that my life is meant to be an evolutionary development of my soul to higher states of being. I'm extremely compassionate and sympathetic because I understand the universality of life—that we are all one with each other. Some people of a coarser nature think that is silly, but I know because it's what I actually experience within myself.

Call me a romantic; you won't hurt my feelings! I like romance and I believe in true love. In fact, for me there is only one kind of love— the true, forever-after kind. I'd never marry for money or because a guy was Mr. Pecs. He could be a chimney sweep covered in soot and if we truly loved, it wouldn't matter. I don't care what he does for a living, though if he's a poet or a musician it would be nice. Whatever he is, he has to understand my love of all the earth's creatures and not make fun of my sympathy for the animals, the birds, even the fish. I'm one of those who works to save the whales and the dolphins. I feel that if it's a living creature we should respect its right to live.

My idea of the perfect man is someone who is sensitive and understands that there is an eternal life flowing through everything. My problem is that I can confuse myself in my desire for this, thinking that someone who just gets high and talks a good line is the real thing. I have to be careful because I'm so easily taken over by my empathy that I can become self-sacrificing for love. Intimacy is very important to me also, and I can't deal with coldness or distancing. I have to feel close and *be* close to the man I love. At the same time, I have to be allowed to be my own shifting and changing self, to have my moods and altered states of consciousness. When I love, I give myself totally.

VENUS IN ARIES MAN

Action is what I like, whether it's in a relationship or watching sports or films. And I want the newest, the latest, the most avant-garde, the farthest out. I thrive on new experiences. The here and the now is where I live, a lot more than most people. Surprise me! Give me something I haven't experienced before. And if it is totally exclusive, a one-of-a-kind thing, so much the better. I fill my life with energetic things, from loud music to loud colors. Weapons of all kinds attract me, whether I use them or not. Their firepower represents the ultimate action. I'm also into head-tripping, getting off on what's completely conceptual. So long as it's new. And different.

When I fall in love, I'm romantic and impulsive. I fancy myself a dragon-slayer, and I'd like to be able to go on a quest for my ladylove. To say I'm idealistic in love is an understatement. I put my woman up on a pedestal, even if I know that eventually she will fall off, being only human. I confess I'm a bit macho. I want to take care of her. I want my love to be tested, like knights of old. I can make any woman feel like she's the only woman in the world, and she is to me. I'm a very enthusiastic lover and I hate being bored, so I take her out. We go places together and have adventures.

I know exactly what attracts me in a woman. She has to be vibrant and alive, exciting and a challenge. If she likes to fight, that's okay too, because I enjoy a good fight. It's stimulating and gets the juices flowing. If she gives me a hard time, it's all in the game and I love the competition because in the end I can't see how she could resist me. I'm an active lover and I like the banter and playfulness of it all, including a bit of wrestling. Whatever keeps the relationship on a high edge keeps me interested, even if it's battling. Conflict. I probably shouldn't admit it publicly, but I find conflict, even in the bedroom, stimulating, and making up is half the fun! We keep each other interested, because we never know what to expect!

VENUS IN TAURUS MAN

I like a calm, secure, and stable life, with enough money to buy comforts. I feel the same way about love relationships. Emotional security is just as important to me as financial security. I like things that can stand the test of time, what's classical—whether it's music or beauty—comfortable, and traditional, such as fine fabrics that last for years.

Actually, I'm not very aggressive about lovemaking. I'd rather attract than pursue. But I love to touch and be touched. I enjoy physical contact, and my sense of touch is highly developed. I can be romantic, but I've got a practical nature. For example, I'll bring my lady a bottle of good wine for us to share over dinner and a potted plant instead of cut flowers. We will both enjoy the wine and the plant will last. Flighty women who can't make up their minds about what they want turn me off. I like a wholesome woman with good values, from the right background, one who's built for comfort, not for speed. I'm a sucker for rounded beauties (especially curved necks and shoulders), and I don't mind if she's security- and money-minded. I'm artistically inclined and I feel a close kinship with the earth, so my woman appreciates beauty and growing things. A family man by nature, I want to settle down.

My home is my haven. I want it to be beautiful in a tastefully conservative way, and I want my woman there. I'm possessive, I admit it. I have a strong sense of what's mine. Jealousy sometimes rears its head in my relationships, but only if my emotional security is threatened. I'm affectionate, giving lots of hugs and kisses. I may not always *tell* you I love you, but I'll show you. I'm always reliable. You can depend on me through thick and thin. I'm slow to anger. I like to keep everything on an even keel. I'm a lover, not a fighter.

VENUS IN GEMINI MAN

Most of all, I want mental stimulation. Without it, I die. But keep it light. Nothing heavy, please. No dark and moody conversations— they're so depressing! Lots of variety is what I like, in all that I experience. Whatever's new and trendy fascinates me, and I enjoy change for change's sake. Change is life's blood to me, for without constant change and the stimulation it brings, I wither on the vine and my mental grapes go sour. This craving for variety extends to my social and romantic life, and I'm insatiably curious about people. All people, even ones I just pass on the street or sit across from on a crowded bus or train. In fact, I'm likely to strike up a conversation with a complete stranger just to satisfy my curiosity.

Romantically, I'm a bit fickle, though I hate to admit it. It's hard for me to settle into a permanent relationship because there's always so much left to experience and I don't like to cut off my options. Whatever's witty, interesting, informative, or just plain different excites me and I want to be able to experience it, all of it. I fear missing something. I go to the intellectual events, where there's good repartee, take in the newest popular show or concert, whatever's different. There, I've said it again! *Different.* Yesterday's newspaper is old news.

I get around. I travel in pursuit of pleasure. I play with words, play on words. I love humor and cleverness. My tastes are versatile, too. I can go to a classical concert one night and watch "Wrestlemania" the next.

I'm not naturally monogamous. Though I interact with those I love, they have to allow me my space or I get stifled. I guess you'd call me a mental claustrophobic. Whatever limits me mentally stultifies me.

I'm an idealist at heart and I'm looking for my one true love. She can discuss philosophy, play Trivial Pursuit, watch baseball, and cook a gourmet meal all at the same time. Her mind is agile and she's got a razor-sharp wit. She behaves like a lady and lets me fly. But I'll always fly home if she doesn't pin me down, appreciates my puns, and loves my changeability.

VENUS IN CANCER MAN

It's easy to hurt my feelings, even if I don't let on. My sensitivity is sometimes a sore point with me. I want closeness and sensitivity from others, but I don't always get it. Because I like nurturing and being nurtured, I'm called "too sensitive," but most often I hide my vulnerability in a dignified manner. I know that I'm often unpredictable, both emotionally and mentally, and so I seek a stable domestic situation. I want financial security so that I can make my home a shelter from the storm. Marriage doesn't put me off. In fact, I welcome it as a way of creating a safe haven. I cherish my family and my home is my castle.

My taste may be somewhat old-fashioned, even sentimental, but I like things that are personal. I like mementos, and I enjoy remembering the little things that people like. If my ladylove favors pink tea roses, she'll always get them from me. But I like to use my imagination too, and create nice experiences that way. Comfort and beauty are important to me, especially in my home environment, and I'd rather entertain at home than go out to restaurants or public places. It's so much cozier. I even like to cook, and I don't mind doing the grocery shopping. If it's for my home, I enjoy it.

I even call my mother regularly without being reminded to do it. I have a great sense for family.

The woman of my dreams is delicate and sensitive, a real *lady* in the old-timey sense of the word. She likes to keep house, even if she has a career, and she likes to nurture me and her children, if she has them. Family is important to her and she appreciates the deep intimacy of a loving relationship. She gives me a sense of being taken care of, and in return I take care of her. Our home is our bastion against a cold, cruel world, and we keep it as pleasant and lovely as possible, entertaining our friends there and giving them the same sense of security we enjoy together.

VENUS IN LEO MAN

Whatever I do, I do on a grand scale, I like monumental architecture like the Taj Mahal and the idea of dedicating such a structure to love and romance. People who are small-minded in their affections or their outlook on life get on my nerves. So does stinginess, whether of pocket or of purpose. I can always see the big picture, the bigger the better. I'm one who deals in large-scale undertakings, and I put my whole heart into whatever I'm doing. I don't skimp, neither on the expense nor on the emotional content. I'm proud of all I accomplish, and though some may accuse me of being too proud, I can also, I confess, be silly and playful like a kid. In fact, that's why I like kids so much. Just because they are so spontaneous. They express themselves directly and with open hearts. I identify with that a lot.

I'll give a woman anything I've got, including the shirt off my back, which incidentally will be of the very highest quality, so long as she treats me with respect. I can put up with a lot, but not that. I have to have respect. *Loyalty* is my watchword, and I'm not suspicious by nature, but because I am susceptible to flattery and appearances, I can be misled or taken advantage of. That's because I need attention, and a lot of it. A woman can get to me that way and it really hurts if anyone is insincere.

My ideal woman knows how to make an entrance and take center stage. I love to show her off. She has presence and acts like a noble-woman regardless of what class she was born in. She's got spirit and breeding. If she's somewhat imperious that's okay by me. She is queen to my king. I treat her right and I expect the same treatment in return. But so long as we make a beautiful-looking, powerful-seeming couple, I can overlook incompatibility for the sake of the image we present. But when love is true, it is *grand* in style, like opera. I'll always be an incurable romantic.

VENUS IN VIRGO MAN

I tend to be critical of those I love. I want perfection and purity, even though I know that most humans can't attain my standards. But it's so important to me that I get to criticizing, thinking I'm helping them to improve. That comes of my tendency to analyze—some say over-analyze—emotions. But I like to be thorough and that's just how I go about it. Sometimes I can make other people self-conscious, even though I only mean to be helpful, and that stifles the flow of communication between us. Sometimes I may get too fussy, but I show my feelings by paying attention to details and taking care of things, by noticing small things, which are just as important as the big ones. And I like to be useful to those I love—to do something practical, like building a bookshelf, that will make their lives happier.

I'm shy and not aggressive about making dates and going out, so it's easy for me to get wrapped up in my work to the exclusion of a social life. I don't have much flash to me. I work hard and I like nice things, but I'm not a good "mixer." I lavish affection on my animals and give them the uncritical love I can't give people.

I have a hard time being close because my standards for myself are so high. I'm afraid my faults will show, so I often push people away only to want them later. It's said that cleanliness is next to godliness, and I believe that. Personal hygiene and order are important to me. I can't stand sloth. A woman with a soiled dress or unwashed hair can turn me off completely—forever.

I am most comfortable with a woman who has a simple, honest way about her and who is orderly and precise. I've been hurt by women who have used me, so I look for sincerity. I don't want to sound prudish. I love to think about what goes on underneath her orderly exterior and high-buttoned blouse! My love is pure and once my guard is down and my heart is won, I'm not so uptight. I let myself be cared for, and I return the favor. I'll drive her around, do her laundry, pick her up at the airport. No service is too much trouble for the woman I love.

VENUS IN LIBRA MAN

You might call me a gentleman of the old school. I'm polite and discreet. I'm known for my charm and good manners as well as for my sense of fairness. My style is courtly and I am quick to reciprocate any gesture made in my direction. The theory of relationships of all kinds, from the personal to the legal and artistic, interests me and I love discussions about relationships. It's my favorite topic, conversationally and intellectually. For this reason, I enjoy small, intimate dinner parties that foster good conversation at a high level, where ideas are the foremost. I'm a mainstream kind of guy and I don't go in for the weird and outré. Beauty and balance are my style. I like to share cultural pursuits.

I'm not averse to marriage, for partnership is my preferred way of life. I like being in a relationship. In fact, I'm much happier that way. I can rarely tolerate being alone for long. Love is a beautiful concept, and I love beauty wherever I find it—especially in the female of the species. But don't look to me for exotic sexual experiences. Just for loving affection and quiet sensuality. Coarseness turns me off completely, except for once in a while, when a small dose of it is necessary to balance things if they have gone too far in one direction.

My ideal woman is first and foremost a lady, even if on the very rare occasion she can be a harlot in the bedroom. She is good at discussing and debating ideas. Nothing is more of an aphrodisiac for me than a really good conversation. I'm a bit inconsistent, I admit. Sometimes I want a woman who is ultra-feminine, all ruffles and lace, the perfect "little woman," a helpmeet. Other times I want an intellectual, someone who's my equal, to talk to as well as to look at. I like to share my thoughts and feelings, for I confess I'm a romantic, in love with love.

VENUS IN SCORPIO MAN

Sex is a major issue with me at all times, no matter what I'm doing otherwise. My thoughts are never far from it. I find sexual undertones or overtones in most everything, especially daily life. That's because I can see below the surface and mentally ferret out what's really going on. This ability to see deeply draws me into the unknown and unexplored, whether it's moody and difficult art and music or the dark side of the human personality. I'm known for my intensity, but what you see is only the tip of the iceberg. Inside, I'm a deeply feeling and very passionate person, even if I keep it a secret, which I do sometimes because I'm into secrecy. And I'm naturally suspicious. But you can trust me. If I give you a compliment, it's no bull. Flattery is not my style. I hold back until I get the lay of the land, then I advance or make a move. When I do make a commitment, it sticks. I don't take anything lightly and I don't give my word unless I mean it.

Love to me is a very big word. I can be intensely jealous and even vindictive if I'm hurt or betrayed. I know how to wait and then strike. On the other hand, I can let go completely and forgive the old hurts and be healed from within. Mostly, I keep this to myself, but I am something of an occultist. I believe in my ability to make myself over and rise up from my own ashes, like the Phoenix. That's because I live close to the source of my own power and I understand how to create and to destroy.

The woman who will attract me has an aura of mystery and depth. Usually I like strong-featured looks—something out of the ordinary, not your usual prettiness of the generic blonde. Actually, I prefer brunettes. They're more classical and intense and have soul and substance. This is what excites me. When I see a woman I want, I may not be at all obvious, but if I sense she is interested and available, I'll put out a strong energy field to her and then make my move. My strong powers of attraction come from my instincts. I rarely make a false move.

VENUS IN SAGITTARIUS MAN

Freedom is high on my priority list. I have a spiritual nature and I'm always seeking the ideal, not the real. I want all the good things in life—adventures, good times, travel, fun, spontaneity, romance. And I want those things to be vehicles for my personal growth. I don't always *talk* about being spiritual, because not everyone understands, but it's an important part of of me. I'm sociable, and generally outgoing. I like to be friendly with everyone. But I'm not superficial or light-headed. I'm a thinker, and my thoughts run deep. I travel to far-off places to stimulate my mind. I love to get to know foreigners, especially women.

My tastes run to the lavish, when I can afford it. I like lots of color and things that show my eclectic taste. I take a bit from one culture, a bit from another, and bits from lots of others and combine them in an individualistic way that's tasteful and interesting.

I'm not afraid of getting involved in a relationship with someone different from myself, with a foreign background, or of some other religious persuasion. Others' philosophies and theologies interest me, and I like to experience these through the people who live them in their own milieus. I'm always as open and honest about my feelings as I can be. I don't hide or try to deceive. I'm ethical in whatever I do, whether business dealings or romantic relationships.

My ideal woman has her head in the stars but her feet on the ground. She is outdoorsy, maybe likes horses or just backpacking. She loves to travel with me. We have fun together while doing our spiritual seeking. I want to share my adventures with her and give her joy. Most of all, I want us to laugh together, for that's the mark of true love. We know how to give each other the space we need. And, oh, yes! Even if she's not a beauty, she is smart and well-educated. She takes me to visit her stars, and I take her to mine.

VENUS IN CAPRICORN MAN

I want financial and emotional security, no question about it. Success is important to me. I have to have status in my organization and be paid the money I deserve. I work hard and always do my share so I deserve any advancement I get. I contribute fully, and my contribution is always useful, never wasteful. I genuinely prefer the best of everything. Some people accuse me of being snobbish but I don't mind others' opinions. Sticks and stones. I'm ambitious. I mean to get to the top so I can provide for my myself and my family in a solid and secure way. Nothing showy, mind you, just quality.

Forget the fancy titles (unless, of course, it's CEO!). Just give me the raise and the bonus. I'm conservative in politics and at home. I treasure the wisdom of the past, from furniture design to economic theory. I like things to be elegant, understated, functional, and durable. I'm not one to show a lot of affection, but I'm a loyal and devoted friend or lover. I'll do whatever I can to further your ambitions. I'll be there for you and I'll take responsibility.

I'm not above choosing a woman who is superior to me in wealth or social position. I like class and high achievement. The woman I seek is refined in public and able to let herself go in private. She also is basic and real, a hard-working woman who earns respect, the salt of the earth. I'm very sensual and I like plenty of sex under the right circumstances. Sometimes, though, I hold myself back. I fear failure or ridicule, and I always keep my dignity intact, no matter what. That may make me seem remote, even mysterious, but underneath I'm as vulnerable as the next man. I need a woman who can see that and respond with loving kindness.

VENUS IN AQUARIUS MAN

I take pride in my special outlook on life. I'm willing to experiment with all kinds of relationships. I give people freedom to be who they are and I expect the same in return. I can champion monogamy while realizing it isn't the only way to have a sexual relationship. Lots of people in different cultures over time have found other ways that worked for them. We're human, and in humanity there is diversity. Whatever my choice of love style, I rarely get jealous. Jealousy is against my principles and I won't inflict it upon a woman if I can help it. I use my gift of reason to avoid negative feelings by discussing things rationally. I make an effort to live up to ideals of brotherhood.

I hate emotions running all over the place. They make objectivity hard to come by and difficult to maintain, so I avoid the overtly emotional. That makes intimacy something of a problem for me. It's often easier for me to fall in love with an ideology than a real person. I never compromise my principles, and I need someone who can deal with that. I'm accused of being cold and unfeeling, but I don't much relate to that. I work hard at my objectivity—maybe it gets in the way. I'd rather be *friends* with the woman in my life.

I value friendship above all else. It's stimulating to the mind, and the more and different friends of both sexes I have, the better. I often fall for an unusual woman far from my own roots.

My ideal woman can love me and let me be free. She's independent, an original type, and it makes no difference if she's from another social class or ethnic group. I like a woman with a strong male side, and I appreciate intelligence, even a scientific bent or radical streak. However, if we break up, I'm always willing to stay friends. That's what's really important!

VENUS IN PISCES MAN

For me, there is only one possible reason for marrying or getting seriously involved with someone, and that is *love*. Not your sentimental, gooey, simplistic version of it—the kind that is really just kids' play—but the Real Thing. Transcendent. Spiritual. Two souls joined as one. All the things you've heard about and maybe thought weren't possible. They are, and I know. I have a deep understanding of the unity of life. I connect with this. And I know how to connect with it through love. My romantic nature has a flowing aspect, and I'm idealistic in my approach, but this isn't pie in the sky. It comes from a deep knowing of inner matters, from my empathy with others and even with the creatures of the earth. I can talk to the birds and the flowers because I see life in the universe as all-encompassing, fluid, merging. It is all One and I am in touch with that One. That may sound a little silly, but it's true nonetheless. I don't always *express* my feelings like this, but they are always there.

I'm a romantic at heart, sensitive to others and their needs, sometimes to the point of being self-sacrificing. People's needs can really get to me. I can't shut them out. And then I forget myself and who I am and what's good for me. I can get so caught up in them. Objectivity isn't one of my good points, but sympathy is. Sometimes my own sympathy for someone in need overflows and I *become* that person.

I'm drawn to sensitive, empathic, quiet women with psychic sensibilities, who go with the flow, so to speak. My ideal woman is the one I fall for totally. I don't care what size or color she is, what her background or education is, if she works or doesn't work—as long as she touches my heartstrings and our love is complete and sincere. Then I'm an erotic and tender lover, imaginative to the point of being psychic. So long as she allows me my shifting moods and feelings, we will make beautiful music together.

chapter nineteen

ASTROSCRIPTS FOR MARS

Bold MARS has fashioned
Every sting and nettle—
Every fragile peace
He can unsettle.
God of War, he acts
In the name of power and order.
Crosses he every private border.

MARS IN ARIES WOMAN

I'm a warrior woman. I could have led the Charge of the Light Brigade. I start fast and I can stop on a dime. Whatever I do, it is with quickness and speed. I'm impetuous, impatient, and impulsive, sometimes to the point of being rash. I go where the action is, and I usually am in the lead. I often charge ahead without looking behind to see who, if anyone, is following me. I leave the details to others, but first I motivate them to finish what I start. There's always something new to go on to, a project that will challenge me once again. I thrive on the challenge, like a knight-errant.

I don't go in for game-playing. When I want something or someone, I go for it or him. I act and react spontaneously, even if I have regrets later. My first response is usually the true one. I'll fight if a fight is necessary, because combat turns me on. But I can make up just as easily. I'm no shrinking violet or clinging vine. I'm an independent woman with a mind of her own. Yet, I'm a true romantic. I like men who are on quests, who have goals and a vision for life. I don't like threatening a man, so he's got to be his own person to deal with me. He doesn't have to be macho, though. He can be a gentle person like an artist or a poet. Just as long as he knows who he is and is secure in that. I do like a man who looks like a man and acts like one.

I respond to romance if the situation is right. If I'm truly his lady and his Number One, then my passion is aroused to white heat. If I'm not his sole focus, I wilt like a daisy without water. I just have to be first in his heart and in his mind.

I'm able to make the first move if necessary, but I'd rather not. The idea of being swept away thrills me and then I like to alternate between who is assertive and who is receptive. Dominance and passivity as a love game appeals to me, as long as we both know it is only a game. I don't want to be dominated in reality, only in fancy. I'm a warrior, but I'm first a lover.

MARS IN TAURUS WOMAN

"Give me land, lots of land," could be my song. I'm a real Earth Mother type, very grounded. I like my comforts and I'll gladly share them with you. Count on me for the long haul. But don't rush me. I have more endurance than any other ten people put together, but I'm lazy. At least until I decide to act, which might take quite a while. I'm a bit like the Little Engine That Could. I just keep right on chugging away, no matter what. If I'm committed, I don't stop or waver. I may be slow, but I'm steady and sure in my progress, and

I continue on long after the competition has fallen by the wayside.

Patience is one of my virtues, but it can turn into rock-hard stubbornness. I can really dig in and make a big hole for myself. But if a man is mine, I'll stick with him through thick and thin. My common sense makes me a veritable Rock of Gibraltar. My needs are simple and basic. Give me reality. Land. Money. Food. Sex. And lots of all those things. My endurance qualities extend to sex as well. I am a woman who can make love all night and again in the morning. I'm in touch with my body and I take care of it. I'm a world-class hugger. I love to touch. My touch can be healing. I give great massages.

If a man wants me, he has to talk straight or, better yet, show me. He can touch me, hold me, make me comfortable, help me set up my house, pick me up at the airport, take care of me when I get sick, and come through for me when I need him. He'll never regret it. I'll be there for him. I'm a steadfast woman, loyal and true.

I need a man who can make me feel secure, who is more traditional than experimental. He can be macho or the strong, silent type, but he has to be successful and have something to show for his efforts. I especially am attracted to a man who makes something with his hands, like a craftsman. But it's okay if what he makes is only money. My problem is that because I'm so strong I attract the momma's boys and if they satisfy me sexually and sensually, I overlook their weaknesses. I'm such a lover of beauty and comfort that I can be seduced by a handsome build with a strong neck and massive shoulders, or by financial success. If I'm dazzled I forget to worry about my inner person and if we are communicating well.

MARS IN GEMINI WOMAN

Talk to me. Help me get the ideas flowing! I love a conversation, even if it's one-sided. I'm a world-class talker. I dazzle with my insights, my wit, and my ability to mix ideas and fly from thought to thought. Mental stimulation and doing lots of different things individually or simultaneously gets my juices flowing. I juggle a lot of mental things at once. Apples and oranges or whatever. Variety is my lifeblood. I can do punk rock today and browse old bookshops tomorrow. Then I'll be off to see the whales migrating, or catch a high-falutin' art auction. As long as it's a change.

I'm a woman with a brain. No one turns me on without intriguing my mind. I don't say a good body doesn't help—I take care of mine to look youthful. Neither does a smart, versatile mind.

Ideas and mental gyrations are my thing. Trivial Pursuit is a favorite pastime. I love puns and puzzles, especially crossword puzzles.
As long as it's nothing heavy or depressing, I like figuring things out.
Light, that's me. I need to circulate, like the air, and I need my social
life like a flower needs water. My life's a constant battle against
boredom. If I get bored, I'll curl up and die!

I flirt because I like to explore every option and I flirt with ideas
the same way I flirt with men. That's why my ideal man must be
nimble of mind as well as of foot. Nothing clumsy, *please*. Actually,
I might have several flirtations going at once, with women as well as
men—nothing serious, mind you—and then drop the whole lot and
go to bed with my books and magazines. Just reading a book with a
lover turns me on. Sometimes I think I could be happy being celibate,
that maybe I don't need sex at all. That's because I'm such an independent thinker. Still, he can send me flowers and I'll appreciate
them—as long as he includes a brilliantly clever card! It's the thought
that counts, and thoughts count with me more than with most women.

MARS IN CANCER WOMAN

I get angry when my feelings are hurt or my security is threatened.
And because I'm so sensitive and easily hurt I've developed a crusty
exterior. But beneath it lurks a real hearts-and-flowers person, a
sentimental and romantic dreamer. Though I'm often moody and shy,
don't underestimate me. I'm original and creative and can be psychically tuned in. People mistake my being thin-skinned for weakness,
but I'm ambitious and very tenacious. I'll hold on longer than anyone.
I'm a survivor. I protect me and mine. And I have a long memory
when I've been wounded.

Financial security is uppermost with me and I'm driven by the need
for it. If I'm feeling overwhelmed by insecurity I can seem quite selfish,
but even then I'm always a sucker for someone or something that
needs my help. I identify with stray cats and the world's orphans and
homeless persons. My mother was a consummate worrier and she
passed it on to me, so I get caught in the there-but-for-the-Grace-of-
God syndrome and try to mother everyone. I guess you'd consider
me old-fashioned. Domesticity turns me on even if I find myself traveling a lot. Home is where the hearth is and children are a strong
instinctual drive for me. I'm very home-oriented and like to cook. A
good meal can fix just about any of life's ills. And a Teddy bear is
always a comfort. Coziness shuts out the world's harshness.

The traditional he-man appeals to me—the kind of a man who can provide a good home for me and my children. I find nothing sexier than making a baby. He's courtly and romantic, somewhat patriarchal even. I know that underneath there's always a little boy lurking. I fall into the mother-caretaker-helper role very easily, even if I'm a liberated woman philosophically opposed to it. It's an automatic tea-and-sympathy response that I can't help. Once I feel secure with a man, I've got an active imagination with a love of erotica and a loony sense of humor, but I can't bear impersonality or detachment. I merge with my lover at a very deep level sexually, and afterward I want him to hold me, not roll over and go to sleep.

MARS IN LEO WOMAN

I was born to rule, no matter what domain I find myself in. The grand gesture becomes me and I am always personally involved with whatever I do, setting my individual stamp on it. I live by the dictum "Whatever is worth doing is worth doing well." I admit that I like to run things, and that I'm a woman to be reckoned with. I'm ambitious and proud. My honor is topmost, and I'm not afraid to take a stand or assume a position of power. I can handle it because I have vision and leadership abilities. I take my responsibilities seriously and I can take the heat, too. Even though I can be self-centered, I'm not really selfish and I'm never stingy. I'll open my home and heart to those I like and shower them with warmth and attention. I enjoy seeing others glow with happiness.

Since I'm so honorable, I expect the same from others. Once I've formed an attachment I put my trust in the relationship. I'm loyal to a fault and sometimes I have to be proved wrong in a particularly nasty way before I see the light. That's because I do everything whole-heartedly. Nothing short of the best will do. I'd rather fail magnificently than succeed in a mediocre way. I need outlets for my creativity, and I'm strongly motivated to express myself in whatever mode I choose. I lean toward extreme situations of the "larger than life" variety—anything to avoid everyday-ness.

My loves tend either toward the soap opera or the grand opera. I'm a sucker for romantic fantasies. The ordinary and common completely turn me off. It will be on the grand scale, if only in my imagination. No matter what other qualifications he has I've got to have sexual chemistry with a man. I'm playful and passionate in bed. I love to romp and act silly, wrestle to see who's stronger. I have a giving nature. If he makes me feel adored I'll cater to his whims. He has to be strong with a definite personal style. He can be a film mogul, or an out-of-work actor, as long as he's bold, we look good together, and enjoy passionate sex.

MARS IN VIRGO WOMAN

I do everything with great attention to detail, whether it's organizing a corporate meeting or making a cup of tea. Perfection comes naturally to me, and I'm efficient and highly skilled in my work and in my personal life. That translates into my being very practical. I'm a woman who believes that form follows function, and therefore I like things that work and I want to know what makes them work. The proof of the pudding is in the eating, and the pudding will be right if the ingredients are the best and the correct instructions are meticulously followed. Everything must be performed in the right sequence. I'm a sequential person, very good at the concept of going from A to B to C and so on, not skipping around. I like order and I bring a rational intelligence to bear on creating it all around myself. My drawers are neat and well-arranged, my desk is clean and uncluttered, my files are properly labeled, my kitchen is handy and practical. Method is second-nature to me, and I don't mind taking the time to do what has to be done properly. Why do it slapdash? Attention to life's little details can be a meditative or spiritual experience for me, because I know its importance to the big picture. Someone once wrote, "It's the little things that count. We can sit on a mountain but not a tack." I understand that notion very well and incorporate it into my daily life.

The idea of master craftsmanship appeals to me and I will spend the necessary time to develop my skills in every area of life, including the sexual. I'm one of the best lovers around because I pay attention to details. I notice and remember what people like, whether it's a special brand of coffee or two lumps of sugar in their tea, and I provide it. Sometimes my attention to detail may make me seem fussy or even prudish, but when I let go of my inhibitions, I'm very earthy and sensual. And I care a lot and show it by serving those I love. The men I like are fastidious. They use logic and strive for excellence no matter what their work. I appreciate a sense of craft as well as intelligence and kindness. I can be critical and so can a man I like, but that's okay because nothing is nicer than something when it's right, be it a kiss or a concert.

MARS IN LIBRA WOMAN

I am not a pushy person and I don't like pushy people. I like to be nice. To me, being nice means doing what other people want or what makes them comfortable. I always try to keep in balance and I'm always very aware of when things get out of balance. What gets me mad is unfairness of any kind. Though I don't like to argue, I'll take a stand on any issue of injustice. But I'd rather have a civilized debate than a heated argument. It's always better to keep the atmosphere pleasant and unriled. Strife upsets me and I have a nose for its presence when it's brewing. I try to motivate others to work out their difficulties in a nice and refined way, and I usually succeed because I'm such a rational person. I can see both sides of the problem and I'm a good mediator. People respect and value that.

The men I like are from opposite poles. Either they are very masculine with traditional good looks or they are gentle and artistic, maybe with long flowing locks. I alternate between being attracted by brains and by handsomeness. I go first one way and then the other in my search for the right balance. But I like being in a relationship. In fact, it's hard for me not to be in one, whatever kind it is. I can compromise easily, sometimes too easily, because it's so important for me to have a relationship. I bend over backwards to avoid confrontation because I hate negative feelings. So much so there are times I can't feel my own, and then I get evasive in my tactics, burning dinner or forgetting telephone calls just to get even. But as soon as evenness is restored, I revert to my natural good manners and tact.

Sexually, I'm fairly conventional and I don't go for the experimental side. Sex, like life, should be mutually enjoyable and refined, not too boisterous. It should be another form of communication and include all the nice trimmings like good restaurants, excellent conversation, well-groomed good looks, and proper manners. I like finding out about my partner and how he feels about our relationship. I'm always open to discussion, as long as it's objective and carried on in a civilized manner. Don't make me mad, though, or I'll dredge up every slight from the last twenty years that I was too polite to mention at the time!

MARS IN SCORPIO WOMAN

I'm a woman who's not afraid to take chances. In fact, I love being on the edge of riskiness. I'm an either-or person. For me, there's no middle ground. I am totally into the moment and I invest it with great intensity of feeling and passion of action. It doesn't matter if it's good or bad, joy or sorrow. I have a relentless quality in my actions and reactions—I do nothing by halves. Life is something I experience intensely from either pole, negative or positive. If I'm in love, I'm obsessed. If I'm out of love, I'm remote. When I go after something or someone, I get it. There's a magnetism about me that surrounds the object of my desire and pulls it irresistibly to me. I know that and I depend on this power of attraction to get me what I want. To say I'm naturally sexy is an understatement. Sex oozes out of my pores, even when I'm not particularly thinking about it. Which is rare. Sex is a big issue for me all the time, or almost all the time. Whichever way, total passion or complete celibacy, I go to the extreme. I like to test myself and others, for the sake of probing beneath the surface to find out what's really going on down there in the depths.

Disaster doesn't faze me. I'll even push things to the brink and let them collapse. So something better can take its place. Things fall apart, but life always goes on. I like to be in control because I've been in the position of not being in control. I've dealt with abuse and I know about the power syndrome. Life is a dangerous business and I leave little to chance. I analyze all the different angles. Maybe I'm not always objective, but my insights are deep and penetrating and I live close to their instinctual source. When I hate, I do it with passion, to the point of becoming self-destructive to get my revenge.

My ideal man is powerful in some way, with great charisma. He may have an air of mystery and intrigue, leaving a lot to the imagination. He's dedicated or obsessed with an idea or work, and he takes risks or lives on the edge. He might be a religious fanatic or a relationship addict. But when it's good, sex can be a truly spiritual experience, like being reincarnated together. We may have to struggle, but that only makes our love stronger.

MARS IN SAGITTARIUS WOMAN

I'm a woman on the move, mentally and philosophically as well as physically. Even if it's only in my mind, I'm a great traveler and I visit a lot of foreign lands. I like the great out-of-doors, camping trips, hikes, woodland excursions. Whatever's foreign—cultures, languages, food—turns me on. I do things in a big way and I'm always striving to reach beyond myself. I confess I often trip, sometimes over my own feet. I'm a klutz. But that's only because I've got my sights set on the far distance and don't look at what's in front of me. Luckily, I've got a great sense of humor and can laugh at myself.

Spirituality is important to me, and I feel I've got a mission in life. But I'm an independent thinker and I won't be bound by anyone else's ideas of what is right. I make my own decisions, follow my own path, once I find it. I'm a true believer, but it can take me a while to discover what I believe. Then I become a bit of a proselytizer or can turn into a missionary, for I act on my beliefs. I speak bluntly and freely, and I don't care what others think. I say what I mean regardless of who doesn't like it. This makes me seem irrelevant, but I'm really like the kid in the story about the emperor's new clothes. I speak the truth and that often upsets the status quo.

I like sex and take it in my stride. I have my standards, but I'm not exactly a shrinking violet. I don't necessarily think monogamous relationships are the only way to live. I'm restless and I need my freedom. Especially if the man I'm with isn't stimulating enough for me. But I always have hope and faith in the future, no matter where I am today. If this relationship doesn't work, the next one will. My men must be active and have scope and vision. Foreigners attract me, especially if they fly a lot or teach philosophy. Most of all, a man must be able to have fun. And he has to be someone I can believe in. Together we can do great things and go fabulous places. Life will be a continuous challenging adventure of learning and growing.

MARS IN CAPRICORN WOMAN

I'm a woman with definite plans and goals, and my plans include financial success and security. That may seem materialistic, but one of life's realities is that you need money. I'm not afraid of hard work and when I set my mind to a goal, I accomplish it, no matter how long it takes. I'm serious about all that I do, I have patience and discipline, and I can hold out for what I want because I know how to realistically appraise a situation and how to wait.

Since I was a child I've been mature, and I know that it's best to work within the system and adjust, so I keep to the status quo. I respect authority and I aim to become an authority figure myself. I know about the bottom line, and I'll do the necessary dirty work. There's a workaholic streak in me, but I'm no clone. I'm also an individualistic person with the stamina to go the distance and reach the top.

If need be, I'll dress for success—elegantly. I'm proper in my behavior and I have strong ethics. In fact, I'm sometimes rigid in my moral code, a bit of a puritan. That may be because I'm afraid of destitution. I need to succeed in order to feel safe. This can make me act as if I don't need anyone because I always had to be competent as a child and I became self-sufficient. Rejection terrifies me, so I protect myself.

Truth to tell, I long for a man to take care of me and be protective, but it's hard for me to let go of my fears and allow that to happen. I don't like being dependent—that's scary. Besides, I'm usually the most competent person around and I end up taking charge just because everyone else is dithering.

I'd like a strong man who knows how to handle himself and doesn't go to pieces in a crisis. Someone responsible and reliable, maybe a corporate type. Or a very individualistic loner who knows the ropes and can get us safely across the border if shooting starts. With such a man I could be totally unrepressed, let go of my strict controls, and unleash my earthy sensuality. Then I can *undress* for success.

MARS IN AQUARIUS WOMAN

Freedom means a lot to me. It's my principal motivating factor. I'm highly individualistic and I hate to be told what to do. I'm altruistically minded and very attracted by ideas and theories on how to improve humanity's lot. I abhor selfishness. I have a conscience and my scope of understanding leads me to do my duty to the group voluntarily. I don't need to be coerced or reminded. I like to analyze actions—my own and everybody else's. It gives me an edge because I'm good at dissecting things on the mental level. My favorite color is cool and I use a combination of intuition and logic to fuel my intellect. There's an electricity about me. Fire without heat. I can come up with an explanation for just about anything and make it sound good, but I don't care for emotionalism since it gets in the way of reason. And reason is what separates us from the beasts. Because of this penchant of mine for rationality, I hate to get angry and blow my cool. It's much neater to analyze the situation without getting involved.

Trouble is, once I've analyzed and dissected a man mentally, I'm usually bored and ready to move on, collect another specimen, and begin the process all over again. It's a technique I use to feel free, and that feeling of freedom is as necessary to me as breathing air. Even if I'm in a committed relationship. Because of this, I'm interested in different sexual life-styles. I'll consider open marriage, no marriage, group sex, bisexuality, homosexuality, asexuality. Even communal sex. Communes appeal to me whether they're into group sex or completely celibate and devoted to the study of some religious idea.

Groups in general suit me, even if it's only a health spa with all the latest gadgets and techniques.

I like men who are different or special in some way: geniuses, rebels, idealists, iconoclasts, scientists on the leading edge of new thought. Ideally, I'd like a man who is all of these things. I need him to turn on my mind, and then my body will follow along. My brain is the sexiest organ in my body.

MARS IN PISCES WOMAN

I'm an idealist and a romantic. I need inspiration in order to do anything. When I am inspired I have limitless energy, no matter what I'm doing. When I have inspiration I can go on forever. Ordinary tasks seem imbued with meaning for me, for I have a great sense of what it means to be truly humble, and I am elevated by it. My vibes are so strong that I can tune in to almost anything, like a psychic. Altered states of consciousness appeal to me because I like to lose myself in whatever I do, whether it's my work or lovemaking. I can submerge myself in a cause or a lover. Because I hate confrontation some people find me passive, but it's passive resistance. I'd rather wear down or confuse than fight head on. I'm evasive. I flow with a situation and go right into it, like water can flow downhill and inundate a road, blocking traffic for miles. I'm like that when I need to be.

Life's not direct. It's all shadings and subtleties, grayness and soft contours. I find direction by indirection, and come up with creative solutions no one else would have imagined. I'm good at strategy. Even when I am being most indirect, I'm busy sensing the atmosphere and smelling things out. I'll act according to what I pick up intuitively and with my feelings.

The erotic interests me, as long as it's poetic and filmy. I like sex props like sexy underwear and visual stimulation, smells, and sounds. I have the urge to merge and I'm not always that discriminating, especially if I've had a few drinks or am high on something. I go for men who reflect my sensitivity—the sweet, gentle, idealistic poet or musician. My ideal man is someone with a vision who will be kind to me. His inspiration turns me on and makes me feel great passion by fueling my need to be inspired. Then I idealize him. The trouble is that I can blind myself to reality. I have to be careful that the man I see as a magical artist with a message for humanity doesn't turn out to be just one more alcoholic who's having a nightmare rather than a true vision. Still, if he needs me. . . . There's that flow again!

MARS IN ARIES MAN

I know *what* I want when I want it. And I want what I want *when* I want it. Anything that gets in my way doesn't stay there for long. I have a true warrior spirit.

Often I think I was born in the wrong time, because I'd have loved to have been a knight in shining armor, fighting battles for beautiful damsels, killing dragons, storming citadels. But it doesn't matter. I find my own battles in this day and age. I'm a person who's not afraid to act, not afraid to show anger, not afraid to move in when there are things that need doing. I'm the last person in the world who needs to take a course in assertiveness training!

I like a woman who can appreciate a real man, a man with this kind of get-up-and-go. Timid ladies aren't for me. Too fragile. I don't like to have to worry about crushing a poor butterfly. Crusades thrill me. I like the chance to fight for what I think is right, no matter what the obstructions. I'm not big on patience. When I see a woman I want, I don't beat around the bush about how I feel about her. Right away I let her know I'm interested.

If she enjoys sports and activity, that's good, because I'm not one to sit around a lot unless I'm watching an action movie or reading an adventure book. Projects I can work on inspire me because I can put passion into anything I do, even if it's not a woman!

I'm an enthusiastic lover and I come on strong. I'm aggressive in bed and get turned on by dominance and submission games.

Passion is my middle name, and I've been called domineering more than once, but I have a playful side and, though this may come as a surprise, I'm really sweet and somehow innocent in spite of all my energy.

My perceptions are quick—too quick for some people but that's too bad. They'll just have to get used to it. I go with my gut reactions and I'm seldom wrong. If I make a mistake, I just start over. I don't cry in my beer.

I go for two kinds of women and maybe one day I'll find both in one gal. One is the warrior type, like me, a real challenge. The other is the super-feminine, with all the ruffles and frills. I don't see any reason she can't combine the two, do you?

MARS IN TAURUS MAN

Slow but sure might very well define me. I don't get rushed. I like to be definite and I'm very motivated by issues of security. I like things that are real and palpable. Possessions are important, and I admit to being possessive about the people I love. They are *mine*. And I take care of them. Money is always something of a concern to me, no matter how much I have or don't have. I get fixated on it. I like nature and can rough it at times, but I'm always aware of where the money's coming from. That's because I like my creature comforts as well as my financial security. I pay attention to tomorrow. My approach is conservative and cautious, and I want facts and figures, not pie-in-the-sky theory. Give me concrete examples.

I like what endures, whether it's good, solid furniture or a meal that sticks to your ribs. I don't need anything fancy. Good home cooking is better than gussied-up "cuisine." My home is important to me and I like to keep it stable. I'm a caring guy, very sensual and sexual, and I can go the long mile. Because I love to touch and hug I'm a calming influence with animals as well as people. Once I make a commitment, I can't be budged off dead center. Stubborn is an understatement—I'm the original immovable object.

I need sex and I appreciate it. Massage is a specialty of mine, and the gentle touch. I'm aware of my body and its connection to the earth. I love doing things with my hands, like gardening or cooking. The beauties of nature invest me with healing vibrations. My appetites are strong, but I'm not an ostentatious person. I show a woman that I care by taking care. By doing real and practical things that make her life more comfortable. If she's sick, I am there. She can always count on me for the long haul. I may not express my feelings eloquently, but my presence is solid and comforting.

I like doing the traditional male things for my woman, like opening doors and holding chairs. Being the provider is natural to me and it's a role I like. I may be more of the strong, silent type, but my feelings are real and strong. Some people mistake me for passive because I'm slow to act. It's a big mistake. When I blow, the earth rumbles. I prefer peaceful tactics because I'm dangerous when I erupt, like a volcano.

MARS IN GEMINI MAN

I'm the sort of guy who can have the TV, the stereo, and the radio all going at the same time, while talking on the phone and having a conversation with someone in the same room. I'm the guy with a telephone in every room and six lines to choose from for outgoing or incoming calls. If I could afford it, I'd have my own Fax machine so I could communicate worldwide instantly. And get the answer back just as quick. Information is my lifeblood and I think my brain is the

most sexual organ in my body. My greatest passion is for ideas. Intelligence turns me on quicker than feminine pulchritude. In fact, if
a woman is intelligent enough she can be ugly or odd and have a
chance with me. If she can stimulate my mind, she can stimulate my
body. And I'll love her for it. As long as she doesn't try to pin me
down.

Good conversation is more of an aphrodisiac to me than anything
else. Without it, I can't get turned on at all. That's my favorite
foreplay—before, during, and after sex. Sex for me is as much of a
mental experience as it is physical, because I see most of life as a
mental exercise anyway. I'm logical to a fault, and I can argue seven
sides of any issue and agree with them all. I don't get emotional. It's
a waste of time.

I like to keep my options open and that's why I'm an inveterate
flirt. What's the harm? It's all in the game. You know, how you play
it. And I play it very well and with a light touch. Don't count on me
for anything heavy.

Boredom is my enemy and I'll do almost anything to keep it at bay,
even having a sexual relationship. But I'm not really sure I need to
do sex. I can just as well think about it and talk about it. Give me
good talk first and foremost. If what follows isn't so great, well, we
can talk about that too, and it will at least be interesting. I'm a good
catch, if you can catch me. But you'll have to do it by going through
my mind. And by letting me circulate. Otherwise, I'll stagnate. Keep
the information flowing. Let's consider all the possibilities of both the
body and the spirit. After all, they're just two sides of the same coin,
like me.

MARS IN CANCER MAN

I'm determined to survive, and even when I get stomachaches from
worry, I get out there and take care of business. A big motivating
factor for me is having others to take care of. I make sure the people
I love are provided for, to the point of being overprotective. I like
having my family around me, my wife and children nearby. I believe
in conjugal bliss. Even when I have to travel, my home is very important and I usually take some mementos with me to keep in touch
emotionally. I call home a lot. I'm ambitious because I need to succeed
to feel secure. My mother had a lot to do with that. She was always
worried. So, I work hard to get money in the bank and keep food on
the table. Disaster always threatens just around the corner, so I like

to stock up, especially on foodstuffs. My mother always kept a well-stocked larder "just in case."

Once I feel secure, I help others in need. Because I'm myself so sensitive to hurt, I feel for others' pain. I don't always show it, for I've got a thick protective shell, but I'm really shy and very sensitive. I put a lot of feeling into everything I do and I have a strong psychic sense. Because of my sixth sense, I'm often indirect and because I've been hurt a lot, I can be very macho, but underneath I'm a sucker for romance and children. I'm old-fashioned in my behavior and traditional in my manner. I look to the past for guidance on how to do things.

When I feel insecure, I can turn into a whiny baby just looking for someone to take care of me. I'm tenacious and when I get ahold of someone, I don't let go. I can really get my hooks in and hang on. But when I've got myself together, this tenacity is only healthy persistence. I work long and hard until I reach my goal. I may get there crabwise, but I do stick to it until it's achieved.

Domesticity turns me on and I like a womanly woman with big breasts who can cook a good meal and provide a romantic atmosphere. Once my security is assured, I can get into intimacy in a big way. I like staying home, cuddling, using erotica. I'm not aggressive, but I can get wrapped up in lovemaking for hours on end. I'm a sentimental dreamer.

MARS IN LEO MAN

I like being a man. I'm proud and passionate and I always do everything in a big way. I hate to fuss with the details. I go for the big picture and I go for the gold. I never settle for second best. I'd rather have a grand failure than a small success. I hate what's mediocre and tawdry. Whatever I do, I put my whole heart and energy into it, and I work hard to bring all of my creativity potential to bear on whatever it is. I get totally behind a project when I believe in it. In fact, I can get so fired up with a sense of mission that I become somewhat fanatical. I've got to put my personal stamp on what I get involved in. Leadership comes easily to me and I gravitate toward the power center. I know I was born to rule, and because of this I am generous and open. I believe in benevolent rule. My honor is unimpeachable and I'm never afraid to take the heat. Being important brings heavy responsibilities.

I confess to being hot-tempered, self-centered, and sometimes imperial-seeming, but I'm never petty or stingy. I give with an open heart and I'll share what I have with those I like. I'm affectionate and give out a lot of attention. I like to see people respond to my warmth and love—they can get a tan just from my glow. I'm trusting to a fault, and once you're an intimate of mine you've got my full trust. Only an overt betrayal will make me default on that, for until I'm hit over the head with the evidence, I expect everyone else to be as loyal and honorable as I am.

Sexually, I'm a passionate man. I crave romance and drama and I want to sweep my lady love off her feet and give her the movie version of life and love. Glamour and power turn me on, in a woman and in life. I like trips to exotic places with luxurious surroundings as part of my love life, and I'm always in charge. I'm not afraid to show my affection and I'll fight for my rights. I can overpower those who can't stand their ground. I don't need a woman to shore up my ego by being a doormat. I want her to be queen to my king, and I want us to look good together and give off an aura of power. I need to love and be loved in a big way that's affectionate and demonstrative.

MARS IN VIRGO MAN

I'm an exacting sort of person with a great sense of technique. I like using my rational mind to reason things out or to make things happen. I'm very practical and I like to know why things work. Working with my hands gives me pleasure, whether it's crafting something, typing, even cooking. I am a hands-on guy and I don't mind getting my hands dirty, for afterward I can enjoy getting them clean again. Whatever I do, I like to make sure it's done in the correct and proper sequence. For that reason, I like to study manuals that explain clearly what to do or how to use a special piece of equipment. Using a tool properly is a craft in itself. I can be creative, but it is the master craftsmanship kind of thing, not spontaneous artistry. I work methodically and sequentially, always striving to be the best I can be at whatever it is I am doing.

There are those who find me prim or call me a prude, but it's not true. Underneath my meticulousness hides a satyr, a Pan, who can play the pipes of earthy sensuality. Clean and neat turns me on, but don't be fooled. I give great back rubs and know just which oils are best. I'm very thorough when it comes to making love, for I pride myself on being effective and reliable. I'm gentlemanly and naturally intelligent, though I have trained my mind to be a disciplined and useful tool. I like to keep my body in the same condition. A fit mind in a fit body is my goal.

I like old-fashioned women, the kind that are both competent and intelligent. I know a lady when I meet one, and I can recognize class. Though I don't like to show off, I'll pay a lot of attention to her details and compliment her on a pin she's wearing or notice she's had her hair dressed differently. I'll be sensitive to what she likes, whether it's at the dinner table or in bed, and do it for her to the best of my ability. I'm a perfectionist, and I always want her to have the perfect experience with me. Sometimes this gets in the way of my pleasing myself, because I'm so critical to make sure it's just right. Still, when I do get it "just right" it makes me and my partner very happy. That's worth working for, isn't it?

MARS IN LIBRA MAN

I'm a lover, not a fighter. The only thing that will make me stand up and fight is injustice. I'm good at fighting for others' rights, not so good at fighting for my own. That's because I was brought up to be polite, with good manners—a person who did not offend or hurt someone else. I'm a gentleman, and a gentleman always takes the other person's feelings into consideration before his own. I don't mind doing this because I prize equality among people. It's the best way to achieve grace and harmony in any situation, and I do this with considerable finesse. Because of my natural charm, I'm a good mediator, for I can acutely appraise what's really going on and act accordingly to keep or restore the balance. I hate to lose my cool and it's very hard for me to show anger. Despite this, I'm often caught in the middle. I'd rather kill with kindness than get mad at someone. You catch more flies with honey. Because I want people to like each other, I turn the other cheek.

This trait is a great advantage in social situations, but it's not so great for me personally. In my zeal to bend to the other guy's position, I often neglect *my* needs. Then I get mad at myself for being so easy. When this happens, I become devious and do subversive things, like being late for dates or forgetting something that's important to the other person. Accidentally on purpose, as it were. And when I finally allow myself to know that I'm mad, I recall every slight and disappointment of the last decade—which, of course, I was too well-mannered to mention at the time they happened!

Grace and beauty turn me on in a woman, as does her intelligence and aesthetic taste. Sexually, I always remain a gentleman. I'm affectionate and want lovemaking to be mutually enjoyable, in elegant, sensual surroundings. No kinky stuff for me. My ideal woman is very feminine with a sharp brain. In my search for the perfect balance, I swing between extremes, first going for the brainless beauty queen and then for the plain-Jane scholar. Still, I *must* be in a relationship. Sharing and equality are vital to me.

MARS IN SCORPIO MAN

I am a prime risk-taker in all areas of my life, but sex is the main one. I test myself constantly and go to the extreme. Polarities attract me powerfully. Love and hate. Life and death. Birth and rebirth. Light and dark. Good and evil. I experience them in myself deliberately, for I must plumb the depths of any experience. My gaze can undress people, but it not only takes off their clothes, it goes down into their souls and sees what they are hiding there. I'm a natural psychoanalyst. I'm a builder, but I also like tearing down things so they can be rebuilt better. I recycle everything, from my garbage to my love life, to squeeze out the essence of meaning. Whatever I do, it's with great intensity and feeling. *Passion* is the word—lots of it. I can even go so far as to give up sex altogether for a long time, just to test myself and exert self-discipline. Or I can debase myself in exotic or far-out situations. I seek the dark side the better to know the light. Since I've lived close to the edge, I know the need for self-control. I can be secretive, because there's always much more going on with me than meets the eye, and there's a lot I keep to myself.

The saying "Be careful what you wish for, you may get it" applies to me. I have a talent for making things happen. My desire nature is so powerful it can run my life, which is why I practice discipline. But I have to be careful I don't then over-control. I walk a tightrope between the dangerous and the divine, which is why I'm attracted to fanatical religions. I've a taste for vengeance so look out. I can wipe you out with sarcasm or simply decide you don't exist. Fire or ice. I'll get you even if I have to destroy myself in the process. It will still be satisfying.

Sex for me is often a place to act out my power issues, and I can dominate or be dominated. The right woman can make it a spiritual experience that will transform me into the sublime human being I really am. We have to go through a lot together before I can trust her, but once I do we rise to the heights and join the company of angels. And that's worth everything.

MARS IN SAGITTARIUS MAN

Mine is an adventurous spirit. Whether it's mental or physical, I've got to keep moving around. I travel constantly, even if it's only a commuter's drive or in my mind. I like to learn about everything and anything, for that keeps me moving forward. Other cultures, other countries, other languages all interest me. I know that there's nothing, and I mean nothing, that I can't do if I set my mind to it and want it badly enough. I just don't believe in the word *no*. I'm a positive thinker and an optimist. I'm always looking for the pot of gold at the end of the rainbow, because I know it's there somewhere. I have a special mission in life, even if I haven't yet figured out what it is. That's why spiritual issues are important for me. But they have to be of my own choosing, not something someone else tries to ram down my throat. I'm independent and I won't be led by anyone else's ideas. I develop my own. Then, when I'm satisfied, I'm very true to what I believe. I confess it's hard for me to stay in one place long enough to find out what I need to know, and I'm not always realistic about what I choose to believe.

Still, I'll risk my all to get to the higher truth, for I crave the excitement of exploring the unknown and I'm greatly motivated to understand everything I contact. You always know where you stand with me, and I'll always tell you what I think, even if not asked. I'm blunt and free with my speech and my thoughts—honest to a fault as they say. Sometimes I say too much or the wrong thing, but I know how to temper it with humor. I love to laugh and most everybody laughs with me.

Even when I make love, I laugh and have fun. Especially when I make love. If sex isn't fun, why do it? On the other hand, I can be very spiritual about my sexuality and lovemaking, to the point of practicing spiritual rituals connected with it. I see sex as an expression of the highest we humans can reach as well as the most carnal. I don't make a commitment until I'm sure, for I'm a ramblin' man by nature. Limitations frustrate me unbearably and I like my freedom—too well. Of course, I'm searching for my true love and the love I can believe in forever, but in the meantime I need to explore many different women. How else will I know when I meet the right one?

MARS IN CAPRICORN MAN

Count on me for stability and endurance. I may not be the flashiest guy on the block, but I'm probably the most reliable. And the most ethical. I'm very success-oriented, but my idea of success may not be the other guy's idea. Though I stick within the establishment and I work hard, I'm basically a loner and an individualist. If it goes against my moral code, I simply won't do it and no amount of outside pressure will make me cave in. My primary interest lies in creating a power base for myself founded on my own stringent determinations, so I'm realistic in my actions. If I have to kowtow to the corporate dress code, it doesn't bother me. I'll grow a beard on my vacation. I know how to do a lot with very little, and I know the true meaning of *conservative*. It means "conservation," basic, down-to-earth ideals. I was raised on the work ethic and money and prestige mean a lot to me. That's how you survive in this world. And I mean to survive and thrive, and be able to protect those I love.

I'm not the world's fastest starter. Remember the tortoise and the hare? I'm the tortoise. I go slow but I get there. The race is not always to the swift, remember that. In the long run, it's endurance and stick-to-it-iveness that count. I'm a planner and therefore not very spontaneous, but I'm well-organized and I know what's expected of me. The spotlight doesn't interest me. I prefer to work behind the scenes. I'd rather be kingmaker than king. And I'm in no hurry. Because I know I'll make it.

I'm the same with relationships. I take my time and wait to see that things are right and will work out. I like a woman who is proper and knows and respects appropriate social behavior. Acting out in public is one sure way to chase me off in the opposite direction. I confess I'm not the most confident of men. I can fade into the woodwork in my desire not to be too obvious, and this makes me repressed about my feelings. I had to learn self-control early as a survival tool, but along with it came a whole set of inhibitions. Once released, however, I can romp in the hay in a most earthy way! On the job or in bed, I'm good for the long haul.

MARS IN AQUARIUS MAN

Mr. Cool, that's me. I even identify with extraterrestrials. I like all sorts of typical male-type things, like motorcycles and aerodynamics, but my interest is purely mental. I'm not at all a macho man in reality. What I am is detached and intellectual. My approach to life is mostly theoretical. It's safer that way. I don't like to get involved. It's too messy and when emotions get heated it's impossible to figure out what's going on. I hate being confused or losing my cool, and I rarely get angry because being involved breeds subjectivity and that blows my style. You might say I am a scientist of life, because I can create a theory to explain almost anything. I prefer keeping things mental and objective.

I'm caught up in my humanitarian ideals and trying to live up to them. I believe in brotherhood and universality, at least in theory. Practice is another thing, but I don't worry about it. I like experimentation of all kinds, including sexual. I'll explore the idea of bisexuality or asexuality. I may not bother to actually do it, but I'll consider it as a possibility. I like to look at all the options because I might want a change tomorrow. Change is my thing. I have a hard time relating to individuals as such, but I like the idea of joining a celibate community devoted to higher ideals. Study appeals to me when it is of a spiritual nature—just so long as things don't get too personal. I'd rather make a major commitment to a community than to an individual.

My ideal woman is both brilliant and beautiful, but not in an ordinary, generic blonde way. Something exotic, special, or far-out attracts me. I like unusual people and unique anything. I've no trouble being a man but I don't go for the macho behavior. It's too crude and nonintellectual. I think the mind is the sexiest. It's the mind that determines what we find erotic. The body is just a follower while the mind is the leader. My main problem is that I tend to dissect everything, and once I've analyzed a woman and learned what makes her tick, I'm likely to get bored and move on to the next specimen. Or I can turn myself on by just thinking about sex. I don't even have to do it.

MARS IN PISCES MAN

I have the soul of a poet. I don't always show it, but I'm a sensitive man. I feel my way through life. Logic isn't one of my strong points. I follow my hunches and usually get where I'm going, even if it takes me a bit longer by an indirect route. But the scenery on the winding country lane is much more attractive than on the highway. I like to put my toe in the water before I step in all the way, and I wave my mental antennae around to pick up the currents in the air before I make a definitive statement. I have to fight my own indifference, because I'm prone to just float and fluctuate in an unmotivated state. Like a sailboat, I have to catch the breeze before I can move. Then I'm quick and sure and to the point. And I constantly adjust to which way the wind is blowing, using strategy rather than confrontation to get things accomplished.

I don't always understand why I do things because I'm not partic-

ularly straightforward but sort of multidetermined, and I'm guided
by my imagination and inner sensitivities. I come up with creative
solutions this way, but I usually have no clue where they came from.
Ambiguity isn't a problem for me because nothing is what it seems,
and things can have multiple meanings anyway. I like to be helpful
and kind, and I can be self-sacrificing for those I love. My idealism
carries me through hurts and disappointments but I have to watch
out for my anger sneaking up on me unawares. I have a propensity
for violent response when negative feelings get loose in me and become
overwhelming. Especially if I've had one too many.

I'm in love with being in love, and the romantic atmosphere inspires
me to write poetry and send flowers. Give me the works—sexy lingerie,
lovely fragrance, candlelight, the moon and roses, imaginative sex
play. Especially by the sea. Being submerged is a wonderful feeling
and I can really get into the flow of true intimacy. Under the right
conditions, I can go for a long time. Afterward, I like to send beautiful
cards or flowers or special gifts to commemorate our blissful experience.

part five

THE REVIEWS

chapter twenty

RAVE REVIEWS

Now that you have read the Astroscripts for your Star Self and your Co-Star, and have begun to understand each other's Play Within, you are ready to review the relationship.

Below is your Basic Astropoint Relationship form. List the signs in which your Star Self and your Co-Star's Astropoints fall:

BASIC ASTROPOINT RELATIONSHIP FORM

Star Self	Co-Star
SUN in _____	SUN in _____
MOON in _____	MOON in _____
ASC in _____	ASC in _____
VENUS in _____	VENUS in _____
MARS in _____	MARS in _____

When filled out, the form will look like this one, which we filled out for our sample couple, discussed in Chapters 12 and 13.

Sample Woman	Sample Man
SUN in CANCER	SUN in SCORPIO
MOON in AQUARIUS	MOON in TAURUS
ASC in SAGITTARIUS	ASC in LEO
VENUS in TAURUS	VENUS in LIBRA
MARS in VIRGO	MARS in SAGITTARIUS

Using your filled-out Basic Astropoint Relationship form, you will go through the next four chapters, comparing your and your Co-Star's Astropoints to see how they make contact with and affect each other. To do this, you will need to prepare a blank form for each chapter. We have provided one fill-in line for each, but you should use as many blank lines as you have Astropoints to compare. This is likely to differ in each chapter. We suggest that you use separate sheets of paper for each chapter. These forms will give you your Basic Astropoint contacts for scoring each chapter.

When you have totaled your score for each chapter, you will enter it on the Master Scoresheet on page 321.

SCORING YOUR RAVE REVIEWS

To compare your Astropoints for Rave Reviews, list all the Astropoints between your Star Self and your Co-Star that *match* (that is, that are found in the same sign).

For example, if your Sun is in Leo and your Co-Star's Moon is in Leo, your Sun *matches* your Co-Star's Moon.

Use the form provided below, and be sure you compare *all* of both of your Astropoints.

Rave Reviews Form

Star Self   Co-Star

───────── matches ─────────
Astropoint   Astropoint

Our sample couple's *matching* Astropoints are:

Star Self		Co-Star
ASC	matches	MARS
VENUS	matches	MOON

Note that we are listing *only* the Astropoint and *not* the sign on the Rave Reviews Form. For purposes of our scoring system, it is not necessary to note the sign on any of the forms we'll be using in this and the next three chapters. In fact, it can even be confusing. So just use the Astropoint alone, and use as many blank lines as you need.

MIRRORED PAIRS

Once you have listed all of your and your partner's Astropoint matches, look over your Rave Reviews Form for Mirrored Pairs.

A Mirrored Pair involves not one but *two* sets of Astropoint contacts that "mirror" each other. If, for example, your Moon matches your Co-Star's Venus, then look to see if that Moon/Venus match is "mirrored" by a Venus/Moon match (that is, your Venus is in the same sign, or matches, your partner's Moon).

Diagrammatically, these Mirrored Pairs form a diagonal cross:

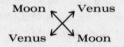

Because our sample couple has no Mirrored Pairs in their Rave Reviews, we will use a hypothetical Rave Reviews Form from a different couple to show you how to find a Mirrored Pair.

Star Self		Co-Star
SUN	matches	*ASC*
SUN	matches	MARS
MOON	matches	VENUS
ASC	matches	*SUN*
VENUS	matches	ASC
VENUS	matches	MARS

Notice that we have underlined the *SUN/ASC*, *ASC/SUN* Mirrored Pair so that you can see it quickly.

Now look over your own Rave Reviews Form to see if you have any Mirrored Pairs. List them at the bottom of the form like this:
Mirrored Pairs—*SUN/ASC*
ASC/SUN

SPECIAL COMBINATIONS

Special Combinations are Astropoint pairs that have special significance. They have a stronger effect, for good or for ill, on your relationship than ordinary Astropoint pairs.

If you and your Co-Star have any of the following matches, you have a Special Combination.

Special Combinations for Rave Reviews

Star Self		Co-Star
SUN	matches	MOON
MOON	matches	SUN
MOON	matches	MOON
MOON	matches	VENUS
VENUS	matches	MOON
VENUS	matches	MARS
MARS	matches	VENUS

Our sample couple has one Special Combination under Rave Reviews.

Star Self		Co-Star
VENUS	matches	MOON

Using your Rave Reviews Form, list any Special Combinations below your Mirrored Pairs: Special Combinations—Venus/Mars.

SCORING

Here's how to score your potential for a Rave Review:

1. Score 10 points for each pair of matching Astropoints.
2. Score an *additional* 10 points for each Mirrored Pair.
3. Score an *additional* 20 points for each Special Combination.

Your scoresheet for Rave Reviews should look like this:

Rave Reviews (_____ @ 10 points)   = _____
Mirrored Pairs (_____ @ 10 points)   = _____
Special Combinations (_____ @ 20 points) = _____
   Total Rave Reviews   + _____

For example, our sample couple's score is:

Rave Reviews: 2 @ 10 points   = 20
Mirrored Pairs: 0 @ 10 points   = 0
Special Combinations: 1 @ 20 points = 20
Total   + 40

Now turn to the Master Scoresheet on page 321 and fill in your own Total Rave Reviews score.

chapter twenty-one

GOOD REVIEWS

Congratulations! You've gotten this far, and even if your relationship didn't pull any Rave Reviews (we hope it did!), you are now ready to find out what the potential for Good Reviews is. Remember, not every show has to get Rave Reviews to have a long, profitable run. But it will need at least *some* Good Reviews.

Good Reviews are the *compatible* Astropoints between partners. The *compatible* signs are:

ARIES	and	LEO/SAGITTARIUS/AQUARIUS/GEMINI
TAURUS	and	VIRGO/CAPRICORN/CANCER/PISCES
GEMINI	and	LIBRA/AQUARIUS/LEO/ARIES
CANCER	and	SCORPIO/PISCES/VIRGO/TAURUS
LEO	and	SAGITTARIUS/ARIES/LIBRA/GEMINI
VIRGO	and	CAPRICORN/TAURUS/SCORPIO/CANCER
LIBRA	and	AQUARIUS/GEMINI/LEO/SAGITTARIUS
SCORPIO	and	PISCES/CANCER/VIRGO/CAPRICORN
SAGITTARIUS	and	ARIES/LEO/AQUARIUS/LIBRA
CAPRICORN	and	TAURUS/VIRGO/PISCES/SCORPIO
AQUARIUS	and	GEMINI/LIBRA/SAGITTARIUS/ARIES
PISCES	and	CANCER/SCORPIO/TAURUS/VIRGO

Using your Basic Astropoint Relationship form and the Good Reviews Form below, list all the Astropoints between you and your Co-Star that are *compatible*. For example, if your Moon is in Aries and your Co-Star's Venus is in Sagittarius, your Moon is *compatible* with your Co-Star's Venus.

Good Reviews Form

Star Self		Co-Star
——————	compatible with	——————
Astropoint		Astropoint

In addition to the preceding listing of compatible signs, certain combinations of Venus with *any other Astropoint* become compatible. So check your Basic Astropoint Relationship form for any of the following *Venus-Compatible* placements and add these to your list of Basic Astropoints for Good Reviews.

VENUS-COMPATIBLE PLACEMENTS

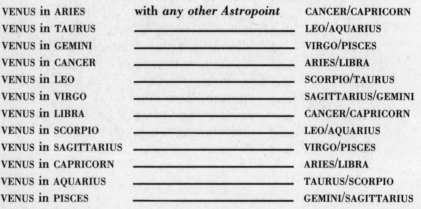

VENUS in ARIES	with *any other Astropoint*	CANCER/CAPRICORN
VENUS in TAURUS	——————————————	LEO/AQUARIUS
VENUS in GEMINI	——————————————	VIRGO/PISCES
VENUS in CANCER	——————————————	ARIES/LIBRA
VENUS in LEO	——————————————	SCORPIO/TAURUS
VENUS in VIRGO	——————————————	SAGITTARIUS/GEMINI
VENUS in LIBRA	——————————————	CANCER/CAPRICORN
VENUS in SCORPIO	——————————————	LEO/AQUARIUS
VENUS in SAGITTARIUS	——————————————	VIRGO/PISCES
VENUS in CAPRICORN	——————————————	ARIES/LIBRA
VENUS in AQUARIUS	——————————————	TAURUS/SCORPIO
VENUS in PISCES	——————————————	GEMINI/SAGITTARIUS

For example, if *either person* has Venus in Aries and the other person has Mars in Cancer, that pair of Astropoints is *Venus-Compatible*.

Our sample couple's *compatible* Astropoints are:

Star Self		Co-Star
SUN	compatible with	SUN
SUN	compatible with	MOON
MOON	compatible with	VENUS
MOON	compatible with	MARS
ASC	compatible with	ASC
ASC	compatible with	VENUS
MARS	compatible with	SUN
MARS	compatible with	MOON

Our sample couple's *Venus-compatible* Astropoints are:

Star Self		Co-Star
SUN	Venus-compatible with	VENUS
VENUS	Venus-compatible with	ASC

Once you have compared all your compatible Astropoints, and those that are Venus-compatible, look for Mirrored Pairs as you did in Rave Reviews. In Rave Reviews we were looking for Mirrored Pairs that were *matching*. Here we are looking for Mirrored Pairs that are *compatible*. Use your Good Reviews Form to find any Mirrored Pairs and list them beneath your Basic Astropoints (which include the Venus-compatible points).

For example, our sample couple has *two* Mirrored Pairs:

Star Self		Co-Star
MOON	compatible with	MARS
MARS	compatible with	MOON

and

ASC	compatible with	VENUS
VENUS	compatible with	ASC

Note that the Venus/ASC from the second Mirrored Pair comes from the Venus-compatible list in their charts.

After listing your Mirrored Pairs, check your Good Reviews Form for these Special Combinations. The Special Combinations for Good

Reviews are *different* from the Special Combinations for Rave Reviews.

Special Combinations for Good Reviews

Star Self		Co-Star
SUN	compatible with	MOON
MOON	compatible with	SUN
MOON	compatible with	MOON
MOON	compatible with	VENUS
MOON	compatible with	MARS
VENUS	compatible with	MOON
VENUS	compatible with	MARS
MARS	compatible with	MOON
MARS	compatible with	VENUS

Note that Special Combinations may be found in either your Basic Astropoint list or in your Venus-compatible list.

Our sample couple has *four* Special Combinations:

Star Self		Co-Star
SUN	compatible with	MOON
MOON	compatible with	VENUS
MOON	compatible with	MARS
MARS	compatible with	MOON

Next, list any Special Combinations below your Mirrored Pairs. Here's how to score your Good Reviews potential:

1. Score 5 points for any pair of compatible Astropoints.
2. Score an *additional* 10 points for any Mirrored Pair.
3. Score an *additional* 15 points for each Special Combination.

Your scoresheet for Good Reviews should look like this:

Good Reviews (_____ @ 5 points)   = _____
Mirrored Pairs (_____ @ 10 points)   = _____
Special Combinations (_____ @ 15 points)   = _____
     Total Good Reviews   + _____

Our sample couple's score is:

Good Reviews: 10 @ 5 points   =   50
Mirrored Pairs: 2 @ 10 points   =   20
Special Combinations: 4 @ 15 points =   60
Total   = 130

Now turn to the Master Scoresheet on page 321 and fill in your Total Good Reviews score.

chapter twenty-two

MIXED REVIEWS

If your relationship was not "made in Heaven" (and few are!), then even though you may have some Good Reviews, you are likely also to have some Mixed Reviews. Mind you, they aren't terrible. The Astropoints involved in Mixed Reviews provide the spice in a relationship. If *all* your Astropoints fell under Rave Reviews and Good Reviews, you'd be bored to death with each other in short order. So, a few mixed reviews are like the pepper in the soup or the salt in the pie crust!

Mixed Reviews occur when Astropoints between charts are in *opposite* signs. You may remember our discussion of opposites in Chapter 3 and, although we have said quite a lot about opposites being complementary and that opposites attract, nonetheless they remain *opposite* and therefore are subject to a Mixed Review.

The opposite signs are as follows:

ARIES	LIBRA
TAURUS	SCORPIO
GEMINI	SAGITTARIUS
CANCER	CAPRICORN
LEO	AQUARIUS
VIRGO	PISCES
LIBRA	ARIES
SCORPIO	TAURUS
SAGITTARIUS	GEMINI
CAPRICORN	CANCER
AQUARIUS	LEO
PISCES	VIRGO

Once again, use your Basic Astropoint Relationship form and the Mixed Reviews Form below to total your potential for Mixed Reviews. For example, if your Sun is in Leo and your Co-Star's Moon is in Aquarius, your Sun is *opposite* your Co-Star's Moon.

Mixed Reviews Form

Star Self		Co-Star
_____	opposite	_____
Astropoint		Astropoint

Our sample couple's *opposite* Astropoints are:

Star Self		Co-Star
MOON	opposite	ASC
VENUS	opposite	SUN

After listing *all* your pairs of *opposite* Astropoints, cross out any that include Mars, except for Mars with Venus or Venus with Mars. Disregard the crossed-out Mars combinations since they do not apply to Mixed Reviews.

Now, check for Mirrored Pairs that are in *opposite* signs, and list any you find. Note that our sample couple has no Mirrored Pairs under Mixed Reviews.

After listing your Mirrored Pairs, check your Basic Astropoint Form for Special Combinations, as follows:

Special Combinations for Mixed Reviews

Star Self		Co-Star
SUN	opposite	SUN
SUN	opposite	MOON
MOON	opposite	SUN
MOON	opposite	MOON
VENUS	opposite	MARS*
MARS	opposite	VENUS*

*See No. 3 in the scoring instructions.

Here's how to score your Mixed Reviews potential:

1. Score 15 points for any pair of opposite Astropoints, remembering to *exclude* the Mars pairs as instructed.
2. Score an *additional* 10 points for each Mirrored Pair.
3. Score an *additional* 5 points for each Venus/Mars or Mars/Venus Special Combination.
4. *Subtract* 10 points for each regular Special Combination.

Your scoresheet for Mixed Reviews should look like this:

Mixed Reviews (_____ @ 15 points)   = _____
Mirrored Pairs (_____ @ 10 points)   = _____
Mars/Venus Combination (_____ @ 5 points)   = _____
Special Combinations (_____ @ −10 points)   = −_____
     Total Mixed Reviews   + _____

Our sample couple's score is:

Mixed Reviews: 2 @ 15 points   = 30
   Total   = 30

Now turn to the Master Scoresheet on page 321 and fill in your Total Mixed Reviews score.

chapter twenty-three

BAD REVIEWS

Well, into each life some rain must fall. . . .

By now you've gotten an idea of the most compatible components between your Star Self and your Co-Star, and now it's time to look under the rug. Bad Reviews result when signs between charts are in *incompatible* positions so that they *conflict*.

The incompatible signs are:

ARIES	conflicts with	CANCER/CAPRICORN
TAURUS	————	LEO/AQUARIUS
GEMINI	————	VIRGO/PISCES
CANCER	————	ARIES/LIBRA
LEO	————	SCORPIO/TAURUS
VIRGO	————	SAGITTARIUS/GEMINI
LIBRA	————	CANCER/CAPRICORN
SCORPIO	————	LEO/AQUARIUS
SAGITTARIUS	————	VIRGO/PISCES
CAPRICORN	————	ARIES/LIBRA
AQUARIUS	————	TAURUS/SCORPIO
PISCES	————	GEMINI/SAGITTARIUS

For example, if your Moon is in Leo and your Co-Star's Sun is in Scorpio, your Moon conflicts with your Co-Star's Sun.

However, as Venus is *always* benevolent and she never conflicts with any other Astropoint, *do not count any Venus combinations in Bad Reviews*.

Use your Basic Astropoint Relationship form and the Bad Reviews Form below to list any of your own conflicting Astropoints.

Bad Reviews Form

Star Self   Co-Star

———— conflicts with ————
Astropoint   Astropoint

In addition to the preceding listing of conflicting signs, certain combinations of Mars with any other Astropoint become conflicting.

So check your Basic Astropoint Relationship form for any of the
following *Mars-conflicting* placements, and add these to your list of
Basic Astropoints for Bad Reviews.

MARS-CONFLICTING PLACEMENTS

MARS in ARIES	conflicts with *any other Astropoint* in	LIBRA
MARS in TAURUS	————————————————	SCORPIO
MARS in GEMINI	————————————————	SAGITTARIUS
MARS in CANCER	————————————————	CAPRICORN
MARS in LEO	————————————————	AQUARIUS
MARS in VIRGO	————————————————	PISCES
MARS in LIBRA	————————————————	ARIES
MARS in SCORPIO	————————————————	TAURUS
MARS in SAGITTARIUS	————————————————	GEMINI
MARS in CAPRICORN	————————————————	CANCER
MARS in AQUARIUS	————————————————	LEO
MARS in PISCES	————————————————	VIRGO

For example, if your Mars is in Aries and your Co-Star's Moon is
in Libra, that pair of Astropoints is *Mars-conflicting*. However, *do
not count* Mars/Venus or Venus/Mars combinations. These, as we
noted earlier, are always positive because of Venus involvement.
Merely skip these in your listing if they occur.

Our sample couple has *three* conflicting Astropoints:

Star Self		Co-Star
MOON	conflicts with	SUN
MOON	conflicts with	MOON
MARS	conflicts with	MARS

Check your listing for conflicting Mirrored Pairs, as before. Our
sample couple has no Mirrored Pairs.

Now check for these Special Combinations:

Special Combinations for Bad Reviews

Star Self		Co-Star
SUN	conflicts with	MOON
MOON	conflicts with	SUN
SUN	conflicts with	MARS
MARS	conflicts with	SUN
MOON	conflicts with	MARS
MARS	conflicts with	MOON
MOON	conflicts with	MOON*
MARS	conflicts with	MARS*

*See No. 4 in scoring instructions.

Please note that all of our sample couple's Basic Astropoint pairs are Special Combinations.

Here's how to score your Bad Reviews potential:

1. Deduct 15 points for any pair of Astropoints.

2. Deduct an *additional* 10 points for any Mirrored Pair.

3. Deduct an *additional* 10 points for each Special Combination, including Moon/Moon and Mars/Mars.

4. For Moon/Moon or Mars/Mars Special Combinations, deduct *another* 15 points.

Your scoresheet for Bad Reviews should look like this:

Bad Reviews (_____ @ −15 points) = −_____
Mirrored Pairs (_____ @ −10 points) = −_____
Special Combinations (_____ @ −10 points) = −_____
Moon/Moon or Mars/Mars
  Special Combinations (_____ @ −15 points) = −_____
    Total Bad Reviews −_____

Our sample couple's score is:

Bad Reviews: 3 @ −15 points = −45
Special Combinations: 3 @ −10 points = −30
Moon/Moon or Mars/ Mars Special
  Combinations: 2 @ −15 points = −30
    Total = −105

Now turn to the Master Scoresheet on page 321 and fill in your Total Bad Reviews score.

chapter twenty-four

THEME AND VARIATION

In addition to the numerical scoring system, another way to review your relationship is through understanding the themes that occur between you. Knowing your themes will give you even more information about what's good, not so good, or bad.

There are three kinds of themes: your Astropoint Theme, your Element Theme, and your Mode Theme. Each of these will affect the general tenor of your relationship.

To determine your Astropoint Theme, you will need to refer to your forms for Rave, Good, Mixed, and Bad Reviews. Using the Astropoint Theme Scoresheet that follows, count the number of times *the same Astropoint* (that is, Sun, Moon, ASC, Venus, Mars) occurs in *all* the review categories, for both yourself and your Co-Star. Enter these totals for each Astropoint accordingly, then choose the highest number—it tells you the Astropoint Theme of your relationship. If, for example, your relationship scores 9 Suns, 8 Moons, 6 ASCs, 10 Venuses, and 5 Mars, you have a Venus Astropoint Theme.

Our sample couple has a Moon Astropoint Theme.

If there is *no highest number*, and two of the numbers are *equal*—that is, if you have two Astropoints totaling 6 and none higher—then you have a mixed Astropoint Theme, or for example, Sun/Moon Theme.

If you have *more than two* Astropoint totals that are the same, and none higher, then you have a multiple Astropoint Theme, and you will need to read all of the theme analyses involved.

Astropoint Theme Scoresheet

ASTROPOINT	SUN	MOON	ASC	VENUS	MARS
Rave Reviews	___	___	___	___	___
Good Reviews	___	___	___	___	___
Mixed Reviews	___	___	___	___	___
Bad Reviews	___	___	___	___	___
Total	___	___	___	___	___
Astropoint Theme =					

Astropoint Theme = _____

Astropoint Theme Scoresheet for Sample Couple

ASTROPOINT	SUN	MOON	ASC	VENUS	MARS
Rave Reviews		1	1	1	1
Good Reviews	5	4	4	4	3
Mixed Reviews	1	1	1	1	
Bad Reviews	1	3			2
Total	7	9	6	6	6

Astropoint Theme = *MOON*

ASTROPOINT THEMES

SUN THEME   Your relationship supports both of your life purposes—you feel you can be yourselves with each other. The person whose sun appears more often feels this more strongly. There is also a lot of vitality between you two. You stand out together, attracting attention whether or not you try to. You find it easy to express yourself with each other. Clashing egos can be a problem as is the lack of ability to compromise with one another.

MOON THEME   This is a very emotional relationship. You really feel for each other. One or both of you mothers the other, and children are often important in the relationship. You feel at home together, whether or not you are from similar backgrounds. Home, food, family, and security are important. Infantile, fearful, clannish, or control with care-taking behavior a problem.

ASCENDANT THEME   When the Ascendant is the theme, the two of you match well, often looking good together. Even if you are of different races or social classes, people see you as a set, and your public image is strong. You like to do things together and going out in the world and facing life is easier when you have each other. You strengthen each other's identities. Superficiality and focusing mainly on what you do and how you appear can be a problem.

VENUS THEME   A Venus relationship feels good, and life is beautiful when you are together. Love, romance, pleasure, art, affection, pleasantness—plus aesthetic pursuits such as dance, art, film, and music—are important. You feel attractive and attracted in this relationship. It's natural to be sweet. Being lazy and overly self-indulgent together, pampering each other to the point of not accomplishing anything, even if it is important, can be a problem.

MARS THEME   When Mars is the relationship theme, action and passion rule. You need to be active and like to do things together. Sex is a big deal, positively or negatively—if you're not making love you're battling each other or fighting for some cause together. You do well with goals to achieve. Danger is attractive, and power games in fun and for real abound. Selfishness, violence, and insensitivity to each other can be a problem.

SUN/MOON THEME   You feel like a matched set. It seems you are *supposed* to be together, the epitome of *man* and *woman*. You complete each other. Others also see you in this light. There is a wonderful feeling of complementarity—where one is soft, the other is strong; where one is aggressive, the other is gentle. You may polarize too much, setting up your own little universes, and that can cause problems.

SUN/ASCENDANT THEME   This relationship supports your identities. Your impact together is strong. Your social front as a couple and how you appear to others is important. In fact, you're a high-profile pair. You appear more important and better connected when you are together. You get a lot of response from other people about your relationship one way or another. Superficiality and too much concern about your social masks can be a problem.

SUN/VENUS THEME   You both feel and express lots of love, appreciation, and affection for each other. You feel supported in your value systems and well-liked. You acquire money or possessions as a couple. You beef up your identities with discussions about values, and share an interest in beauty, luxury, fine things, or the arts. The good life is yours—at least it feels that way—whether or not you have money. Be careful not to get hung up on your image as a couple and neglect your individuality.

SUN/MARS THEME   The two of you never stop doing things together. Energy, sexuality, drive, and ambition are major forces in your relationship. You are definitely a dynamic duo. The amount of heat you two produce needs directing, and sometimes fights ensue if it's not used constructively. Create together, be adventurous together, challenge yourselves together. The danger with this theme is being in competition with each other and beating each other up, physically or emotionally.

MOON/ASCENDANT THEME There is mutual support in this relationship. You two appear to be a romantic match, caring for and nurturing each other. You create a safe haven for one another, which allows you both to deal with the public better. In fact, together you make a home that is comfortable for others as well as yourselves, and you mother everybody. Being too dependent on each other or too clannish together can cause problems.

MOON/VENUS THEME With this combination, you both love *and* like each other. This theme helps overcome differences. You deal with problems in a loving and supportive manner. The bond you feel for each other is deep and positive, making it easy for you to appreciate one another. You feel natural together and like to make things—a lovely home, children, or creative projects. However, you may be too nice and ignore strife for too long, causing problems.

MOON/MARS THEME In this combination, emotions are at a high pitch. It's supercharged sexually— steamy and exciting. You are passionate and get into each other's vulnerable places. Your feelings are strong and the whole relationship will probably move quickly. This is a fertile and creative match— but not very calm. You may irritate each other on a daily basis, with neither of you feeling really safe. One may push, the other fear being pushed.

ASCENDANT/VENUS THEME With this theme, you appreciate each other. Because you're mutually supportive, it's easy for you to be personal. You like going out and doing things together. Life is more pleasant when you're around each other. Individually, you seem more beautiful when you are together. As a couple, you present a lovely face to the world. But you can fall into the trap of being too sweet and superficial as a couple, causing problems.

ASCENDANT/MARS THEME There's never a dull moment in this match. You are an exciting and challenging pair, doing things together and moving out into the world of action and adventure. You push each other to grow and are more aggressive as a couple than apart. At best, you have a unified front that will help you achieve your goals. If you don't channel all the heat you two generate you could wind up fighting, just to use the excess energy.

VENUS/MARS THEME This theme epitomizes "woman needs man and man needs woman." Your combined passion, love, and liking make for a grand romance. A very sexy combination, this is hot and sweet, and you quickly bond as a pair. You are drawn together on a primal level. Knowing you belong together as lovers can ameliorate other difficulties. The intense sexual haze may blind you to reality. Try to let it settle before making a major commitment.

If your Astropoint Theme for the relationship is repeated in an Astropoint pair in any of the Review categories, there is an *extra-theme emphasis*. An example of this is a Moon Astropoint Theme and a Moon/Moon pairing (such as Leo Moon matches Leo Moon under Rave Reviews).

Our sample couple has a Moon Astropoint Theme and under Bad Reviews, her Aquarius Moon conflicts with his Taurus Moon.

In the case of a mixed Astropoint Theme, if the two Astropoints are paired anywhere in the Reviews, it will emphasize whichever category (Rave, Good, etc.) is involved.

If the extra-theme emphasis involves Moon, Venus, or Moon/Venus mixed themes, being related is often the dominant factor of the relationship, and it is easy for one or both people to lose their individuality. A way to avoid this is to make sure each partner has some separate interest or activity to call his or her own.

If the extra-theme emphasis involves Mars or Sun/Mars mixed themes, being right may be more important than being related. If this is the case, give yourselves room to move and respect each other's independence and the right to a differing opinion. Practice consideration of each other and learn the art of compromise, knowing that sometimes it's necessary to do what you don't want to.

If the extra-theme emphasis occurs with Astropoints paired under Rave or Good Reviews, the theme will support the best expression of both parties in the way described for the theme. If the extra-theme emphasis occurs with Astropoints paired under Bad Reviews, it will make the relationship more difficult in the way described for the theme.

To determine your Element and Mode Themes, you will need to refer to your Basic Astropoint Relationship form. Using the form and the table below, make an extended Astropoint Relationship form where you list, in addition to the sign, the Element and Mode of the sign. For example, Leo is in the Element Fire and the Mode Fixed.

TABLE OF SIGNS, ELEMENTS, AND MODES

SIGN	ELEMENT	MODE
ARIES	FIRE	CARDINAL
TAURUS	EARTH	FIXED
GEMINI	*AIR*	*MUTABLE*
CANCER	*WATER*	CARDINAL
LEO	FIRE	FIXED
VIRGO	EARTH	*MUTABLE*
LIBRA	*AIR*	CARDINAL
SCORPIO	*WATER*	FIXED
SAGITTARIUS	FIRE	*MUTABLE*
CAPRICORN	EARTH	CARDINAL
AQUARIUS	*AIR*	FIXED
PISCES	*WATER*	*MUTABLE*

Here is your Element and Mode Themes Scoresheet:

Star Self

ASTROPOINT	SIGN	ELEMENT	MODE
SUN	_____	_____	_____
MOON	_____	_____	_____
ASC	_____	_____	_____
VENUS	_____	_____	_____
MARS	_____	_____	_____

(Example: LEO   FIRE   FIXED)

Co-Star

ASTROPOINT	SIGN	ELEMENT	MODE
SUN	_____	_____	_____
MOON	_____	_____	_____
ASC	_____	_____	_____
VENUS	_____	_____	_____
MARS	_____	_____	_____

Using this list, fill in the following chart with the number of times each Element and Mode occurs in your and your Co-Star's signs. Then total the two. The *highest* number in each category is your Element Theme and your Mode Theme. If you do not have a single highest number among either the Elements or Mode, you have a mixed Element or a mixed Mode Theme. For example, our sample couple has a Fire/Earth mixed Element Theme and a Fixed Mode Theme.

Element Theme Scoresheet for Sample Couple

ELEMENT THEME	FIRE	EARTH	AIR	WATER
STAR SELF	1	2	1	1
CO-STAR	2	1	1	1
TOTAL	3	3	2	2

ELEMENT THEME = *FIRE/EARTH*

Mode Theme Scoresheet for Sample Couple

MODE THEME	CARDINAL	FIXED	MUTABLE
STAR SELF	1	2	2
CO-STAR	1	3	1
TOTAL	2	5	3

MODE THEME = *FIXED*

Element Theme

	FIRE	EARTH	AIR	WATER
STAR SELF	_____	_____	_____	_____
CO-STAR	_____	_____	_____	_____
TOTAL	_____	_____	_____	_____

ELEMENT THEME = _____

Mode Theme

	CARDINAL	FIXED	MUTABLE
STAR SELF	_____	_____	_____
CO-STAR	_____	_____	_____
TOTAL	_____	_____	_____

MODE THEME = _____

ELEMENT THEMES
SINGLE ELEMENT THEMES

FIRE THEME   The two of you enjoy many activities and are able to be independent of each other as well. You both need space to breathe. You're romantic and expressive—sparks fly sexually and otherwise because you have tempers and spirit. If you fight, it's a good idea to do something physical while you work it out—take a walk, for example. Action will help quickly dissipate bad feelings.

AIR THEME   Your relationship involves much discussion. You love to talk to each other, you enjoy socializing. The quality you most like in your relationship is the mental stimulation. Words are an aphrodisiac. You learn together, exploring interesting ideas and concepts. However, you're not very practical as a couple. You can get lost in the mental stratosphere and forget the real world.

EARTH THEME   You're a stable, solid couple with a tendency to conservatism. A practical and reliable team, you are useful to each other, helping each other out by giving massages or doing the laundry. You feel very real together, and everyday life—or getting your act together—seems easier. Hanging on to the status quo and resisting anything new can make you inert and dull.

WATER THEME   This relationship is full of *feeling*. You don't have to do much more than be together. It's naturally intimate—you synchronize and flow into each other. You can even have the same moods. You're sensitive and perceptive, to each other and the world, so you create a haven for yourselves. There's danger of clinging, being dependent, and emotional excess.

MIXED ELEMENT THEMES

FIRE/AIR—AIR/FIRE THEME You two communicate well with plenty of give and take. The Fire inspires the Air's logic and ideas, and the Air feeds the Fire's flames. You are easily supportive of each other's projects and ideas. Air provides understanding of Fire's spontaneous expression. You have fun together, brainstorming ideas and putting them into action. You can overdo the extroverted couple role, running madly around and paying no attention to your feelings or whether things make sense.

FIRE/EARTH—EARTH/FIRE THEME   You are different, yet drawn to each other. At best, Fire's inspiration helps Earth move, and you two can make your dreams come true. Both have what the other lacks: Fire has the vision, hope, and spontaneity that Earth desires; Earth has the solidity, practicality, and usefulness that Fire wants. You need to be careful that Fire's speed and ardor don't burn Earth, that Earth doesn't put out Fire with heaviness and resistance.

FIRE/WATER—WATER/FIRE THEME   This is an emotional combination.   You are an extremely expressive couple, exciting and passionate. Together you can be creative and intuitive, with enough feeling and inspiration to share with others. The steam heat you produce can power a lot of things, but be careful of hysteria. You can lose the sense of how far to go and just keep acting and emoting. Water may drench Fire's heat, and Fire can evaporate Water's feeling. Both of you tend to get out of control.

AIR/EARTH—EARTH/AIR THEME You two put ideas into reality.   You're logical and practical as a couple and can be depended upon as a source of calm and reason when all about you are losing their heads. There is little wasted action with you, because you reason things out to find the most sensible solutions. Earth and Air have a difficult meeting of the minds. You may be dry and uninteresting, alienated from each other and other people. Earth and Air have a difficult meeting of the minds. It can seem you each come from different planets, because together you lack feeling and inspiration.

AIR/WATER—WATER/AIR THEME You are an intuitive and sensitive couple. Water understands feelings and compassion, Air understands ideas and concepts. You are fascinated with each other because of your differences. You react quickly, sometimes overreacting. You combine feeling and analysis, discerning subtle undercurrents. Water may become frustrated with Air's distant cut-and-dried approach, and Air may feel trapped by Water's constant emotional need to connect.

EARTH/WATER—WATER/EARTH THEME You are a solid and warm couple. Your relationship has a comfortable, homey quality to it. You are fertile together, figuratively and literally, and so you can seem like everyone's parents. You deal with practical matters in a feeling way. Water moistens and refreshes Earth's dryness, and Earth gives stability and security to Water's sensitivity. There is danger of getting insular and wrapped up in your own safe world, not letting in new ideas.

MODE THEMES
SINGLE MODE THEMES

CARDINAL THEME This relationship happens fast and is one of action. When you are together, you are spontaneous and original, always thinking of new things to do. You inspire each other to try new activities, think about things a new way, or see the world in a new light. There is danger of battles of will and power struggles when your enthusiasms collide.

FIXED THEME Your relationship is deep and meaningful. A powerhouse team, together you stand up to the world as a unified front. Once you get involved, which may take time, your relationship has great staying power. There is danger of rigidity and fear of change, for one person's growth can threaten the other. You both are strong, so try not to control each other.

MUTABLE THEME   Your relationship is flexible and interesting. You're a two-person band doing many different things, even looking different ways. Often you find you are involved without having noticed. You both adjust easily to changes in the relationship. There is danger of being too loose and letting the whole relationship dissolve because you never confront anything or commit to each other.

MIXED MODE THEMES

CARDINAL/FIXED THEME   A dynamic combination of will and power, one of you probably is the initiator, the other the finisher. You alternate between action and inaction. There can be power struggles if one person doesn't want to be pushed, or if one needs action and the other won't move.

CARDINAL/MUTABLE THEME   You're never bored. New ideas and flexibility combine to make a creative team. You may go constantly from one thing to another, never completely resolving the first before you're on to the next. You need to focus together, then you can accomplish whatever you want.

FIXED/MUTABLE THEME There's complementarity here. The person with more Fixed energy tends to get stuck in a rut, but the Mutable person can always flow around the problem. This combination has guts and the ability to identify problems and make changes. This will work well if you take risks together and try new things.

chapter twenty-five

THE REVIEWS ARE IN!

If you got quite a few Bad Reviews, cheer up. You might still win some extra bonus points!

Go back over your forms for the reviews and check for Mirrored Pairs. If any of your Mirrored Pairs are Moon/Venus–Venus/Moon or Venus/Mars–Mars/Venus, you get extra bonus points.

If one of these Mirrored Pairs occurs, score an extra 25 points. If *both* occur, take the grand slam of an extra 50 points.

Fill in these extra bonus points on the Master Scoresheet and then add up your grand total.

MASTER SCORESHEET*

RAVE REVIEWS (Total, page 298)   +_____

GOOD REVIEWS (Total, page 302)   +_____

MIXED REVIEWS (Total, page 306)   +_____

BAD REVIEWS (Total, page 309)   −_____

EXTRA BONUS POINTS (above)   +_____
Grand Total   _____

When you have the total, read on for what the numbers mean:

OVER 160—IT'S A HIT!

Top-of-the-line harmony prevails here, but this score needs a sexual charge to make it *romantic*. You'll remember Mars, the planet of sexual energy. If he appears with the Moon or Venus, under "Rave" or "Good Reviews," this can be fantastic—the best of all possible worlds. You are not only lovers but good friends. You make great companions for each other, for you are similar in many, many ways. However, if you don't have that Mars injection of *sex*, you could be so harmonious that it is ultimately *boring!* The pizzazz a love relationship needs would be missing, and though you'd be great buddies, the steam of passion just wouldn't be there, so you'd feel more like sister and brother than lovers.

*It is necessary for you to have *both* your own and your partner's ASC placements in order for the scoring system to accurately reflect your relationship review.

125–160—STANDING OVATION

Congratulations! Probably you already know you have a great thing going. Love and romance score high in this category, and your relationship could go down in history as one of *the* great love affairs, right up there with Cleo and Tony, Liz and Dick. It's got the whole nine yards—steamy passion, true love, and just plain liking each other. The harmony quotient is *high*, but there are enough differences between you to keep you both zestily interested. With just the right balance of sex, love, and friendship there's no place to go but up. Add a healthy dose of mutual respect and good companionship, and you're right off the charts with a long-running production. If you've a Mars or a Sun/Mars Theme, your relationship will be as hot and spicy as a Mexican dinner. On the other hand, if you've a Venus, Moon, or Venus/Moon Theme, things will be as sweet and creamy as a hot fudge sundae.

60–124—YOU GET APPLAUSE

This relationship has great potential! It's looking good. Though there are areas to be worked on (hey, nobody's perfect!), you share mutual interests and have good feelings about each other. This will make the working out a lot easier. You're not alone—most people fall into this category because most relationships are a mixture of good and not-so-good, and they need to be worked at to accentuate the positive and eliminate the negative. In any case, if you have a Venus/Mars combination anywhere, it might be wise to wait a bit for the overtly sexual haze to clear before making a major commitment. In the good news department, a Moon/Moon or Moon/Venus pair under Rave or Good Reviews will tilt the scales more in the direction of positive, as will a Venus or Moon/Venus Theme. The bad news is that a Mars/Mars pair under Bad Reviews or a Mars or Mars/Sun Theme will make things more difficult.

30–59—REHEARSAL CALL

There's good potential here, but it won't be realized without some hard and serious work. If you want to keep this show from closing after a few nights, you need more rehearsal time to understand the characters you *both* are playing. Study your scripts and play them together to help smooth out performance difficulties. You have big plusses in this relationship along with big problems, but that doesn't mean you have to give up. With proper attention, you can still get this show on the road. Venus/Mars in combination anywhere is a caution light indicating that it's necessary to let the sexual dust settle before making major decisions. Moon/Moon or Moon/Venus paired under Rave or Good Reviews will put love on your side in disputes and make them much easier to settle, and a Venus or Moon/Venus Theme will help similarly. Alas, Mars/Mars paired under Bad Reviews or a Mars or Mars/Sun Theme will make it all the more difficult.

0–29—BRING IN A PLAY DOCTOR

This show needs work or it may close early—or never open at all. To get this into production, you'll need lots of patience and the will to work at it. You may have reasons for being in this relationship that you yourself do not understand; you may be working out issues in your own life through the relationship. This is not unusual, for often two people come together to learn more about themselves through relating to the unexpressed parts of themselves which they attract in another person. This is known in psychological terms as projection. Study the Astroanalysis of our sample couple (pages 170 and 178), paying especial attention to the discussion of projection. Then schedule some rehearsal time. Study your individual scripts to learn more about how the characters in your internal drama behave and react, which of them you identify with, and which seem odd or unrelated to you. Study the scripts of your Co-Star to clue into projections you may be making. A Moon/Moon or Moon/Venus pair under Rave or Good Reviews means you have a good chance of working it out, as does a Venus or Moon/Venus Theme. However, a Mars/Mars pair under Bad Reviews or a Mars or Mars/Sun Theme can escalate frustration to the point of no return.

0 OR LESS—MAY CLOSE OUT OF TOWN

If your score falls below zero, this is an indication that either there are very few contacts between your charts, and those that are there are mostly in Bad Reviews, or that you have lots of contacts in "Bad Reviews." Either way, this relationship needs work, for you are very different people in your approaches, both to everyday living and to life itself and how it should be lived. Read the suggestions for "Rehearsal Call" and "Bring in a Play Doctor" for clues on how you can better understand your inner conflicts and those in the structure of the relationship. This relationship need not be a total loss. If you are together, there are reasons, and they may not be evident from your score. Remember that there are other planets that can affect you as well as the ones discussed in this book. Also, if you have a Moon/ Moon or Moon/Venus pair under "Rave" or "Good Reviews," or a Venus Theme, it will help enormously. With a Venus Theme, there will be love and affection to help work things out.

Note: If you feel that your score does not accurately reflect your relationship, you may be strongly influenced by the other planets, not discussed in this book. If such is the case, see Appendix II.

chapter twenty-six

REPRISE

Now that you've completed all the scoring for your Star Self and your Co-Star, let's take a look at our sample couple's Master Scoresheet:

RAVE REVIEWS	+ 40
GOOD REVIEWS	+ 135
MIXED REVIEWS	+ 30
BAD REVIEWS	− 105
EXTRA BONUS POINTS	+ 0
Grand Total	100

THEY GET APPLAUSE!!!

Astropoint Theme = Moon
Element Theme = Fire/Earth
Mode Theme = Fixed

Now, it's time to reveal who our sample couple is in real life.
They are a *real* couple known to everyone—Princess Diana and Prince Charles. As everyone knows, they married when Diana was

very young—only nineteen—and she quickly became the toast of the media. She was "Shy Di" and a former teacher of children—both characteristics fitting her Cancer Sun. Although younger than her prince, she is herself exciting and charismatic, and the media have focused a lot of attention on her. At first, Prince Charles was relegated to side stage, the glare of publicity lifted from him, but then his more retiring side (which we saw in Chapter 13, *"Your Co-Star"*) began to be discussed.

Charles and Diana settled in and had a family very soon. As time passed, their problems were revealed to the public. Being a royal couple, they have no privacy about their lives. At the time of writing this book, there is discussion about how they spend much time apart and about the strains and stresses in their relationship. Diana is suspected of having an affair, Charles of staying away from her. Diana is accused of being shockingly undignified and rowdy with her friends at social events. Charles is described as serious and private, loving nature and attracted to farming, painting, and metaphysics.

On our scale, their relationship scores a 100 or, They Get Applause. They have a Moon Astropoint Theme. Their Element Theme is Fire/Earth, and their Mode Theme is Fixed. Their overall score shows that their relationship has areas that need to be ironed out, but they love and like each other, sharing many mutual interests and attitudes to balance their differences. Chances are they have huge fights, then make up. Their Fixed Theme shows them to be a powerful couple who will get into struggles of control. Yet they have staying power and a serious commitment to each other.

They have to let each other grow, being careful not to squelch change in the relationship or in each other. Because they are royalty, they have special problems. The public exerts pressure on them to appear stable. The fixity between them will help them present a united front to the world. However, it makes it harder for them to go through the inevitable changes of a relationship.

Their Element Theme—Fire/Earth—shows up their differences. At best, they can combine inspiration and solidity in their marriage, becoming a stable royal couple, with the vision rulers need, and being the pillars of their society, while still having fun with each other. At worst, they can "dump" on each other, each blocking the other's efforts, either squelching vibrant fire or blasting earth's security.

However, with Moon/Venus and Venus/Moon in both Rave Reviews and Good Reviews, they have a strong dose of benevolent energies to help work things out. They have on their side love, appreciation, and a basic comfort and familiarity between them. Despite their differences, they feel right together, especially when they are affectionate, loving their children, and sharing resources.

With a Moon Theme, lunar issues are important to them. Sensitive feelings, nurturance, raising children, comfort, and security are emphasized. They certainly established themselves quickly as parents! In fact, their children sometimes seem to be the strongest bond between them.

Because of the Moon Theme, they may feel that no one is taking care of the caretakers. *Each* might feel uncared for. They are an emotional couple, with much feeling between them and, despite whatever individual rationality they may have, because the Moon is their relationship theme, they aren't very rational with each other. With each other they are sensitive, moody, loony, feeling—all the things the Moon represents.

Their Moons *are* related to each other, but under "Bad Reviews." This indicates a basic conflict regarding *needs*. Because their Moons are in an uneasy relationship, the more difficult Moon traits can pop up between them, causing irrationality and infantile behavior.

Diana has an Aquarius Moon, Charles a Taurus Moon. Diana—despite her more conservative and homey Cancer Sun (which loves having a brood of children around her) and her Taurus Venus (also conservative)—has a rebellious, unconventional, mental, and emotionally distant Moon nature. She needs her space in order to express her individuality. Her tendency to shock at conservative events, while expensively dressed to the nines (Taurus Venus), is an expression of her Moon.

Charles's Moon hates show, shocks, or surprises, inappropriate behavior, or anything that is overdone in public. His Taurus Moon likes what is familiar and stable; he loves nature and comfort. His Moon is a homebody and bastion of tradition, needing to sit in the fields, smell the flowers, dig in the garden. Because his Moon is conventional and responsible, he will do what is expected of him, such as attend the requisite social events. He will never make a spectacle of himself. Still, with his Leo Ascendant, he is comfortable being the center of attention but, with his Taurus Moon, never controversial.

His wife, however, *enjoys* controversy, but not intentionally. Her Sagittarius Ascendant provides an extra dose of free spirit, encouraging her Moon. And to make things harder on *his* Moon, she is unpredictable because Aquarian Moons are unpredictable.

For her part, she would feel Charles's conventional attitudes to be stodgy and stifling. At times he may seem dull or uninspiring to her. He might also try to keep her in line.

Fortunately, they have a Special Combination Moon/Venus under Rave Reviews (her Venus and his Moon) and *also* under Good Reviews (her Moon and his Venus). This adds harmony, appreciation, and love. Although their Moons are at odds, their Moons get along famously with each other's Venus. Moon/Venus is one of the best pairings for harmonious relationships, for needs (Moon) and wants (Venus) are harmonious.

Despite their problems, it is easy to see why they married. They have many Good Reviews, plus the happy Moon/Venus–Venus/Moon Special Combinations. It is widely rumored as well that Diana announced at age sixteen that she was going to be Princess of Wales. With her tenacious and ambitious Cancer Sun, she accomplished it.

The most difficult part of their relationship shows up in Bad Reviews. This reveals their Moon/Moon differences and their Mars/Mars conflict, which causes fights and opposite behaviors. Diana's Virgo Mars is careful, tidy, practical, and a perfectionist, while Charles's Sagittarius Mars is wild, free, blunt, uncareful. He will throw things to the wind when she is trying to sweep up. Or she will try to straighten his tie when he wants to go hunting or horseback riding.

Just as each of their Moons relates well to the other's Venus, Charles's Mars matches Diana's ASC under Rave Reviews. They share the grand, optimistic Sagittarian energy. Diana's Mars is compatible with Charles's Moon under Good Reviews. Although they may seem at odds, they have a positive Mars effect upon each other, which energizes, stimulates, and turns on sexuality.

Each has both independent and homey streaks, different ways of feeling comfortable, and different ways of acting. Spending time apart gives each room to breathe. When they are together, they can enjoy each other's energy, share their love for their home and children, while not stifling or harassing each other.

How might an average couple cope with these astrological dynamics?

They could achieve breathing space by socializing separately with friends or pursuing individual interests and activities. A separate area for each could be set up in their home to cater to their different Moon needs.

By becoming aware of their differing needs and wants, they could make room for them in the relationship, allowing for necessary sep-

In addition to our method of comparing your PLANETS OF LOVE—the Sun, Moon, ASC, Venus, and Mars—it is possible to compare entire charts, which can give you further insights into your relationship. This technique is called "synastry." In Appendix I, you will find titles that address this subject in different ways. In addition, our computer can give you a print-out chart of the planets of *both* people in a relationship, on one wheel. This way, it's easy to see how *all* the planets in both charts relate to each other.

If you are interested in having a personal computer chart calculated, our computer can do that for you.

In addition to the basic computer chart, we offer computerized interpretative services of various degrees of detailed complexity from a Relationship Profile to an Ultimate Personal Profile.

Also, our computer can give you a printout chart of the Planets of *both* people in a relationship, on one wheel. With this "bi-wheel" chart it's easy to see how all the Planets in both charts relate to each other.

We also offer *individualized* interpretations prepared by a professional astrologer *on tape*, covering specific areas such as Relationship Guidance—for interpersonal problems and potentials; and Individual Guidance—for the person who wants to focus on a particular area of life.

Telephone consultations can also be arranged.

In addition to aspects and intraspects, there are what we call "transits," which are the everyday movements of the planets in the sky as they relate to and affect your chart. Transits can affect relationships, too, and it's wise to pay attention to them, especially if they involve the "outer" planets—Saturn, Uranus, Neptune, and Pluto. Transits are *temporary*, but they can be very powerful.

If, for example, you, your partner, or your relationship is having a transit of Saturn—the planet of restrictions and frustrations—you might be going through a rough patch that will be over and done with in a few months or a couple of years. If you know this, you can weather it rather than assume what is affecting you is permanent or terminal. This can be a great comfort and make things easier.

There are, of course, beneficial transits as well. For example, when

Jupiter transits the Seventh House of your chart, you might find that your relationship works very well indeed, or it might be a time when you would form a new partnership.

For an informative brochure listing all services, prices, and complete ordering information, please send a #10 *stamped, self-addressed envelope* to:
HAZELWOOD PRODUCTIONS
P.O. Box 0000
New York, N.Y. 10021

We are sorry, but requests that do not include an SASE cannot be processed.

a p p e n d i x I I I

HOW TO FIGURE TIME CHANGES

The time given in this calendar is U.S. Eastern Standard Time. This is always five hours less than Greenwich Mean Time, which is the "basic" standard time for the world. If you were born on or near the United States east coast (in the Eastern Time zone), you do not need to make any time corrections unless Daylight Saving Time or Wartime Daylight Saving Time was in effect at that particular time. If you were born in the Central Standard Time zone (unless Daylight Saving Time was in effect), add one hour to your birth time to convert to Eastern Standard Time. For Mountain Standard Time, add two hours, and for Pacific Standard Time, add three hours.

For Yukon Standard Time, add four hours. For Central Alaska Standard Time, add five hours. (Hawaii now uses Central Alaska Standard Time. However, before June 8, 1947, parts of Hawaii used Hawaiian Standard Time. For a birthplace in Hawaiian Standard Time, add five and a half hours.) For Nome Standard Time (western Alaska), add six hours.

If you were born in a place in the world with a different time zone, it may be more convenient to convert to Greenwich Mean Time (since this is the way most world time-conversion charts work) and then subtract five hours to get United States Eastern Standard Time.

After you correct your time for Eastern Standard Time and if you were born in the United States and if your birth time is within an hour of a Moon sign, Sun sign or Moon phase change, you should check to see if there is a possibility that Daylight Saving Time might have been in effect when you were born. This can be one of three kinds:

1. Summer Daylight Saving Time
2. Wartime Daylight Saving Time
3. Fuel crisis Daylight Saving Time

Although it is a very complex operation to determine whether any given locality did or did not have Daylight Saving Time (within a state different communities might elect, in a given year, to be on or off, or begin and end Daylight Saving Time on different dates), it is relatively simple to eliminate the possibility when and where it was not in effect. Find your state on the map on page 335. If there is "NO" indicated, it means that Daylight Saving Time was not observed anywhere in the state for the years before 1967 (except wartime). If your state does not have a "NO," you will have to check with relatives or local records to find out if you need to subtract one hour from the time of your birth (already corrected for time zone differences) to conform with Eastern Standard Time. If your state does not have a "NO" listed, you will still be all right if you were not born within the outside dates listed for each year below the map. These are the dates when summer Daylight Saving Time could have started and ended.

During both World War I and World War II, Wartime Daylight Saving Time was standard throughout the country during the following times:

1918, 3/31 to 10/27
1919, 3/30 to 10/26
1942 to 1945, 2/9/42 to 9/30/45

334

Since 1967, automatic nationwide Daylight Saving Time has been in effect from the last Sunday in April to the last Sunday in October. An exception was the fuel crisis Daylight Saving Time in 1974 and 1975 (see dates after map). An entire state can exempt itself. In 1967 Arizona and Hawaii were exempt, and in 1968 Michigan became exempt as well.

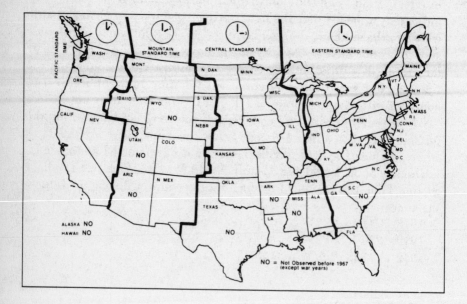

OUTSIDE DATES
FOR DAYLIGHT SAVING TIME

1920	3/28-10/31	1940	4/28-9/29	1961	4/30-10/29	1981	4/26-10/25
1921	4/24-9/25	1941	4/27-9/28	1962	4/29-10/28	1982	4/25-10/31
1922	4/30-9/24	1942 to 1945	**WAR TIME**	1963	4/28-10/27	1983	4/24-10/30
1923	4/29-9/30			1964	4/25-10/25	1984	4/29-10/28
1924	4/27-9/28			1965	4/25-10/31	1985	4/28-10/27
1925	4/26-9/27	1946	4/28-9/29	1966	4/24-10/30	1986	4/27-10/26
1926	4/25-9/26	1947	4/27-9/28	1967	4/30-10/29	1987	4/26-10/25
1927	4/24-9/25	1948	4/25-9/26	1968	4/28-10/27	1988	4/24-10/30
1928	4/29-9/30	1949	4/24-9/25	1969	4/27-10/26	1989	4/30-10/29
1929	4/28-9/29	1950	4/30-9/24	1970	4/26-10/25	1990	4/29-10/28
1930	4/27-9/28	1951	4/29-9/30	1971	4/25-10/21	1991	4/28-10/27
1931	4/26-9/27	1952	4/27-9/28	1972	4/30-10/29	1992	4/26-10/25
1932	4/24-9/25	1953	4/26-9/27	1973	4/29-10/28	1993	4/25-10/31
1933	4/30-9/24	1954	4/25-10/31	1974	1/6-10/27	1994	4/24-10/30
1934	4/29-9/30	1955	4/24-10/30	1975	2/23-10/26	1995	4/30-10/29
1935	4/28-9/29	1956	4/29-10/28	1976	4/25-10/31	1996	4/28-10/27
1936	4/26-9/27	1957	4/28-10/27	1977	4/24-10/30	1997	4/27-10/26
1937	4/25-9/26	1958	4/27-10/26	1978	4/30-10/29	1998	4/26-10/25
1938	4/24-10/2	1959	4/26-10/25	1979	4/29-10/28	1999	4/25-10/31
1939	4/30-9/24	1960	4/24-10/30	1980	4/27-10/26	2000	4/30-10/29